KU-KLUX

KU-KLUX

THE BIRTH OF THE KLAN
DURING RECONSTRUCTION

Elaine Frantz Parsons

The University of North Carolina Press Chapel Hill

This book was published with the assistance of the
Anniversary Endowment Fund of the University of North Carolina Press.

The paper in this book meets the guidelines for permanence and
durability of the Committee on Production Guidelines for Book Longevity
of the Council on Library Resources.

The University of North Carolina Press has been a member of the
Green Press Initiative since 2003.

Jacket illustration: Courtesy of the North Carolina Museum of History

Library of Congress Cataloging-in-Publication Data

Parsons, Elaine Frantz, 1970– author.
Ku-Klux: the birth of the Klan during Reconstruction / Elaine Frantz Parsons.
    pages cm
"This book was published with the assistance of the Anniversary Endowment Fund
of the University of North Carolina Press."
Includes bibliographical references and index.
ISBN 978-1-4696-2542-3 (cloth : alk. paper) — ISBN 978-1-4696-2543-0 (ebook)
1. Ku Klux Klan (19th century) 2. Domestic terrorism—United States—History—
19th century. 3. Racism—United States—History—19th century. 4. United States—
Race relations. I. Title.
HS2330.K63P37 2015
322.4′20973—dc23
2015026763

Portions of this work appeared earlier in somewhat different form in
Elaine Frantz Parsons, "Klan Skepticism and Denial in Reconstruction-Era
Public Discourse," *Journal of Southern History* 77 (February 2011): 53–90, and is
reprinted here by the permission of the publisher.

To my parents,
Janet Elizabeth Frantz and Carl Daniel Frantz,
who taught me what I need to know

Contents

Illustrations and Figures

KU-KLUX

Introduction

The Ku-Klux Klan remains a ghostly presence in U.S. history. Like a ghost, it commands attention: 150 years after the Klan's beginning, the Klansman still evokes a powerful response when he appears and reappears in popular films and writings. And no U.S. history textbook is complete without discussions of the Klan in the Reconstruction era, around World War I, and in response to the civil rights movement. The Klan is solidly entrenched as part of our national narrative, where it has come to represent the most violent aspect of white racial oppression. And yet few are confident that they know what they have seen. Discussions of the Klan tend to resolve into discussions of its covert nature: we spend as much time contemplating what we imagine is hidden from us as we do describing the Klan based on the ample information we have. The Klan's secrecy is as large a part of what makes it interesting to many as is its violence.

The Klan emerged after the Civil War as a solution to the problem of southern white defeat. We know now that white political, economic, and social dominance of black southerners would long outlast slavery, but white southerners, lacking the benefit of hindsight, were not at all certain that they could maintain their grip on resources and power in the South after losing the war. They had reason to fear; black southerners had reason to hope, and northerners looked on with mixed feelings. White southerners still had immense advantages over their black neighbors: they owned the vast majority of land and other capital; as a group, they were considerably more literate and numerate; they had experience controlling and working within institutional structures such as local governments, the military, and other voluntary organizations; and they had important allies—many had active networks of personal and business ties to influential people beyond their local area, in neighboring counties and even distant states. Together, these white advantages in property, education, organization, and connections would seem insurance enough against black competition even without the formal system of slavery.

Yet white southerners shared a widespread fear that their former slaves would rapidly overtake them. They worried that all of the remaining pillars of their power could be chipped away if freedpeople took full advantage of their new freedoms and the federal government and other sympathetic northerners supported them. The federal government engaged in widespread talk, and much more limited action, around land redistribution in 1865. Some exceptional black families who had been free before the war, and even some slave families, had accumulated enough capital before or during the war to rise to the top half of their community in property holdings in the 1870 census: as few as their numbers were, these relatively prosperous postwar black southerners loomed as large in the white as they did in the black imaginary. Meanwhile, what felt like a second army of schoolteachers flooded into the South, where they passionately set about educating freedpeople in hopes of narrowing the yawning gap between black and white education.

And many freedpeople approached their new freedom with tremendous boldness and energy, determined that they would have all of its fruits. Freedpeople eagerly attended classes and amassed their limited resources to board teachers and to build them schoolhouses. While black southerners had little experience running formal institutions, the experiences many had gained in collective life during slavery equipped them well to organize and participate in formal groups, most notably Union Leagues but also militias, religious associations, and self-improvement societies. White northerners again provided assistance in getting many of these groups started, but southern black communities needed little encouragement. The sight of organized black groups of any sort in the early Reconstruction years made many Democratic whites sweat. Freedpeople traveled in order to rebuild their family structure; those black southerners who were literate quickly began to form ties with one another and with sympathetic white leaders, corresponding with new allies in nearby counties, state capitals, and even Washington, D.C.

As the props of their power began to feel less secure, white southerners became preoccupied by the new threat posed by freedpeople's strength. During slavery, whites could count on their control of slaves' mobility, associational life, and access to weapons, paired with their largely unquestioned right to punish or control slaves or free people of color based on the slightest suspicion, to ensure that black southerners could not use physical force to claim rights or property. Before the war, they also had recourse to local and state governments organized largely around maintaining the slave system. After the war, with these traditional forms of control gone, whites feared that black southerners, in small ways or large, would overpower them and demand resources and rights.

Southern whites developed many strategies to prevent this. Making the most of the economic power inherent in their continued possession of the land was crucial: at a time when many freedpeople were dying from the effects of malnutrition and exposure, whites who held the key to food and housing could make broad demands of those they hired; freedpeople were hardly in a position to walk away even from a cruel employer.[1] Economic control often included physical violence; if employer violence was not always as dramatic as collective violence, it could rival its devastation and horror. Alabama freedman John Childers testified on the death of his nine-year-old daughter eight days after her employer beat her severely for losing the hat of the white baby she was watching. "I saw the rest of the children playing in the yard, and she was in the door sitting there and I thought that was strange, because she was a mighty playful chap, and I asked 'what are you sitting here for' and she says, 'Pap, Mr. Jones has beat me near to death.' [The witness weeping]."[2]

Most white-on-black violence took such humble forms: individual white men (and women and children) attacking black men (and women and children) to assert their private interest, confident that they would not be punished. Kidada Williams has called this private racial violence "the ordinary violence of emancipation."[3] This individual white-on-black violence was largely a continuation of violence that was common during slavery. In addition to continuing to use violence on the bodies of those working for them, many postwar whites illegally continued their traditional role as judges and enforcers of black public behavior, challenging and assaulting black people who did not adhere to white standards of propriety or violently breaking up public meetings of black people as they would have done under slavery.

Whites did continue to have substantial, though less predictable, access to the state's capacity for violence to assist them in dominating their black neighbors. While most state and local governments came under the temporary control of Republicans during the early Reconstruction era, both state and local governments continued to be important perpetrators of white-on-black violence. Juries after the war were mixed-race, and some show of due process was required, but justice was hardly color-blind in the postwar period. By necessity, convictions relied on local reputations and rumors. Whites often blamed their black neighbors for thefts or fires and arrested them on thin or no evidence. Black jury members might hold the line against conviction, but the pressure on them to convict could be tremendous. Jails and prisons began to fill up with black southerners. As Michael Trotti notes, "In the half-century after the Civil War, three-quarters of [the 2,768 people] executed in the South were African Americans."[4]

But while many patterns of white-on-black violence persisted, racial violence in the South did transform dramatically with the end of slavery. Everyone came out of the Civil War terribly more familiar with deadly violence than they had been. Black men's participation in combat had given them skills, confidence, and plausibility as effective users of violence. But, in the South, the number of black men who had taken up arms was dwarfed by the number of whites who had done so, and whites were also much more likely to have participated in informal collective wartime violence like guerrilla warfare; despite white anxieties, combat experience enhanced rather than detracted from the white monopoly on violence. Through these experiences, white southerners in particular had learned to ambush, to stalk, to mobilize and move efficiently, and to fire a building. They had also developed skill with weapons, both on battlefields and to intimidate or control civilians. At the same time, it became more common during and after the Civil War to own guns and to carry them on the street. Before the war, whites in plantation counties of South Carolina and Georgia had used guns in 37 percent of the homicides they were convicted of. After the war, they used guns in 80 percent.[5]

Perhaps informed by the lessons learned in war, white southerners increasingly turned to collective violence. Race riots surged in the early Reconstruction years. The massive and deadly 1866 riots in New Orleans and Memphis received the most press, but other such riots occurred throughout the early Reconstruction South. In Camilla, Georgia, between eight and twelve black people were killed, and over thirty wounded, when whites assaulted a Republican political rally in September 1868. That same month, white rioting left many black men dead in Opelousas, Louisiana; so chaotic was the situation there that estimates of the dead ranged from 52 to 227. In March 1871, rioting whites in Meridian, Mississippi, killed thirty black people. In April 1873, in a dispute over the validity of an election, a large group of white men in Colfax, Louisiana, attacked a large group of black citizens, killing at least 70, and perhaps more than 165. At least 48 of the men killed had surrendered and been disarmed before being shot. In all of these riots, whites suffered negligible bloodshed, since they were substantially better organized and armed.[6]

The private nighttime attack, however, would be the form of collective violence most closely associated with the Reconstruction era. It was not a new form: the rural South had a long-standing tradition of collective nighttime attacks.[7] In the charivari tradition stretching back to early modern Europe and imported to both the northern and southern United States at the time of settlement, costumed men would surround the homes of those who had offended the community, clanging pots or playing rude music, and sometimes forcing the inhabitants out to beat or humiliate them. In the years before and during the war, groups of men sometimes arrived at the home of a target, yelling obscenities, throwing rocks, shooting at the house, or assaulting its inhabitants. People who were suspected of sexual immorality, gambling, drinking, or socializing across racial lines; of theft, fraudulent trading, or fencing stolen goods; or of holding unpopular views risked a nighttime visit from outraged community members. For that matter, a nighttime attack hardly needed to represent community consensus: whenever two people were involved in a serious dispute, one party might gather a group of friends to menace or attack the other party's home during the night. This tradition of nighttime collective attacks continued, particularly in the rural South through the antebellum period.

During the war, guerrilla violence, which often took this form, plagued many parts of the South, particularly along the borders and in areas near more formal combat. Like most antebellum collective nighttime attackers, these groups were often nameless. Newspapers, letter writers, and government officials referred to them in any number of ways: as "slickers," "guerrillas," "regulators," or "gangs." These groups raided the homes of political enemies, stealing from, terrorizing, beating, raping, and sometimes killing inhabitants. With governments otherwise occupied, they could grow much larger than vigilante groups before the war or after, and they could attack entire neighborhoods or communities, sometimes even during the day. These groups could be more or less persistent over time, gathering for one raid or many.[8]

Sporadic small-group nocturnal violence continued to be practical and effective in the postwar rural South. It required little organization or planning, could respond quickly and easily to specific local conditions, and drew on community networks that the northerners interested in suppressing it found difficult to decipher. Early in the postwar period, particularly in 1866 and 1867, former Confederate soldiers and others took advantage of the weakened state to spawn groups of "vigilantes" or "guerrillas" throughout the South. Most were nameless, but some took names, or had names given to them. The Black Horse Cavalry wore blackface while terrorizing laborers in Franklin Parish, Louisiana. The Pale Faces emerged in 1867 in Middle Tennessee. The Knights of the White Camellia began in Louisiana in the spring of 1867.[9] Countless other groups of unnamed "slickers" roamed rural regions throughout the South in the early Reconstruction years.

All of these forms of violence, however, shared a significant shortcoming as a means of reasserting white racial dominance. Individual white-on-black attacks, riots, or slickers demonstrated and asserted local white control and intimidated and disheartened black southerners, yet the same qualities that made these types of violence attractive in the early Reconstruction era—they skirted potential northern interference by being seemingly unplanned, sporadic, and deniable—also neutered their coordinated political force. The many thousands of individual white-on-black attacks, the several bloody riots, the hundreds of slicker groups failed to add up to a coherent whole. Rather than representing the voice of a defeated-but-not-prostrate white South—an emergent southern white leadership—they conveyed a message of inchoate southern white fury.

The Ku-Klux Klan would solve this problem. It revalued collective local nighttime attackers, allowing Ku-Klux to effectively remain small, local, and difficult to detect or suppress, and yet to imagine and present themselves as part of a single pan-southern resistance movement. Wedding small-scale organization with an insistent discursive claim to regional coherence, the many small groups that comprised the first Ku-Klux Klan would together become the most widely proliferated and deadly domestic terrorist movement in the history of the United States. From 1866 through 1871, men calling themselves "Ku-Klux" killed hundreds of black southerners and their white supporters, sexually molested hundreds of black women and men, drove thousands of black families from their homes and thousands of black men and women from their employment, and appropriated land, crops, guns, livestock, and food from black southerners on a massive scale. Klan groups aimed many of their attacks at black people who expected and demanded political rights and social dignity. As Ed Ayers has argued, "the Klan was indirect testimony to black assertion and autonomy in the old plantation regions, not to black powerlessness." Black southerners who mobilized to vote, organized their peers, or ran for office were particular targets of Klan violence, along with those who defended their property and failed to defer to white Democratic southerners in private conflicts and public spaces. As black victim Simon Elder testified, the Klan targeted him because, as a prosperous renter able to hire white labor, "I was getting too much for them."[10]

In addition to those thousands whom the Klan targeted, countless others responded to the widespread terror the attacks generated. They learned about the attacks through newspapers or personal networks and reshaped their lives in large ways and small to avoid Klan violence. White-on-black violence, particularly as it took on the malignant form of Klan violence, therefore limited how all black southerners and their white allies used public space and resources, participated in political life, and defended their interests against white employers and neighbors. It shaped not only what they could do and where they could go but how they could walk and carry their bodies, how they could speak, and where they could look.

THE KU-KLUX KLAN began in Pulaski, a town in Middle Tennessee, in mid-1866, and Klan groups began to spread beyond the immediate neighborhood of Pulaski by early 1868. That summer, an explosion of Klan demonstrations, announcements, warnings, and occasional but sometimes deadly acts of violence in scattered areas throughout the South marked the Klan's proliferation. As summer turned to fall, and the federal elections approached, Klan violence further spread and dramatically increased in intensity. The Klan's presence in this early period was most notable in middle and western Tennessee, parts of the South Carolina Upcountry, North Carolina, eastern Georgia, northern and western Alabama, various parts of Kentucky, northern Louisiana and the New Orleans area, eastern Texas, and southern and northeastern Arkansas.[11] After the 1868 elections, Klan violence in 1869 and early 1870 dwindled in Tennessee (where influential Democrats attempted to disband it) and South Carolina, but persisted in Alabama and Georgia, increased in North Carolina (particularly in Alamance and Caswell Counties), and spread more substantially into Mississippi and Florida.[12] In late 1870, in the wake of the federal elections, through mid-1871, Klan violence surged in many areas, most prominently Upcountry South Carolina and western Alabama. In other areas, such as Kentucky and Georgia, Klan violence also persisted into mid-1871.[13] The spread of the Ku-Klux was incomplete and uneven: Virginia and Louisiana saw little Klan violence. Even in states and regions with the most Klan activity, many communities never suffered a Klan, while some communities had multiple Klan groups. Klans had an ideal habitat: rural places where the ratio between black and white residents was fairly even, and where white Democrats were not functionally holding substantial political power. And while Klan violence was often deadly, even in the most Ku-Klux infested areas, the outbreak of Klan violence was rarely more than one terrible night, or a week, or a few months. Very few communities suffered Klan groups that visibly persisted for longer than a month or two at a time.

Agents of the federal government first made note of the Ku-Klux in mid-1867, but they became much more substantially interested in it with its spring 1868 proliferation. Working together with state governments, Washington tried several strategies to counter Klan violence: forbidding newspapers to advertise it, making it a federal crime to forcibly prevent people from voting, employing detectives to infiltrate Klan groups, raiding suspected Klan dens, and, finally, arresting Klan participants on a substantial scale in some regions. These efforts weakened Klans even as elite Democratic whites began to move back into more conventional powerful roles, making informal Klan violence less attractive to them. While occasional Klan attacks would continue for decades, particularly in the old border states, Ku-Klux violence would rapidly dissipate after mid-1871. While the Klan was a major issue in the 1872 presidential election, local reports of Klan violence after mid-1871 were very low. The Klan had all but ended by the beginning of 1872. Klan violence would appear sporadically through the late nineteenth and early twentieth centuries, but the Klan would not again be a substantial force until a "second Klan" emerged decades later at the time of the First World War.

The nature and the targets of Ku-Klux violence differed from one community to another and one region to another. Some Klans warned or whipped, targeting political actors. Some Klans shot at the homes of freedpeople to frighten them away after they had gathered their harvest. Ku-Klux violence in Florida, which was still thinly populated and even less effectively governed than much of the South, tended to involve little costuming and ritual. Rather than dealing out warnings or whippings, Florida Ku-Klux committed assassinations. Similarly, Klans in the trans-Mississippi South were usually more deadly than those to the east.[14] And while Klan violence in most places was sporadic, showing little evidence of planning and organization, Alamance and Caswell Counties in North Carolina and the South Carolina Upcountry hosted several large-scale costumed and orchestrated attacks that required substantial advance planning. The shape Ku-Klux violence took in a particular area followed local patterns of violence. Klans followed local traditions in their choices of weapons, in their behavior during their attacks, and even in their selection of victims. Certain locations that had been important to prewar cultures of violence, like muster grounds or hanging trees, continued to play an important role in Klan violence.

It is tempting to see Klan attacks as the idiosyncratic and desperate acts of defeated rural whites left behind by history: as victorious northerners, eyes to the future, embarked on the long, slow, and always-imperfect process of recognizing that all men were citizens whatever the color of their skin, white southerners stuck in the backwaters had not yet begun this path, and the Klan was their decisive rejection of its logic. This book questions that dichotomy. The violent events in these rural southern communities were not simply a southern white rejection of northern good intentions. They were part of a white-dominated national culture still quite far from recognizing black agency and rights, which often recognized the necessity of systematic white-on-black violence, even where it was loath to explicitly endorse it.[15] Northerners neither substantially participated in Klan violence nor generally approved of it. They passed legislation, spent money, and sent troops to suppress it. Yet they created a broader culture in which the Ku-Klux thrived; they eagerly integrated the Ku-Klux into their cultural understandings, played a crucial role in publicizing it, and were quite reluctant, in the end, to substantially punish the Ku-Klux for their violence.

The Ku-Klux Klan was created by white people and for the promotion of their interests. It is patently obvious that the purpose of the physical Ku-Klux Klan was to promote white political, economic, and social interests over those of their black neighbors. What is less obvious is that the same is true of the idea of the Ku-Klux. The decision to label white-on-black violence as Ku-Klux violence was made in order to serve white more than black ends. While at the beginning, white Democratic southerners found themselves threatened by the label, within a few years even many of them had come to realize that the "Ku-Klux" label could serve their interests.

The Ku-Klux's liminal status enabled northerners to maintain an ambiguous relationship to southern white-on-black violence. The Ku-Klux movement was substantially about this negotiation between northern and southern whites. Ku-Klux claimed the ability to move undetected through the silent and darkened rural southern landscape, but they intended for accounts of their deeds to be published and circulated through a national newspaper exchange and wire system. That is, they claimed to be invisible to their local southerners, but visible to a national audience. They were well aware that what they did during the night would make its way into this news system: a broader national audience would "see" them through evidence and testimony better than locals ever could. The central fascination of the Klan, and the quality that made it so effective in the environment of the early Reconstruction period, is that it was at once invisible and impossible to ignore, a powerful force shaping the future of the South but at the same time deniable. The Klan's influence rested on violence as deliberately refracted through discourse. The national discussion about what the Klan was and what it was doing, and the violence committed by Ku-Klux on the bodies of black southerners and their white allies, shaped, limited, and reinforced one another.

There were two Ku-Klux. First, the embodied Ku-Klux consisted of thousands of real men on the ground inflicting real pain, injury, and death on the bodies of freedpeople and those who allied with them. These men were embedded in community structures and local power relationships. Their speech and actions had been shaped by their local environments and cultures. When they became Ku-Klux, they banded together with other men they trusted in the belief that the shape black emancipation was taking threatened their interests. The Klan's actions bore many similarities from place to place and person to person. Yet because they were different men in different communities with different problems, interests, and values, each man was a distinctive sort of Ku-Klux, and each group a distinctive sort of Klan. Together these thousands of violent individual men committed thousands of violent deeds against those people who they found most interfered with their own interests.

The second Ku-Klux was the disembodied Klan: the abstract idea of the Klan as it was represented in public discourse. Some contemporaries sarcastically referred to it as the "newspaper Klan," but it was not to be lightly dismissed. Like the embodied Klan, the disembodied Klan was produced by thousands of individuals who each spoke, wrote, drew, and performed their distinct idea of the nature and meaning of collective white-on-black violence. Together they created a composite notion of the Klan that defined the white southern men committing the violence as organized, powerful, mysterious, bizarre, and almost undetectable, their victims as passive and helpless.

These two Klans were utterly entangled with one another: representations of the Ku-Klux had a separate though dependent relationship to the thing itself. From 1867 through 1871, eyewitness reports and physical evidence of violence committed on the ground would both fuel and limit the construction of the disembodied Klan. Early representations of Ku-Klux as puckish and playful, for instance, would lose their plausibility as more accounts of Klan atrocities came into circulation. Accounts of Ku-Klux as invulnerable would disappear as agents of the government routed and arrested them. Challenging recent work on the construction of the memory of the war and Reconstruction often places memory construction in the wake of the events themselves. Yet contemporaries produced usable narratives of collective postwar violence even as it was occurring. The disembodied Klan would just as thoroughly fuel and limit what embodied Ku-Klux could do on the ground. If Ku-Klux wanted their actions to be understood, they would have to take a form and behave in a manner that made sense to their public audience. Real Ku-Klux reliably conformed to newspaper tropes. Those who did not could not claim the title "Ku-Klux."

THIS BOOK MAKES four claims about the Klan. First, the ideas and priorities of northerners powerfully shaped and influenced what the Ku-Klux became. Northerners neither created the Klan nor themselves inflicted Klan violence against black southerners, but they played a crucial role in making the Klan what it was. They turned eagerly to the image of the Klan to interpret the situation in the South, and their own role in it; the challenges facing the Reconstruction-era North; and the changing nature and capacities of the postwar federal government. Northern reporters, authors, songwriters, and orators wrote and spoke about the Ku-Klux, but did so selectively, suppressing some acts and characteristics and embellishing others. At a time when northerners so dominated the national discourse, northerners' interest in the Klan enabled it to circulate broadly. Were it not for northern-published newspapers and other popular texts' intensive interest in the Klan, and that of northern political and cultural leaders, the Klan probably would have remained just one of many contemporary local southern slicker groups.

The idea of the Ku-Klux thus produced was a powerful tool for shaping the postwar state. The postwar period was a time of growth in both federal and state capacity both in and beyond the United States. Government entities had been compelled and enabled by the war to develop substantial new capacities, from establishing more elaborate working bureaucratic infrastructure, to making communications clear and efficient, to developing information-gathering and information-storage systems.

The Ku-Klux seemed to necessitate and justify the extended use of these new capacities. But the Ku-Klux also mirrored much that seemed threatening about the new state: its use of violence, its allegedly highly organized and top-down structure, the often opaque and arcane nature of its decision-making process. Writings about the Klan could serve as either justifications or critiques of Republican governments in Washington or state capitals. National newspaper discourse of the Klan in major northern papers was often more closely tuned to events in Washington than to the suffering of the Klan's southern Republican victims.

Second, the Klan was part of a modernizing process through which rural white southerners learned, appropriated, and inhabited cultural forms from the urban North. Ku-Klux and their supporters used deliberately reactionary rhetoric, yet the idea of the Klan felt like a way for rural Democratic white southerners to move out of the Confederacy and into a new and integrated nation.[16] Ku-Klux drew on southern-coded honor culture, but they also fiercely parodied it, becoming deliberately comic versions of noble knights, dressed in ridiculously exaggerated faux finery and attacking foes for whom they had only the deepest contempt. They frequently appropriated tropes, language, costume, and even technology from northern urban cultural forms such as the minstrel stage and even from the brand new burlesque performance style.

Cultural gatekeepers in the North at first considered the Klan to be *au courant*. Not only urban newspaper and popular song writers but also baseball teams, advertisers, individual maskers, and even college eating clubs adopted Ku-Klux imagery. While northerners very rarely became "Ku-Klux" themselves, the Klan became popular in the North, particularly in 1868, when word of the "mysterious organization" was beginning to spread. Thus the Klan simultaneously took the form of white southern resistance to northern authority while serving as white southerners' contribution to a unified culture.

Third, despite the reasonableness of the conventional understanding of the Klan as a group representing white southern interests against white northern claims to authority, the idea of the Klan also served the purpose of sectional reconciliation and the construction of a shared set of political understandings between northerners and southern Democratic whites. Many northerners found in the idea of the Ku-Klux a useful way to frame events in the South: the Klan was a distinct, identifiable enemy, and the sort of entity that the government imagined it had the tools to suppress. It was a southern cancer, but one that could be excised from a body otherwise returning to health. Southern Democratic whites, who experienced the Klan as modern and northern-inflected, found in the Klan a way to see themselves as a part of a postwar nation. Even while the Reconstruction-era Ku-Klux Klan thwarted the realization of freedpeople's and northern Republicans' dreams of a new and more just nation, the idea of the Klan and its violent actions on the ground helped to piece together the postwar nation that would instead emerge. This new order would violently oppress black people and those whites who allied with them in new ways, and Klan groups set up those new practices of oppression.

Because the Klan's very existence was always an open question in popular discourse, the political discourse over the Ku-Klux also became a liminal space, or "space of displacement": it threw truisms into confusion, provoking new ideas and alliances.[17] Even as it highlighted rifts in postwar views of the role and rights of freedpeople, the national conversation about the Ku-Klux was also building something, in that the debaters shifted terrain over time in response to one another. The debate over the Ku-Klux would substantially begin in 1868 and end in 1872; the terms of that debate would be dramatically different by the end of its existence. Public conversation about the Ku-Klux allowed northerners to express dissatisfaction with Reconstruction, and ultimately to empathize with and work alongside conquered white southerners.

Ku-Klux supporters and participants changed their stances during the debate as well. They were well aware of the national interest in the Klan; cultivating a national audience was one obvious effect of consolidating discrete local violent groups into that single entity. To claim a Ku-Klux identity while committing an act of violence against a freedperson or white Republican was to precisely place that act in a national context and deliberately draw the attention of an audience who did not typically consider acts of violence in a distant community relevant. A generic group of rural southern white men attacking a black man was unlikely to make the national press; a Ku-Klux attack, however, might well do so. Most who became Ku-Klux appear to have been interested in how this national idea and attention might help them improve their local position. Yet those who saw themselves as a part of a translocal community, such as elites and politicians who spent time following events beyond their county seat, were also at times aware that the publicity surrounding the Klan could enable them to communicate to the North their own views of race, violence, and government.

Black Republican southerners and their southern white allies also used the Ku-Klux to position themselves within the national story of Reconstruction, in different ways at different times. Many quickly came to understand that northerners responded more energetically to acts of violence and oppression against them committed by Ku-Klux than to the same acts committed by those who did not claim a Ku-Klux identity. But just as quickly, many also came to understand that the Ku-Klux narrative framed its victims in ways detrimental to their claims to dignity, capacity, and citizenship. Rural southern Republicans were expected to provide the fuel for Klan discourse, in the form of victim testimony. Over the course of the Reconstruction Klan debate, many provided that testimony and encouraged others to do so, but often did so gingerly, observing that the Klan narrative was being used as a tool for white reconciliation and black exclusion.

Fourth, looking at the Klan through contemporaries' language provides a critical view of what it meant to be a Ku-Klux. Who came to be called, or to call themselves, "Ku-Klux"? When and why did they gain or embrace that name, and what difference did the name make to their capacities, resources, actions, and self-conception? While historians know little about the identity of attackers, the best evidence would suggest that Ku-Klux attacks were often carried out by contingent groups of men; these groups perhaps committed only one attack, perhaps several in a single night, or perhaps a long and terrible series over the course of months. Communities and outsiders debated over whether a given attack was a "Ku-Klux" attack, and several different groups of people who had some claim to be "Ku-Klux" sometimes coexisted, often not peacefully, in a particular southern community.

"Ku-Klux" was a brand-new identity in an old and defeated region. The Civil War created a crisis in identity. Even as freedpeople and their former masters struggled for resources and rights, discursively they redefined themselves and each other.[18] In this time of bureaucracy's youth, personal names were unstable. This was true of nonelite whites as well as black men and women. Often semiliterate at best, many had no standard spelling of their name. Even elites shifted names situationally, using "Jr." or "Sr." or a middle initial only when they thought it necessary to distinguish themselves from others, adding "Dr." or "Esquire" on some legal documents but not others. The same man might, in different circumstances, be called by his initials, his first name, his middle name, a nickname, and alternative phonetic spellings of each of these. The changes in names were by far the greatest, however, among freedpeople. They had a new need for last names. Often whites referred to them by the last name of their former master; often freedpeople themselves chose differently. With striking frequency, freedpeople went by more than one first name as well, whether because others chose to call them what they did not call themselves, because like whites they shifted names situationally, or because they renamed themselves over time. And just as their personal names changed, so too did the titles, descriptions, and categories by which southern men defined themselves. Veterans took their military titles home with them. Large groups of postwar southerners suddenly found that they had become "freedpeople," "veterans," "cripples," "widows," "vagrants," and "Union Leaguers," not to mention "Republicans" or "Conservatives." "Ku-Klux" became one of many new identities conservative white men could lay claim to.

THE IDEA OF the Ku-Klux Klan emerged from a set of discursive conventions more cultural than political. It was influenced by an array of cultural practices and popular figures of the day, including sensationalist fiction, the minstrel stage, phonetic writing, contemporary fashion, Sir Walter Scott, Mardi Gras, and bureaucratese. Its resonance and power grew, in large part, from its success in offering up these often comfortable and appealing tropes to frame parts of the postwar political situation that Americans, North and South, experienced as strange and threatening. Specifically, the stories of the Ku-Klux that circulated through the press mapped out, and began to implement, approaches to the twin problems of how the nation might absorb two seemingly difficult types of citizens: freedmen and former Confederates.[19] The embodied Ku-Klux, in practice, would confront these two problems in an all-too-straightforward way: it would perform and enact the exclusion of freedmen from the body politic and negotiate, with a mixture of violence and rhetoric, the reintegration of former Confederates. The disembodied idea of the Ku-Klux, which circulated through popular texts even as the embodied Klan circulated through parts of the South, worked in a more nuanced way, often amplifying or clarifying, but also shaping and limiting, and sometimes becoming radically disconnected from or even in tension with the work of the embodied Ku-Klux.

A remarkably small number of professional historians have written substantial studies of the Reconstruction-era Klan. The Klan played an important role in the writings of the Progressive Era and interwar historians: several Dunning School studies describe Klan violence as a regrettable but understandable and inevitable reassertion of white southern power in the face of the wrongs committed by uneducated and insufficiently civilized black political leaders and their followers. As Dunningite Paul Haworth wrote, in the face of northern support of "negro equality," "open resistance was hopeless. Some indirect and hidden means must be found. The outcome was the formation of such secret societies as the Invisible Empire or Ku-Klux-Klan, the Knights of the White Camelia, the Pale Faces, and the White Brotherhood."[20] By contrast, W. E. B. Du Bois's *Black Reconstruction* refers to the Klan as the violent means through which elite whites co-opted poor whites in their effort to impose an economic order hostile to workers.[21] In 1939, amateur historian Stanley F. Horn, with *Invisible Empire: The Story of the Ku Klux Klan*, created the first serious full-length treatment of the Klan. Not until 1971, with the publication of Allen Trelease's *White Terror*, did the Reconstruction-era Ku-Klux have a scholarly treatment with any claim to comprehensiveness. In the more than four decades since, popular books have explored the Ku-Klux, academic and popular books have focused on the Ku-Klux in particular states or regions, and scholarly monographs have treated the Ku-Klux as an important aspect of larger arguments about the Reconstruction era.[22] Yet no scholarly monograph has approached the Reconstruction-era Klan critically and comprehensively.

Trelease's text, therefore, not only continues to dominate the historiography of the Klan but is the sole work to take an intensive scholarly approach to a number of important questions in its history. Fortunately, *White Terror* is brilliant, exhaustive, and painstakingly careful. Yet Trelease wrote before the rise of cultural history. This reveals itself, above all, in his stiff relationship to his often ambiguous primary sources. Later cultural historians, acutely aware that texts are shaped by generic constraints and multiple competing cultural narratives, developed more nuanced textual interpretation. Trelease is a sophisticated reader. He appreciates that some newspaper accounts of the Klan were not intended to be read "straight," that Democrats trivialized the Klan at some times and defended it at others, and that Republicans tended to exaggerate the Klan's centralization, organization, and political orientation. Yet he does not engage with the relationships among these competing narratives. He also sometimes makes factual claims based on questionable, much later narratives without interrogating the context in which they appeared, as when he describes the rather complex organization of the Oglethorpe County Klan based on John C. Reed's 1908 article "What I Know of the Klan," from *Uncle Remus' Magazine*.[23] This lack of sensitivity to discourse causes substantial interpretive problems: contemporary texts written about the Klan have complicated forms of representation. Not only are they participating in a broader national political discourse, but they often draw on sensational and comic genres.

Trelease's work also precedes the development of black studies, with its critique of privileging the actions and ideas of white men while representing others as the objects of their actions and ideas, and Trelease can unconsciously reproduce racist analysis, even though he was motivated by a powerful antipathy for white supremacy. At some point around 1960, Trelease began a book radically challenging the almost uniformly sympathetic existing historiography on the Klan. In 1967, he accepted a position at tumultuous University of North Carolina at Greensboro.[24] To write a book so very unflattering to the Klan at this moment was a charged and even a physically dangerous act. *White Terror* stands in sympathy with black Klan victims, and, in a sharp break from previous work on the Klan, insists on their humanity, dignity, and intelligence. Yet the black men and women in Trelease's account largely lack both agency and a cultural orientation or organization of their own. They are menaced and attacked, and they sometimes fight back, and sometimes plea for redress, but they do not otherwise substantially contribute to the unfolding of events and analysis.

It is time to revisit the history of the Reconstruction-era Klan. One key issue requiring revision is the basic question of what sort of thing the Klan was: should it be considered as an organization, or was it a decentralized pattern of violence? There is little doubt that the Klan consisted of organized and disorganized elements. Important people worked to organize Klans, with at least some limited success, yet Klans quite often emerged where no one had organized them and developed no connection to any broader organization. Trelease acknowledges that most Klan groups were probably not highly organized and avoids calling it an "organization." Yet his book's structure privileges organized elements of the Ku-Klux and presents "volunteer" Ku-Klux as anomalous. He begins by describing formal elements of the Klan, then moves through the South chronologically and geographically, apparently including any evidence he can find of organization. While he finds expansive claims of organization less than credible, he allows the organized Klan to occupy a lot of his book's real estate and to shape its narrative. Where Trelease discusses less organized Klans, or claims that all Klans in a given area lacked central organization, he finds himself with rather little to do with them beyond note their existence and describe their deeds. Structurally, more isolated and less persistent Klans find themselves stragglers at the tail of Trelease's more organized army, presented as exceptional and as less significant even though they may well have surpassed the organized groups in size.

My book's approach to evaluating evidence of organization is a mirror image of Trelease's. While acknowledging the existence of sometimes intensive and sometimes successful efforts of organized Ku-Klux, I structure my book based on discourse, which I take as the organizing principle around which Ku-Klux groups formed. Where I find Grand Wizards, written constitutions, coordinated actions, and other evidence of organization, I acknowledge it as evidence of a local investment in bureaucratic structure, of local elite support for and participation in the local Ku-Klux, or as an expression of hope that the Ku-Klux movement could be a centralized and organized one, but I also treat these organizational efforts, even when successful, as epiphenomenal; I rarely consider them important in pushing the narrative forward. While Trelease's analytical energy went into organization, mine goes into discourse; while his framework hangs on the evidence of coordination and prominent leaders he could find in various places, mine hangs on accounts of the Ku-Klux as they circulated through the North and South, in different ways at different times.

Whereas Trelease gave considerable weight to contemporary and later claims to widespread or elaborate Klan organization and ritual, I approach it with skepticism. Ku-Klux and their supporters frequently made exaggerated claims about the Klan's scope and capacity. They at times winkingly embraced a tall-tale tradition: the primary sources swim with examples of Ku-Klux controlling lightning bolts, wearing hats the tops of which disappeared into the clouds, leaping over trains, clandestinely controlling the Johnson impeachment proceedings, possessing an elaborately articulated infrastructure from Maine to Texas, and meeting in massive and elegant underground vaults. These ridiculous claims are sometimes segregated into humor pieces but usually blend seamlessly into other claims with various levels of plausibility. These statements awkwardly straddle the line between earnest assertions and outlandish jokes. All historians have had to choose where to make the cut in reading Klan accounts with elements of exaggeration.

This book reads accounts of Klan organization and capacity through a lens of suspicion.

Several people had a compelling interest in imagining the Klan as more organized than it was. Contemporaries who in 1865 had confidently taken on the charge of protecting freedpeople in the wake of the war soon, in 1868–72, for instance, could only take solace in contemplating the impossible power of the Klan: Benjamin Runkle, the head of the Memphis Freedmen's Bureau office, reported after the devastating 1866 Memphis Riot, "I have endured the mortification of turning away the poor people who came to me for protection and whom I was sent here to protect, and I am now enduring the mortification of placing it on record that I was powerless and did nothing; And have only to add that the Freedmen's Bureau in this City during the riot was a mockery."[25] Countless government officials and private citizens would be similarly mortified at their failures over the following years and would find in the Klan an alleviation of their failure. The more powerful the Klan was understood to be, the more it monopolized responsibility for postwar injustice.

There are other reasons to be wary of claims that the Klan was an organization meaningfully and effectively directing local violence. For such an allegedly complex and expansive institution, it left behind strikingly few artifacts of its internal organization. Very occasionally a letter emerges representing communication between Klan leaders, or a prescript or membership list surfaces, but for the Klan to have been as organized as some have claimed, there should have been thousands of such letters and documents in existence, along with account books, the originals of letters sent from Klan dens to presses, even some form of minutes or meeting notes. The Ku-Klux Prescript insisted that each den include a scribe and a corresponding secretary, after all. The suggestion that local den chiefs or secretaries, together with individual members who had received correspondence, reliably and comprehensively destroyed them in 1871 to avoid prosecution and that almost none concealed them only to bring them out again in the Ku-Klux-loving period a few decades later suggests a pervasive internalized bureaucratic discipline that would be surprising to see anywhere, but particularly in the postwar South.

Reading the Klan as less organized makes Klan violence seem less like an orchestrated and intentional act and more like a pattern of self-interested response to the postwar situation. Yet arguing that the Klan was often epiphenomenal rather than causal—one part of a larger system of oppression in motion; a name used to organize and interpret seemingly incoherent streams of evidence of white-on-black southern violence—in no way diminishes the violence Ku-Klux caused. The racial violence pervading the postwar South demanded an explanation and response. The idea of the Klan framed it in a way that was at times useful and therefore attractive to many groups: northerners and southerners, Republicans and Democrats, black and white. And emphasizing the organized, centralized nature of Klan violence can lead historians to absolve the broader society of responsibility for the intense oppression of postwar freedpeople. If Klans indeed had managed to organize most white men in several areas, assumed a paramilitary form, and perfected a structure of surveillance and communication, then neighboring whites' claims that they were too intimidated to stop them would make a good deal of sense, and the Freedmen's Bureau, even with the occasional support of federal marshals and detachments of U.S. soldiers, could hardly be blamed for failing to protect freedpeople.

Reframing and renarrating the Klan in terms of a national discursive process opens it up in several productive ways. Not only does it spread the responsibility for Klan violence beyond a single terrorist movement and suggest how antiblack violence was embedded in a broader national culture; it also addresses a question that historians of the Klan have never been able to confidently answer: how it began and spread so quickly at a time when the South was broadly understood to have been barren soil for voluntary associations, or organizational life more generally.

I most frequently refer to the Klan neither as an organization nor even as a movement, but rather as a sometimes-embodied "idea." I refer to "the Klan" or "the Ku-Klux" in the singular only when I am talking about it as cultural object. When I discuss groups on the ground, I refer to them in the plural. The Ku-Klux Klan was most frequently shortened to "Ku-Klux" in this period, though publications sometimes used the full name, "Klan," "Kuklux," or, rarely, "K.K.K." Individuals who participated with these groups were referred to as "Ku-Klux." The term "Klansman" was not in common use during this period. The difficulty in remembering not to use this term anachronistically underlines the degree to which our understanding of the Ku-Klux has been influenced by twentieth century representations: most notably in Thomas Dixon's *The Clansman*.[26]

THIS BOOK'S SEVEN chapters trace the major sources of the Ku-Klux idea: those who began the first Ku-Klux Klan in Pulaski, Tennessee;

the northern newspaper press, which covered it heavily, selectively, and strategically; existing popular cultural tropes that were appropriated by Ku-Klux and their supporters; those Klan victims and their questioners who produced a huge body of testimony describing Klan attacks; and influential figures in local communities that hosted Klans, who struggled with one another about how to tell the story of their Klan to outsiders.

The first chapter confronts the fact that the Klan was founded not by southern plantation owners but by politically moderate, fairly cosmopolitan, border-state professionals. These young men, facing the political, economic, and cultural collapse of the South in the wake of the war, developed the Klan as a diversion. Yet from the beginning they understood the potential political significance of southern social and cultural organizations such as the Klan. Throughout the South, in the early Reconstruction period, defeated southern nationalists were throwing their energies into precisely such cultural initiatives. Because of their liminal position between North and South, the Pulaski Ku-Klux, in their organization and performance, framed the crisis of the South and the position of the southern white man in a way informed by and resonant with ideas circulating in the urban North. The Pulaski Ku-Klux understood the problem of the Reconstruction-era Klan as a problem of modernity and provided a way for the defeated southern white man to position himself in terms of the modern. This perhaps accounts for the success of the Klan in outcompeting alternative groups. Chapter 1 explores the transformation of the Klan to a violent and explicitly political organization a bit more than one year after its founding.

The second chapter focuses on why so many Klan attacks took on such distinctive cultural forms. Ku-Klux borrowed their costume and violent performance not only from local culture, but also from popular cultural tropes in national circulation and heavily featured in minstrelsy, burlesque, circus, and carnivals. In deliberately mimicking these cultural forms, they put themselves in conversation with the northern, urban centers where so much of the naturally circulating popular culture was produced. Many of the images Ku-Klux borrowed were already weighted with a host of meanings about race, gender, and social order. Ku-Klux imported these meanings into their attacks, which they frequently used to reinforce racist cultural narratives: depicting black victims as comically overembodied and lacking in integrity. Klan victims responded not only to the violence of their attacks but also to the cultural meanings embedded in them. Depending on their circumstances and strategy, they could try to save themselves suffering by performing the minstrel roles they understood to be expected. Or they could refuse to inhabit those roles, and instead use the attack itself, and their later narration of it, to challenge the assumptions inherent in the popular cultural tropes the Ku-Klux were mobilizing.

Chapter 3 traces how Klan attack narratives were produced, from the moment of violence to the moment of testimony, by each of the three key participants in this narration: attacking Ku-Klux, government officials eliciting testimony about the attack, and the victims who alone were in a position to publicly narrate the attack. Members of each of these groups had broadly shared motivations in producing the narrative of Klan violence, and each had both an interest in shaping, and a substantial ability to shape, its telling. Through their narrative, they believed that they could not only read southern racial life but also influence it. Ku-Klux, of course, dictated many of the terms of the attack and, through violence, forced victims to behave in certain ways and constrained them from behaving in others. Government officials taking testimony would only hear certain sorts of stories, and used their formal control of the venue of testimony, their broader social power and expectation of deference, and their mockery, disbelief, insult, and approval to elicit certain sorts of narratives of the attack while preventing the expression of others. Victims, while the least powerful of these three, were usually the only ones who had been present for the attack and could speak of it without incriminating themselves. While sharply constrained by their fear of Ku-Klux, their need for government officials' support and the necessity of speaking in a way that to some degree both reflected the moment of violence orchestrated by the Klan and was considered "relevant" by those taking testimony, they nevertheless were the only tellers of the story both willing to speak and recognized as authentic, and therefore had the nontrivial power to choose to speak certain words, in certain ways, and to withhold others.

Chapter 4 takes up the story of the Klan as it entered the national discourse, arguing that northern newspapers used the Klan to talk about the nature of citizenship, the expansion of the state, and their anxieties that the individual was subject to manipulation by an increasingly robust and centralized government and centralized newspaper press. The national conversation about the Klan largely occurred during two periods—the first from early 1868 through early 1869, the second from late 1870 through 1872—and the nature of the discussion differed dramatically between those two periods, revealing changing approaches to Klan violence.

Chapter 5 highlights and explores one crucial aspect of the national press coverage of the Klan: the persistence of the plausibility of Klan denial throughout and after the Klan period. This chapter will also deal with the ways in which the states' information-gathering mechanisms expanded during this period, partly in order to deal with the challenge of the Klan. It will argue that the image of the Klan as at once apparent and invisible, and the status of Klan accounts as detailed and rigorously documented yet also incredible, was a productive feature of Klan discourse. The very ambiguity of the Klan's status played an important role in the reconciliation of North and South.

The last two chapters zoom in for a close view of one southern county both before and after the arrival of the idea of the Ku-Klux and the explosion of terrible Ku-Klux violence. The translocal, disembodied idea of the Klan had to take root in specific local communities. Chapter 6 explores the Klan's emergence in Union County, South Carolina, a community with its own robust and articulated culture of racial violence. Based on a network analysis of social relationships taken from the county's criminal indictment records, this chapter explains what, structurally, happened to patterns of violence in Union County when the Klan emerged there in 1868 and then again in 1870. In the wake of the Civil War, an effective black leadership emerged in the county that gained desirable elective and patronage positions, made meaningful connections with powerful leaders beyond the county, and began to prosecute white criminal actors and vice businesses that had long been tolerated in the county, and that many whites in the county depended upon. While much Klan violence seems to have been committed by small local groups, two incidents were notable exceptions to this pattern: the two deadly jail raid executions conducted by large groups of socially elite Ku-Klux. This chapter argues that in these larger attacks, these elites worked in collaboration with local established violent actors to suppress the threat of the new black leadership.

Chapter 7 explores how journalists and political leaders outside Union County responded to and represented its violence, and how Union County elites controlled how their violence would be understood and appropriated by outsiders. Labeling violence as "Ku-Klux," and therefore as a fundamentally extralocal conflict, had powerful practical consequences: both Republicans and Democrats in Union showed an initial reluctance to apply the label. By late 1870, however, both sides were deliberately using the definition. Political leaders and the state and national press both showed great interest in Union events, sending a bizarre array of representatives from the outside, including detectives, gold miners, a couple dozen armed Bowery Boys, a former filibuster leader, and three U.S. congressmen and their entourage, into the county to assess and intervene in events in the county.

In their desire to frame the postwar oppression of black southerners and their allies in useful and compelling ways, northerners inadvertently helped to construct and proliferate the idea of the Ku-Klux. We cannot know what southern racial and political violence would have looked like in the early Reconstruction era in the absence of Ku-Klux. Yet this book argues that the Klan idea energized white violent actors, made their violence meaningful, valorized extreme displays of black pain, and spread the idea of the Ku-Klux through culture. There is good reason to suspect that, absent the Klan, anti-Republican violence would have been less common, less sadistic, and less terrifying.

This gives me pause as I write this book into the popular discourse of the twenty-first century. I imagine myself to be writing for a sympathetic and like-minded reader, though an acute and critical one. But once words have been made public, they become available to anyone, and for any purpose. When I have published parts of this research in the past few years, it has occasionally found its way onto racist websites, where snippets of it have been used free of context to support deplorable claims. The idea of the Klan is still alive, now, perhaps, more than a decade ago. Some people, dangerously, still adopt an identity as Klansmen. Klan organizations, rallies, and parades, with their toxic combination of racism and the glorification of violence, are a decidedly marginal but persistent part of American life. Discussing the historical Klan, however critically, keeps the idea of the Klan alive in the public discourse, making it feel, to a potential recruit, like a relevant identity in a way that, say, becoming a Molly McGuire might not be.

At the same time, the Ku-Klux remains a powerful symbol within antiracist discourse. Opposition to the Klan is so nearly universal that it serves a crucial function in building and maintaining public awareness of the dangers of racial oppression and violence. These dangers are, unfortunately, still with us, and being able to mobilize an image of a centralized, powerful Klan, one not muddled up by a historian, might have real practical value. Revealing the complexities of the historical actions of the Ku-Klux, and of the idea of the Ku-Klux, could make the symbol less easily available for these purposes. It also, however, makes the symbol less easily available to a small but tenacious group of people who would defend the Ku-Klux today.

The Ku-Klux was not as centralized or institutionalized as many non-historians today believe it was. But the fact that false and exaggerated claims circulated made actual Ku-Klux attacks no less real or deadly. Thousands of Ku-Klux groups existed. They killed, raped, brutalized, robbed, and terrorized black and white Republicans throughout the South. While the idea of the Klan was culturally constructed, the suffering caused by those who assumed that constructed identity was palpable. It is the very definition of terrorism that it produces surplus fears. Many false claims were made a few years back about the scope and capacity of al-Qaeda. As we struggled to understand the 9/11 attacks in its immediate aftermath, based on thin information, many of us saw al-Qaeda everywhere. This overreaction, however, does not call into question the existence of an actual al-Qaeda and the catastrophe of the 9/11 attacks. Some conspiracy theorists did, and do, make that claim, believing that our own government orchestrated the attack as an excuse for aggression and federal expansion, but this conspiracy theory has remained marginal. It is perhaps an indication of the extent of the cultural damage done by the Civil War that Reconstruction-era publics, north and south, took the parallel claim, that the Klan was simply manufactured by the federal government to justify its continued control in the South, much more seriously.

Many people were able to think about the Klan without focusing on the extreme suffering that the Klan was perpetrating only because they were able to ignore or dehumanize Klan victims and dismiss their suffering. In discussing the discursive significance of the Ku-Klux, this book potentially risks doing the same thing. Why care about parades, false facial hair, and Ku-Klux euchre? What mattered about the Klan was the pain and oppression that it inflicted. Every distraction from that core reality is in some sense an act of disrespect to the victims. From this perspective, it is troubling that the Ku-Klux and their supporters, distracted northerners and their mixed motives, loom much larger in this manuscript than do the rural freedmen and white republicans who were the Klan's victims. When they do come into clearest focus, in chapters 5 and 6, their words and perspectives are loud and powerful and do in fact disrupt the intentions and framings of Klan supporters and northern observers. But we spend most of this book dwelling on the intentions, concerns, motivations, and interests of the victims' attackers and observers, rather than on their own experience.

It is important to resist Ku-Klux claims that there was anything bizarre about it. The Klan was deeply implicated in, and drew from, seemingly innocuous or positive elements of American culture. The idea of the Klan, if not its actions, served the purposes of many Americans of many regions and political alignments. Contemporaries and historians have liked to imagine the Klan as appearing out of nowhere, plaguing the devastated South for a few years after the war, and disappearing again until it was evoked anew in the early twentieth century. The truth is much less comforting. Mardi Gras parades, modern business practices, the Masons, the burlesque, baseball, the professionalization of reporting, the establishment of a functional federal government infrastructure, and sensational fiction all played a role in helping the idea of the Klan, and therefore the reality of the Klan, to circulate and operate. The Klan did not materialize out of nowhere, and neither did it really go away.

ONE

The Roots of the Ku-Klux Klan
in Pulaski, Tennessee

I will only add that nearly all the BLOOD AND THUNDER proclamations
and general orders issued in circular form or printed in the columns of THE
CITIZEN when the order was in its incipient form and before it had assumed
political significations, originated in the brain and were written by the Faber of
the then editor of THE CITIZEN, solely for fun and sensational effect. What
editor, pray tell me, imbued with the least journalistic enterprise, would have
failed to take advantage of the circumstances and enlivened his cou[rse] with
these sensational fulminations? Would you? This is my excuse and defense.

—From "Mr. Frank McCord Tells What He Knows about the Kuklux,"
    Pulaski Citizen, clipping dated December 18, 1892

The Ku-Klux began as a name. It was chosen by a group of young former
Confederates in Pulaski, Tennessee, in May or June 1866.[1] Pulaski, the
seat of Giles County, is seventy-four miles south of Nashville, connected
to the city by the Nashville and Decatur Railroad. The war's shadow fell
heavily on the nation, but Pulaski bore a disproportionate share of suffering. While it was never itself a battlefield, Federal troops had occupied
it, and it was in close proximity to some of the war's most deadly fighting. Union troops camped in Pulaski in the days before the bloody Battle
of Nashville, and were a frequent presence throughout the war.[2] These
strains may have contributed to the area's fraught postwar atmosphere.

Giles County saw more than its share of "the ordinary violence of
emancipation."[3] As early as 1866, Giles County experienced particularly
heightened racial conflict and noteworthy resistance to federal control. A
group of black leaders emerged in Giles during the war, including Dangerfield "Danger" Rhodes (a brickmason, aged fifty-three at the end of
the war, who had been buying his time from his master for some years

before the war and owned several horses and mules; he sharecropped with his sons during the war and would report $1,900 in property on the 1870 census), Henry Webb, Orange Jones, and others. These were, as one of their number was described, "active energetic m[e]n with good hard homade Sense," who had won the respect not only of other black Giles Countians, but also of some Union officers (some of whom had stayed on Danger Rhodes's place during the war).[4] They also worked to support less well-positioned freedpeople: Freedmen's Bureau superintendent R. C. Caldwell described Danger Rhodes as "a very deserving colored man . . . who beyond his means has been alleviating the wants & necessities of the poor of his race. During the winter he has had under his roof one man (crushed in the tornado . . .), & a nurse for the same, a lying-in woman with three children; all of whom he had to feed & furnish fuel. They sought his house for refuge in their distress, and he would not turn them away from his door."[5] They reported local problems to sympathetic federal officials. By early 1866, they sent a collective letter to Freedmen's Bureau assistant commissioner Clinton Fisk: "There is a disposission on the part of the white Citizens some of them to impose and [sic] the colored citizens."[6] They reported that whites refused to let them use the church basement that had been promised to them for their own church services (after allowing them to renovate it for the purpose), and also refused to allow a black-owned grocery to sell alcoholic beverages, despite its proper licensing.[7] They gave several compelling accounts of abuse. A black saloonkeeper in Pulaski hung a sign out that said "Equal Rights," which whites immediately tore down. Pulaski was the kind of place where such a sign would have been pulled down, but it is perhaps even more significant that it was the kind of place where someone was going to put it up to begin with.[8]

Freedmen's Bureau agents consistently identified whites in Giles as particularly oppressive of freedpeople. Superintendent Caldwell took the freedmen's part, and they considered him well-meaning but complained that he was ineffective. Finding Caldwell unable to stop "gross outrages" in the county, the Bureau removed him in June 1866, and soon replaced him with Captain George E. Judd, a man of firmer mettle and backed by a cavalry.[9] Reporting to his commander Michael Walsh in December 1866, Judd was struck by the unreconstructed nature of Giles County whites, even compared to whites in nearby counties. "It can almost be said that there is no law in Giles County all do just as they see fit without regard to law or decency."[10]

Freedmen's Bureau officials could not agree on where to assign blame for aggression against freedpeople in Pulaski. Sometimes the perpetrators were clearly landowners. Prominent Confederate leader John C. Brown lived in Pulaski, and the local editor of the Democratic paper, the *Pulaski Citizen*, Frank McCord, was believed to be drumming up antiblack sentiment.[11] But those same Freedmen's Bureau officials also pointed to lower-class whites, "roughs," as the heart of the problem. Captain George E. Judd, soon after his arrival in Pulaski, fingered poor whites, "men who amount to nothing, have no property and no principle," or "the low class of whites."[12] The *Pulaski Citizen* agreed with the Freedmen's Bureau that street violence by rowdies was a major problem. Their town was overtaken with the "horse-thieves, housebreakers, loafers and whisky-heads of this community" indulging "their propensities for committing depredations upon the public and reveling in their midnight orgies," the paper said. It called for Pulaski's more publicly inclined citizens to put an end to it: "Our citizens should take the matter in their own hands and endeavor to rid the country of such villains."[13]

Events nearby contributed to the tension and disorder. The Memphis Riot in May 1866, followed by the New Orleans Riot in July, each left dozens of black people dead at the hands of white mobs: many more black urbanites suffered rape, beatings, arson, and theft during these sprees of intense racial violence. The urban race riot was a novel form of violence for the South, a response by whites to freedpeople's new claims and practices, and it was hard not to notice that the federal government was unable or unwilling to protect freedpeople from such extreme violence, nor even to find and punish wrongdoers in its wake. As one black Pulaskian worried, "Those Memphis Riots are having their effect here."[14] Organized white violence began to feel attractive and pragmatic to strong southern partisans, and unfortunately inevitable to many others. By the summer of 1867, some political leaders were calling quite publicly for organized resistance to black claims to political, social, and economic rights, and to federal authority. Influential former confederate general Albert Pike advised Tennessee's conservative whites to form themselves into civic guard companies.[15]

The Ku-Klux Klan was created at this moment and in this place. As the story goes,

One evening in May, 1866, a few . . . young men met in the office of one of the most prominent members of the Pulaski bar. In the course of the conversation one of the number said: "Boys, let us get up a club of society of some description." The suggestion was discussed with enthusiasm. . . . The committee appointed to select a name, reported that they had found the task difficult, and had not made a selection. They explained that they had been trying to discover or invent a name which would be, to some extent, suggestive of the character and objects of the society. They mentioned several which they had been considering. In this number was the name "Kukloi" from the Greek word *Kuklos*, meaning a band or circle. At mention of this, some one cried out: "Call it Ku Klux." "Klan" at once suggested itself, and was added to complete the alliteration. So instead of adopting a name, as was the first intention, which had a definite meaning, they chose one which to the proposer of it, and to every one else, was absolutely meaningless.

The men who first became Ku-Klux—Frank O. McCord, Richard Reed, John C. Lester, Calvin Jones, John Booker Kennedy, and James Crowe—presented themselves as elites and intellectuals, above and opposed to the violence of rough men, but also as men who felt the stern responsibility to restore their collapsed society. All were Confederate veterans who had returned to a devastated and depressed Pulaski. They came from comfortable backgrounds and were in their mid-twenties through mid-thirties. Frank McCord, who was thirty-three in 1866, was listed in the 1870 census as an editor of the *Pulaski Citizen*, and had $3,000 in property. The paper was owned by his younger brother Luther. While never listed as a founding member, Luther would play a crucial role in the beginnings of the Klan. Twenty-seven years old in 1866, he boasted $10,000 in combined property on the 1870 census. Calvin Jones and John Lester appear in the census as attorneys. Richard Reed was thirty-six in 1866. He alone does not appear in the 1870 census, but in 1860 he was a thirty-year-old attorney reporting no property and living in a boardinghouse with other professionals. Calvin Jones in 1870 would still be living with his very wealthy lawyer father (who reported $35,000 in 1870); in 1866 he would have been twenty-five. Thirty-three-year-old John Lester was his close neighbor and also lived with an older male relative, probably his father, and reported no property in 1870. James Crowe was twenty-seven in 1866. By the 1870 census he would call himself a cotton broker and report $10,500 in property. There are a few John Kennedys in the 1860 and 1870 Giles Census, but the correct one is probably the one who appears in

1860 as a twenty-year-old living with a prosperous farmer and personally claiming $20,000 in combined property (an inheritance: his three younger siblings each also had $20,000). Luther and Frank had attended two years of Lagrange College in Alabama, and Crowe and Lester too had some higher education, the former at Giles College, the latter at Center College in Danville, Kentucky.[16] They were seen by those sympathetic to them as educated elites. Luther McCord's younger brother Lapsley, in an obituary, would praise him as "widely read."[17] Pulaskian Mildred Ezell Reynolds later proudly recalled that the early Klan "was composed of the nicest and most cultured young men in the town and country, thus the origin of the club's name is Greek."[18] Mrs. S. E. F. (Laura) Rose similarly noted years later that "the very conception of the Ku-Klux was amid influences elevating and refining, and its charter members were gentlemen of education and refined tastes."[19] None of the founders was a plantation owner, and only Crowe (at least by 1870) had a position directly tied to agriculture, so the impact of the end of slavery was perhaps less direct on them than on many others.

These men may, early on, have been joined by George W. Gordon, who had been a general in the Confederate army. He was a lawyer in Pulaski at the time, so in such a small community he would have known the original group well. While early texts do not mention him as among the original members, a prescript and pin that have been passed down by his family and are now held by the Tennessee State Historical museum suggest that he had early involvement with the group. Historian Stanley Horn suggests that he was the author of the original Prescript.[20]

The men who conceived of the Ku-Klux Klan were naturally worried not only about public order in the streets of Pulaski, but more generally about the explosive political situation of Tennessee, the dire situation their community found itself in, and the extent to which former Confederates would have the right to participate in the new state and national governments. They also worried about the role freedpeople would take in the new social, political, and economic order, and how they might relate to them.

These men coexisted uncomfortably with the confident emergent class of black leaders, yet the violent oppression of the latter by the former was perhaps not seen as inevitable by either group just after the war. When an 1866 article in the *Pulaski Citizen* referred to "Danger Rodes" as "one of our most honorable and industrious colored citizens," the designation may have been intended as parody. But it seems likely that it was not.

The article approved of his having shot a man stealing from his watermelon patch, and the joke was at the thief's expense.[21] As long as Rhodes and other black elites were in close and positive communication with a nearby military force that was potentially willing to intervene on their behalf, white Democratic elites were motivated to take them seriously.

The first Ku-Klux was likely not founded for the direct purpose of racial conflict. The nonpolitical origin of the Ku-Klux is one of the few areas where historians have largely agreed.[22] Allen Trelease could not have been clearer: "The Ku-klux was designed purely for amusement, and for some time after its founding it had no ulterior motive or effect. All the evidence supports this."[23] Yet the evidence is so scant and unreliable that it must be approached with care.

Mainly, historians have based claims to the Klan's innocent origins on brief accounts of its founding written by former members more than a decade later for the explicit purpose of celebrating the Ku-Klux's role in redeeming the South from Reconstruction. Original member James R. Crowe, for instance, wrote, "The first meeting was purely social. We would frequently meet after the day's business was over in some room or office. We would have music and songs. [Frank] McCord was one of the finest violinists I have ever known and [Calvin] Jones was equally gifted as a guitarist. We would go and see the pretty girls of Pulaski or go serenading and amuse ourselves as best we could."[24] Frank McCord claimed that the group was "longing for some kind of amusement and recreation, and organized for the purpose mentioned."[25] John C. Lester (with his collaborator D. L. Wilson) wrote that all members agreed that "the end in view" was "diversion and amusement."[26] In his unpublished 1911 historical novel about the Ku-Klux, Frank McCord's younger brother Lapsley remembers that in its early days "there were parties of them out nearly every evening calling upon their sweethearts."[27] The one outsider who claimed to have seen Ku-Klux before 1867 (he testified to having seen them in the fall of 1866, though he was most likely mistaken in his date and meant fall of 1867) had witnessed their appearance at a "moon-light pic-nic in a beech-grove, where they emerged to enjoy the entertainment."[28]

There is material evidence that the Ku-Klux's founders participated in the minstrel tradition: Frank McCord's fiddle is in the collection of the Tennessee State Historical Museum. A contemporary image further supports this account of the Ku-Klux's origins. The image, labeled "Midnight Rangers, Pulaski, Sept. 3, 1866," depicts seven young men with

A *carte de visite*, on the reverse of which is written "Midnight Rangers, Pulaski, Sept. 3rd 1866," that shows what may have been the earliest members of the Ku-Klux Klan in Pulaski, Tennessee: (*back row, left to right*) John Lester, Calvin Jones, Richard Reed; (*front row, left to right*) Frank McCord, unidentified, John Booker Kennedy, and James Crowe. Thank you to Bob Wamble for pointing me to it. Courtesy of the Giles County Historical Society.

musical instruments, including fiddles, a guitar, and a banjo. Discovered by Pulaski historian Bob Wamble, the *carte de visite* likely represents an early incarnation of the Ku-Klux. Comparing the *carte de visite* with the few available contemporary images of the original Ku-Klux, Wamble provisionally identifies six of them as John Lester, Calvin Jones, Richard Reed, Frank McCord, John Booker Kennedy, and James Crowe. He was unable to identify the seventh.[29] While their faces are not blackened, their informal dress, jaunty poses with hats askew, and choice of instruments suggest that they are performing in either the minstrel tradition or a related genre. If the Ku-Klux founders were not the men depicted in this image, they were down the street doing the same thing; if the men in the picture were not the future Ku-Klux, their name (to Civil War–era Americans, "rangers" meant "informal militia") associated them with nocturnal violence. If this group is the Klan founders, their choice of a paramilitary name shows that anger and the idea of violence were present from the beginning, even though the evidence (or the absence of evidence) suggests that the idea of violence was as far as they went.

Whatever the Pulaski Ku-Klux did or intended in this earliest period, the lack of mentions of them in other sources up through the spring of 1867 indicates that they did not gain much attention. No violence during this period was attributed to "the Ku-Klux." They could have been engaging in political or violent behavior anonymously. Some Ku-Klux members may have been committing violence, perhaps against freedpeople, perhaps even collectively, but the qualities that would make Ku-Klux violence distinctive—an excessively performative quality, together with claims on the part of the attackers that they were part of a larger movement—were not present in any attacks that Ku-Klux members may have perpetrated in these early days. Unless one imagines Ku-Klux were consciously staying out of the limelight while planning (a posture that would suggest a remarkable ability to predict the explosive future of the thing they were creating), Ku-Klux members through the spring of 1867 did nothing to differentiate themselves from other white social and fraternal orders of the time.

Still, the professed innocence of Ku-Klux origins does not fit easily with what we know about the men who began it or with the circumstances of early Reconstruction-era Tennessee.[30] The Pulaski founders saw themselves as having an important role in civic affairs. Frank McCord was the local news editor for Pulaski's newspaper. Reed, Jones, and Lester were lawyers. Kennedy would be elected clerk of the Lawrence County Circuit Court in the 1880s. Crowe would become an insurance salesman. They were organizers and joiners, the rising generation of Pulaski's leaders. It seems incongruous that, during such a crisis, these men would have invested their time and organizational energy in something purely for entertainment.

There is a way to reconcile the Ku-Klux founders' seriousness with the apparent frivolousness of their actions: they were engaged in entertainment with a purpose and saw the very act of organizing themselves as having a publicly significant end. Forming a social group might get young white elite potential leaders moving. Letting the community know about such a group's existence might remind them that they matter. At the time they conceived of the Ku-Klux, Pulaski's elite young men not only were unhappy about their troubling political and economic situation; they were also deeply worried about their own lack of occupation. Many traditional paths through which they might distinguish themselves were closed to them. The original Ku-Klux were attempting to reestablish their careers: one of them went to work for his younger brother as a local news editor; two others, Richard Reed and John Lester, took up law offices around Pulaski's central square. But they were hardly beginning their careers in a promising environment. In addition to the South's general stench of defeat, Pulaski's tiny business district had sustained a lot of damage during the war, and no one had rebuilt it. To make matters worse, a fire would sweep through the district in the spring of 1867, destroying, among other things, the law offices of both Reed and Lester, apparently leaving Reed with nothing but a suit of clothes and his pocket watch.[31] The men of Pulaski, according a *Citizen* article in January 1867, needed to "break the monotony of this work and eat style we have gotten into."[32] A letter written by a pseudonymous Pulaski resident to the *Nashville Union and Dispatch* more than a year after the Ku-Klux's beginnings, in October 1867, mentioned that Pulaski residents were finally dealing with buildings damaged in the war and since, and claimed hopefully, "Pulaski is arousing from the lethargy which seemed to have been characteristic of its people since the war."[33] The Ku-Klux was "got up" at least in part to provide its members with something to do. The Pulaski Ku-Klux recognized the South's cultural collapse and state of lassitude as a serious problem demanding a collective solution, and also as a more tractable problem than its political collapse. What better way to address it than to form some of the best young men in the town into a secret society to pursue this purpose?

Many former Confederates saw rebuilding a southern culture as an important social good. Antebellum political mobilization had been closely tied to public entertainments like parades and picnics: the categories of "entertainment" and "politics" were not neatly segregated in Reconstruction-era Americans' minds.[34] The politically utility of organizing an association for amusement would have been apparent to any socially engaged adult in the nineteenth century. Tournaments, balls, masquerades, parades, and the like played a prominent role in the activities of politically minded former confederates.[35] These early Reconstruction-era entertainments were frequently patronized, organized, and endorsed by Confederate political figures. They had various immediate and concrete benefits: it was often possible to sneak the content of southern nationalism or contempt for northerners into these seemingly innocuous cultural forms, and cultural events could likewise be used to raise money for southern causes like the support of war widows and orphans. But they also had the larger purpose of unifying and invigorating demoralized southern society. The willingness of former Confederates at the highest level to spend substantial energy organizing and participating in entertainments suggests that they too appreciated the political utility of popular culture to the South's future. To take one of many possible examples, two of the elite men who would later be portrayed as crucial to the Ku-Klux's growth beyond Middle Tennessee, Nathan Bedford Forrest and John C. Brown, were, at the time that the Ku-Klux was being created in Giles, occupied in judging and awarding prizes to participants in a jousting tournament for the benefit of an Orphan Asylum.[36]

The men who thought up the Ku-Klux shared in this broad belief in the political valence of entertainment. In January 1867, the *Pulaski Citizen* expressed the sense that entertainment was a necessary civic good. In a richly significant article called "Amusement Wanted," Frank McCord wrote, "We need an organized theatrical club in our midst—something of the drama—to teach that vice will not go unpublished and that virtue will meet its reward. If we can't have anything else, let us have one of the stroling [sic] minstrel bands of the country. . . . We shall advert to this subject again and try to stir our young men up to an effort to organize a dramatic club, such as we were proud of when the war cut short our social amusements."[37] The call for a theatrical club to combat vice (very close to what these men would come to believe they had created with the Ku-Klux) is here tied to an assertion of the civic value of creating an organically southern cultural space—something to be "proud of."

In fact, some early Ku-Klux were already using entertainment for political purposes. The first time after the Civil War that future Ku-Klux founders appeared in the public record working together was in May 1866, just about the time when the Ku-Klux is believed to have been founded. Three of the six founders, "R. R. Reed, J. C. Lester, and James Crow," appeared in the *Pulaski Citizen* on the list of organizers of a series of tableaux staged to raise funds for artificial limbs for maimed Confederate veterans.[38] Crowe appeared in one scene as the Emperor Aurelian, and Lester appeared in "Queen Elizabeth Discovering Her Favorite's Marriage." Most of the scenes were selected for their expression of domestic sentiment or the opportunity they provided for the young women of Pulaski to display themselves. Parts of it, though, such as Crowe's Zenobia and Aurelian tableau, also had an obvious political message. The scene of the conquered warrior princess "raising her deprecating, but manacled hands" inspired McCord's newspaper to reflect that "the fetters degraded not [her] but the haughty Roman who had imposed them."[39]

Pulaski founders later explained their decision to begin the Ku-Klux in similar terms. In 1884 original member John Lester and his coauthor D. L. Wilson published what is by far the most thorough account of the Ku-Klux's founding,

> When the war ended in 1865, the young men of Pulaski . . . returned home and passed through a period of enforced inactivity. In some respects it was more trying than the ordeal of war which lay behind them. The reaction which followed the excitement of army scenes and service was intense. There was nothing to relieve it. They could not engage at once in business or professional pursuits. Their business habits were broken up. None had capital with which to conduct agricultural pursuits or to engage in mercantile enterprises. And this restlessness was made more intense by the total lack of the amusements and social diversions which prevail wherever society is in a normal condition.[40]

Lester and Wilson's description of the nature of Ku-Klux founders' motivations is jarring in that it is distinctively modern. If the condition of the modern is the "disembedding . . . of social relations from local contexts of interaction," a sense of discontinuity and rupture with the structures of the past, a break with a providential view of history, an adoption of a belief in the contingent nature of historical change, and a move from status-based to contractual relationships, the Lester and Wilson passage gestures toward many of these things: a clear sense of rupture, a sense that the forces that controlled their future were not in Giles County itself, secular framing, and a search for a role that indicates no expectation of secure status.[41]

Another indication of the modernity of Lester and Wilson's account is the term "restlessness." The word had a modern feel. Its rate of usage had been increasing substantially and consistently through the nineteenth century.[42] But the passage evokes the modern in other ways as well: "They could not engage at once in business or professional pursuits. Their business habits were broken up." This is not the language of the plantation-house parlor, or, if one believes that southern plantation practices had been surreptitiously modernizing in just this way in the late antebellum period, it was not language that evoked plantation culture, as it was already coming to be idealized. Rather, it gestured eagerly toward the urban, industrialized Northeast. At the time, Lester and Wilson were writing almost two decades after the founding of the Ku-Klux—perhaps they were projecting the New South back onto its origins. But its consistency with complaints about purposelessness in the *Pulaski Citizen* of 1866 suggests that the sense of personal crisis among local young men feeling their lack of occupation was a key impetus for Ku-Klux. The young men of Pulaski suffered after their defeat, but those who founded the Ku-Klux framed their suffering in terms evoking a modern northern business ethic.

To appreciate this modern framing, consider the potential framings that Lester and Wilson and the *Pulaski Citizen* notably neglected: theological language and the language of honor. Reading through both the *Pulaski Citizen* and later accounts of the Ku-Klux's founding, one finds remarkably little evocation of the idea of honor or of God's will. This language sometimes comes through in poems, letters, and articles reprinted in the *Citizen*, but rarely in the editorial voice itself. Making sense of the South's defeat, and beginning to imagine how to rebuild, the *Citizen*'s columns did not bemoan the war as humiliating and unmanning. While the paper complained frequently of disorder and loitering on the streets of Pulaski, it did not seem particularly troubled, specifically, by the lack of deference displayed by black people toward white. Nor did it excruciate over the fact that God had allowed the North to prevail. The problem with the defeat, to the *Citizen*, was not that it had interrupted traditional relationships among men or between men and God. It was that it had left them without a meaningful and usable society.

Lester and Wilson's text presents the Ku-Klux's founding in a crisp, matter-of-fact tone that feels so modern in part because of the only scattered and ornamental references to divine purpose or romantic notions of honor, and in part because of the writers' shrugging acknowledgment that power and culture were translocal, in flux, and circulating in strange and inscrutable ways. As Lester and Wilson said at the beginning of their discussion of the Ku-Klux's proliferation, "A wave of excitement, spreading by contagions till the minds of a whole people are in ferment, is an event of frequent occurrent."[43] The Ku-Klux's purpose was conceived of by its founders in relationship to a dynamic changing culture rather than to a stable and status-based one.

The idea of the Ku-Klux was not the product of plantation culture. Neither its founders nor many of its key early supporters were the sort of southerners that southerners themselves considered typical. Rather, the Ku-Klux's ideas, structure, and early energy came from professional young men living in the Upper South, in town, inhabiting an intellectual universe in which northern ideas and institutions played an important part. Part of the effectiveness of the Ku-Klux idea would be that it explosively applied northern framings to the southern situation. It made the Ku-Klux feel fresh and powerful to southerners, and caused northerners to find it relevant and fascinating.

The member of the Pulaski circle about whose political and social views we know the most is Luther McCord, the younger brother of original leading member Frank McCord and the owner and editor-in-chief of the *Pulaski Citizen*, for which Frank would serve as local editor during the Reconstruction era. Luther McCord had held many ideas that resonated with urban northern culture before the war. He had been very much part of an antebellum liberal and cosmopolitan conversation. While some caution may be called for in reading his views onto the rest of the Pulaski Klan founders (about whose ideas we know much less), knowing his positions, they joined him in forming the Klan and used his paper as their group's mouthpiece.

McCord's paper, in the last years before the war, had been reformist and antisecessionist. The *Citizen* called repeatedly for women's rights, arguing (à la Margaret Fuller) that every woman needed "a purpose in life,—a business—some industrial pursuit" in order to become "a type of [her] kind."[44] The paper actively participated in and advocated for an antebellum temperance movement that was dominated in the South by the minority of elites with a professional or industrial orientation.[45] It also consistently opposed the Democratic Party. As Frank and Luther's younger brother Lapsley McCord later remembered, the paper "gravitated quickly toward Whiggery or Knownothingism and [Luther McCord] became a strong partisan of [Constitutional Union Party candidate] John Bell."[46] Luther McCord most dramatically demonstrated his orientation to the North in his passionate and consistent objection to secession. McCord went so far as to travel to Washington, D.C., in May 1860 in hopes of contributing to a sectional compromise.[47] As late as March 22, 1861, the *Citizen* was still desperately arguing against secession.[48]

Though they never use the term itself, the way in which Lester and Wilson, and also Frank McCord, describe the experience of the Ku-Klux founders is similar to what people a few years later would call boredom. It may seem as though boredom has been always with us, but the term "boredom," which had long specifically referred to the experience of being spoken to by a bore, or to an imagined collection of bores, had only in the 1840s begun to take on its broader modern meaning. Even by the late 1860s, it was used almost exclusively either in this older sense or to refer to two specific situations to which "boredom" was frequently applied in popular novels: disenchantment with marriage and the emptiness of fashionable life.[49] It is unsurprising that Lester and McCord did not use this term to describe the mental distress of the men who created the Ku-Klux, but rather two closely associated terms, "restlessness" and "longing."

Boredom was a concept closely tied to modernization and industrialization. As Walter Benjamin pronounced, "In the [1840s] boredom began to be felt on an epidemic scale."[50] Elizabeth Goldstein relates the rise of the idea of boredom in Western culture in the mid-nineteenth century to broader cultural shifts that fit under the rubric of modernism. First, as traditional understandings of the self and of the value of one's life's work ceased being theological and became fundamentally social, a language of boredom replaced theologically valenced descriptors of the failure to internalize and adhere to norms. A fundamentally new experience emerged, of suffering because one is spending time in a way disconnected from socially-valued goals, failing to enhance one's position within the broader society. Second, as people began to experience their world as transitory, to believe that stable old forms were passing away, replaced by fleeting "modern" styles and fashions, boredom expressed a sense of purposelessness or alienation. Finally, boredom often expressed the failures of the much-touted new regime to deliver satisfaction: the thwarted promise of science to give human beings control over nature and of the era's political revolutions to give individuals agency within their societies.[51]

All of these meanings were relevant to the founders of the Ku-Klux. They were Presbyterians and Methodists, but they did not speak of the world in religious terms: they lived in secular rather than sacred time, oriented toward their relationship to the dynamic political, cultural, and social world surrounding them. One can easily imagine how the fleetingness of historical forms would have occurred to them as they spent their days in a burned-out town square, and how they might have had the sensation of perpetually wasting time, unable to use it to achieve goals they found meaningful. Finally, if boredom emerges "whenever the promise of political emancipation is frustrated" and "marks the discrepancy between the actual and the imagined," those young and able Pulaski men, defeated soldiers and civic boosters with precious little to boost, were prime candidates for the very modern experience of boredom.[52]

Later southerners who adopted the Klan identity knew little or noth-ing about the McCords or their ideas. Few had any idea that the Klan had began in Pulaski, and certainly did not consult them as authorities, to the first Ku-Klux's chagrin. Nevertheless, the Pulaskians' urge to bring the trappings of the modern to their southern conditions and practices would shape the Klan's performative identity in ways identifiably modern and with a northern valence. Though the Ku-Klux itself was instrumental in reestablishing an antebellum status quo, those who built the idea of the Ku-Klux were not so much wishing they were in the land of cotton as they were "restless" for "business and professional pursuits." It is no coincidence that southerners who supported the Ku-Klux they created would sometimes claim that it had originated in the North.[53]

WHAT, THEN, DID these young white men of Pulaski create during that crucial first year? Despite the thinness and unreliability of descriptions of their earliest meetings, we know what they had to offer by the time they "went public" in the spring and summer of 1867. This tells us that they must have focused, during this first year, on organization and ritual.

There is no definitive answer to where the name "Kuklux" (as it was first spelled in the *Pulaski Citizen*) came from. Since lying about the Ku-Klux would almost immediately become constitutive of being a Ku-Klux, the first Ku-Klux's accounts of their origins need to be taken with skepti-cism. Yet their account makes sense. The nonsense of the name was understood by early Ku-Klux as a feature. The name, Lester and Wilson claimed, was "utterly meaningless" but had an air of the "mysterious." While the choice of such a name was "apparently accidental," "the mem-bers of the Klan themselves were the first to feel its weird influence." The name had a power Ku-Klux founders did not understand but nevertheless felt and made use of, to such a great extent that "the original plan was modified so as to make everything connected with the order harmonize with the name."[54] Ultimately, Lester and Wilson tell us, it was this name, and the mystery it evoked, that would fuel the Ku-Klux's growth: "a wave of excitement, spreading by contagion."[55]

Even the name evoked the modern. Spelling "Clan" as "Klan," and the peculiar orthography that would come to be associated with the Ku-Klux (switching *c*'s to *k*'s and spelling things based on their sound rather than on a conventional dictionary spelling), was very much of the period. Many mid-nineteenth-century Americans, including many southerners, were interested in the relationship between the spoken and written word.

Replicas of Robert J. Brunson's Ku-Klux Klan robe and hood produced by the Conservation Workshop, Inc., of South Salem, New York, in 1993. The original, dated 1866, is from the collections of the Giles County Historical Society and housed at the Tennessee State Museum. The replica is owned by the Tennessee State Museum. The front of the original hood is made of ecru cotton and decorated with paint, fabric, and tape to resemble a face. Eye holes are cut out, and the eyebrows are made of black fabric. The nose is burgundy and applied with a running stitch. The beard is made of gray paint, and tape fragments are stitched around the perimeter of the face. The top of the hood is burgundy and ecru striped, and terminates in a striped tassel.

The original robe is a full-length burgundy cotton trimmed in ecru. The collar fastens with hook and eyes. The fourteen ecru-cotton-covered, nonfunctional buttons are arranged, evenly spaced, in pairs to just below the waist. A two-and-one-half-inch-wide strip of ecru cotton fabric is appliqued down the front of the robe and along the hem, on either side of the neck, and continues on the back to form a point; a covered button sits just below the point. A five-pointed star below a crescent is on the breast, and a small embroidered floral motif is in the center of the star. The robe sleeves are slightly gathered at the arms and each has a five-pointed star at the shoulder. A band of ecru cotton fabric is around each cuff, and a single covered button is above the band on either sleeve. Courtesy of the Tennessee State Museum Collection, Nashville.

Dialect literature flourished at this time, as did philology.[56] It was a major idea in the nationalist mid-nineteenth century that culture, and particularly language, was constitutive of regional identity, and the idea that a nation's identity resided in its cultural traditions and language had been an important component of the development of southern identity. Contemporary German Romantic ideas about culture, language, and nation had flowed into the antebellum South.[57] The *Pulaski Independent Citizen* had participated in the project of imagining a southern vernacular by carrying a number of stories in dialect, including "darky," "yankee," and foreign dialects as well as those of Crockett-like southern and Western figures, from 1859 through 1861.[58]

The "Klan" also gestured toward self-consciously nostalgic writer Sir Walter Scott, making the name discursively rich. Scott was the quintessential advocate of an old honor-based cultural tradition, and his major novels had been around for decades, but he was at the same time a popular writer and a foreigner whose own origin and writing about exotic places gave his work a whiff of the cosmopolitan. To take his "clan," transform it with a fashionable substitution of a k for the c, and join it to two nonsense words gestured playfully toward the modern.

Ku-Klux costumes also evoked the modern. Ku-Klux, from the beginning, dedicated substantial time and energy to creating and describing their costuming. At the 1866 picnic described by the early witness (which was likely actually in 1867), they apparently wore "very tall hats . . . covered with spangles, with stars, and it was rather a pretty and showy costume . . . [with] a kind of talma or cloak thrown over their bodies, and then a tunic running down to their feet nearly."[59] The first article about them in the *Citizen*, in March 1867, reprinted a notice calling for them to assemble "in costume."[60] Lester and Wilson claim that "each member was required to provide himself with the following outfit: A white mask for the face, with orifices for the eyes and nose; a tall, fantastic cardboard hat, so constructed as to increase the wearer's apparent height; a gown, or robe, of sufficient length to cover the entire person. [Each member selected his own material, aiming to inspire] the greatest amount of curiosity . . . often of the most flashy patterns of 'Dolly Varden' calicos."[61]

The reference to "Dolly Varden calicos" is telling. Dolly Varden calicos were "creton chintzes of black or dark ground, with figures of Cupids, birds, butterflies, flowers and tendrils, all in the most vivid colors, and grouped as fantastically as the imagery of an opium eater's dream . . . just such materials as our grandmothers used to make their old fashioned bed curtains of."[62] The Dolly Varden costume, named after a character in a minor Dickens novel of the 1840s, became briefly fashionable in the late 1860s and early 1870s, so if they did in fact adopt Dolly Varden chintz in 1867, Ku-Klux were remarkably au courant for small-town Tennesseans. Probably, however, Lester and Wilson are projecting later fashions back onto the Ku-Klux. It makes the most sense to read this "Dolly Varden" reference as "printed calico in the latest fashion." "Dolly Varden calico" had other connotations as well. By the time Lester and Wilson were writing, it was associated with the loud and grotesque: comic rural characters in plays were costumed in it.[63] Still, while it was garish, it was also novel—the acid-washed denim of the Reconstruction era. Its very loudness marked the intrusion of modern manufacturing and international commerce on dress. The "Dolly Varden" costume appealed to rural Americans as cosmopolitan and new. As they eagerly appropriated it, the sophisticated began to see it as tacky and unsubtle, confirming rather than transcending the backwardness of the rural Americans wearing it. Lester and Wilson's claim that Ku-Klux had been clothed in it implied a (failed) gesture toward the fashionable. Whether this gesture should be taken as deliberately ironic, or whether the Ku-Klux was implicated in an ultimately embarrassing rural claim to the cosmopolitan, is not spelled out.

Historians have understood the period between March 1867 and early 1868 as crucial both in spreading the idea and organization of the Ku-Klux beyond Pulaski and in bringing order and a unified purpose to the many impromptu Ku-Klux groups emerging through the region. No one pins down precisely when the Ku-Klux began to threaten and commit violence upon freedpeople and white Republicans, but discussions of the timing of the transition tend to work from the understanding that Ku-Klux had turned to both politics and violence by late 1867.[64]

The claim that the Klan had begun to take on its violence and political character by 1867 rests on the much later claims of founding members and on three events. First, the *Citizen* began to print notices about the Ku-Klux beginning in March 1867. Second, an organizational meeting was apparently held in Nashville sometime that spring. Finally, the Ku-Klux apparently put on its "first public demonstration," a parade in Pulaski, in the summer of 1867. The sources relating to all three events are themselves deliberately opaque and prove much less about the nature of the Klan in 1867 than they seem to do. While they are immensely useful in filling out what the idea of the Ku-Klux had become by the spring and summer of 1867, they are substantially less informative about what Ku-Klux were actually doing.

The first of the three events was the Ku-Klux's decision to embrace publicity. In June 1866, almost exactly as the Ku-Klux was beginning, the *Citizen* published a column reflecting on sensationalism. It advised, "Whenever you wish to get up a sensation story, do it in this style."[65] But it was not until March 29, 1867, that the *Citizen* mentioned the Klan in its pages. After this first mention, it continued to print stories about the Ku-Klux roughly once per week until the early summer. These articles were decidedly nonserious. The first, "What Does It Mean?," playfully expressed the editor's (Frank or Luther McCord's) puzzlement at a cryptic Ku-Klux notice he had received (or, likely, written), seemingly calling a meeting. "Will anyone venture to tell me what it means and if it means anything at all? What is a 'Kuklux' and who is this 'Grand Cyclops' that issues his mysterious and imperative orders?"[66]

The following weeks' articles continued the bemused tone but introduced a darker note: the missives from the Grand Scribe (who sometimes materializes in the editorial offices, hands over the text, and vanishes without a trace) that the still-baffled editor "reprints" now contain new phrasing: "The hideous fiends of night are holding high carnival over a world that is all their own," and "Be conscious! Our Holy Den has been invaded by Spies!"[67] This sensational feel remains in subsequent articles into the summer. These early articles make no reference to politics or race. At least through June, the Ku-Klux's message was limited to conveying the very fact of its existence and a sensationalist style.

The second event that purportedly established a transition to politics and violence in 1867 was the Nashville organizational meeting. Here the contemporary sourcing is, at best, quite shaky. Almost all that historians know about the Nashville meeting comes from sources created years later: Lester and Wilson's book, Wilson's account printed in *Century Magazine* in 1884, and letters by Luther McCord and John Kennedy.[68] There is one piece of putatively contemporary evidence of the meeting: the Ku-Klux's original Prescript (its constitution), was apparently adopted there and given to George W. Gordon to draft.[69] This document is undated, however, and its provenance is in question; though Lester and Wilson tell us that it was distributed to "all known dens" after it was produced, almost all copies were allegedly destroyed when Forrest disbanded the Ku-Klux in 1869. The only two known copies were the one given to early Ku-Klux historian Walter Fleming many years later by Alabama Ku-Klux leader and *Tuscaloosa Independent Monitor* editor Ryland Randolph, and another handed down through George Gordon's family and currently held by the Tennessee State Museum. Randolph apparently used it in his capacity as Grand Giant in Alabama.[70] Randolph claimed his had been "issued by the headquarters of the Ku-klux (Memphis, I believe)" and sent to him.[71] He made no mention of the Nashville meeting. Gordon, of course, was from Pulaski and could just as well have written it from the comfort of home. A year later, this Original Prescript was apparently revised. The "Revised and Amended Prescript" included most of the text of the first (though it cut half of the Latin epigraphs), but also had an addition of about eight pages of material mainly relating to the Ku-Klux's ideology. This "Revised and Amended Prescript," which was reprinted at the time in local newspapers, is of much clearer authenticity. That is, we cannot be sure even that the original was written, as claimed, in 1867, and even less can we be sure that it was conceived of at a meeting in Nashville. We know for certain only that a document called a Revised Prescript had been written by mid-1868.

While the Original (like the Revised) Prescript projects a future, more elaborately organized Ku-Klux than ever came to realization, the style in which it is written and the plans it reveals tell us a good deal about the nature of its author(s). One of the most striking formal features of the Prescript is its display of erudition. Whoever wrote it not only had an elite education but took pains to convey that fact. It begins with quotations from *Hamlet*—

> What may this mean
> That thou, dead corse, again, in complete steel
> Revisit'st thus the glimpses of the moon
> Making night hideous; and we fools of nature
> So horridly to shake our disposition, With thoughts beyond the
> reaches of our souls?

and from "Address to the Devil" by Scottish poet Robert Burns:

> An' now auld Cloots, I ken ye're thinkin',
> A certain Ghoul is rantin', drinkin',
> Some luckless night will send him linkin',
> To your black pit;
> But, faith! he'll turn a corner jinkin',
> And cheat you yet.[72]

It ends with a brief passage from Scottish poet Philip James Bailey's well-known 1839 work "Festus" and a dedication ("L'Envoi") to the "shades of the venerated dead."[73] Each of its pages features a Latin header and footer that seem to refer not specifically to the content of the page on which they appear but to the Klan more generally.

Damnant quod non intelligunt
    (They condemn what they do not understand)
Amici humani generis (Friends of the human)
Magna est veritas, et prevalebit (Truth is mighty, and will prevail)
Nec scire fas est omnia (We are not allowed to know all things)
Ne vile fano (Bring no vile things to the temple)
Ars est celare artem (It is true art to conceal artistry)
Nusquam tuta fides (Nowhere is there true honor)
Quid faciendum? (What is to be done?)
Fide non armis (Faith, not arms)
Fiat justia (Let justice be done)
Hic manent vestigia morientis libertatis
    (Here lie the remains of Dying Liberties)
Curae leves loquntur, ingentes stupent
    (Slight griefs talk, great ones are speechless)
Da[bit]t Deus his quoque finem
    (To these things too, God will grant an end)
Cessante cause, cessat effectus
    (The cause ceasing, the effect must cease)
Droit et avant (Ahead and forward)
Cave quid dicis, quando, et cui
    (Beware what you say, when, and to whom)
Dormitur aliquando jus, moritur nunquam
    (A right sometimes sleeps, but never dies)
Deo adjuvante, non timendum
    (God helping, nothing should be feared)
Spectemur agendo (Let us be judged by our acts)
Nemo nos impune lacessit (No one attacks us with impunity)
Patria cara, carior libertas
    (Dear is my homeland, but liberty is dearer)
Ad unum omnes (All to one end)
Deo duce, ferro comitante
    (With God as my leader, and the sword as my companion)

Tempo mutantur, et nos mutamur in illis
    (The times change, and we change with the times)
O tempora! O mores! (Oh what times! Oh what customs!)
Ad utrumque paratus (Prepared for either [study or the sword])
Cavendo tutus (Safe through caution)
Astra castra, numen lumien
    (The stars are my camp, the gods are my light)
Ne quid detrimenti Respublica capiat
    (In order that the state should not suffer any loss)
Amici usque ad aras (Friendship until death)

Like the front matter, the quotes show off the author's erudition. Given the legal orientation of many of them, whoever did the selecting was likely a lawyer. Many had been used as mottos on battle flags or for universities or other organizations. The quotes are obviously political, positioning Ku-Klux as members of an oppressed people whose liberties have been violated and who are steeling themselves to defend them.

The main body of the Prescript also revealed much about the writers. If the text is framed and ornamented with literary and Latinate references, its body is bureaucratic, showing a comfortable familiarity with modern business culture. Terms like "disbursement," "appropriation," "dissemination," "hereinafter," "subsequent," "biennially," and "incumbent" are used confidently and correctly throughout the text.[74] The Prescript projects a highly centralized organization, with local dens at the bottom of the rigidly hierarchical structure regularly sending up that information required by the Grand Wizard to decide how it should be controlled. The Prescript described the first duty of the Grand Dragon as "to report to the Grand Wizard . . . the condition, strength, efficiency, and progress of the [Ku-Klux] within his realm."[75] It made provisions for dedicated organizers, "Special Deputy Grand Titans," to focus on "the more rapid and effectual dissemination and establishment of [Ku-Klux Dens]."[76] It called for the establishment of departments within the Ku-Klux and stated that the ghouls of each den must produce "quarterly report[s]."[77] This bureaucratic language was common to fraternal orders of the day, and it is possible that Ku-Klux adopted it not directly because they desired to be like modern businesses but rather because they desired to be like the Masons. It would not be surprising to find that this document was modified from another group's constitution. The fact remains, however, that the Ku-Klux who produced the Prescript were looking to transform their local group into an expansive modern bureaucracy.

These two elements—Latinate ornamentation and a description of how to establish a functional and efficient bureaucratic hierarchy—form the bulk of the document's content. Two other features are also revealing: calls for secrecy and sobriety on the parts of members, and sensational elements. The substitution of an asterisk for the Ku-Klux's name throughout the document and a list of code words to enable secret communication give the document a clandestine air. The insistence on secrecy and sobriety suggests that the members are to perform their membership obligations as serious, weighty ones. "Any member who shall reveal or betray the secret purposes of this * shall suffer the extreme penalty of the law." Like the bureaucratic language, though, it was generic: many fraternal orders of the day made that sort of claim on their members, and the level of seriousness with which it was really meant to be taken was complicated. The substitution of the asterisk for particularly mysterious aspects of the order was also used in Masonic ritual manuals of the time.[78]

Though having code words was, again, generic to fraternal orders of the day, the particular code words selected ("Dismal" for "1st," "Dreadful" for "7th," "Startling" for "2,," "Hideous" for "9") were not derivative of Masonry or Odd Fellowship and had an ominous and literary quality, as though they had been extracted from sensationalist fiction. The part of the Prescript written in English avoids any reference to the purpose of the Ku-Klux, to any activities the Ku-Klux might engage in, or to the political orientation of potential members. It does not refer to the war or to the South, and its only reference to the federal government is the preamble: "We recognize our relations to the United States Government and acknowledge the supremacy of its laws."[79] The Latin quotations more clearly suggest that the writers of the preamble felt oppressed, unjustly treated, and forced into a position in which they would have to fight to defend or regain their rights, but nowhere did the Prescript point to the Ku-Klux's specific situation, goals, or grievances. Like the early Ku-Klux itself, then, the Prescript was devoted much more to form than to content. And the form it took gestured to the modern, the urban, and the cosmopolitan, blending literary sensationalism, erudition, and bureaucracy.

Beyond the Prescript that some later claimed to have been produced there, we know very little about the putative Nashville meeting. We certainly do not know when it happened. A letter from James R. Crowe reprinted in Mrs. S. E. F. Rose's 1914 book places it in the fall of 1866.[80]

Walter Fleming says April 1867 in his introduction to the Lester and Wilson book, then in a later footnote says May 1867.[81] On May 24, 1867, the *Citizen* refers to a gathering of representatives of new Ku-Kluxes from Elkton, Lynneville, Franklin, and Columbia that month, though it does not give a location. This could be the same meeting, though it sounds considerably less ambitious than the one later described.[82] Trelease speculates that April, when so many Tennessee conservatives gathered for the Nashville meeting, would have been a convenient time: "Whether this was the chosen occasion or not, it was the ideal opportunity."[83]

Neither can we be confident in the identity of even a single person who was present at, or contributed from a distance to, the Nashville meeting.[84] James Crowe mentions the presence of Nathan Bedford Forrest and Confederate war hero John W. Morton in his much later letter to Mrs. S. E. F. Rose, but he makes many demonstrably false claims in that letter.[85] Lester and Wilson do not mention confederate elites' role at the meeting; this is consistent with their practice of not mentioning individuals' names, ostensibly to protect them from potential prosecution, but they also do not make the claim, even in general terms, that elites were present at, or in communication with, the meeting. The only description they gave of the "delegates" is that "they were present from Tennessee, Alabama, and a number of other states," a claim gesturing toward large plans and great things, but notably thin in detail.[86]

Those who know one thing about the earliest Ku-Klux Klan know that it was headed by Nathan Bedford Forrest.[87] Yet I have found little more evidence that he was in any way connected to the purported meeting than I have found for anyone else. Forrest deliberately, though coyly, presented himself to the national press and to the government as the Klan chief in his *Cincinnati Commercial* interview published in September 1868. He was part of a group of Memphis elites, including *Memphis Avalanche* editor Matthew Galloway, and Memphis intellectuals Elizabeth Avery Meriwether and Minor Meriwether, who later came to realize the political value of the Klan and deliberately support and propagate it.[88] But I have found no evidence that Forrest associated himself with the Klan before 1868, after it had spread throughout the South. There is also no compelling contemporary evidence to establish that Forrest ever exercised any leadership functions, besides offering himself up as a figurehead.[89]

The third event that has been taken to demonstrate the Ku-Klux's move toward a more organized form and a more public posture by the spring and summer of 1867 was a parade it apparently held in Pulaski in mid-1867. The primary sources are stronger here than with the Nashville meeting but, again, highly unreliable and self-contradictory. To begin with, they conflict about the date on which the parade occurred. The *Citizen* provided thorough coverage of the parade in its June 7 edition, establishing that the date of the parade was June 6. Lester and Wilson mistakenly claim that it occurred on July 4. Pulaski Ku-Klux member R. J. Brunson decades later claimed to have been in the parade and concurs with the July 4 date (his account is, throughout, closely plagiarized from Lester and Wilson's).[90] Though we can be sure from the *Citizen* coverage that the parade occurred in June, people remember it on the later date: Klan groups in the following years would later frequently parade on July 4, likely because it would have seemed fitting for it to have been on that date. Just after the war, Fourth of July parades became associated with freedmen asserting their political rights. The Fourth of July parades, and perhaps even Klan parades that did not occur on the Fourth, could have been intended as challenges to or even parodies of freedmen's political parades.[91]

If the date of the parade itself was fuzzy in memories, descriptions of its content also leave much to be desired. Mildred Ezell Reynolds, for instance, whose family was socially close to Klan founders, hazily described the parade in her Second World War–era memoir. She recalled: "The whole town was on the 'qui vive' to see the great parade. . . . It is needless to say such a demonstration had a wholesome effect on unruly negroes or other depredators."[92] Frank McCord later remembered their first decision to "make some kind of demonstration before the public." Each member "provided himself with a long robe of decided colors and a tall paper hat and domino."[93]

The *Citizen*'s account, the only description written at the time and by far the most detailed one, has its own serious limitations as a source. It claimed that the parade featured seventy-five Ku-Klux. "No two of them were dressed alike, all having on masks and some sort of fanciful costume." The costume of one marcher was "a robe of many colors, with a hideous mask, and a transparent hat, in which he carried a brilliant gas lamp, a box of matches and several other articles." Another wore "a blood red hat which was so tall that we never did see the top of it."[94] Because the *Citizen*'s account was resolutely written in the tall-tale tradition so popular among southwestern newspaper writers at the time, it is hardly a reliable account of the parade. Can we take out the obvious exaggerations to get an accurate picture? Was there a man in a tall red hat? Did a parade occur? McCord's style deliberately obscured this.

Lester and Wilson later published a very different description of the parade. Notably, during their depiction of the parade they take a moment to, seemingly innocuously, warn readers about how easy it is to deceive people and "how little even the testimony of an eyewitness is worth."[95] They claimed, first, that the Pulaski parade was just one of many simultaneous parades in many towns, in response to a demand by the Grand Dragon. According to Lester and Wilson, people from the region came to the Pulaski parade in large numbers. They saw an impressive show. First, a "skyrocket" (strikingly, not worthy of mention by the Pulaski coverage the next day) was launched to start the procession. The parade they depicted was much more military, much less carnivalesque than the one described by the *Citizen*. Displaying complete discipline, the Ku-Klux marched and countermarched through the town streets with funereal slowness and in impressive silence. Most impressively, "by crossing over in opposite directions the lines were kept up in almost unbroken continuity. The effect was to create the impression of vast numbers."[96]

These accounts are patently fictive. Just as the *Citizen*'s story is presented in the tall-tale tradition, so Lester and Wilson's description of the parade is not straight. Take, for instance, the claim that townspeople were fooled by countermarching into imagining that they were witnessing much greater numbers than were in fact present. The ridiculousness of that ruse is apparent to anyone who has seen Pulaski and has a sense of its very small scale and low density. Surely some people were standing where they could see that the seventy-five or so Ku-Klux were doubling back. Those who were not could presumably communicate with those who were, or maybe even stroll down a few yards to satisfy their curiosity about the origin of this spectacular and seemingly endless stream of men through their tiny downtown (in which some of the buildings had recently burned down). The claim that the Ku-Klux had some sort of inscrutable marching tactic is a fantastic claim rather than a real one, from the genre of sensational fiction, in the same category as a claim that a detective had an India rubber mask that could disguise him as any person. It is a literary device: the authors are asking the reader to tacitly accept it in order to enable the creation of a satisfying larger narrative.

Exaggerations and lies about the Ku-Klux were fundamental to the idea of the Ku-Klux. Ku-Klux lied about themselves even before they were doing illegal things that they would want to conceal with lies; the broader culture of disguise, secrecy, and audacious misrepresentation was constitutive of the meaning of the Ku-Klux. Luther and Wilson, and all of the original members who later wrote about the Ku-Klux, carried on this tradition. Their book is full of stories of implausible pranks against freedpeople which are simply not physically feasible and not meant to be taken as such. Given the literary license in the two texts that provide the most detail on the parade, all we can take away is that there may have been some sort of parade, and if there was, it strove for the "fantastic" in its form and almost certainly involved costumes. None of the accounts even suggest a political message for the parade, though Lester and Wilson and some other later writers remember it to have been aimed at intimidating freedmen.

In addition to the stories in the *Citizen* and the evidence surrounding the Nashville meeting and parade, there are bits and pieces of other evidence of early organization, largely from celebratory twentieth-century sources. For instance, R. J. Brunson, according to his memoir published in 1913 by W. T. Richardson, claims to have joined the Pulaski Klan in July 1867. Apparently, he was in "Den no. 4. That was the fourth den of the original K. K. K. that was organized."[97]

So much, and no more, is what we know about the Ku-Klux's activities in the spring and early summer of 1867. Ku-Klux were publicizing themselves in their local paper, presenting themselves as fantastic and mysterious, and, if we choose to accept the validity of the Nashville meeting and original Prescript, they were also taking steps to organize and to portray themselves as modern and erudite. They were perhaps making vague gestures toward the political: this is particularly true in the Latin epigraphs of the prescript, and if an organizing meeting occurred, it would suggest an emergent political orientation. Even if a meeting did not occur, the *Citizen* was beginning to claim that regional organizing was taking place, which gestures to the political. Yet there is no evidence from this period of any sort of articulated political program or idea about a role for the Ku-Klux in state or national politics. There is also no credible evidence that the Ku-Klux had expanded in any substantial way beyond Pulaski.[98]

This is one point that previous histories have gotten significantly wrong: while most claim that the spring of 1867 was the moment at which the already well-established, already politically oriented Ku-Klux "went public," the Ku-Klux made hardly a ripple in even local public consciousness throughout 1867, and there is precious little evidence, all of it from claims made later, of anything more political than some general concerns about its potential voiced by newspapers and Freedmen's Bureau agents, and the sense of injury and potential for resistance expressed in the Latin quotes in the prescript. Not only is this is at odds with the claim that the Ku-Klux had grown out of control by mid-1867; it also strongly suggests that the Ku-Klux's efforts to publicize themselves in the mid-1867 were ineffective. Pulaski resident William Thomas Richardson's 1913 book, *Historic Pulaski*, claims that "during the months of July and August, 1867, the Ku-Klux was much talked about by the citizens of Pulaski. Its mysteriousness was the sensation of the hour. Every issue of the local paper contained some notice of this strange order."[99] He is of course correct that the *Pulaski Citizen* was publicizing the Klan. Apparently, though, appearing regularly and dramatically in the pages of the *Citizen* did not ensure even local fame. Either the *Citizen's* circulation was too small to effectively spread ideas through the community, or articles promoting yet another local voluntary society, however bizarre and dramatic, failed to catch readers' attention.

And assuming it occurred at all, the parade was seemingly not the profound social experience that some recalled. Perhaps it was ill-attended and something of a flop: a few local young men self-consciously wearing strange cardboard and calico costumes, blowing on whistles while marching through the burned-out business district. Few people, even locally, seem to have known about the existence of the Ku-Klux for several months after the various efforts to publicize it in the spring of 1867. Anybody had the opportunity to know about it—if nothing else, from regular mentions in the *Citizen*. And the *Citizen* was increasingly demanding that the Klan be noticed, beginning to frame it as a political entity by the late summer of 1867.

At least a few people, particularly those working in journalism or government who had a professional interest in racial violence in Giles, did read the *Citizen* and learn about the group it was working so hard to promote. In August 23, the *Citizen* quoted the *Nashville Press and Times* as saying that concern about an (unnamed) vigilante group in Pulaski justified the continued presence of the militia there. The *Citizen* asked if perhaps they were referring to the Ku-Klux.[100] In September the *Citizen* described, in some detail, purported concerns on the part of the Freedmen's Bureau about the Klan and published a letter by the mayor claiming that they had done no harm and had a right to exist.[101] They also strongly refuted claims that the Klan had ever had anything to do with alleged local attacks on state militia, though they did absolutely insist that when freedmen's bureau's officials complained of "organized companies" of ruffians, they meant Ku-Klux.[102] Captain J. J. Mankins, stationed in Pulaski with the Twenty-First Army Corps, testified in 1869 that he had first learned about the Ku-Klux in the spring of 1867.[103]

If Freedmen's Bureau agents and other governmental officials had heard the term "Ku-Klux" and identified it as a potential resistance group by the spring of 1867, they do not seem to have found it very interesting. The Citizen had to insist on labeling as Ku-Klux the ruffians the Nashville paper had complained of before indignantly denying its allegations. The first named mention of the Ku-Klux by federal officials that I have found was in December 1867, when a Freedmen's Bureau officer in Columbia, H. A. Eastman, worried about the "kuKlux" and asserted that there was no doubt their purpose was "to annoy and intimidate the colored people." He did not in his December report attribute to them any general violence or any specific activities.[104] In August 1868, when he reported about the previous year's acts of violence in Maury and Marshall Counties, he listed seven specific murders committed by the Ku-Klux. The first, the hanging of a white man named John Courtney, was dated "December 1867." The August 1868 report, written during a period of great national interest in the Ku-Klux, could have assigned an agency to the earlier attack that it would not have done at the time it occurred. The fact that the date is so ambiguous (the other, later murders of white victims have specific dates, though the murders of black victims often do not) would also suggest that the report of the attack was an oral report given well after the event.[105]

The most decisive evidence that the Ku-Klux was largely unknown, even in Giles and surrounding counties, long after the beginning of the Citizen coverage, the parade, and the putative organizational meeting, is the testimony before the Tennessee state legislature in July and August 1868 about the Ku-Klux in Middle Tennessee. The Ku-Klux victims and witnesses and local elites from Giles and surrounding counties who were called before the legislative committee universally testified to having first learned about or encountered the Ku-Klux in 1868. One, George F. Bowles, a teacher at a colored school in Giles County, claimed to have been visited, threatened, and robbed of his papers by the Ku-Klux "about the 15th January" 1868. No one else claimed to have been aware of them earlier than February or March 1868, many dating the Ku-Klux only back to April and others claiming not to have known of the Ku-Klux's existence until that summer. Anderson Cheatham of Maury County claimed in his early August testimony, "I have been seeing them for the last 6 months," which would mean February 1868 was the earliest sighting. Mr. Charles Marchbanks of Warren County claims that it was active in the "last days of March."[106]

Several people place their knowledge of the Ku-Klux in April. Pink Harris of Giles County does not specifically state that he did not know about the Klan before April, but when asked to state "all you know" about the Klan, he recalled seeing a very large assembly of Ku-Klux at a church in April, and then to have encountered and been threatened by two later that same month. Moses Boddy, a twenty-eight-year old farmer in Giles, claimed to have been visited in April by thirty costumed men attempting to take his gun. Walter Scott, also of Giles, was asked to "State what you may know of an organization known as the Ku Klux Klan, and whether they have done anything to you, and what was it? State all you may know about them. When did you first see or know them?" In his response, he discussed his attack in April and some events since then. It may be that he was focusing on the first part of the question and not responding to "when did you first see or know them."[107]

Men from outside of Giles similarly traced their knowledge of the Klan back only to early 1868. William Wyatt of Lincoln County recalls hearing of an attack in March, and of hearing about the existence of the Klan when he was in Nashville at some indeterminate point before that. When asked if he had ever heard of the Klan "until the State Militia was mustered out of service in the Fall or Winter" of 1867, he said he had not. Richard Moore of Lincoln County recalls the Ku-Klux appearing "sometime last spring." Charles E. Robert, the city editor of the *Union and American*, referred to publishing a Ku-Klux notice "about the time the organization appeared in the Spring." A white wheelwright named Jacob M. Davis from Tipton County said, "The first I ever saw or heard of these Ku-Klux organizations, was about the 1st of May, 1868." Nim Wilks of Maury County did refer ambiguously in this late-summer 1868 testimony to a Klan attack "June last," which could refer to 1867, but his later testimony (where he refers to having seen the body of the man who "killed Bickner" before that; John Bicknell was killed on February 29, 1868) shows that he was referring to 1868.[108]

Absence of evidence is not evidence of absence. Yet the timing given by these Giles County men, the absence of any discussion of events prior to January 1868, and the failure of those calling witnesses to find anyone with earlier accounts does seriously weaken the claim that the Pulaski

Ku-Klux were political, violent, or even locally well known before that period. Presumably, if these men had had stories to tell about a Ku-Klux parade or a Ku-Klux raid at an earlier point, legislators would have been happy to hear it.

This source has its limitations: the group of witnesses who testified before the Tennessee General Assembly may have been assembled with more haste than care. In the absence of any reason to think the committee would have deliberately avoided calling witnesses who knew about the Ku-Klux at an earlier date, though, or that witnesses would have been intimidated into suppressing knowledge about earlier Ku-Klux activity, this testimony confirms what was also suggested by the Freedmen's Bureau reports and the lack of other evidence: that most freedpeople and others, even in Giles and surrounding counties, did not know of the existence of, and did not feel threatened by, the Ku-Klux until early to mid-1868.

IF SO MANY people in the area did not learn about the Klan until early 1868, its early proliferation was much less dramatic than its founders suggested. This is not just a small interpretive error. It is vital to Lester and Wilson's argument that the Ku-Klux's spread was organic and preceded the organizational and publicity efforts of 1867. Southern nationalists like that chronology, which positions the Ku-Klux as a collective expression of the renewed self-respect of the southern people. In their telling, the newspaper publicity, Nashville meeting, and parade were efforts to bring coherence and control to a movement already spiraling out of control. Lester and Wilson's second chapter, "The Spread of the Klan," insists that "during the fall and winter of 1866, the spread of the Ku-Klux was rapid. It spread over a wide extent of territory. Sometimes, by a sudden leap, it appeared in localities far distant from any existing dens.'"[109] As it spread, people came to appreciate its political potential and to use it as a vigilante force. Its growth and transformation was "natural" and "not at first remotely contemplated by the originators of the order." Their third chapter, "The Transformation," presents baffled founders, concerned by the size and emerging vigilante character of the Ku-Klux they had created, discovering that the "spirit" they had evoked "from the vasty deep . . . would not down at their bidding" and realizing that the best they could do would be to organize it under the leadership of "prudent men. . . . In this way, it was hoped the impending dangers would be effectively guarded against."[110] Historians since have generally accepted Lester and

Wilson's false claim that the Ku-Klux's organic spread preceded attempts in spring 1867 to organize it.[111]

If the Klan would not be widely known even locally until early 1868, the *Citizen* was sporadically continuing to publicize it, and the Klan was gradually developing, in its pages, its character as a violent and political entity. The *Citizen* had first mentioned the Ku-Klux in print in its cryptic, prepolitical spring 1867 articles. The articles began to take on a more ominous tone in the summer. On June 12, Governor William Gannaway Brownlow, immensely unpopular with Tennessee conservatives and a favorite target of ridicule in the *Citizen*, declared the registration of voters in Giles County null and void, as there was evidence that the county had been illegally registering former Confederates. A supposed "proclamation of the Grand Cyclops" published on June 14 parodied Brownlow's proclamation and the political ambition that they believed underlay it: "Every man in our county of Giles . . . shall be provided with a box of Dr. John Bell's Worm candy and a bottle of Dr. Jeems' Alternative, and regulate themselves. . . . Those who will pledge themselves . . . that they will support me as a candidate for the Emperor of Mexico, will be furnished certificates."[112] An article on June 21, 1867, referred cryptically to a Ku-Klux named "Alla Hassan" who was banned from the Ku-Klux for intemperance.[113]

After this, there was silence on the Ku-Klux until a July 26, 1867, article apologized, "As we hadn't heard from the Ku-klux in some time, we, with others, had begun to conclude that they were played out."[114] The article reassured the public that Ku-Klux had recently been spotted about town "maneuvering about the square [speaking] gibberish." Afterward, the paper did not mention the Ku-Klux for almost another month. On August 23, it printed a letter from "A Kuklux." The letter asserted the Ku-Klux's existence and its position as the true defender of "the interests of freedom, the hopes of civilization, and the happiness of the whole country" and mocked those who it claimed were beginning to worry that the Ku-Klux was a danger to radicals.[115]

This article was followed by one per week over the following month. The articles from late August through September are the first to describe an encounter between the Ku-Klux and federal officials. Federal officials, the paper claimed, were beginning to complain that "there is organized in this county several companies, whose object is to murder Union men." Though they did not use the name "Kuklux," the *Pulaski Citizen*, reprinting their complaints, insisted that "of course these 'organized companies' are the Ku-klux." The *Citizen* denied the allegation.[116] Captain

J. J. Mankins later recalled having seen men in costume, presumably Ku-Klux, in Pulaski around October 1, 1867, but they did not seem to have been up to anything of note.[117] There is some reason to suspect that the Klan was not active: the one time the Ku-Klux is mentioned between early September and the end of 1867, on December 17, is in an article entitled "Obnoxious," which complained that some parties "wearing the garb of, and pretending to be, Kukluxes" were "rendering themselves odious" by crashing private parties. The Citizen reminded these so-called Ku-Klux that this was impolite and called on the Grand Cyclops to officially disclaim the real Ku-Klux's participation in it.[118] We have other glimpses of what the early Ku-Klux were doing late in the year: the November 15, 1867, issue of the Citizen covered a Giles County tournament in which John Kennedy competed as "Knight of Ivanhoe" and James Crowe as "Knight of the Lost Cause."[119]

White men in Giles County committed a great deal of violence against black men in 1866 and 1867, some of which involved collective attacks that structurally resembled Ku-Klux attacks. In March 1866, freedman Allen Abernathy complained to the Freedmen's Bureau that white planter James Scruggs had shot him after taking offense at his whistling, and that thereafter, "ten or fifteen" armed whites assaulted and threatened a group of freedmen who were friends of Abernathy.[120] On July 7, 1866, white men Jonathan Gilliam, Jack Keith, and others allegedly murdered a colored man named Dudley Kimbraugh.[121] And Giles was seen as a regional epicenter of violence: one Freedmen's Bureau agent complained in January 1867, "Roughs collect in Pulaski from this and adjoining counties. They have their own way here, threaten to kill and drag out all who disagree with them."[122]

And there is evidence that the men who were creating the Ku-Klux in Pulaski were also involved in racial violence: Captain Judd reported that on May 13, 1867, Frank McCord had incited a riot against a black male schoolteacher who had whipped a white male student. The child, who was attending the black school, was the son of a white prostitute. When the child stole money from a fellow student, his mother asked that the black schoolteacher, named Clark, whip him. Yet she later complained to other whites about the whipping, leading Frank McCord and others to threaten to whip Clark in retribution. The encounter did not go as McCord had planned: "The negroes had got wind of what was going on and they gathered together in such force that the white miscreants dare not attack them. . . . The best citizens did not uphold the would be mob, and the crowd of negroes was so large that there was a good prospect of their [whites] getting whipped, consequently they gave it up. . . . I was told this morning that a party of young men had said they would mob Clark and myself tonight, but I think this is all blow."[123]

Still, through 1866 and 1867, freedmen's agents and, it seems, freedmen themselves described this violence as disorganized acts by "roughs," on the one hand, and greedy landowners, on the other. There was as yet little interest in connecting the dots between the antiblack violence pervasive in the county and the "Ku-Klux Klan" that the *Citizen* was beginning to take pains to present as a potentially dangerous menace to freedpeople and their white allies.

AS THE *CITIZEN* reduced its Ku-Klux coverage from June 1867 through December 1867, a few papers beyond the Ku-Klux founders and their immediate circle were just beginning to take note of it. Some few Tennessee newspapers mentioned the Ku-Klux beginning in mid-1867. In August, the Republican *Nashville Press and Times* had apparently described it as a group similar to the "Knights of the Golden Circle," which "bodes no good to those who may be known as Union men." In response, the *Citizen* mocked "Mr. Press and Times" as a coward: "Dismiss your fears and sleep as sweetly as you ever did upon your mother's lap."[124]

At least one paper well beyond Tennessee took notice of the group. On August 22, 1867, the *Milwaukee Daily Sentinel* printed a single story about the Ku-Klux. The article, entitled "From Tennessee," contains two paragraphs, not explicitly connected to one another. The first notes that a grand jury in Giles County had found a bill for assault with intent to kill against Clark for the whipping. The second states, "A mischievous secret society, called the Ku-Klux, had been organized in Giles County, composed of young men of rebel proclivities. A gentleman from that county says that he is confident they mean mischief and requests the government not to withdraw the militia."[125] The paper chose not to explicitly connect the first part with the second, though the editor must have been aware of why they went together, but the *Sentinel* thought its readers would be interested in the potential for violence by this "mysterious" group.

Even in Middle Tennessee, though, only a few newspapers mentioned the Ku-Klux in 1867, and those only sporadically. The *Nashville Union and Dispatch* mentioned the Ku-Klux six times in the last half of 1867. The first mention, in August, claimed, "This clan, whose terrible name imports death and destruction, are at their favorite pastime again . . . [creating] consternation among Radicals and negro school teachers." It went on to note that the Pulaski "Ku-Klix Klan" had caused the Freedmen's Bureau agent, Captain Judd and his party, to be kicked out of their lodging by "inform[ing] his landlady . . . that she would consult her interest by discharging them."[126] The second August piece claims that Captain Judd had deliberately frightened the freedpeople in Giles with false rumors about the Klan, and they had come out in large numbers to defend themselves, causing real troubles.[127] In September, the paper published a letter from "Fides" defending the Ku-Klux from charges made in the *Press and Times*: "It is true that there exists here an organization called the 'Ku Klux' but having no such object as that mentioned in the *Press and Times*—On the contrary they have conducted themselves in a remarkably quiet manner, molesting no one."[128] In November, the paper mentioned four costumed Ku-Klux's presence at the jousting tournament, the proceeds of which were to support a Confederate memorial.[129] The fifth Ku-Klux article, in December 1867, printed a "letter from Columbia," which described "some general and undefined dread among the negroes of a secret order that has recently made its appearance, known as the 'Ku-klux Klan.' No one, as yet, states publicly who compose the 'Klan,' or what are its purposes. . . . They have extended themselves all over Maury and Giles counties. Some [call them] 'Rebel bush-whackers.'"[130] A week later, a correspondent from Maury County noted the presence of Ku-Klux "who as yet . . . have done nothing" but who, according to a "negress," "were dead Rebels who had come up out of the ground and brought their horses with them."[131]

A review of all Tennessee newspapers housed in the Tennessee State Library and Archives yielded only one other Middle Tennessee paper, beyond the *Union and Dispatch* and *Press and Times*, that mentioned the Ku-Klux once in 1867: The Democratic *Winchester Home Journal* first mentioned the existence of the Ku-Klux in September 1867 in an article condemning militia activities in Pulaski.[132] Beyond the *Milwaukee Daily Sentinel* reference in August, I have been able to find only two other mentions of the Klan beyond Tennessee.[133] Both appeared in the last weeks of December, and both are significant. A *Press and Times* article reprinted in the *New York World* on December 17, 1867, reported the beating of a black man and the killing of a white man in Maury County (directly north of Giles, and the county including Nashville) by men wearing the uniform of the Ku-Klux Klan. The paper introduced the Klan to its readers, explaining, "The Klan is a secret organization which has been in existence for some time in Maury and the surrounding counties. What its object is no one knows, though outsiders have generally looked upon it as an outlandish but harmless order, whose chief aim was sport and frolic."[134] The *Tuscaloosa (Ala.) Independent Monitor* named the Klan on December 30, 1867, claiming that a group calling itself the Ku-Klux had played a prank against Ryland Randolph, the paper's editor (and the future Klan leader who would later offer one of the two extant original Prescripts).[135] Tuscaloosa is well over a hundred miles south of Pulaski, so word of it had spread some distance by the end of December, though I have found no other sign of organization than this teasing reference.

The Nashville papers and the *Winchester Home Journal* likely learned about the Ku-Klux from exchanges sent by the *Pulaski Citizen*, or letters sent to them by locals. At least the *Union and Dispatch* was relying on letters received from "Fides" in Pulaski. Because telling false or exaggerated stories about the Klan, on the one hand, and keeping facts about the Klan secret, on the other, were expected of Ku-Klux and their allies, stories about the Klan that rely on Ku-Klux's self-representations have to be approached with care. All of the *Citizen*'s writings, and the 1867 articles other than the *Press and Times* pieces, fall into that category. Some later writings of the Ku-Klux founders support the theory that the difference between newspaper claims and the events they described might have been extreme indeed. Most notable is Frank McCord's much later letter (see the epigraph at the beginning of this chapter) in which he confessed having fabricated "nearly all" of his early articles. "Nearly all the BLOOD AND THUNDER proclamations and general orders issued in circular form or printed in the columns of THE CITIZEN when the order was in its incipient form and before it had assumed political significations, originated in the brain and were written by the Faber of the then editor of THE CITIZEN, solely for fun and sensational effect."[136] He does not specify in this letter when the incipient period ended, and for that matter has established himself as an unreliable narrator, but since the *Citizen*'s coverage began in March 1867, it surely included, for instance, the events of that summer.

In later years, early Ku-Klux seemed to confess that their written claims about the Klan had been less than veracious. Lester and Wilson's warning that witness responses to the parade "illustrates how little the testimony of even an eyewitness is worth in regard to anything which makes a deep impression on him by reason of its mysteriousness" falls into this category.[137] When Mrs. S. E. F. Rose wrote to James Crowe and

John B. Kennedy in 1909 to ask them for an account of the founding, Crowe wrote back with a fairly vague response (the details he did give were demonstrably false), but Kennedy's response was completely evasive and comically fulsome. While giving not a single fact about or description of the founding, he described the Ku-Klux as endeavoring to "protect the women of the South, who were the loveliest, most noble and best women in the world. . . . Pardon me for speaking once again of the dear southern women, the heroines, who so bravely bore the heavy burdens and hardships of those long years of war. The world has never known lovelier, braver women than they were. They were ministering angels. . . . They were our inspiration. . . . Their memory is a sweet benediction to our lives as we near the last river. We would say to younger women, teach your children to love and honor the memory of those noble women of the South, the women of the '60s."[138] Kennedy was an old man by that point. Perhaps he had lost his mental acuity, but it is tempting to read his letter as a deliberately over-the-top performance of flattering evasion.

It is in December 1867 and January 1868 that contemporary evidence of Klan violence begins to appear. The Freedmen's Bureau report from the summer of 1868 names the Klan as having been responsible for the death of a white man in December 1867. The December 17, 1867, piece in the *New York World*, reprinted from the *Nashville Press* was the first to explicitly suggest that Ku-Klux might have committed violence: "We learn that a white man was killed some days ago near Bigbysville, Maury County, and that a negro was terribly beaten at the same time, by a gang of men disguised, according to the latter's statement, in the dress of the Kuklux Klan. This Klan is a secret organization which has been in existence for some time in Maury and the surrounding counties. . . . Outsiders have generally looked upon it as an outlandish but harmless order, whose chief aim was sport and frolic," but if it is actually a "band of outlaws," it needs to be speedily suppressed.[139] The transition of the Klan from social group to terrorist group was not inevitable, but by December a good deal of the groundwork for it had been laid. For months, the *Citizen* had suggested that the Klan had a political purpose. Its sensationalist language had become increasingly foreboding. Other newspapers and authority figures had begun to vocally anticipate that it might begin to commit violence. White-on-black violence continued to the streets of Giles County. Frank McCord himself had been fingered as a leader of antiblack public opinion. To begin to commit violence in the name of the Klan, by the end of 1867, was to fulfil the expectations of government officials and newspaper editors alike.

The first Ku-Klux attack to be reported occurred north of Giles, in Maury County, in mid-December, and though the brief account of it was picked up by the *New York World*, no more is known about it. Pulaski exploded in violence on January 7, 1868. That day a fatal attack in Pulaski became the first act of white-on-black violence that would gain substantial national attention as a Klan attack. Tellingly, the victim was Orange Jones, sometimes called Orange Rhodes, one of Pulaski's bold but precarious black leaders. The attack began with a dispute between a black man named Calvin Carter (either the mulatto farm laborer, then twenty-eight, who would report $125 in property on the 1870 census or the mulatto man, then twenty-one, who in 1870 was in jail) and a white man named Calvin Lambert (a twenty-two-year-old listed in 1870 as a grocer with $1,000 in property) that was apparently about some matter of business, and possibly also about a black woman named Lucy Reynolds. Lucy Reynolds would be labeled a "colored strumpet" in a report of the event. The 1870 census names a twenty-three-year-old mulatto woman named Lucy listed as a "housewife" to a forty-five-year-old mulatto man of the same name. She may have been a single daughter mothering the many younger siblings in the household. Apparently, Calvin Carter threatened to whip Reynolds if he "caught her going to Calvin Lambert's house." As friends of the two men gathered, the dispute mushroomed, and within hours the downtown was in an armed standoff. A group of poorly armed and outnumbered black men, including Orange Jones, took defensive shelter in a grocery owned by a black man named John Carter. A group of white men shot at them, injuring several, including Ben Nelson (probably B. H. Nelson, a then twenty-six-year-old carpenter who would report $100 in property in 1870) and killing Jones. No whites were injured or killed.[140]

Brevet Major General W. P. Carlin, stationed in Nashville and responsible for maintaining peace in Tennessee, sent his subordinate, Captain Michael Walsh, to Pulaski to investigate the attack. We cannot be sure how Walsh went about his investigation when he arrived on January 9. Presumably he called on locals, perhaps witnesses, government officials, or prominent Republicans. Perhaps he even talked with the editors of the local newspaper, Luther and Frank McCord. Walsh's description of events, in his report to Carlin, emphasized that the incident had demonstrated an unusual degree of coordination. He believed that the final stage of the violence, the assault on the grocery, had shown telltale signs of military discipline on the part of the whites. As he put it, "it could only be done by an organization well matured and drilled." Walsh would have been familiar with the Ku-Klux before his investigation, since his subordinate, George Judd, had been reported in the papers as having been driven out of his lodgings in Pulaski by the Klan. He likely would also have recognized, though he did not mention it in his report, that the victim of the shooting, Jones, was a political actor and a frequent signatory on freedmen's petitions. Summarizing his report, Walsh attributed the violence to an organization "called the Ku Klux Klan, having for its end the expulsion of loyal men whites and blacks from the counties of Giles & Maury and thus terrorizing similar to that which was general in this county about the breaking out of the rebellion."[141] Though he did not provide concrete evidence of a connection, and though he acknowledged that little was known about the Ku-Klux, he reasoned that they must have been responsible for the shooting.

It is best to remain agnostic about whether the Pulaski Ku-Klux were involved in the killing of Orange Jones. If one accepts Walsh's claim that the coordinated violence of so many white men would suggest prior planning, his imputation of that violence to the Ku-Klux makes sense. The Ku-Klux by this point had likely physically existed in Pulaski, in some form, for at least several months, and those speaking for the Ku-Klux in the Pulaski Citizen had taken an aggressive stance against Brownlow's Republican government. Frank McCord had a few months earlier been named as leading a failed, but menacing, antifreedman mob: his white neighbors had failed to follow his leadership, so he likely would have felt the need to redeem himself.[142] No other similar group in Pulaski is known to the historical record. The town had Odd Fellows, Masons, Sons of Temperance, churches, and dramatic clubs, but there is little reason to imagine that any of those might have been violently inclined. If there was a prior organization at the bottom of assault on the grocery and the killing of Jones, the Ku-Klux is the strongest candidate. At least two of the men arrested for involvement in the riot, John Kennedy and May Ezell, are known by historians, and may or may not have been known to Walsh, as important early Klan members.[143] And the fact that another Klan attack had been reported a few weeks prior strengthens the claim that this attack was a deliberate and orchestrated Klan act.

Walsh's report is quite different from the report of the event given in the Citizen on January 10. That article had claimed that the actions of the black men were orchestrated, while the actions of the white men were not. Walsh should absolutely be given the benefit of the doubt over the McCords; not only would the casualty list support Walsh's account, but the McCords were in the business of defending Pulaski's white citizens and of printing deliberate falsehoods about the Ku-Klux. Still, this is not the sort of falsehood they were in the habit of printing: until this point, their claims had been trivial and humorous, not pertaining to any event their readers would want to know about. Their deliberate false-hoods tended to be delivered with a stylistic wink that was not present in the January 10 article. The paper had a local reputation to uphold. The McCords had an interest in controlling the meaning of this important event and had practical reasons to give an account reconcilable with local consensus. The size of the discrepancy between their account and Walsh's may suggest an ambiguity in local knowledge regarding the basic facts of the attack.

More important, Walsh's report does not fit well with what is known about the pre-1868 Ku-Klux. Even assuming it was actively meeting, it is doubtful that the Pulaski Ku-Klux at this point was sophisticated, extensive, or disciplined. Whatever it was, it was likely not "an organization well matured and drilled." There is little evidence beyond the mid-December report from nearby Maury and the later Freedmen's Bureau report that the local Ku-Klux had done anything more than boorishly crash parties since the previous September. Furthermore, Walsh's central premise—that the speedy emergence of eighteen men from their homes with guns already loaded, their formation into a straight line, and their coordinated attack was evidence of prior planning—is itself questionable. By his own account, armed men had been running through the streets throughout the day. Guns would have been at the ready. Houses in Pulaski were scattered enough that all men could hardly have been witnessed emerging simultaneously, or even have coordinated a simultaneous emergence, and it is hardly unusual that men who found themselves in spontaneous conflicts less than three years after the war were drawing on military tactics.

Another way to interpret the event in Pulaski would be to regard it as a riot. While much smaller in scale, the Pulaski event resembled in character the Memphis and New Orleans Riots of 1866. Indeed, "riot" is the term Walsh himself used at the beginning of the report and is what newspapers immediately labeled it. While calling an act of collective violence a "riot" often misleadingly imputed spontaneity to events that in fact depended on preexisting social structures, claiming that it could only have been done "by an organization well matured and drilled" likely erred in the other direction. It is easy to imagine how Walsh might have misread the shootings. By the time he arrived two days after the killing, he was hearing from Pulaski residents a story that already had been repeated and negotiated many times, as Pulaskians worked toward a (messy) common narrative. Armed with this contextual information, along with his own set of expectations, he presumably nudged and shaped this common narrative himself. Military officers have an interest in imputing structure and competence to their opponents: perhaps he influenced interpretations in that direction, selecting from competing or flexible accounts.

Walsh may have been correct that this represented the bloody beginning of the Pulaski Ku-Klux's violent turn. There is no evidence to dispute the claim that the whites who brutally shot the group of black men huddling in the grocery in self-defense had been formally initiated, met and drilled regularly, and would have understood themselves to be acting as "Ku-Klux." The fact that the one man killed was politically active may support the idea that the killing was not a random and spontaneous one. And there is no question that the Pulaski Ku-Klux would be violently intimidating black citizens by March 1868.

While the Citizen's original account of the attack was straight, its second story evinces a darkly winking tone. "The report of Capt. Walsh lays the blame upon the poor 'Kuklux Klan,' which is so supremely ridiculous that we will not insult our readers with a refutation of the charge."[144] Perhaps the shootings fell somewhere between a riot and a paramilitary operation: some of the attackers were members of the Ku-Klux, and they drew from the Ku-Klux's organization, such as it was, and were motivated by its belligerent rhetoric and sense of purpose, but they had not planned the attack in advance, and the attack was not ordered by the Ku-Klux leadership.

On January 11, another attack occurred just a few miles outside Pulaski, in Lynnville, that more closely anticipated the form of later Klan attacks. According to a January 14 letter from a Frank Dickerson,

> about 16 white men with masked faces & armed came to said
> White's house and took me from there together with Eph Johnson,
> Judd Grisby, Tom and Jack White (col'd), they then selected Jack and
> Tom White (col'd) and myself—stripped down our pantaloons—
> laid us on logs—tied our hands behind our backs and then whipped

us severely with beech limbs, four of them whipping Jack White at the same time. They kept us in this condition for nearly two hours off and on, threatening at the same time to kill us because we belonged to the Union League and voted the radical ticket. Three of the party who attacked and punished us in this unmerciful manner belong to the "Ku Klux Klan."[145]

Collective white-on-black violence in Pulaski would follow this example, continuing through 1868 and for years thereafter. Much of the violence in 1868 would be called Ku-Klux violence. After 1869, when white elites called on Klans to cease, the violence would continue but usually would not be labeled as Klan violence. A message from a public meeting in Giles County read aloud at a state convention in 1871 declared, "Oh, gentlemen of the convention, we, the colored citizens of Giles County, insist that you will use every influence you can bring to bear upon Congress to put a stop to the doings of these desperadoes. For God's sake help us ere we perish."[146]

This evidence that the nature of the Ku-Klux's early proliferation has been mischaracterized alters our understanding of how and why so many southern white men would soon choose to call themselves Ku-Klux. As later chapters will show, the Ku-Klux came to widespread national attention between January and May 1868, at the same time that it was emerging to local recognition. Word of mouth and personal networks were much less important, and national media networks much more important in the Ku-Klux's local establishment than has been understood.

But even if, until the end of 1867, the Klan was largely a bluff, tragically it did come into concrete existence, and did spread, very soon afterward. Chapter 2 will explore the national proliferation of the Klan through the press, and on the ground, in 1868. This proliferation had some peculiar effects: a man named Idel Brite, fleeing the Ku-Klux in June 1868, took refuge in Pulaski. The birthplace of the Ku-Klux idea served, for him, as a safe haven from the now embodied Ku-Klux.[147] There is reason to think that, not too long after the Ku-Klux metastasized from its local roots, some original members became dubious about their creation. The following month, around the time that a black man who worked for Luther McCord was attacked by drunken Ku-Klux from another town, the *Citizen* complained that violence had gotten out of hand: "There are many things done by them, or in their name and garb, which we do not hesitate to pronounce wrong. . . . If this Kuklux Klan has any organization, with a responsible person at the head of it, we call upon him, in the name of the law-abiding and orderly people of the community, to have such outrages as these stopped."[148]

At least some of those who embodied the Pulaski Ku-Klux idea, they claimed, were not real Ku-Klux, but were only using their "name and garb." Or, alternatively, though they were Ku-Klux, they were doing things that their creators condemn. That is, Ku-Klux founders made some rhetorical attempt to negotiate a meaningful relationship between the once locally embedded form of the Ku-Klux and the actions of those who had appropriated it, or even to imagine that the former might exert some authority over the latter. This tone of disapproval and regret for at least certain "excesses" of Ku-Klux violence, paired with an attempt to claim some of those appropriating the Ku-Klux identity they had launched free-floating into culture as "real" Ku-Klux and to reject others as false, would be a staple in the writings of Ku-Klux founders in future years.

This position ultimately became the basis of a contemporary Ku-Klux defense, but also of a body of Pulaski Ku-Klux support that endures among some to the present. Historian Walter Fleming and others kept up an extensive and quite congenial correspondence with these early members, which clearly rested on an assumption that their hands were clean.[149] Those who condemned the Ku-Klux and accused it of atrocities, these supporters maintained, failed to differentiate between the high-minded "true" Ku-Klux envisioned by the founders and the crude and violent men who would illegitimately claim the identity. As Mildred Ezell Reynolds wrote in 1942, "After the need for protection was over the 'Clan' was disbanded: but for many years deeds of violence were done in the name of 'KU KLUX' which was no more. The name lived for years and was used for violence that was charged to the clan but was the work of marauders using the name."[150]

There are two serious problems with the "real" Ku-Klux imagined by these defenders. First, it is a post-hoc patching together of Pulaski ideas, which were entirely or almost entirely just ideas, with a practice that was largely post-Pulaski and was, from the first, inextricably intertwined with the other consequences of the Ku-Klux's embodiment. With the limited exception of winter 1867, the "real" Ku-Klux from which the rest of the Ku-Klux, according to these supporters, would be a tragic falling away kept its purity precisely because it never moved from idea to practice. The narrative of a Ku-Klux that began as a lark by elite young men, moved into a stage of respectable nonviolent political action, then declined into violence as it was taken up by the underclass, is dangerously misleading. It imputes a middle stage during which Ku-Klux controlled black men simply by exerting their intellectual superiority over an ignorant and superstitious people. Imagining this as the way some "real" Ku-Klux could have operated is both profoundly problematic and without credible evidentiary support.

Second, the "Pulaski ideas" that serve as such an important part of this ideal image of the early Ku-Klux do not resemble what the historical records suggest actually motivated the early Ku-Klux. Later Ku-Klux idealizers projected back onto the Pulaski founders a nostalgic, white-supremacy-oriented focus that leaves out much that was there and adds much that was not. Gone, most strikingly, is the early Ku-Klux's modernizing framing, their restlessness and bureaucratese, and their non–iconically southern background. Instead, the Pulaski Ku-Klux become southern white everymen who created the ceremonial aspects of the Ku-Klux on a lark but then immediately realized its potential to challenge freedpeople's and their allies' claims to power. While the audience for the Pulaski Ku-Klux from the spring of 1866 through December 1867 was, first, each other and their close friends, then perhaps some readers of the *Citizen*, then, very gradually, newspaper editors from beyond the county, these later celebratory images of the Ku-Klux imagine the Ku-Klux as performing before (specifically, intimidating) freedpeople.

Both racist idealizers of the early Ku-Klux and historians have imagined too much continuity and too smooth a transition between the Pulaski form and its appropriation. Some might argue that this is not important—that the violence and destruction of the Ku-Klux from 1868 on is what makes it worth understanding, and if this is projected incorrectly back on its beginnings, it only damages the packaging. But the packaging matters. It was what enabled the Ku-Klux's appropriation by the press, which the next chapter will trace in detail. And while the national press, in adopting the idea of the Ku-Klux, would radically alter it, certain elements of the original Ku-Klux form would persist, fortifying, but also shaping and limiting, the Ku-Klux's cultural and political significance.

For the first year and a half of its existence, until 1868, the Pulaski Ku-Klux's spread was not much like wildfire, even though many of its performative elements were in place. Perhaps the performance alone held little novelty for Reconstruction-era southerners. As future chapters will discuss, the Klan's costumes, rituals, and performative behaviors were derivative of existing cultural institutions; only when those theatrical elements were wedded to collective violence did the Klan become culturally fascinating. So, for all the opportunities they may have had to learn about the Ku-Klux through 1867, the existing evidence suggests that many residents of Giles and nearby counties in fact learned about the Klan only around March 1868, just as national newspaper coverage was hitting its stride.

TWO

Ku-Klux Attacks Define a New
Black and White Manhood

> On the way, they asked me how I liked their flag, pointing to the flag they
> carried, flesh colored and in the shape of a heart. I told them, very well, for all
> the use I had for it. They said it meant Ku Klux.
>
> —Testimony of John Dunlap, in *Report of Evidence Taken Before the Military
> Committee of the Tennessee General Assembly*, 1868

After a small group of white men in Pulaski developed the Ku-Klux from
1866 to late 1867, Klan groups in and around Pulaski began to commit
acts of violence. The violence began sporadically and was still, at the
beginning of 1868, limited to Giles and closely surrounding areas, with
the exception of the one incident in Alabama and perhaps a few more as
yet unknown. It would dramatically intensify and proliferate in the spring
of 1868. From then until mid-1871, the Klan took on the form not of an
idiosyncratic local group but of a daunting national movement.

To the victims themselves, every attack was profoundly local. Their terror, the pain they felt, and the danger and damage to their bodies that the
terror and pain signaled was what mattered about the Klan attack. Every
action by the Klan involved particular men using physical force to break
down specific bodies that housed memories, sensations, words, and wills
and that enabled them to feed and house themselves and their dependents. Caswell Holt, a freedman in Alamance County, described the physical nature of his attack: a group of men pulled him from his bed by the
neck, choking him, then nearly put out his eye. They carried him outside
and partially hung him repeatedly, bucked him (that is, tied his hands
together over his folded legs and ran a stick behind his knees), then
formed a line and whipped him with sticks and switches before partially
hanging him again and rubbing a stick up and down his raw back while

he choked. They then demanded that he run back to his house, which he could hardly do. His back was "cut all to pieces," and his wife found a splinter as long as his finger buried in his hip.[1] Columbus Jeter, then a forty-year-old black preacher who also taught night school in Douglas County, Georgia, told of being painfully jerked from his hiding place in his chimney, pulled around by his hair, and shot with a shotgun as he ran away. He lost most use of his left arm.[2] Henry Hamlin of Madison County, Alabama, working on a railroad, told of being whipped with a leather strap so many times that his back was permanently injured.[3] Robin Westbrook did not live to tell his story, but the wife who watched him die later told of how he had armed himself with a dog-iron and managed for a time to fight off the several attackers who had broken down his cabin door. Ultimately they hit him in the head with a gun, then managed to sneak around behind him and shoot him in the shoulder; once he fell, they shot him fatally in the neck.[4]

The pain was what must have mattered to the suffering men in the moment; if they survived and the crisis abated, they could assess the damage to their bodies. Perhaps they would be in constant pain, or would not be able to lie on their left side at night, or would not be able to use one of their arms, or would be impotent, or deaf, or would walk with a limp, or would always have a scar across their forehead. Perhaps their body, in a few hours or several days, would fail them entirely as internal injuries did their work or infections set in. Or perhaps nature would heal their bodies from the injuries caused by the brutality, allowing them to resume their role in their family and community and the plans they had made.

Pain and physical damage did not mark the Klan as a new form of white-on-black power. It was consistent with the many private white-on-black attacks, some of which were collective, which both preceded and coexisted with Klan violence. Those who were doing well in the new regime, who were hopeful and confident and kept trying to lift their heads had kept a look out for such violence since the war. Rather, what made Klan violence uniquely powerful were the rich networks of dark cultural meaning with which Ku-Klux surrounded this moment of pain and violence.

A Klan attack was part of something larger, more inscrutable, and perhaps inescapable than the act of any individual or small group. The alchemy of the Klan attack was to transmute a specific violent act inflicted by a group of white men on the body of an individual victim into an attack by abstract men on an abstract body. The Klan attack was at once the infliction of pain and damage on a specific person and an act of national political and cultural meaning and significance. It was both embedded in the fleshy local and the creature of a disembodied translocal discourse.

The Klan's claim to be not-from-here was central to its terror. If an attack were motivated by local struggles and oppressions, the victim might imagine that he or she could anticipate or control it. But small American communities, economically, culturally, and socially, found themselves more tightly interconnected after the war; in the same way, Ku-Klux claimed that the logic of their attack lay far beyond any one local community. Whites liked to speak of freedpeople's response to Klan violence as "dread."[5] The mayor of Columbus, Mississippi, Henry B. Whitfield, claimed that a Klan raid "frightens [black people] nearly to death."[6] The pain and damage to single bodies was amplified by a "general feeling of dread and terror."[7] One black man who witnessed a Klan attack believed that one of his attackers, "a kind of drunken, desperate man," revealed his identity during an attack "to let me know that he was really in the gang, and to make me hold him in dread."[8] The pain and damage was not enough, attackers feared. It was crucial that victims and others who heard about attacks recognize them and fear them as larger than single local events.

Capitalizing on the layers of cultural meaning which encased their violence, both real Ku-Klux attackers and individuals or groups who wanted to make use of the dread occasioned by others posted countless threatening notices in central places in town and left them at the doors of isolated cabins. The more literary among them penned mysterious notices of Klan meetings for publication in local newspapers. They marched in costumed procession through the streets of the town at midnight to show their numbers. They circulated rumors of attacks to come, or sent allies with stern warnings for people who refused to understand the inevitability of white control. Sometimes they dressed in costume to deliver these warnings themselves, armed and at nighttime, demanding that too-confident black people or their white allies cease their behavior, renounce their views, or even leave town immediately.

So, beginning in early 1868, many groups of white men in a diverse set of local communities declared themselves to be Ku-Klux and took steps to either terrify or physically attack black southerners and their allies throughout the former Confederacy and even occasionally in the loyal border states. As the victims of these attacks, in turn, reported their suffering, newspapers eagerly passed along these stories as well, contributing to the evolving national discourse on the nature of the Ku-Klux.

Because all people who chose to call themselves Ku-Klux were affiliating themselves with what they thought they knew about the Ku-Klux elsewhere, Klan attacks bore certain resemblances to one another. Many, though not all, Ku-Klux wore costumes; many used their costumes or behavior to mark themselves as bizarre; and almost all made a fetish of secrecy. Rather consistently, they chose as their victims men (and sometimes women), usually black, who were affiliated with the Republican Party and therefore with northern power. Despite the fact those claiming a "Ku-Klux" identity were, by definition, presenting and imagining themselves as part of a translocal movement, the Klan attack was always the imposition of a translocal idea not only onto the bodies of real victims but also onto concrete communities with their own fully elaborated practices, conflicts, and norms.

Bruce Baker and other historians have discussed the profound localism of cultures of violence: acts of violence, particularly collective violence, have always worked to define communities to themselves. They identify insiders and outsiders, dramatically illustrate group values, and often become central to communal memory.[9] Klan groups worked in the same way. They self-consciously drew on a translocal grammar, but their attacks could be coherent and effective to their victims, community members, and even to themselves only when they fit the ideas they borrowed from elsewhere into local cultural ideas and meanings, community perceptions of individuals in their own communities, and the local significance of certain places and certain phrases. Much of the context that would enable historians to understand the local meanings of Klan violence was oral, or not preserved, and cannot be recovered. Who knows, for instance, why a Ku-Klux group in North Carolina attacked a woman in North Carolina who had given birth to a stillborn baby that was reputed to look like a Ku-Klux, or why another group poured tar in the vagina of a supposed prostitute, another brutalized a highly educated quadriplegic man, or another gloated that they had caught a preacher? Local groups who committed these idiosyncratic acts were motivated by local reasons that may be beyond historians' capacity to recover.

But every locale had its grammar of violence that was meaningful only to insiders and deliberately opaque to outsiders. Certain phrases were popular in certain areas: in some regions, it was common for a potential attacker or combatant to tell his victim or opponent that he intended to "rip his damned [various body parts] out."[10] Certain places or events, like estate sales, parade grounds, certain grocery stores, or lynching trees, became expected forums for violence in some places more than others: episodes of violence committed there would have evoked past bloody scenes. Certain forms of violence were more common or resonant in some areas than others. H. W. Guion testified that Mecklenburg County, North Carolina, was "famous for rape."[11] Though historians cannot read all of the local dialect of violence, it shaped how locals reacted to attacks and understood what they suffered, perpetrated, or witnessed.

It is easier to unpack the common, intralocal elements woven through Klan violence. Much of that intralocal language of Klan violence traveled through newspapers. The national newspaper discourse about the Ku-Klux had a close relationship with mid-nineteenth-century popular culture. Ku-Klux were violent and clandestine, ghostlike and difficult to verify, but they were also costumed. The costumes, and the cultural ideas they evoked, shaped the Ku-Klux and public responses to it as much as ideas of the nature of the state, the press, and freedpeople did. The specific character of Ku-Klux costumes was meaningful enough to Ku-Klux that they labored to produce them, meaningful enough for Ku-Klux victims and witnesses that they later described them in detail, and meaningful enough to a national audience that newspaper reporters and political figures sent south to gather information about the Ku-Klux spent substantial time asking about their dress and performative behavior.

Ku-Klux did not dress and perform as they did simply to avoid identification or to frighten superstitious freedmen. While Ku-Klux's desire to conceal identity motivated some elements of their costume and performance, such as masks and disguised voices, it sheds little light on why so many Ku-Klux adopted such baroque garb and routines. Likewise, Ku-Klux's hopes to frighten freedmen into submission only partially explains the elaborate displays and claims they made not only to their victims, but also to one another and to their own supporters.[12] A northern congressman who expressed his incredulity that southern whites actually believed that black victims were fooled by the costumes was no doubt correct.[13] Freedmen hardly required such a supplement of terror. Indeed, it could be argued that the addition of costume and theatrics made less difference to the victims of the violence than to any other group that witnessed or learned of the Ku-Klux's attacks. It is not clear that costumed, theatrical Ku-Klux changed freedmen's behavior in ways any equivalent violent racist vigilante movement would not have done.

Ku-Klux used costumes and performance for reasons far beyond their hopes to obscure their identities or cow their victims.

Ku-Klux performance has usually been interpreted as though its intended audience consisted of its actual and potential victims, yet Ku-Klux were well aware of the close scrutiny of two other audiences. One of these was northerners; the Ku-Klux committed their violence during those years when the North's Reconstruction policy was most indeterminate. As a conquered people trying to determine how far they could reassert white Democratic political and economic control, wary that northerners would suppress any direct display of organized violence, Ku-Klux had everything to gain by encouraging northerners to read their attacks as theatrical rather than political or military. By couching their attacks within often-elaborate performances derived both from mid-nineteenth-century commercial popular culture and from the long folk tradition of "rough music" or charivari, Ku-Klux adopted a time-tested strategy of the weak.[14] As James Scott has argued, "Actual rebels mimic carnival—they dress as women or mask themselves when breaking machinery or making political demands; their threats use the features and symbolism of carnival" to "conceal their intentions" from those in power, who delay their response while attempting to determine whether the rebels are "playing or in earnest."[15] Ku-Klux performance blended old and new. While the specific popular cultural forms from which they borrowed were very much of the moment, the idea of grotesquely costumed violence was an essentially premodern form of protest.

Even as Ku-Klux theatricality confused northern response, the type of performance the Ku-Klux adopted did discursive work at home: Ku-Klux were performing as much for themselves and other southern whites as for anyone else.[16] As in Pulaski, performance sometimes logically and chronologically preceded the adoption of racial violence by Ku-Klux in a particular area; it was not simply a ploy to frighten freedmen or to distract the occupier. Ku-Klux used their attacks both to violently reimpose white male Democratic dominance and to explain their new roles to themselves and their allies.

Ku-Klux performance was, in part, an expression of white southern men's sense of disempowerment and failure as patriarchs after the war.[17] Men were expected to protect and sustain dependents, but many southern men could not do this during the war and its aftermath.[18] And many southern white men had grounded their manhood on their right to inflict unmanning violence upon slaves.[19] It was not only the violence itself, but also their right to use it casually and on a whim, that set off their manhood against that of their black victims. As one attacker told his victim, forty-two-year-old black man John Childers, "I'd rather kill you right here now than eat a fried chicken."[20] Ku-Klux drew from popular culture to reconstruct their destabilized gender identities and reaffirm the racial dominance at its core. At the same time, Ku-Klux performance expressed a new relationship to violence. Violence had always been constitutive of the southern gentleman, but the war and white men's temporarily weakened grasp on the reins of mastery during the Reconstruction years made that violence stark and public. Ku-Klux performed violence to insist that it restored their mastery. Ku-Klux blended popular cultural tropes like minstrelsy and the carnivalesque with local traditions of violence and rituals of dominance to negotiate their new identities in relationship to freedpeople and to present their violence as constructive of a new and stable southern social order.

Klan violence was very much about restoring a lost mastery while also building new postwar men. The tactics were largely the same: whites remembered how to whip with branches, leather straps, and whips, to threaten and to shoot, to whip a woman's bare thighs or to rape, to hang a man either long enough to kill him or just long enough to make him experience the extremes of moral terror then cut him down. But the meanings were different. Klan attackers were using violence not to define themselves as masters and black men as slaves, but to define themselves as dominant and their victims as compliant within the new postslavery order. Sometimes Klan attackers were interested in forcing their victims to labor more or better or with more deference, but far more frequently, they were interested in forcing their victims to recognize them as rightful leaders and themselves as rightful followers in the new free order.

How Ku-Klux Attacks Defined the New White Man

Southerners, both black and white, were widely perceived as backward, traditionalist, and behind the times. Ku-Klux did many things during their attacks to push against this definition, marking themselves not as backward-looking planters but rather as modern men. The Ku-Klux was secular, separate from a religious framework in a way that future iterations of the Klan would not be. It regularly mocked forms deemed traditional, such as the idea of the "gentleman." Individuals who chose to become Ku-Klux intentionally appropriated an identity marked as being from elsewhere. And they appropriated most energetically from commercial and media networks. A Ku-Klux was a man who decided to adopt as his own an identity he had read about in the paper.

Ku-Klux costumes, as the Pulaski men had intended, situated their wearers in a world of international commerce, idiomatic humor, and the high production values of the New York stage. The Ku-Klux served to alleviate the restlessness of southerners as it had that of the Pulaski founders by reframing problems in a way that made meaningful action seem possible. At a time when so many defeated white men felt that they had not had the opportunity to do meaningful work, Ku-Klux's ritual and other performative elements recast young adult white southern men's identities in a way that enabled them to feel capable of playing a public role in the postwar landscape. Northerners were also attracted to its performative freshness. Even as they encountered the Klan's performative elements directly alongside reports of ruthless violence, the stench of the oppression did not mask the whiff of the new. The Klan served an energizing function in part by building a new southern white male identity that was drawn self-consciously from the newest trends, from popular entertainment to contemporary forms of organizational structure. To these men, the particular shape that the Ku-Klux Klan gave to the violent racial oppression so pervasive in their world felt vibrant and hopeful.

Ku-Klux were most obvious about appropriating northern popular entertainment. The Columbia (S.C.) Daily Phoenix in February 1867 reprinted a Brick Pomeroy column that reviewed the blockbuster burlesque hit The Black Crook, playfully insisting that everyone has to see it because "not to have seen it is to be prudish, old-fogyish, behind the times."[21] Ku-Klux costumes would soon be compared to those in The Black Crook. Costuming was itself a modern fixation. The mid-nineteenth century was a time of great anxiety about the dangerous ease with which a person could present themselves as someone who they were not, but not coincidentally it was a time of great interest in disguise.[22] There was nothing new about masquerade balls or the use of costumes in theatrical productions, yet the cultural centrality of costumes generally—and also, more specifically, the use of costume to fully obscure identity—had increased in the late antebellum period. The first public carnival processions in the United States began in the 1830s in Mobile, became institutionalized into planned parades in the 1840s, and spread to New Orleans in the 1850s. At the same time, masquerade balls spread through northern cities, in part due to German influence.[23]

A hood/mask associated with John Campbell Van Hook Jr., a Confederate colonel of the Fiftieth North Carolina Troops and a farmer in Roxboro, North Carolina. The mask, or hood, is made of fabric and rabbit fur. The three "horns" are stuffed fabric, and red and black ribbons are sewn on; the eyebrows are made of black fabric, the eye openings are rimmed with red ribbon, and the nose is made of red and black fabric. The fangs are made with the same fabric as the horns, and the sideburns and beard are made of brown rabbit fur. The North Carolina Museum of History, Raleigh.

National interest in costumes was not limited to carnival and masquerade balls. Costumes were central to the sensationalist fiction so popular during those years. It was in the 1850s that popular fiction in the United States began to feature detectives. These detectives were not yet the sort that sat in offices smoking, drinking, yearning, and philosophizing: rather, they were assuming false identities, often in costume, in order to infiltrate dangerous spaces and gather hidden information. Many of the same papers that carried accounts of the Klan ran detective stories alongside them, both as news and as fiction. The *Philadelphia Daily Evening Telegraph* on Christmas Eve of 1869 printed a story about a detective who disguised himself as, among other things, a dissenting minister, a naval officer, and a lady.[24] Costuming carried with it a modern, urban feel.

Ku-Klux regalia, like that proliferating in carnivals and on the stage, was diverse, wild, and often festive. Some costumes are close to the image of the Klansman that has come down to us from *Birth of a Nation*: J. J. Hinds of Decatur, Alabama, was surrounded by a group wearing "paper, or paste-board hat[s], about eighteen inches high, in funnel shape . . . covered with a black mask, with eye and mouth holes." On their legs they wore red flannel pants with white stripes along the seams, and over that was a brown belted gown.[25] Costumes ranged from lavish gowns and headpieces with matching disguises for horses to a piece of cheap cloth over the face. Some Ku-Klux wore pants with short jackets or a normal suit of men's clothing turned inside out. Some members of a South Carolina group donned masks made of squirrel skin.[26] One extant mask held by the North Carolina Museum of History incorporates rabbit fur.[27]

Some costumes featured "all kinds of fixings"—fake beards or tassels, for example, or one to four horns pointing up or down.[28] Some Ku-Klux wore "scarlet stockings" underneath their costumes.[29] Some attached pieces of reflective metal to their disguises. Some had red paper hats with "square stars tacked about on" them. One victim described the costumes of the men who attacked him as "white gowns, and some had flax linen, and red calico, and some red caps, and white horns stuffed with cotton. And some had flannel around coon-skin caps, and faces on, and next to the caps their gowns came down so that I could not see only the legs below the knees . . . only a little hole at the eyes, not bigger than a man's finger nail."[30] Another witness described a band as wearing "a mass of white, red, and black on the face. I think probably it was ribbon fitted over the face, and head and hair covered, and large horns on. Some horns were red and some black, and some of the tassels were black."[31]

Ku-Klux sometimes interpreted their costumes for their victims. It is well known that Ku-Klux frequently claimed to be ghosts of the Confederate dead. A visitor to Pulaski in the Ku-Klux's early months claimed that its members decided to pose as "miraculous persons—spirits and ghosts, and things of that kind," and other examples of Ku-Klux posing as ghosts abound throughout the South.[32] Historians have less often remarked on the fact that Ku-Klux frequently also assumed the identity of moon-men.[33] Ku-Klux in Alabama, Mississippi, and Georgia told their victims that they

Historian Katherine Lennard came upon this bonnet/mask that may have been either a Klan costume piece or a contemporary costume piece that evoked the Klan. She describes it as "a cream muslin bonnet categorized as a Klan costume that has very muddy provenance. It is a mid-nineteenth century shape, with boning across the top of the crown, and a simple muslin mask—fabric aging just different enough to suggest that it may have been added later—hanging to cover the face. The fabric is definitely old and it has real nineteenth-century silk ribbons that would tie under the chin. The donors claimed to have gotten it from a Connecticut man whose father was a member of the Klan, but they provided no exact dates. . . . It is not much to go on, and could easily be some sort of masquerade costume piece that somehow ended up at the Schomburg as a Klan costume." Schomburg Center for Research in Black Culture, New York Public Library.

This robe and hood is said to have belonged to Joseph Boyce Steward (1845–1939) of Lincoln County, Tennessee. The item description is: "a) Robe of dark brown linen. Trimmed with white linen bands with center row of cut-out diamond shapes. b) Hood of dark brown and white linen. Top part of hood is brown with stiffened triangular piece in front. Bottom part is white linen with eye slits and features outlined in brown linen." Courtesy of the Chicago Museum of History.

had come from the moon.[34] Repeatedly, Ku-Klux supplemented their identity as ghosts of the Confederate dead and moon-men with the claim that they had come from battlegrounds to their victims' homes by way of hell. One Alabama Ku-Klux characteristically told a black railroad worker, "We have just come from hell, and we rule you all."[35] The idea of posing as a denizen of hell to frighten freedmen seems indeed to have preceded the formation of the Ku-Klux. The *Pulaski Citizen* reported in early 1866 that a huge, monstrous, fire-breathing creature with cloven hooves and horns had visited four freedmen's households in Bracken County, Kentucky.[36]

Other recurring Ku-Klux performative identities also marked them as threatening outsiders. One common conceit of Ku-Klux was that they were "outlanders," or foreigners. To give this impression, they assumed foreign accents that victims identified as Irish, German, or French.[37] Other Ku-Klux dressed as or acted like Native Americans, an identity that in contemporary minds combined foreignness and amoral savagery. Some of Warren Jones's Georgia attackers called themselves "Big Injun" and "Little Injun."[38] A memoir-writer recalled encountering a (non-Klan) vigilante in 1874 wearing "a black gown that came to his knees and a mask of an Indian face with long horsehair for hair."[39] When white schoolteacher Sarah Allen claimed that the Ku-Klux who warned her away "yelled like Comanche Indians," it is unclear whether her attackers were deliberately imitating Native Americans, or if she was insulting them with the comparison, or both.[40]

Many other Ku-Klux assumed the characteristics of animals. Interestingly (and reflecting the materials they had ready access to in making their costumes), their tastes ran less toward savage animals than toward domestic ones, such as cows, mules, and goats. A number of Ku-Klux costumes sported cows' and mules' tails or mules' ears. The favorite animal feature, however, was that most phallic of accessories, the bull's horn. Some Ku-Klux also mimicked animal behavior and sounds. Mississippi victim Joseph Galloway claimed that some of his attackers "shook their heads and horns at me, and acted like cows."[41] Another Mississippi group "bleated like billy-goats."[42] Twenty-six-year-old Gadsden Steel of York County, North Carolina, recalled a Ku-Klux leader who "bowed his head down to me, (illustrating with a very low bow,) and says, 'How do you do,' and horned me in the breast with his horns [which were two feet long and attached to his head]."[43] When the Ku-Klux attacked freedman Columbus Jeter in Georgia, they made the "most curious howling of dogs I ever heard."[44] Former Confederate general Samuel Ghoulson of Mississippi had heard that the Ku-Klux had made an attack, "some hooting like owls, some howling like dogs."[45] A North Carolina man recalled that attacking Ku-Klux "made a kind of noise like these little screech owls. Then they came up and poked their horns at me, like they was trying to hook me."[46] An admiring young white Louisiana man claimed in a letter to his family that a group of Ku-Klux had "made all kinds noises [sic] from an ant to a buffalo, & finally ended by bellowing like oxen when they smell blood."[47] A devilish figure who visited Kentucky freedmen some months before the Ku-Klux began was reported to have hairy arms, cat paws, horselike legs, and a serpent hiss. At each appearance, it sported a different head: an ape, a horse, a vulture, and an elephant.[48]

All of these costumed identities—foreigners, Indians, animals, and ghosts—were staples of popular culture. When contemporaries described Ku-Klux costume and behavior, they often recognized its links to popular entertainment. Congressman James Justice described the costume of one of his attackers as "a red suit out and out—a great deal like those I have seen on clowns in circuses. There were a number of stripes on each arm; I do not know what number; something bright like silver lace, like stripes on a sergeant's sleeves. There was something on the breast of one of them, something round."[49] An Alabama Ku-Klux sympathizer, asked if he had ever before seen a Ku-Klux costume, replied, "No, sir, only in the circus."[50] Because vigilantism and popular culture had influenced one another so heavily over the nineteenth century, Ku-Klux were able to place themselves within both traditions at once.[51] Indeed, Ku-Klux costumes were so perfectly situated at the intersection between folk vigilante disguise and the costumes favored by contemporary popular entertainers that observers became confused. When Thompson C. Hawkins, a postal agent who was attacked by the Ku-Klux in Alabama, first saw the group, he thought they were traveling entertainers. "They had on caps or hats . . . and in front something like a white paper. . . . That attracted my attention, or called it to believe that they belonged to a band of music."[52] A Freedmen's Bureau agent in Huntsville mistook a Ku-Klux group for an "advance of some circus company."[53] When a group of "masked serenaders made its appearance on the square, with horns, bells, tin pans" in a Mississippi town, locals attacked them in the belief that they were Ku-Klux (whether the musicians in fact had violent intentions is unclear).[54]

Ku-Klux drew on popular culture in their behavior as well as their costume. One of the first public appearances of the Pulaski Ku-Klux was apparently a parade in which members wore a variety of bizarre and elaborate costumes and played makeshift musical instruments.[55] References to other parades pepper the 1871 congressional testimonies: congressional investigators frequently inquired of their witnesses whether they had witnessed "parades of disguised men," and their responses were resoundingly positive. A Noxubee County, Mississippi, planter claimed that there had been "several parades" of Ku-Klux in his county in the past year.[56] A Radical politician in Greene County, Alabama, said that he knew of "a great many," though he had never seen one.[57] Most of these parades were probably more like political processions than like parades of popular entertainers: fairly straightforward displays of force and numbers unadorned with carnivalesque elements. Yet such adornment was not uncommon. Ku-Klux leader Randolph Shotwell was disgusted that other vigilante groups who falsely (in his opinion) claimed to be Ku-Klux "marched into villages in masked processions with stuffed elephants and other grotesque animals."[58] Ku-Klux mimicked contemporary showmen in other ways as well.[59] One Alabama Ku-Klux "commenced some mystical flourishes with his pistols . . . and in a few minutes returned again and went through the same performance."[60] Ku-Klux attacking a white farmer amazed him with a fireball.[61] In the course of a particularly sadistic attack, Ku-Klux staged their own circus, first forcing their black victims to act like horses, then performing for them, "puking" fire out of their mouths.[62] A South Carolina Ku-Klux band "jumped around" its victims "and asked them whether they liked liquor. . . . They took them out and danced around them; they behaved like fools."[63] While the reference to liquor reminds us of one factor contributing to many Ku-Klux's grotesque behavior, Ku-Klux went to great lengths to establish a theatrical atmosphere. Writing a fictionalized account of the Ku-Klux's Pulaski beginnings in the early twentieth century, Lapsley McCord described Ku-Klux as using torches and fireworks to make a "wholesale spectacular [performance of] demonical theatricals."[64]

The Ku-Klux's costume and theatrical behavior resounded in many registers. To be sure, each of these costumes and identities had its individual valence. Moon-men evoked the idea of lunacy, dead soldiers the ravages of the recent war, Indians savagery, animals brutality. Yet all of them told observers that their wearers had adopted the role of the unfamiliar, unpredictable, and uncontrollable. By marking their attacks as performative through costume and behavior, Ku-Klux created a liminal space in which, as Richard Schechner, following Victor Turner, has argued, "cognitive schemata that give sense and order to everyday life no longer apply, but are . . . suspended."[65] The Ku-Klux's theatrical behavior also signaled that they were meant to be watched rather than interacted with and that they intended to astonish their viewers. It conveyed that the events about to unfold would be more like a show than like a political meeting, a marketplace, a battle, or a brawl. In this way, Ku-Klux instructed their victims and witnesses as to how they would be expected to behave during their attack, establishing a distance between themselves and their viewers and suggesting that the "visit" was pre-scripted. In a Reconstruction-era South where freedmen were increasingly asserting their own agency, the very form of the Ku-Klux attack relegated them to passive spectatorship. Both their decision to wear costumes and their specific choices of costume ensured that Ku-Klux attacks would be read, in part, as theatrical and understood in terms of contemporary popular culture.

Ku-Klux were selective in their appropriations from popular culture. In choreographing their attacks, for instance, they drew not from prize-fighting or domestic fiction but from minstrelsy, the carnivalesque, and related genres.[66] Not coincidentally, these types of performance were deeply implicated in the work of racial and gender redefinition. Drawing from them enabled Ku-Klux to mobilize the cultural messages they had already refined over many years of performance. The success of Ku-Klux in sending their rather complex and potentially treacherous cultural messages—asserting their manhood by wearing scarlet stockings or waving a pink heart-shaped flag, and their suitability as leaders of a new civilized South by giving a Comanche war whoop—was due to their ability to use the framework already built by minstrel and carnival traditions.[67]

Connections between the Ku-Klux and the carnivalesque abound.[68] Elizabeth Meriwether, Memphis Ku-Klux insider and author of a pro-Ku-Klux farce featuring a Ku-Klux trickster figure, hinted at a connection between the Ku-Klux and carnival by setting her play in New Orleans. Though the play does not include any direct reference to Mardi Gras celebrations, her adolescent sons, corresponding about her play the year it was written, referred to it as "a book . . . on Mardi Gras."[69] Sally Bedell, of Columbia, Georgia, described having seen a man accused of involvement in a Klan murder on the night of the murder with a "masquerade suit"—"calico pants and a worsted coat," and a pasteboard hat with a facial covering of black fringe. He said he was planning to wear that, going out in that evening with a large group of other costumed men.[70] Ku-Klux riders sometimes wore disguises that had been manufactured for private masquerades. Congressmen interrogated a suspected Ku-Klux from Union County, South Carolina, Joseph F. Gist, at length about the nature of the costumes he had seen at a local "fancy dress" party. As chapter 7 will discuss, his description of the "dominos" closely matched victims' and witnesses' descriptions of Ku-Klux costumes in the same area. "The men, most of them, had on gowns" of "various" colors, including black, white, blue, and red. "The hood was drawn over [the head] with holes for the eyes."[71] A local Union County black seamstress had made some of these costumes; though she was understandably reticent with the congressional committee, her description of the dominoes she produced was quite consistent with descriptions of Ku-Klux costumes.[72] A local white, William A. Bolt, insisted that the masquerade costumes were the same as those worn for local raids.[73] There were other examples of the appropriation by Ku-Klux of elements of masquerade costumes: two witnesses from elsewhere in South Carolina claimed that the Ku-Klux group they saw wore "dough-faces like you see in the stores," presumably for masquerades.[74] A Georgia man claimed that someone had displayed "some clothing that some young men wore at a masquerade ball" in Atlanta, falsely claiming that they were Ku-Klux costumes.[75]

At the same time, as the story of the Pulaski Ku-Klux's minstrel origins suggests, there were numerous ties between minstrelsy and the Ku-Klux. One memoirist claimed he had been recruited for the Ku-Klux on the basis of his skill as a blackface minstrel.[76] The congressional committee interrogated professional minstrel John Christy about his role in a Ku-Klux attack in Meridian, Mississippi.[77] Ku-Klux's favored "ghost" identity and the costumes that went with it had roots in antebellum minstrelsy. Many Ku-Klux bands resembled traveling minstrel troupes also referred to by contemporaries as "serenaders."[78] Some of these Ku-Klux groups performed music—oddly, one anti-Ku-Klux freedman claimed that "it was the prettiest music you ever saw."[79] Ku-Klux bands were also closely associated with the minstrel serenading tradition in Mississippi. In August 1867 diarist Samuel Agnew, a white rural Mississippi minister who controversially preached to freedmen, wrote, "A crowd of the Baldwyn boys came down in the train" and "serenad[ed] our citizens tonight," "playing a few tunes" outside his own home. Within a year, Baldwyn would emerge as the local hotspot for Ku-Klux violence, and in 1869 Ku-Klux would pay a visit to Agnew's home.[80] Ku-Klux in other regions retained some memory of their minstrel origins. North Carolinian Ku-Klux leader Randolph Shotwell, one of the few men to spend substantial jail time for Ku-Klux activities, dismissed the Pulaski Ku-Klux as having been nothing more than a "burlesque association" that lacked the serious political purpose of the later group.[81]

THE ENTIRE PROGRAMME RECEIVED LAST EVENING WITH

SHOUTS OF APPLAUSE AND ROARS OF LAUGHTER!

LAST APPEARANCE IN THIS CITY.

This, Friday Evening, July 8th, 1864

OF THE EVER POPULAR AND RENOWNED

DUPRES AND GREEN'S

Ghost!!! Ghost!

Ghost! Ghost!

ORIGINAL · NEW ORLEANS AND · METROPOLITAN

MINSTRELS

EVERY MEMBER IN THEIR PRINCIPAL CHARACTERS THIS EVENING IN THE FOLLOWING NEW AND EXTRAORDINARY BILL.

Eisler's Athenaeum playbill for Dupres and Green's Original New Orleans and Metropolitan Minstrels (1864). This Civil War–era New Orleans minstrel show was one of many pre–Ku-Klux Klan theatrical productions that depicted ghosts frightening gullible slaves. Courtesy of the Billy Rose Theatre Collection, the New York Public Library for the Performing Arts, Astor, Lenox, and Tilden Foundations.

WHILE SOME KU-KLUX bands performed music, others gave what they seemed to intend as comic performances reminiscent of the minstrel stage. When Ku-Klux brutally attacked paraplegic freedman Elias Hill, one of them "took a strap and buckled it around my neck and said, 'Let's take him to the river and drown him,' 'What course is the river?' they asked me. I told them, 'east.' Then one of them went feeling about, as if he was looking for something, and said, 'I don't see no east! Where is the d___d thing?' as if he did not understand what I meant."[82] Ku-Klux attacking a white Republican engaged in another strange routine. After roaming around the house in which he was staying, "at last they came to the bed and asked the boys, [in a thin treble voice] 'Who is this?' The boys said they had an old gentleman staying all night there. He said, [in a thin treble voice,] 'What is he?' Another said, [in deep bass,] 'A damned rad.' . . . They came to the bed; one came to the foot and the other to the head; and the one at the foot smelled all around at the foot of the bed, and he says, [in deep bass,] 'He's a damned old rad.' The other one said, [in sharp treble] 'Is he fat?' The other answered, [in bass,] 'Yes.' The other said, [in treble], 'Well, we'll eat him then; get out of the bed.'"[83] These were two of the more striking instances in which Ku-Klux engaged in bizarre routines during their attacks, but Ku-Klux periodically put on such performances on a smaller scale. Speaking in fake foreign accents, or in otherwise altered voices was a fairly common feature of Ku-Klux performance as it was of the minstrel stage. Ku-Klux sometimes went to great lengths to stage their violence as comedy.

But the most explicit way in which Ku-Klux evoked the minstrel and carnivalesque was in their assumption of "female garb" and blackface. So many victims and witnesses, in so many places and over such a length of time, described Ku-Klux costumes as similar to women's clothes that the resemblance could not have been accidental.[84] The congressional hearings alone contain many such references. One South Carolina victim said of his attackers, "Some of them had calico dresses; others had on homespun dresses, paper hats, & c.; every man was disguised."[85] Another described them as wearing "a dark colored something that fitted around them something like a lady's dress and came down about the knee."[86] An Alabama man described his attackers' costumes as "like a lady's dress, only open before."[87] Georgia man Eli Barnes first detected the Ku-Klux's presence when he heard a "rattle . . . like a woman's garment." His suspicion was confirmed when he saw "a great many persons with long gowns on; I did not know whether they were men or women."[88] A Tennessee Freedmen's Aid agent claimed one of those who attacked him was "dressed in women's clothes, and was called the woman of the party."[89] When a white Georgia Justice of the Peace first saw the Ku-Klux, he thought they looked like "a heap of women" and claimed that he mistook them for a midnight bridal party from across the Alabama border seeking his services.[90] A U.S. Army officer looking for evidence of Ku-Klux activity found a "long black cambric dress; it may have been a woman's riding-habit and may have been a Ku-klux gown, we could not tell."[91] A black South Carolina woman whose husband had been killed by the Ku-Klux compared the fabric of the attackers' costumes with that of the white cotton frock she was wearing at her testimony.[92]

It would be tempting to suggest that Ku-Klux had no intention of dressing as women and that their victims and opponents described their costumes as women's clothes as a form of insult in the same genre as the famous story of Jefferson Davis being caught fleeing in his wife's clothes.[93] No doubt many victims did intend insult, but Ku-Klux's appropriation of women's dress was frequently intentional. As scholars of both vigilante violence and carnivalesque performance have emphasized, there were numerous precedents to the Ku-Klux's use of female costume.[94] In addition to many well-known European and early American examples, there were some much closer to home: a September 1865 article in the *Knoxville Whig* claimed that "at a colored ball . . . three colored persons were killed in one night by white men dressed in *Women's Clothes*."[95] Furthermore, some witnesses claimed that their attackers' costumes not only resembled but in fact were women's clothes, which would make their appropriation deliberate. Essic Harris, a Ku-Klux victim, said of Ku-Klux marauders, "Some of them had on some women's clothes."[96] A North Carolina woman recognized a Ku-Klux because "he had his wife's old dress on; a dress that I had seen many a time."[97] A Georgia woman similarly recognized a man by identifying his costume as his wife's dress.[98]

Given the limited number of pro-Ku-Klux sources that describe Ku-Klux costumes, and the small proportion of those that shed light on how the Ku-Klux members and supporters interpreted their costumes, it is significant that three separate pro-Ku-Klux sources liken Ku-Klux costumes to women's clothes. When interrogated in the congressional hearings, former Georgia congressman and suspected Ku-Klux supporter John H. Christy insisted that he knew nothing about the Ku-Klux. Asked if he had witnessed "any man in disguise," however, he came forward with a rather intimate anecdote:

A: No; not under any circumstances whatever that I remember, unless it was a son of mine who was trying to scare his little sister one night.

Q: What did he put on?

A: He put on his mother's dress, or something of that sort; it was a family concern. I do not suppose you want to hear that, but as I am under oath I mentioned it.

Q: How old is your son?

A: Some seventeen or eighteen years old.[99]

Most likely, the son was impersonating a Ku-Klux for his sister's benefit. At any rate, Christy saw enough of a connection between his wife's dress and a Ku-Klux disguise that he was reminded of the incident by the congressman's question.

While John Christy's son's motivation for donning his mother's dress is not certain, J. E. Robuck's assumption of feminine garb is easier to interpret. According to his 1900 memoir, Robuck had been unenthusiastic about secession at the war's beginning. In an attempt to shame him into volunteering, three young ladies had sent him some ladies' garments, including a hoop skirt and a dress, suggesting that his reluctance to fight unmanned him. He claims that he laughed it off at the time. Ultimately, however, he was drafted into the Confederate army. Soon after the war's close, he joined the Ku-Klux. As he put it, "I kept the Mother Hubbard frock until after the war, when it served me a good purpose. I had it transformed into a Ku-Klux robe."[100]

But the most extended reference to Ku-Klux costumes as women's clothes is found in a pro-Ku-Klux comedy written in 1877, a few years after the Ku-Klux's decline. The author, upper-class Memphis woman Elizabeth Avery Meriwether, was the wife of Minor Meriwether, probably the Grand Scribe to Grand Wizard Nathan Bedford Forrest. A friend of Matthew Galloway—the editor of a Ku-Klux organ, the *Memphis Avalanche*—and (off and on) of Forrest himself, she was a Memphis Klan insider.

Most of her play, titled *The Ku-Klux Klan; or, The Carpetbagger in New Orleans*, traces the (ultimately successful) efforts of a Confederate amputee to emerge from his suicidal despair to renewed manliness. The play also includes a set of allegorical characters: "The Widow Secesh" and her five sons, Generl, Kernal, Cappen, Major, and Kuklux.[101] All but Kuklux have been "whipped" by the war: "Their heads hang in hopeless dejection" as they allow "oily" northern carpetbaggers, uppity blacks, and scalawags to run roughshod over them. Kuklux, "grotesque in dress and behavior" is a trickster figure who secretly "performs the most amazing antics" to subvert this new dispensation.[102] His mother, who suspects that he is up to mischief, sees something poking out of his pocket and tells Generl to grab it:

> GENERL collars KUKLUX and pulls a long white garment
>   from his pocket.
> GENERL: [Holding it up] What on yearth is he a doin' with
>   such female toggery?

WIDOW: [Holds up hands in astonishment] If I ever!—No I never!—Wisher may die, ef it aint my old night gownd!

GENERL, KERNEL, CAPPEN and MAJOR all hang their heads in deep shame.

KUKLUX: [Grinning at them] Wat a parcel o' old Tom-cat fools!—a blushin' an' a hangin' yer heads over mammy's old cotton night gound! Wat's the harm?[103]

Soon after this startling revelation, the scene shifts to a courtroom where the brothers (minus Kuklux, who had slipped away) are on trial for a crime against freedmen that they did not commit. At the height of the action, Kuklux enters, dons a lady's hat and shawl, and goes around the courtroom, "play[ing] grotesque tricks, threatening vengeance on the Judge and [all black] JURY."[104] The idea of Klan costumes as women's dress was familiar to at least some influential Ku-Klux supporters.

It was also rather common for Ku-Klux to blacken, tan, or "smut" their faces, or to wear black masks as part of their costumes. Blackface became so associated with the Klan that when, in February of 1872, four men in Minnesota attacked another man while they were in blackface, the *Milwaukee Daily Sentinel* characterized their disguise as "a la KuKlux." Like "female toggery," blackface disguise evoked both popular cultural staples like carnival and, especially, minstrelsy and a long tradition of vigilante costuming. David Roediger and others have described the cultural tradition of "blackface on black violence."[105] In 1866, just before the Klan's beginning, the "Black Cavalry" in Franklin Parish, Louisiana, was known for blacking its face while committing raids on freedpeople.[106]

Blackface emerged early in the Ku-Klux's history: the *Pulaski Citizen* printed an article in early 1867 giving helpful tips on how to remove tan from one's face.[107] A South Carolina victim described some Ku-Klux who attacked him as having "some smut, as it looked to be, from a chimney, rubbed on their hands and faces. Their faces were blackened, but not very black."[108] Other victims and witnesses in South Carolina, Alabama, and Mississippi described their attackers as having burnt cork or other blacking on their faces.[109] Members of a Klan group intimidating voters before the presidential election were "dressed as negroes."[110] Some Ku-Klux apparently went so far as to tangle their hair.[111] Victims and witnesses frequently told congressional investigators that they were unsure of the racial identities of their attackers, because their skin was either colored or entirely concealed from view. This was one practical value of cross-racial dressing; supporters of the Klan loved to claim that black men posing as Ku-Klux to settle private quarrels were responsible for their worst atrocities.[112] Ku-Klux also occasionally (and without much success) attempted to infiltrate the enemy camp by posing as black.[113] And costumes may have evoked blackness in a less direct way as well: William D. Pierson argues that Reconstruction-era Klan costumes' distinctive coloration and shapes may well have been influenced by similarly dressed African "devil maskers" or their Cuban and Haitian derivatives.[114] It seems unlikely that Ku-Klux and their supporters themselves could have articulated the meanings of their costumes. Men would hardly have dressed up in elaborate costume and gone out in the middle of the night to express an idea that they instead could have written in the comfort of their own home or stated at a political meeting. On the most straightforward level, Ku-Klux's appropriation of blackface and female apparel worked as a form of carnivalesque inversion. Fearing that their white manhood had been called into question by their defeat, Ku-Klux assumed a female or black identity, much in the same self-parodying way that nineteenth-century street gangs like the Plug-Uglies or Dead Rabbits defiantly took on degrading monikers. In donning those particular costumes, Ku-Klux emphasized the fact of gender and racial difference. The Robuck story and Meriwether play suggest ways in which Ku-Klux's use of women's clothing worked through inversion to reassert challenged manhood. By assuming the guise of women while exercising physical coercion, defeated white men like Robuck simultaneously owned and transcended their humiliation. By combining female apparel with grotesque performance in order to battle against "hopeless dejection" and to revenge his defeated military brethren, Meriwether's fictional Kuklux made this connection literal. Given the Ku-Klux's project of restoring southern white manhood, it is fitting that the Pulaski Ku-Klux founders may have first gathered to raise funds for Confederate amputees.

Historians of antebellum minstrelsy have noted that donning the minstrel mask could actually reify the wearer's white identity. As W. T. Lhamon has put it, minstrel performers "worked out ways to flash white skin beneath a layer of burnt cork."[115] Similarly, Ku-Klux testified to their white identity even as they performed blackness. Ironically, Ku-Klux, who were terrified by the idea that miscegenation and the end of the status of slave might make racial identity invisible, created with their costumes a situation in which racial identity was indeed invisible. The symbolic, voluntarily assumed whiteness of many Ku-Klux costumes was meant to indicate inner whiteness—a whiteness for which white skin was a necessary but not sufficient prerequisite.[116] Ku-Klux did in fact use their raids to mark some whites as outside the race. One group forced a white man to kiss the private parts of a black man and woman and to enact intercourse with the woman.[117] A group in Mississippi described their schoolteacher victim as "as black inside as that old nigger woman is outside."[118] A Georgia white man thought to be on excessively good terms with his freedmen employees complained that Ku-Klux raiders "treated me rather as if I was a freedman, or worse, perhaps. They called me 'boy' and ordered me around."[119] Whether wearing minstrel cork, shrouding themselves in white sheets, or donning other racially obscuring disguises, Ku-Klux were engaging in a process or racial line-drawing to replace the apparent clarity formerly given by the institution of slavery.

Yet symbolic inversion was not the whole weight of carnivalesque costume. Such costuming sent multiple messages. While the carnivalesque could serve as a safety valve for the disgruntled oppressed and to reify power relations by performing them, even comically, it could be subversive.[120] There was often a slippage between the costume-wearer's everyday and assumed identities and between the audience's desire to distance themselves from and identify with the blackfaced figures they viewed. Dale Cockrell sees wearing a costume as, in part, "a way of actually incorporating the Other into Self."[121] As Lott similarly argues, audiences of northeastern antebellum minstrel shows were involved in a slippery and dialectical relationship with the shows' black subjects: while they feared them, they also used them as figures for their own repressed sexual and violent desires and class anxieties.[122]

It is counterintuitive to imagine Ku-Klux as identifying with their black victims. Yet producing, observing, and ridiculing the suffering black body also allowed Ku-Klux and their supporters to interrupt the traumatic repetition of their own battlefield memories.[123] Ku-Klux identified with the black bodies they simultaneously mimicked and tortured in other ways as well. Many, though not all, Ku-Klux chose to assume the identities of beings—whether bulls, Comanches, or damned soldiers—that were not only beyond the pale of conventional morality but were considered to be particularly strong and violent. Similarly, dressing as a black man, portrayed on the minstrel stage and broadly considered to be controlled by overwhelming physical and sexual nature, allowed Ku-Klux, like antebellum minstrel audiences, to acknowledge and claim their less-than-civilized impulses within a discreet performative space.

White men imagined freedmen, like Native Americans or beasts, as fundamentally outside civilization.[124] Posing as blacks enabled former Confederates to appropriate imaginatively some of this savage power, even while pointing to the difference between black savagery and white civilization. If antebellum whites had turned to blackface-on-black violence to address their class anxieties, Reconstruction-era southern white men were doing the same to address their anxieties about shifting race relations and the associated changes in economic structures. This was a strategy that could easily go awry and needed to be managed with some subtlety. Blackfaced Ku-Klux appropriated the lawless violence they attributed to those outside civilization even while, by committing their atrocities in costumes that could be quickly shed, they distanced themselves from their violent deeds. Ku-Klux may have seen some truth in their frequent claim that their most appalling attacks had been committed by black men.

Dressing like a woman could also serve as a means of appropriating uncivilized characteristics. Natalie Zemon Davis has described early modern cross-dressers as drawing on "the sexual power and energy of the unruly women." In the Reconstruction-era United States, white women were no longer associated with excessive and uncontrolled physical drives.[125] In donning women's clothes, however, Ku-Klux were as much dressing as antebellum vigilantes or participants in charivari as they were dressing as women. Dressing like a woman at once performatively restored Ku-Klux's male identity through absurd contrast and projected the wild lawlessness of mumming vigilantism on its wearers.

Gail Bederman has argued of a slightly later period that Progressive Era white men strove both to show their fitness to compete with "lesser races" in the brutal Darwinian struggle and to prove through their refinement that they represented the highest pinnacle of civilization. They attempted simultaneously to claim their lowest and highest impulses: to be fully muscular, physical, and passionate yet also fully controlled and polite.[126] This attempt to have it both ways was at the core of the Ku-Klux's masquerade.

Dale Cockrell's work on antebellum blackface strengthens this interpretation of Ku-Klux costume and performance. As he has argued, "Masking in blackface was making a statement more about what you were not than about race."[127] In this reading, wearing blackface was similar to dressing as a beast, an immigrant, or, presumably, the damned—these costumes meant that the person behind the mask was not civilized.

Indeed, Ku-Klux repeatedly and vociferously rejected the role of that paragon of civilization, the gentleman. When freedman Elias Thomson referred to his South Carolina attackers (sporting fake teeth, speckled horns, and calico masks) as gentlemen, they demurred: "Do we look like gentlemen?"[128] Another South Carolina Ku-Klux responded similarly, "Don't you call me any gentleman; we are just from hell-fire; we haven't been in this country since Manassas."[129]

Traditionally, gentlemen did not cease to be gentlemen while they engaged in appropriate military or private violence; indeed, it was arguably as soldiers and patriarchs that they were quintessentially gentlemen. The particular costumes that many Ku-Klux chose to don, and their own denials that they were gentlemen while in costume, strongly suggest that they themselves found Ku-Klux raids, unlike warfare or the patriarchal violence of the antebellum period, inconsistent with their gentlemanly identities. One way for Ku-Klux to manage tensions between their usual and costumed selves was to be white men during their quotidian lives and something else during attacks: Christian gentlemen by day, damned souls by night.[130] This instability could be marked and contained through the disguise.

When Ku-Klux's normal and masked identities did leak into one another, they found themselves in an untenable position. Freedmen victims sometimes insisted on recognizing the men behind the masks. When they did, they tended to call on their attackers to live up to their self-proclaimed roles as gentlemanly protectors.[131] When they first entered the home of freedman Columbus Jeter, Ku-Klux "jerked" his twelve-year-old daughter out of bed. According to Jeter, "she knew the young man and called his name. He said, 'Hush, Emily, I will not hurt you.'" Once the attackers had surrounded Jeter, he recognized his former owner through his disguise. "I patted him on the leg as I was lying on the ground, and said, 'Master, don't let them kill me.' I kept getting up by degrees until I had my hands on his shoulders." After the attack the badly wounded Jeter, seeking medical assistance, approached the home of a man who, unknown to him, had been among his attackers. The man had not yet returned, and his wife would not let Jeter enter, but she directed him to go to a near neighbor and tell him that she wanted him to get Jeter a doctor.[132] While this was neither a generous nor even a humane reception of the heavily bleeding Jeter, it is significant both that he hoped for assistance at his attacker's home and that his attacker's wife felt she could not ignore him entirely.

Freedwoman Martha Hendricks found herself in a similar situation when she fled her husband's attackers, baby in arms, to take shelter in the home of her white neighbors, the Grogans. Mrs. Grogan at first discouraged Hendricks from entering, but when Hendricks plead that it was cold and there was nowhere else to go, Mrs. Grogan begrudgingly offered hospitality. Hendricks and her baby sat in a room with Mrs. Grogan and her toddler son to await news. The cause of Mrs. Grogan's reluctance to admit Hendricks became apparent when her son inadvertently revealed to Hendricks that Mr. Grogan was among her husband's attackers. Both women pretended not to have noticed the slip and continued to spend together what must have been an unimaginably painful evening. When Grogan returned, after a hushed conversation with his wife, he assumed a casual and protective role to Hendricks, assuring her that he had heard that her husband had escaped his pursuers (as indeed he had).[133] Perhaps Mrs. Grogan and Jeter's attacker's wife acted more kindly than their husbands would have wanted. Perhaps the white men had joined the attacks reluctantly, or even intervened to spare Hendricks's and Jeter's lives. It seems most likely, however, that the white men were attempting, through their use of disguise, to have two parallel relationships with Hendricks and Jeter.

Another problem with using Ku-Klux violence to reinstate white male domination was that southern white men had always claimed to be superior for reasons beyond brute physical force. While it had always been a gentleman's prerogative and duty to use violence against his inferiors when necessary, the prerogative had been mediated by two key institutions: the private one of slave ownership, and the public one of gentlemanly, even chivalric military service. Neither institution had survived the war. The Ku-Klux, by creating spaces set apart from ordinary life through spectacle and disguise, offered an insecure substitute for these occasions of "civilized," gentlemanly violence.

Ku-Klux's masks hid two things. The first was the fact that they had abandoned the traditional patriarchal duty to protect client blacks from the casual violence of other whites. This dynamic is illustrated the story of a railroad overseer in Alabama in 1869. Some of his white employees had taken to playing pranks on some of his black employees. When one of the whites donned a white sheet and accosted him, a black employee went running to the overseer, "so terrified that he could only gasp out 'oh! Colonel' and was ready to drop." The overseer "gave the men orders they should play no more tricks of that kind." The "Colonel" was defending his economic self-interest in stopping the harassment of his own workers. Yet he was Minor Meriwether, Elizabeth Meriwether's husband and probably Forrest's Grand Scribe. Although he supported the Ku-Klux's terror, he took pride (as he had with his slaves before the war) in defending client blacks against their persecutors.[134] Such Ku-Klux participated in or supported violent attacks, yet were not ready to abandon their self-understanding as benevolent patriarchs. They were discomfited when their victims insisted on seeing through their masks.

The second thing hidden behind the Ku-Klux's mask was a savage violence that, in the years immediately after the war, many were not yet willing publicly to acknowledge. Ku-Klux opponent Hugh Bond was horrified to learn, through accounts of Ku-Klux atrocities, that "the beast was so close under the skin of man."[135] Many Ku-Klux themselves seem to have conceived of the relationship between their violent and civilized aspects in a similar way. Nineteenth-century Americans believed that every man had violent passions within him but that the white man, the civilized man, the gentleman, had rational faculties enabling him to master that violence. The Ku-Klux that Ku-Klux themselves described—a disciplined group that soberly discussed how to control those who threatened the weak or violated public order, then marched off in military formation to dispatch precise and speedy justice—was perfectly consistent with antebellum notions of civilized manhood. But the excesses of Ku-Klux violence and, ironically, the disorder inherent in the performativity in which it was embedded, sent the message that Ku-Klux were controlled not by their rational faculties but by the beast within.

Ku-Klux's use of minstrelsy and the carnivalesque helped to allay these fears. Both of these genres were dramas of controlled savagery. Carnivals featured a motley assortment of apes, apelike blacks, clowns, and wild men who nevertheless basically conformed to the route and marching order of the parade. Minstrelsy's "Ethiopians," particularly end men, appeared barely civilized enough to sit in their chairs. They gave their straight-man "interlocutor" a tough time, but they ultimately managed to play their bones and tambourines in harmony with one another. W. T. Lhamon has aptly described the minstrel stage as enacting a "struggle over the seating of chaotic energy."[136] One Louisiana newspaper editor recognized the nature of the vicarious pleasure many white southerners experienced in watching these pageants of contained brutality when he drew a lengthy analogy between freedmen and the circus animals controlled by "white showmen."[137] Like the British Victorian-era game that invited children to paste bars over the cages of exotic beasts, the minstrel and carnivalesque reassured whites that while the threatening black, Indian, or beast had not truly been civilized, he had been captured; white showmen safely could mobilize savagery for their own purposes.[138]

This was a powerful analogy for Ku-Klux on multiple levels. They wanted to create a South in which the black man jumped through the white man's hoops; they also wanted to believe that the civilized could contain and perform brutality, savagery, or blackness without becoming brutish, savage, or black. This desire to appropriate certain qualities they associated with blackness may explain the odd physical intimacy between attackers and victims that sometimes puzzled freedmen witnesses. The wife of one murdered freedman had at first believed that his masked assailants were black because of their close physical contact with him during the attack. "I thought no white people would pick up such a man and tote him—that they would not lower themselves low enough, as they would say, to pick up a darkey."[139] As they ruthlessly enforced social, economic, and political barriers between black and white, Ku-Klux, whether they were whipping, grabbing, torturing, undressing, or raping, were constantly encountering black flesh.

A Georgia attack suggests how this worked. Like Hendricks and like Jeter's former master, "Mr. Morris" found himself in multiple relationships with his victim, Anderson Ferrell. Ferrell could not believe that Morris intended to harm him. "I heard something falling on my shoulder but I thought it was pitch; I put my hand up and I found it was blood. I said, 'Mr. Morris, what did you shoot at me for? You hit me.'" Unlike the other two attackers, however, the still-costumed but no longer anonymous Morris owned his violence, replying, "'God damn you, I aimed to hit you.'"[140] Morris was deliberately redefining his identity both for the horrified Ferrell and for himself. In claiming his Ku-Klux violence, he made it clear that it was consistent with his white manhood. It was this acknowledgment that would make Ku-Klux costumes superfluous.

Morris's acknowledgment of his violence was a rite of passage.[141] The Ku-Klux's performance enabled southern men to shed the antebellum manhood they had come to idealize for a more starkly, explicitly violent postbellum version. The Ku-Klux's brief reign marked a transitional space between distinct regimes of violence: the threshold between the patriarchal violence of the antebellum years and the chivalric violence of the war, on the one hand, and the public lynchings of the Progressive Era. If performance is a way of figuring loss, representing that which is passing away and may be forgotten, the Ku-Klux's histrionics marked and mourned the fall of antebellum white southern manhood and erected a new modern southern manhood in its place.[142]

How Ku-Klux Attacks Defined the New Black Man

Ku-Klux attacks defined the nature of the white attackers, but they were just as much about defining the nature of their victims. The attacks modeled the roles for black men (and women) in the new order. They did this in several ways, most notably by targeting for violence those black people who most apparently violated that role. But just as they used performance to define their new gendered selves, so they also frequently demanded that victims assume performative roles of their own. By using violence to coerce victims to perform inadequacy and fit themselves into demeaning national popular tropes, Ku-Klux hoped to convince their victims, themselves, and those who learned about the attacks of the justice of white dominance.

As with the freedman they forced to "act like horses" during the circuslike attack mentioned earlier, Ku-Klux demanded that victims perform a minstrelesque role. For instance, Ku-Klux attackers frequently forced victims to feign gullibility. One important argument against citizenship for freedmen was that they were too gullible, too easily manipulated. Ku-Klux endeavored to portray victims' entirely rational fear of their physical violence as though it were superstition or gullibility. The victim, tellingly, failed to "get the joke," allowing himself or herself to be frightened by "ghosts" or "devils." The trope of superstitious freedpeople frightened by ghosts or devils had been a recurring theme on the early minstrel stage. In causing freedpeople to appear to be afraid of ghosts, they were trying to force real freedpeople, and their white allies, to become minstrel caricatures. They wanted bulging eyes, breathless reports of monsters, screams that could be heard in the next county. The standard Klan claims that they came from the moon, from hell, or from Shiloh were all meant to elicit this response. It is an interesting question what proportion of Ku-Klux thought freedpeople believed their ridiculous supernatural claims: mid-nineteenth-century whites expressed such pejorative views of black credulity so consistently that perhaps they were sincere. But it is most likely that making these claims was a means of forcing freedpeople to act as though they were just as ignorant as the Ku-Klux wanted to believe they were.

Ku-Klux attackers regularly required victims to assume minstrelesque roles not only by performing their own credulity but also by demonstrating that the interests, desires, and needs of the body overruled everything else. One of the most jarring commonalities in Ku-Klux attacks is the intensity of the pain and terror that Ku-Klux inflicted upon their victims. As one Tennessee witness noted of a victim, John Dunlap, "He was the worst whipped man I ever saw. I have seen negroes whipped, and badly, too, in the days of slavery, but he was the worst whipped man I ever saw."[143] This degree of pain was neither accidental nor ornamental. Lengthy whippings were excruciating, sometimes deadly, for the victim. Causing such suffering was also real work for the people administering the whippings, which sometimes counted in the dozens or even hundreds. As Samuel Stewart of Georgia recounted, "Before they struck [my wife] any lick, Sam. Rich just raised his mask to wipe the sweat off his face, he had been working on me so hard."[144]

Those who had recently emerged from a slave society in which whipping was central had a nuanced understanding of how it worked and what it meant. The difference between ten lashes and forty, or lashes with one type of branch rather than another, or lashes on a victim in various stages of undress, tied to a tree or not, were not abstract to them. Ku-Klux in these cases labored not only to cause pain, but to cause a particular type and level of pain for a particular purpose. They worked to inflict a pain so great that it disabled the victim's rational function and rendered him radically embodied. Elaine Scarry's work on torture practices a century later explains that torture causes "an almost obscene conflation of private and public. It brings with it all the solitude of absolute privacy with none of its safety, all of the self-exposure of the utterly public with none of its possibility for camaraderie or shared experience."[145] Intense pain is utterly isolating. Generic or fictional accounts of Ku-Klux attacks by Klan supporters often emphasized Ku-Klux victims' expressions of extreme physical pain, transmuted into the language of minstrel comedy.[146] They regularly emphasized precisely the victim's withdrawal into the physical and abandonment of rational control. In the end, Ku-Klux tried to show, black men (and their degenerate white allies) were creatures of passion, not reason, their suffering extensive but amusing.

But what Ku-Klux did during their attacks could only be passed along to a broader audience through victim testimony. And frequently victims used their actions, and their representations of their actions in testimony, to resist Ku-Klux's definition of their manhood. Perhaps the most definitive way in which Klan victims could challenge Ku-Klux efforts to define them through violence was to effectively fight back. As Catherine Clinton has written of freedwomen's resistance to sexual violence more generally, "It is difficult to fathom the fear created by a black woman fighting back." The principle holds for black men as well. Klan victims often planned ahead to resist Klan violence, and often fought for their lives when the violence caught them unawares. They formed into militias, made mutual self-defense pacts, slept in one anothers' homes, picketed on behalf of one another, and fought for one another.[147]

They also denied efforts to characterize them as credulous, another trope borrowed from minstrelsy that was used to degrade black men and women and deny the political value of their speech.[148] They often testified that Ku-Klux had made claims to them during the attacks claiming supernatural status. Rarely did freedpeople, in congressional or other testimony, describe themselves as having accepted, or even having pretended to accept, Ku-Klux's claimed supernatural status.[149] Freedpeople often made a point of mocking those supernatural claims in testimony. When Representative James Alston, a black state legislator in Montgomery, was asked to recall the contents of the threatening note he had received, he was sarcastic: "Wait and let me get it together; it's a long time ago—that the bloody moon and the highway murderers were seeking my blood; that the tombs in the grave-yard was rumbling together against each other to receive my body—have you got the midnight robbers and murders down?—and I had better leave."[150] Major Gardiner of Alabama noted that when Ku-Klux came to drive him away from his crop, they claimed they had not had water since Shiloh, and kept drinking and pouring the water into "some false thing around them somewhere . . . to make us blacks believe that they hadn't any since they come from the devil . . . and everybody knows better than that."[151] Many freedmen were careful to explain that their fear of the Ku-Klux was in response not to their performative claims but to their threats and use of violence.[152] A freedman recounted his attack by Ku-Klux wearing painted meal-sacks over their heads: "The reason I was scared was, that they came in with their pistols, and I was afraid they would shoot me."[153] Alston said of his attackers, "They had no disguises on; they had pistols though, plenty of them."[154]

Some witnesses claimed to have challenged Ku-Klux's self-representations as supernatural beings and told them that they knew they were only men. Elias Thompson, a black farmer in Spartanburg, South Carolina, claimed that he insisted upon playing the part of a social equal throughout his attack. When Ku-Klux ran against his door late at night, he greeted them, "Come in, gentlemen." They corrected him, "Do we look like gentlemen?" But he soothed, "You look like men of some description. Come in." When one of them asked him if he was ready to die, he "told him I was not ready to die." When told to pray, he explained that he was not much for praying. When asked about his voting, he defended the duty of a man to vote what he thinks is right. At two moments during the confrontation, as they threatened to hang him, he started laughing at them. " 'What in hell are you laughing at? It is no laughing time.' I told him it sort of tickled me, and I thought I would laugh."[155] This response was unusual, but not unique: some Ku-Klux victims claimed that they remained calm and even amused during their Ku-Klux encounter.[156] The laughing victim was positioning himself as an audience member, a member of the public, entertained by what he rightly understood to be the Ku-Klux's comic show.

Ku-Klux victims and their allies also often resisted sharing humiliating details of the attacks. It is of course impossible to quantify how much victims suffered, in order to compare it to their representations. Other scholars working on the transcripts have found that freedmen were quite forthcoming in describing their bodies' violations.[157] And there certainly were exceptions: some witnesses gave descriptions of pain so graphic as to be distressing and sickening to the reader. But generally, victims resisted representing their own bodies in pain in a vivid or visceral manner. When testimony describes victims dramatically responding to violence, the testimony is by someone other than the victim himself. An elite white man, for instance, claimed that "the men began to beat him [and he] began to scream and pray and beg."[158] Victims' descriptions of their own suffering often feel constrained and flat in contrast, even dissociated and casual: "They scarred me up right smart."[159] Witnesses insisted on portraying themselves, even while under Ku-Klux attack, as rational rather than overembodied. They frequently displayed wounds, even inviting committee members to touch their imperfectly healed bodies. Peyton Lipscomb, a black Union veteran from near Salem, Tennessee, dispassionately recalled being stripped then whipped, "There didn't but one man whip me. He made me get down on the ground, and he whipped me there, as well as I could tell, fifteen minutes as hard as he could; and then another one came up and whipped me again."[160] Fifty-four-year-old black Spartanburg farmer Joseph Miller recalled that the Ku-Klux "gave me about twenty or twenty-five lashes, I reckon, on the naked skin, and then took me by the arm, with a pillow-case over my head, and turned me around to go to the house at a pretty fast walk." When then told to run for his life, "I stepped off pretty pert, and then they shot."[161] Miller's use of the phrase "stepped off pretty pert" rather than, say, "I fled in terror" deliberately defuses the gravity of his situation. Or, as freedman and Chattanooga Justice of the Peace Andrew J. Flowers described it, "They said they were going to give me twenty-five lashes, and I guess they gave it to me."[162] Many victims describe themselves as having tried to convince or even implore their attackers not to use violence against them; not infrequently, they testify to either having lost consciousness or having been unable to observe and understand the things around them because of their pain. Yet in their accounts, they rarely shrieked, howled, groveled, or lost control of bodily functions. Often they do not even describe themselves as bleeding. If during the attacks they had been reduced to flesh, during the testimony many witnesses allowed their bodies no voice.[163] Instead, their testimony painstakingly performed mastery of self.

Even on the rare occasions on which a sympathetic witness was present at the attack, they tended to elide bodily failures of the victim in their testimony. Augustus Blair described witnessing the sadistic killing of his son, "the only son I had; about eighteen years old; very well grown; as big as I was." In describing unusually and nauseatingly graphic details about his son's torture and killing, he nevertheless took parental pride in his son's self-control and presence of mind. As Ku-Klux were taking him to an isolated area for the attack,

he told them, Oh gentlemen you all carrying me along and here are two men stabbing me with a knife. They said, It's a damned lie nobody is sticking you. He says, Oh yes I feel the blood running down my pants. They said Go on, God damn you; you will have no use for no blood no how mighty soon. He went on up the hill with them and they were punching and cutting him. When they got up there they took him down and beat on his head. I was not further from them than twenty yards. I crept right around behind the patch of briars and laid there. He never hollered but once, but I could hear him [imitating the wheezing rattling sound in the throat] as they were choking him and others were cutting him with a knife as they held him there.[164]

Victims and those who loved them did not readily offer descriptions of their physical responses to their torment at the hands of Ku-Klux. In their narrations, at least, Ku-Klux victims maintained dignity. Perhaps they avoided these depictions because they understood that images of black bodies controlled and unmanned by pain pulled their stories into minstrelsy, as Ku-Klux hoped. These images were regularly used by Ku-Klux attackers and sympathizers not only as an argument against black equality and empowerment but as a denial of black humanity.[165]

Scholars have noted the evasion of graphic description of rapes and other sexual violence in this period but attributed it to the relegation of sexuality from nineteenth-century public discourse. Yet some of the same avoidance of description seems to be true of nonsexual violence as well. In part, victims may have avoided testifying to their pain because, as Kidada Williams has recently argued, they understood that whites simply did not want to hear about their experiences of violence.[166] Ku-Klux committees, like many other white audiences, loved horrible stories of Klan violence, but they were not interested in dwelling long in the subject position of the black victim.

Not only could victims work to unwrite their attackers' minstrel framing; they could also mobilize elements of popular culture for their own purposes. When he was called to testify about his attack before the South Carolina Ku-Klux trials, South Carolina freedman Jerry Clowney determined that minstrelsy was called for. He insisted on clowning for the congressional committee as he described having been forced to clown for his attackers:

> WITNESS: Then, they circled around, with me in the middle,
>   like I was a monkey, or a baboon, or something. Then he
>   [the man with the horns] commenced down here (indicating
>   the legs), and I was jumping and prancing, and begging. . . .
>   [Here the witness lay down.] They jerked me on my face to
>   the ground [The audience laughed at the ludicrous gestures
>   of the witness.] Keep still; I will get done telling it directly.
>   They jerked me to the ground; one man jumped on top of
>   my head and another across my shoulder, and just had me
>   fastened to the ground. Says I, "O, pray! O, master! Do, if
>   you please"—"O, God damn you, I will fix you now." Then
>   right across here, [illustrating the whipping]. . . . The
>   captain stretches off then in front, and all the rest followed

[illustrating their gait,] all making a noise like Oo-oo-oo-oo.
There was one go-dong [go-along?] nigger. I wish his head
was cut off to-day.

MR. CORBIN: That is no testimony.

WITNESS: I hope it will be done! The nigger came back to me
and caught me by the arm. "Now, my friend, you go to work
and make your living honest, and the Ku-Klux will never
trouble you no more—Oo-oo-oo," [imitating their gait].[167]

A lifetime's experience of what elite whites wanted to hear, together with his recent traumatic experience, likely influenced his choice to take a minstrel tone. Adopting such an affect was something like assuming a fetal position—there was no triumph in it, but it might prompt people to give up their attacks out of pity or contempt. It could not allow one dignity, but it might increase one's chance of self-preservation.

In this case, the audience laughed, but Clowney had gone too far, making the elite whites watching him feel uncomfortable, and David T. Corbin, the U.S. attorney for South Carolina, tried to cut him off and denied the validity of his testimony. Clowney would not be the only witness to take that approach, though his was one of the more extreme cases. All testimony was in danger of being pulled into minstrelsy: the scepter of Jerry Clowney's performance hung over all Klan victims. Minstrelsy was arguably the dominant mode in which black people were represented to white audiences in the mid-nineteenth-century United States. When mid-nineteenth-century white people read about black pain or fear, they were usually doing so in the context of a minstrel portrayal. One of the many struggles of the Klan victim called to tell his (or her) story to whites was the struggle to not allow his (or her) words to be interpreted through the lens of minstrelsy.

Jerry Clowney's adoption of a minstrel posture (and others like it) was not only self-abasing, but was also an attempt to strategically employ a powerful cultural language to win the sympathies of powerful northerners. Minstrelsy was primarily a discourse by and for whites used to oppress and degrade black men and women, but it was also a performative language with which black men and women across the South were intimately familiar. They were able to strategically inhabit it when Ku-Klux so demanded, but they also knew it well enough to choose to employ it (as Clowney did) as the medium in which to present their own responses and ideas.

Sometimes victims brought elements of folk traditions into their stories. Just as white Klan narrators sometimes moved in and out of a tall-tale tradition, so, occasionally, black narrators mobilized tropes from black vernacular oral tradition. The trickster makes a regular appearance in victims' self-representations, as victims depict themselves as humbly and calmly acknowledging the superior strength of attacking Ku-Klux and using canny intelligence and humor to convince them to leave.[168] Sir Daniel, a freedman in Alabama, offered a long and rich narration of a freedman named Miles Prior, whom he characterizes several times as a "very brave man." "This Miles Prior says, 'Let them come.' They wanted to burn the school-house. He says 'Fifty men couldn't burn the school-house and let me live.' When they got within about two hundred yards, Miles Prior he pulled off his coat and rolled up his sleeves, and began to laugh, and his wife began to cry, and told him to try to get away, that they were coming. He said he didn't care; let 'em come. They said there were five hundred of them. He said he wasn't afraid of them; the more that come the more he could kill." Ultimately Prior ended up in a jail cell, but when a mob came for him there, he held the door in until he heard the train come, then released it so his attackers all piled up and he could leap out the door and onto the train.[169] This is a simple inversion of Klan tall tales. Sir Daniel recognized that two could play that game. While whites had an enormous advantage in controlling the national discourse, black rural southerners, through their testimony, had a unique opportunity to tweak and destabilize it.

Klan attacks were wrapped in layers of meaning that translated white violence and black agony into an argument for the legitimacy of white power. A Klan attack was simultaneously pain and argument. Many black southerners indicated that they understood this and appreciated that the costume was ultimately as dangerous as the gun. At the moment of the attack, they worked to protect their bodies from white aggression, but many were also keenly aware of the need to refute whites' efforts to define them through their embodied responses

Ku-Klux attacks, then, were not only acts of violence and victimization, but a struggle to define the identity of southerners white and black. Ku-Klux worked to force, their victims to resist, interpretations of these acts as evidence of the inevitability of white triumph and black failure. But this was only one part of the cultural struggle embedded in Klan attacks and their representation. As we will see, they also defined social position, relations, and capacity of perpetrators and victims.

THREE

Ku-Klux Attacks Define Southern Public Life

> They asked another fellow to get down and they asked how did he vote. He said, "I didn't vote at all—I was too young." And he said he come down to the meeting on Saturday. They said, "What were you there for?" And then one of them said, "What sort of a thing is that? What in hell is a meeting? Take off your shirt, and get down here." He got down, and took his shirt off, and they began to beat him—I don't remember how much.
>
> —Testimony of Pinkney Dodd, South Carolina, *Testimony Taken by the Joint Select Committee on the Condition of Affairs in the Late Insurrectionary States*

As stories of aggressors and victims, Ku-Klux attacks are already enormously complex and variable. As we have seen, by drawing from minstrelsy, carnival, and an eclectic array of popular cultural forms, Ku-Klux attacks contributed to many different narratives, even as victims found ways to undermine the story their attackers meant to tell about black and white manhood. Yet this story is incomplete without introducing the third key participants—the elite men who took victim testimony. In their efforts can be traced a single strain of meaning throughout witness testimony: the portrayal of black people as failed citizens, and of white attackers as "the people."

Not only did Klan attacks define postwar black and white manhood; they also spelled out structures of alliance, participation, and exclusion in their postwar communities. Black southerners, through their resistance and testimony, challenged, nuanced, and subverted Ku-Klux claims about the role that they should rightfully play in society. But if they wanted their readings of Ku-Klux attacks to circulate, they had to give them in spaces controlled by elite northern whites, usually as testimony in formal hearings. Most surviving accounts of Klan attacks, then, were unwilling and unwieldy three-way collaborations among attackers who created and largely controlled the situations to be described; victims who experienced the attacks and shaped them into coherent narratives; and elites taking testimony, who encouraged certain narrative accounts while silencing, invalidating, and manipulating others. Ku-Klux supporters and deniers simultaneously needed victims to speak, yet worked to neutralize victims' narrative legitimacy, in part by bringing out the old claim that they were not the true authors of their stories. They alleged that Republican leaders had used deliberate collusion, or even bribery, sometimes in the form of the per diem provided to witnesses, to convince witnesses to produce testimony parroting the national party line.[1] Committee member Francis Preston Blair Jr., former Democratic vice presidential candidate and ardent opponent of Radical Reconstruction, confronted witness Marcus M. Wells with the charge he had been "prepared" for his testimony: "He talked to you as to what you should testify."[2] He did the same to the next witness, James L. Grant, asking if a Republican leader had not "t[old] you what he wanted you to swear to."[3] The extreme prejudice with which the white public approached victim testimony placed on the shoulders of each testifying victim the heavy responsibility of defending the integrity of southern Republicans and freedpeople generally.

Southern Republicans had good cause to collude with powerful northerners, and there is no reason to imagine that they were universally immune to the bribery that was such an important part of mid-nineteenth-century political culture. Yet bribery likely was not the reason so many witnesses so frequently came to say the words that the national Republican Party wanted to hear. There were so many more obvious reasons for witnesses and the national party to be aligned—most notably, what victims experienced and what committee members wanted to hear was usually so similar. Yet there was a distorted truth to Democratic complaints of undue influence on witnesses: Ku-Klux victim testimony was strategic and mediated speech powerfully influenced by the needs and interests of northern Republicans. All speech is strategic and mediated, but acute structural pressures made the strategic and mediated nature of testimony by freedpeople (and their white allies) more obvious. Northern Republicans had so much cultural power immediately after the war that they could set the terms of the discourse that others, including Klan victims, consumed and had either to accept or to actively challenge. But more immediately, southern Republicans recognized that they depended on northern Republicans for their personal safety and empowerment. Victims' speech was powerfully constrained by their very pragmatic desire to say what northern Republican elites wanted to hear.

While Democrats complained constantly that witness testimony was unduly influenced by Republican interests, they had less to say about a second way in which witness testimony was constrained: because victims were invited to have a public voice only for the purpose of telling what the Klan did to them, the scope of their speech was limited and shaped by the words and actions of their attackers.[4] The congressional committee would frequently call elite white witnesses to provide a broad context to Klan violence. Victims, however, were expected to stick to the script of their own attack, and perhaps to list or describe attacks on their neighbors. They were almost never asked to give their views of contemporary politics or local power relationships beyond the narrow scope of the attack itself. Victims' testimony was constrained by their requirement to describe their attack with enough verisimilitude that their veracity (never assumed by their audience) would not be challenged. Ku-Klux victims' ability to be heard rested in their credibly reconstructing the words and deeds of southern Democrats, in ways acceptable to northern Republicans.

Even within the description of attacks, Republican interrogators were usually not interested in listening to several types of things that freedpeople frequently wanted to talk about. They wanted to hear about the acts and words of Ku-Klux but were less interested in the acts and words with which freedpeople responded to them. Some discussion of victims' responses was necessary to the narrative of the attack, but when witnesses began to discuss in any detail their own theories, strategies, understandings, and emotions before, during, or after attacks, they were promptly invited to stop. It is therefore challenging to reconstruct from Ku-Klux testimony either how participants' responses during Ku-Klux attacks may have differed from the expectations of their attackers, or how their private understandings of Ku-Klux attacks may have differed from those of their questioners. To dig down to the victim's voice requires excavation, first of the meanings imposed upon Klan attacks by attackers, and then those imposed upon them by interrogators.

Ku-Klux Attackers Imagine a Postwar Racial Order

Ku-Klux told a story through their attacks. The attackers came prepared to make certain threats or commit certain acts of violence and thereby to force victims to say or do particular things. The audience for the scene they were constructing would be themselves and other attackers, victims, and any witnesses who might be present. Klan attackers had an eye to how the attack would be described. Presumably Ku-Klux expected to tell the story of the attack to others in the community whom they trusted. They might even surreptitiously circulate an account of the attack to a sympathetic newspaper. They also knew that their acts might leave behind physical consequences that would tell their own story: hoofmarks on the dirt road, a door knocked off its hinges, a raw and bloody back, a corpse. Sometimes they was so eager to control the narrative that they left behind a note or threatened their victims to say certain things about what had occurred or not to say others.

The most powerful and common piece of information Ku-Klux attackers communicated through their attacks was simply that they were Ku-Klux. They did this by wearing costumes or by explicitly declaring themselves as Ku-Klux. So when Clem Bowden, a young South Carolina freedman clearing land for himself, was attacked by a group of costumed men, "they asked me if I had heard tell of Ku Klux. They said, 'Here they are. These are the men called Ku Klux.'"[5] Or recall the Tennessee attack in which attackers carried with them a flag that they explained to their victim "means Kuklux."[6] In an attack in Alabama, "they told me that they had Jesus Christ tied, and God Almighty, damned old son of a bitch, chained, and they were Ku-klux."[7] By labeling themselves as Ku-Klux, violent attackers conveyed a great deal about the meaning of what would occur. It was an efficient speech act that pulled themselves and their victims into the well-developed tropes of the national discourse about the Klan.

Another message repeatedly conveyed by Ku-Klux attacks was that Ku-Klux were community members and their victims were not. Ku-Klux groups consistently took pains to present themselves during attacks as organized, disciplined, and well-integrated into their communities and their victims as, by contrast, isolated. Klan efforts to perform organization were quite as central to their costuming and actions as their efforts to portray themselves as savage, manly, or white. At the same time, many Klan attackers went to great lengths to underline the isolation and lack of community of their victim.

Certain conventional elements of Klan attacks make sense only when seen as efforts to demonstrate organization or community embeddedness. Greg Downs has argued that some Klans operated as "literally neighborhood associations . . . recruited from kin and proximate neighbors animated by local anxieties or a desire for neighborhood control." And Ku-Klux sometimes emphasized this to their victims. The Ku-Klux warning, for instance, was almost canonical: Ku-Klux frequently sent an

A Tennessee Ku-Klux Klan rider on horseback and in full regalia, holding a flag with the Latin motto "Quod Semper, Quod Ubique, Quod Ab Omnibus," c. 1868. Courtesy of the Tennessee State Museum Collection, Nashville.

apparent non-Ku-Klux to warn a victim of an impending Ku-Klux attack.[8] "And then he came away along down across below and said to me 'John, I heard a mighty report about you; they are yonder now, talking to Henry Gordon that they are going after you, and are going to kill you; that they are good for you. Now, all I say to you is, look out.' . . . Then I met some more coming from town, and they told me the same thing."[9] This worked as a last warning, perhaps even an effort to avert a physical attack where intimidation would suffice, but it also differentiated a Ku-Klux attack from other common forms of collective violence, clarifying to victims and others that this attack had been planned by an association of men within the community, men with the social capital to meet clandestinely and to command the loyalty of a third party who would communicate to the potential victim only what the Ku-Klux wanted him or her to hear. It marked the attack as, if not the voice of the community, the voice of an established organization comfortably embedded in the community.

During the attack itself, Ku-Klux performed their organization by ostentatiously displaying coordination and military discipline: "They were riding two by two, just as the cavalry ride."[10] They visibly deferred to a leader, explaining to their victims that he was in charge. They often referred to him by a military designation, usually "Captain." Walter Scott of Tennessee claimed that fifteen Ku-Klux came to his door with a rope and asked, "Captain Ku-klux, Shall we hang him?"[11] Ku-Klux sometimes counted off, or referred to one another by numbers: "Well, within a hundred yards of the swamp they all stopped and called numbers, began with number one, and went up as high as number ten."[12] They sometimes communicated through prearranged signals like whistles or animal sounds, which performed prior coordination: "They fired a gun or pistol three times; that is understood to be the signal for the camp to assemble";[13] "I heard them blow a whistle and knew it was the Ku Klux";[14] I "heard an indescribable noise . . . a very singular, grating, discordant kind of whistle which can be heard a considerable distance."[15] When they wore coordinated costumes or costumes that showed evidence of preparation, resources, and labor, they further underlined that the Ku-Klux attack was planned.

A second recurring feature of Ku-Klux attackers was the inverse of the first. In the face of the Ku-Klux's organization, attackers worked to convey victims' isolation. This worked in complicated ways: one of white southern Democrats' common complaints about freedpeople was that they were too organized. And indeed, Klan defenders often argued that the Klan's organization was necessitated by freedmen's organizations like the Union Leagues. At these moments, they portrayed freedpeople as too inclined to follow leaders, marching in lockstep to the polls, too easily manipulated by politicians.

The Klan undermined black organization in part by claiming, and attempting to demonstrate, that freedmen's organization was false, corrupt, inappropriate, or hollow. Freedmen's organizations were a degraded form of association, demagoguery rather than democracy. Ku-Klux attackers wanted to destroy whatever organizational structures freedpeople had managed to build, and expected that in doing so they would reveal that freedpeople lacked the solidarity and integrity to make these associations legitimate and robust; they would thus mark freedpeople as incapable of true civic association. And indeed, the idea of "disorderly" black men coexisted with the idea that black men were too quick to follow manipulative leaders. As James Broomall has argued, the visible organization of the Klan was meant to highlight and contrast with black disorder.[16]

Historians have long noted Ku-Klux groups' interest in attacking those active in formal black associations. The attacks on local political leaders like Wyatt Outlaw have come to be seen as exemplary of Klan violence. This reflects the emphases in primary sources. Newspapers and government investigators alike focused heavily on Ku-Klux attacks, particularly those involving the largest and most formal southern Republican association, the Union League. Ku-Klux attacks on Republican associations and their officers have served as strong evidence that Ku-Klux attackers were motivated by partisan politics. And partisan politics did clearly play an important role in some Ku-Klux violence. Yet targeting those important to Republican organizations could have had subpolitical, local motivations as well. Scott Nelson has shown that even the killing of Wyatt Outlaw was as much about economics and the specter of black self-sufficiency and dignity as about party politics in the abstract.[17] Electing Republican officials and supporting Republican policies and governments was only part of Union Leagues' daily business. As Michael Fitzgerald writes, soon after their founding, leagues generally "took on a less narrowly partisan character and incorporated other local concerns of the black community."[18] While they were involved in an important symbiotic relationship with the national Republican Party, a large part of their reason for existence was not related to politics writ large.

Ku-Klux attacks on those involved in formal associations like the Union League or militias were intentionally political actions, in conversation with a national Ku-Klux discourse. Michael Fitzgerald has powerfully unpacked attacks on Union Leagues, underlining their intensity and effectiveness in Alabama.[19] But attacks on formal groups like militias and the league were also a subset of, and little different from, a much larger body of attacks that targeted all efforts by freedpeople and their white Republican allies to form themselves into coordinated groups. Ku-Klux targeted a broad spectrum of associations. Formal organizations were important parts of broader working networks of freedpeople. They consistently were as interested in disrupting local and informal groups as formal political groups: "Klan assaults . . . were meant to obliterate the solidarities that the league helped to build and maintain."[20] They undermined freedmen's claim to political competence and membership through the ritual of the attack itself, and also through their choice of victims. It was a crucial project of white Democratic southerners to dismiss the social rights and meaningful ties of obligation among black people, in order to bring back a system in which whites could imagine that black people's primary or sole social ties were ties of dependence to white people. As Vernon Burton argued in his work on Edgefield County, South Carolina, freedpeople were unexpectedly effective at organization, using churches, family structures, and schools to provide support for each other. These organizations enabled, among other things, their effective political mobilization. In the rare instances when Ku-Klux attacked people while they were assembled, they attacked any manner of associations dominated by Republicans: church groups, associations to build schools, groups parading on the Fourth of July, groups heading out to have a picnic, or groups to drink together in the town on a Friday night: "They have told, within the last five months, all the colored preachers in the neighborhood, to quite preaching, and they have done so. They have broken up all colored schools."[21] In June 1868, outside Cornersville, Tennessee, a Ku-Klux group broke up a freedpeople's "Debating Club."[22] One interpretation of Ku-Klux's attacks on these nonpolitical groups might be that Ku-Klux were afraid that these groups were secretly engaged in political acts, or that they might lead to political acts. One Ku-Klux victim who was apparently whipped because he was believed to be assisting in organizing a colored school, testified that the men whipping him "said they did not object to the people having the school but that the association of colored people had to stop meeting so often, that if they kept meeting there like they were doing they would form a sort of a league after a while and be for trying to stop them and they were going to stop that."[23]

If Ku-Klux feared what such groups might become, they also focused on the effective power that even nonpolitical informal freedmen's associations already represented.[24] Stephen Hahn points to what could be read as an example of this: local whites, he says, often made "extravagant claims" of dangerous organizations of freedpeople intending to appropriate land and commit violence, but when federal officials examined them, they "often uncovered scarcely more than 'frolicks,' wooden muskets, and community meetings."[25] Yet the act of organization itself, for any purpose, was civically empowering. Walter Johnson has said, "Collective resistance is, at bottom, a process of everyday organization, one that . . . depends upon connections and trust established through everyday actions."[26] Freedpeople and their white allies aspired to give real weight to their interests by developing a pool of sympathetic witnesses and bondsmen and potential allies in violent conflicts, and to gain the ability to spread, stop, and alter rumors and intervene in conventional wisdom by giving people experience in holding leadership and support roles in large groups. Frolics and community meetings large enough to come to the attention of Ku-Klux groups were an effective way to get there. These groups not only created solidarity, but performed and displayed it for others. Whites appreciated that groups of freedpeople, even those with no explicit political program, were relevant to local power relations. In the antebellum period, slave social events had been a locus of resistance; both the whites who had warily tried to suppress or regulate these events and the slaves who had sometimes gone to great lengths to circumvent this suppression and regulation had long been well aware that social events had political meaning.[27] Continuing a long tradition of surveilling and preventing slaves' congregation in groups, whether for religious, social, or other purposes, postwar white Democratic southerners were convinced that any meeting of freedpeople and their white allies was in itself an impediment to their efforts to reassert their monopoly on power.

Ku-Klux were less inclined to attack freedpeople's groups while they were congregated, and more frequently singled out community leaders and organizers. Ku-Klux disproportionately attacked those Republicans who were active in association building, whether they focused on formal politics—serving as officeholders and speechmakers—or were demonstrating in other ways their ability and inclination to organize their fellows. These are Hahn's "prominent freedmen" or "local activists" along with some of their white allies.[28] Many of these prominent freedmen and their white allies were in positions of influence within the Republican Party. The Republican Party was by far the largest and most organized entity in which rural Republicans could potentially hold positions; working for the party was one of the few ways southern rural black men could hope to be paid for their organizational efforts. Whatever else he did, a Republican man with a talent or ambition for political organization would likely play a role within the party among his other leadership functions. When Joseph Williams, "a colored man," was killed by a large mob of masked men, the witness described him as "a little influential in his community among colored people," and also noted that he was a member of the board of supervisors, indicating political activity.[29] But sometimes men of local influence among Republicans would be victimized even if they had deliberately avoiding participating in formal Republican politics. Asked why a merchant had been killed in Florida, for instance, a witness replied, "I will tell you the position I think he occupied in the community. Lucy was a Jew. I think he was in great favor with the negroes. He got a great deal of trade from the negroes and perhaps was rather popular with the negroes." The witness went on to deny that Lucy had involved himself in politics.[30] A group of disguised men similarly attacked another shopkeeper, a white former Methodist preacher: "He had gone to keeping a kind of store on the cooperative system, a stock concern, sustained principally by freedmen, each man putting in so many dollars. . . . A good many people would gather at the store at night, trading. . . . They may have staid there to get information, or something of that kind."[31]

The attack on Henry Lowther, who was forced to choose between castration and death, is well known. Lowther had a particularly powerful position in the local social network. Lowther recounted that the Ku-Klux who castrated him stated the reason for their attack: "They were going to kill out all the leading republican men both white and black. They said I had taken too great a stand against them in the Republican Party." But he immediately added: "I worked for my money and carried on a shop. They all got broke and did not pay me and I sued them. They have been working at me ever since I have been free. I had too much money."[32] The rest of Lowther's testimony suggests that another reason he was selected for attack was his status as an influential and well-connected man in his community. Before the Ku-Klux attacked him, some parties (presumably his soon-to-be-attackers) had caused him to be arrested on the charge of Ku-Kluxing another black man. What is remarkable is Lowther's response: he immediately began calling people to his jail cell, trying to figure out which individuals had arranged for his arrest and how he could manage the situation. A regular parade of townspeople, black and white, came through his cell at his behest, and he made some progress. He gained the support, for instance, of the man he had allegedly Ku-Kluxed, who, we can imagine, was under substantial pressure to ally with Lowther's enemies. Lowther, in other words, was a *macher*. Perhaps he was Ku-Kluxed in part because of his Republican Party support, and in part because of his success as a businessman and his willingness to use the court system to defend his rights (his social stature had made this recourse available to him), but the attack on him was also part of a larger pattern of Ku-Klux attacks on those who were competent and effective local social organizers.

Similarly, when Ku-Klux attacked Alfred Richardson, they were attacking not only a member of the state legislature, but a local community leader. A white man friendly to him warned him of the impending attack, explaining, "You can control all the colored votes and they intend to break you up and they can rule the balance of the niggers when they get you off." The rest of Richardson's testimony further confirmed his role as a community leader. Since the attack, Richardson had gathered a good deal of evidence about the Ku-Klux from his neighbors, who told him about attacks that they were not willing to report to the papers and who brought him parts of Ku-Klux costumes that they had taken or found.[33]

Lowther, Richardson, and many others singled out for attack by the Ku-Klux were active leaders in the Republican Party. And their attacks paralleled attacks on many other men of influence who served as leaders and hubs of organization within their local community. George Houston agreed with his questioner that Ku-Klux victims were "leading, influential men among the colored people," adding, "They were, politically, men who went through the county doing the best they could, keeping the party up." He himself was attacked by the Ku-Klux because "they looked upon me as being the prominent negro of the county." He was a member of the Union League, and he had attended a public meeting opposed to Ku-Klux violence.[34] Ku-Klux target Andrew Flowers was a justice of the peace, and the Ku-Klux who attacked him objected to that, but they were also concerned about his assisting a school board association. "They did not say anything about colored people voting—not to me," Flowers testified. "They said they did not object to the people having the school, but that the association of colored people had to stop meeting so often; that if they kept meeting there like they were doing, they would form a sort of a league after a while, and be for trying to stop them, and they were going to stop that."[35]

Flowers shared another characteristic with a surprising number of Ku-Klux victims: even though he was not asked about serving as a bondsman and did not seem to think it particularly relevant to the attack, Flowers happened to mention that he sometimes served as a bondsman for other Republicans. He had gone the security on a Ku-Klux victim's marriage bond the day before the new groom was killed.[36] Similarly, Ku-Klux victim Henry Reed, who testified that he had been attacked for being "a true Republican, a leading man, and tried to influence men to the best of my ability," also mentioned in passing that he had gone a bond for black Sheriff Calvin Rogers.[37] Chapter 6 will discuss how common going bond was in the histories of the victims of the two large and deadly prison raids in Union Country, South Carolina. This sort of man—who held a position of leadership and influence among his Republican neighbors, who was able and willing to provide bonds and assume structural roles that elite white men had held as masters—empowered his community and increased freedpeople's ability to assert their interests against whites' whether or not he participated in formal politics.

Ku-Klux, then, began the process of destroying black associations by attacking them and their leaders directly. But they also worked to ritually mark all freedpeople's location in society as one of isolation. Most obviously, Ku-Klux usually conducted their attacks when their victims were physically isolated. They did not typically descend on work groups or groups engaging in leisure. They did not tend to, say, attack men congregated in grocery stores or bars. They only rarely attacked Union League members or other community groups while they were congregated.[38] Most attacks occurred at night, when most victims were in the company only of their household. Michael Fitzgerald has discussed how effectively the dispersed nature of postwar agricultural housing patterns enabled these isolated attacks.[39] Ku-Klux victims' households usually contained only immediate family members—spouses and children—though they might also include parents, siblings, or lodgers. Household members who attempted to "halloo" to alert any neighbors within earshot were often threatened or attacked.[40] "He hollered some time, and they said that if he hollered, they would blow his brains out. I hollered for some time, and they slapped me over the head, and told me they would knock my brains out."[41] This was practical; Ku-Klux attacks were more likely to be thwarted when committed in front of people who might support victims. But it was also discursively meaningful: had Ku-Klux violence taken the form of a fight between one faction (Democratic whites) in conflict with another (Republicans), it would have scripted black and white participation as parallel. Ku-Klux and their supporters were much more likely to perform and depict scenarios in which the roles of blacks and whites were radically uneven.

Having found an isolated victim, Ku-Klux further underlined his or her isolation. They frequently took their victim, particularly if male, some distance away from his home, separating him from his most primary community. Taking the freedman from the home was not only part of the process of isolating him; it was also a way to specifically undermine the home. Ku-Klux preferred attacking the freedman at home to isolating him in other ways—ambushing him on the road, say, or while he was out working out in his field. Part of this could simply be that Ku-Klux preferred to attack at night in order to escape detection and resistance, and most men, at night, were in their homes. But Ku-Klux often appeared to be deliberately targeting, and underlining the vulnerability of, the family itself. During slavery, whites' frequent refusals to recognize the standing of the slave family had been an important repressive tool, and the integrity of the black family was an important power struggle in Reconstruction-era local communities, as parents vied with employers for authority over their children, and married couples vied with employers for the right to withhold wives' potential agricultural labor.[42] Ku-Klux attacks, similarly, often appeared to have the purpose of disrupting familial bonds. Ku-Klux rapes of freedwomen presented freedpeople's families as failed associations. In doing so, as Hannah Rosen has argued, they revealed freedpeople's claims to civic competency as fraudulent. The capacity to effectively exercise public power, as a citizen, required that a man be able to interact as an equal with his neighbors while also exerting control over his household. Freedmen, their opponents argued, were "the opposite of independent and masterful men."[43] Ku-Klux attackers "creat[ed] situations that forced black men to fail as protectors."[44] At the same time, freedpeople's supposed lack of commitment to family was a minstrel staple.[45] The Ku-Klux attack sought to demonstrate the failure of freedpeople's familial associations to perform even their most central task: keeping their members safe. And indeed, if their goal was to disperse freedpeople's families, the Ku-Klux accomplished it: one common effect of Ku-Klux violence was the phenomenon of either the man of the house or the entire family "sleeping out" away from the home.[46]

While they were taking their victim out of his domestic space, however, they were notably not bringing him into the public sphere. Victims often noted that the Ku-Klux had not allowed them to don the clothing crucial to public respectability. Sometimes they were not allowed to put on their pants or that quintessential nineteenth-century marker of civilization, the hat. "When [Louis Thompson] desired to put on his clothes, they told him he would have no further use for them, and carried him away in his underclothing."[47] A white victim complained that "they would not give me time to get my hat and coat."[48] "This black man asked them to let him go and get his shoes and pants; no, they said they wouldn't let him, and they carried him on up in his drawers and shirt-sleeves, bare-footed, and wouldn't let him get nothing."[49] Simon Elder, of Georgia, "asked them if they pleased to let me put on my shoes; it was mighty cold. Said he, 'No, God damn you. You need not put your shoes on; we are Yankees from the federal city, and we will have you in Hell before to-morrow night this time.'"[50]

Sometimes Ku-Klux just took their male victim to the yard, but often they took him some distance into a depopulated area, isolating him even from his household. "They carried me about a quarter of a mile from the house may be a little more I cannot tell exactly how far it was it was a good distance from the house."[51] Presumably, if a home was isolated enough that a Ku-Klux group was able to appear in numbers and roust a man by force out of his bed, they could have conducted the rest of their attack right there. Yet Ku-Klux often invested the time, energy, and planning required to move the victim a substantial distance from his home before committing most of their violence. The move was rarely understood by victims as going to someplace; it was moving him away from home, to a place significant only in its isolation.

There was practical utility to this remove. The longer Ku-Klux remained at a victims' home, the more opportunity his allies would have had to organize a counterattack or rescue effort; tracks were difficult to follow until the morning. But isolation also had a symbolic value. The isolated victim was not just practically but experientially completely out-side and beyond hope of rescue by his friends. The Ku-Klux, in sharp contrast, had brought their friends with them. Though the victim might be endowed by the state with citizenship, and though he or she might have made efforts to foster the relationships that would ground abstract citizenship in the local community, the Ku-Klux attack proved that black men's (and white Republicans') claims to membership and solidarity had failed. The Ku-Klux victim was alone and helpless in the hands of his enemies, who claimed to represent "the people."

Ku-Klux seemed less likely to take female victims far from home, attacking them more frequently within the home or in the home's yard. In part this may have been because of the particularly gendered claims they were making on the female victim, which often took the form of demanding her sexual and domestic services by raping her or requiring that she prepare food for them and were therefore meaningfully con-nected to the space of the home. It may suggest that attacks on women were often targeted at their male relations: committing the violence in or near the home would heighten the shame of the victim's kin who failed to protect her.[52] But if the significance of taking a victim to an isolated place was to demonstrate the victim's disqualification for participation in the body politic, it makes sense that Ku-Klux usually did not feel the need to do so with female victims.

Once at an isolated space, Ku-Klux often further emphasized victims' isolation by extracting from them statements of disengagement from civic life.[53] Ku-Klux were always demanding that their victims "publish a card" promising no longer to participate in politics or other forms of public life.[54] They frequently demanded that freedpeople not speak of what had happened to them. Collectively, Ku-Klux, as a terrorist movement, absolutely depended on freedpeople's speech for their acts of violence to circulate and do their work. Yet a particular group of men who chose to become Ku-Klux may well have had a narrower interest (intimidate this man, drive off this family). The not-infrequent demand that their victim not speak forbade them to mobilize community support. Alternatively, Ku-Klux sometimes demanded that a person leave the community entirely.[55] As Gilbert Akin, a thirty-three-year-old mechanic from Columbia, Tennessee, testified, "I have been a marshal in a society I belong to, that is the reason they are so spiteful towards me. They sent me orders to leave; if I did not leave, I would be hung the next night."[56]

Ku-Klux selectively attacked community leaders and structured attacks so as to contrast their own organization with victims' isolation. They also attempted to force victims to demonstrate their unfitness for association by betraying their friends and family members or inflicting Klan-style violence on their fellow southern Republicans. Lewis Stegall of Tennessee recounted that the Ku-Klux had given his mother "50 licks" to make her disclose his location.[57] Alabaman Henry Hamlin was severely whipped by Ku-Klux who believed he could divulge the identity of a Union League leader.[58] Tennessee Ku-Klux threatened to hang Nim Wilks's wife for the same purpose.[59] Edmund Gray was forced to drag his friend out of his home under threat of having his house, with his family inside, axed to pieces.[60] Ku-Klux began their attack on a North Carolina man by claiming that he had just killed a friend of his who, they claimed, had implicated him as reporting the Ku-Klux to officials.[61] Similarly, Ku-Klux regularly used violence or the threat of violence to require some freedmen to assist them by carrying a light for them, whipping one another, providing them a rope with which to hang their victim, or guarding their horses while they attacked their friends.[62]

A Ku-Klux attacking a young freedman (below voting age) responded to his admission that he had been at a political meeting by exclaiming, "What sort of thing is that? What in hell is a meeting? Take off your shirt and get down here."[63] In part Ku-Klux were thus asserting their own uncivilized identity, but they were also suggesting that the young man's life was not one to which this or any other meeting was relevant. His world was to be constricted to bodily pain. After being dragged from his sickbed, severely whipped, and made to run half a mile, William Ford of Alabama was ready for the pain to end, and he understood what was required. When Ku-Klux attacking him "wanted to know my politics, . . . I said 'what is politics sir?'—very ignorant-like."[64] The Ku-Klux victim was made to forget his home, community, friends, and family during his ordeal. Hampton Hicklin recalled that the Ku-Klux had beaten him until "my face was all blood, and my eyes full of blood, and I didn't know a man."[65] After Ku-Klux brutally beat freedman Jackson Surrat, of Spartanburg, South Carolina, they told him, in his disoriented state, where his home was and sent him running toward it. He reflected in his testimony that "the house seemed strange to me."[66] The Ku-Klux attack taught freedmen that they did not have associations, family, or friends, or at least not any who were relevant in the face of white force.

The Ku-Klux attack also worked as an initiation ritual. Mark Carnes has described nineteenth-century American initiation rituals' generic elements: the initiate was blindfolded, taken to an isolated place (usually a hall), and surrounded by men who treated him threateningly. Guides walked him around the hall in "ritualistic circumambulations." Often they threatened to kill him; as part of the performance, they put him through various harrowing trials of his courage, exposing him to "skeletons, skulls, bloody daggers, executioners' devices, and assorted funereal accoutrements." Ultimately, the group, or the group's leader, declared that the initiate was not an impostor but a friend, and welcomed him into the order.[67]

Ku-Klux-themed popular texts made much of the Ku-Klux initiation ceremony.[68] Indeed, these initiations were usually more the focus of these texts than attacks on freedpeople were. In this fiction, initiates are surrounded by disguised men who threaten to kill him and put him through various harrowing trials of his courage. Ultimately, the initiate is reprieved by the den's leader, who declares that he is not an impostor but a friend and welcomes him into the order. Conspiratorial fiction dwelt on how the individual's experience of terror unmanned him. *Terrible Mysteries of the Ku Klux Klan* claims to be based on an account given by a man who has been driven mad by his experience of the initiation ritual and dies of fright before he can finish the story. In *Horrible Disclosures: A Full and Authentic Exposé of the Ku-Klux Klan*, the initiate, referred to as "the poor victim," is "quite beside himself with terror" and "ready to faint with horror."[69] *The Masked Lady of the White House* features black initiates to the order (in this account, the Ku-Klux was a Republican conspiracy) "cring[ing] close down to the floor, while their teeth chattered, their eyes rolled, and the perspiration poured down their ebon faces like rain, so intense was their emotion of dread."[70] The Klan initiation ritual in these 1868 accounts mirrors the Ku-Klux attack.

Some fraternal-style Klan initiations did occur, though no doubt they were considerably more restrained than those depicted in this sensational fiction.[71] Many real Klan initiation rituals could be simpler, if they occurred at all. One witness, asked how new members were initiated in Alamance, responded, "They all in disguise stood around in a ring among the trees, about fifty yards apart. Then two members brought the candidate to the middle of the ring, and left him alone. Then the whole crowd rushed upon him with curious noises, and rubbed him with their horns, frightening him as much as possible. The officers proceeded to administer the oaths."[72] The bare structure of terror, death, and rebirth pervaded even the simpler Klan initiations about which we have information.

The Ku-Klux attack was, on one notable occasion, itself used as a model for an initiation ritual. A group of Yale undergraduates listed in the 1868 *Yale Pot-Pourri* yearbook called themselves the "Initiation Committee." In the image above the list they are pictured dressed in tall pointed hats, masks, and horns in a room bedecked with crescents and skulls, lowering an unfortunate member of the Class of '72 into a coffin. One might argue that they were not specifically evoking the Ku-Klux, but rather evoking the broader body of sensationalist images from which the Ku-Klux had also borrowed. However, four "Initiation Committee" members were also members of Yale's "Ku Klux" eating club. One, Frederick Collin, listed his eating club nickname as "Woe to the Freshman."[73]

The similarity between the initiation ceremony and the Ku-Klux attack collapsed at the end. In an initiation ceremony, after dramatically demonstrating the initiate's isolation and vulnerability, the leader

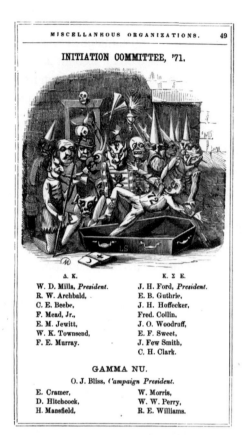

This image, printed in the *Yale Pot-pourri* of 1868–69, purportedly represents a Yale College initiation ceremony. Harry Elkins Widener Memorial Library, Harvard University.

intervenes and, politely ignoring any failures of courage the subject may have evinced during the ceremony, announces that the subject is worthy of membership in their brotherhood. Mark Carnes has influentially read this as a performance of the death of the domestic man and his rebirth as a man among men, and above all it seems to symbolize the shedding or devaluing of old affiliations and identities and the donning of new.[74] The Ku-Klux attack stops with the shedding. As well-connected forty-year-old preacher Columbus Jeter learned when Ku-Klux beat and ultimately shot him in an effort to force him to renounce his claim that "the negro is as good as the white man," Ku-Klux attacks were, among other things, a ritual of exclusion.[75] The victim was not worthy of membership in their brotherhood or any other. While the initiation ceremony was a ritual of inclusion, in which the subject was invited to be part of the empowered, selective group, the Ku-klux attack was, above all, a ritual of exclusion, in which the subject was excised from the body politic.

Northern Elites Imagine a Postwar Racial Order

The political leaders appointed to run hearings on Klan violence had very different interests and priorities than Ku-Klux, of course. Their task, after all, was to reveal Ku-Klux violence in order to end it. Yet their vision of how racial relations would look in the postwar South bore some resemblance to that of the Ku-Klux themselves. Like the Ku-Klux, they imagined that, due to a failure of either character or education, most black southerners, at least for the time being, lacked the ability to act effectively as independent citizens and required northern leadership. On the other hand, they were inclined to take seriously southern whites' claims of organizational competence. This was both ideological and pragmatic: northern elites certainly participated in the racial prejudice almost universally held in the nineteenth century, so skepticism about black competence would come naturally. At the same time, as Democrats complained, Republican political leaders had an interest in emphasizing white southern competence and black vulnerability. It was a powerful narrative for them politically, and it justified their increased involvement in southern affairs. Elite northerners questioning Klan victims, then, often ironically shared the strong tendency to actively elicit victim testimony that represented Ku-Klux as organized and victims as both lacking solidarity and incapable of defending themselves. While the Ku-Klux told that story in order to naturalize southern white control and black deference, congressional questioners used the same story to underline the need for federal resources to prop up vulnerable freedpeople in the face of organized white violence.

Republican elite interrogators were heavily invested in witnesses saying specific things and responding to them in certain ways. For obvious reasons, southern Republicans fled the one and embraced the other, but the Ku-Klux attack and the government hearing mirrored one another structurally. In the attack, the Ku-Klux victim was rousted out of bed by an aggressive group of men whose identities may or may not have been known to him or her; taken from his or her home to an isolated area, often without being allowed to assume respectable public dress; threatened with death; forced to perform his or her own submission; often whipped; sometimes raped or sexually molested; and sometimes killed. In the hearing, the Ku-klux victim was escorted or called into a politically central space (whether a capital or a county seat) by a group of elite men who were usually politically sympathetic to him or her, compensated for time and travel, invited to participate in a political process, treated with a certain structural formality, informed what to expect, asked to tell his or her story, then allowed to leave freely, returning home after the testimony if he or she dared. In both, the southern Republican was alone, extracted from his or her closest ties of community and surrounded by those more powerful than him- or herself. Almost always, those who brought him or her there had things that they urgently wanted him or her to say or perform.

White southern Ku-Klux attackers and white northern elite interrogators shared a sense of superiority and privilege grounded in their race and region. Congressional interrogators made derogatory comments to witnesses and revealed, in the press and in the hearings themselves, the irritation, offense, and disgust they felt during their rural stays. A correspondent for the Democratic *New York World* who visited committee members during their southern travels reported from Spartanburg, South Carolina, that the committee was "getting very tired of their work; they are disgusted at the idea of being sent hundreds of miles to hear 'Old Wives' Tales' and to listen with gravity to long recitations of family feuds and neighborhood difficulties."[76] Many in the federal government responsible for countering the Ku-Klux "shared the [white] Southern worldview more than they ever imagined."[77] Northern elite questioners were ready to listen to southern Ku-Klux victims, but they were not entirely ready to hear testimony that did not fit closely with their own narrative.

Ku-Klux and northern interrogators constrained victims' speech for different reasons and in different ways. Investigative committees provided a rare occasion for freedpeople and their allies to speak. Yet their role as interrogators resembled that of white authenticators of earlier slave narratives. Slave authors struggled to maintain a pure voice even while, to circulate his or her writings, he or she required white authentication. This authentication was never neutral; it constituted a competing text, always threatening to overwhelm the ostensibly primary text of the black writer.[78] White abolitionists established a "discursive terrain" in which slave narratives had to find a place.[79] In the same way, northern Republican committee members both provided a forum for poor southern Republicans to speak and constrained the content of that speech through their control of that forum. Elite white committees were gatekeepers between Ku-Klux victims' words and the ears of the politically minded northern audience who wanted to hear them.[80] Members validated certain of these words, and certain of these witnesses, by obviously accepting some while heaping skepticism on others; they shaped testimony, through their questioning, to fit what they and their constituents expected to hear.

Northern elite Republican questioners wanted to buttress the dominant Ku-Klux narrative. But they were also looking for the language of the national and the political. They asked witnesses not to dwell on local contexts, relationships, and motivations. They were looking for victims who were relatively featureless beyond being Republican and of blameless character. They did not usually require victims to demonstrate their humiliation or gullibility, but their own prejudices led them to expect or even invite evidence of these qualities. Even sympathetic Republicans found it easy to casually describe black people as "worked up to a state of perfect phrenzy with fear."[81]

Elite northerners, like Ku-Klux, also used their interactions with victims to define themselves. In part they wanted to convince themselves of something: in forming themselves into a traveling investigative committee, they were trying out radically new roles. Before deciding to travel to the South, committee members asked Spartanburg native Landon Gentry if he thought doing so would enable them to finally bring the Ku-Klux to light. He refused to answer: "I do not know what kind of power you might have for finding out things."[82] The congressmen, who didn't know either, were taking their new power out for a spin. Their work of self-definition was particularly striking when congressmen headed to rural areas. Their expensive urban clothing was itself a costume. Northern congressmen (and newspapermen) performed supercilious superiority, moral authority, bureaucratic competence, and institutional power. They spoke with a voice of command and demanded deference. They brooked no personal insult. They expressed offence or annoyance at the personal qualities of witnesses.

Questioners conveyed to freedpeople a message about who they were: powerful, canny, provisional allies, but only on certain terms. They could have done that by delivering stump speeches. Instead, these very important men traveled a long distance through the hot summer to gather Ku-Klux victims' words. They did this because they needed freedpeople's speech. Practically, they needed southern Republicans to provide local knowledge that could be framed to contribute to the national Klan narrative that had become so important to their own careers and justifications. They needed witnesses to assume a safely subsidiary loyalty: to participate in an alliance with northern Republicans in which their needs, interests, and words would be distinctly secondary to those of northern leaders. Most of all, they needed witnesses to enact worthy helplessness: while they were sympathetic and appropriate recipients of northern assistance, they were not yet mature citizens capable of self-government without the close guidance and support of their northern allies.

Witnesses usually offered testimony close to what their questioners were looking for. They shared many of their questioners' understandings and motivations, so much of the conformity must have been natural. But they had many other strategic reasons to conform to it willingly even where their experience fit it less clearly. Occasionally it is possible to see this desire to conform at work. White Alabama witness Samuel Horton, when asked, "Was there any persecution of these men who voted the Republican ticket by the Ku Klux?" responded, "Well if that was not what set them on me I can't tell what it was." The bulk of his testimony, however, reveals a wealth of other reasons he might have been targeted for Ku-Klux violence. He was a member of a marginal and isolated religious community that had itself been a rare collective target of a Ku-Klux attack. His daughter-in-law, right before the attack, had given birth to a stillborn grandson who was said to look uncannily like a costumed Ku-Klux. Some had been concerned about the fact that he had displayed the stillborn's body and failed to bury it in a timely manner. Since stillborn cauls were traditionally believed to have magical powers, some may have feared that he was practicing witchcraft. His son, testifying after him, claimed to have been attacked by the same Ku-Klux. Though he harbored Radical views, and though his wife attended Radical meetings, he had scrupulously refused to vote or take any role in politics precisely in the hopes of avoiding such conflict.[83] It was demonstrably not a simple case of Ku-Klux attacking men for "voting the Republican ticket." The Hortons' Republican associational identity was only part of the cluster of tensions they had with the men in their community who adopted the Klan identity. Samuel Horton, though, seemed committed to offering the narrowly partisan explanation that was most comprehensible, welcome, and useful to Republican committee members.[84]

Witnesses like Samuel Horton embraced the national, partisan frame of their questioners rather than focusing on some other narrative that the rich particularity of their local experience might suggest. They willingly offered their own words as "the fulfillment of the prophecy" of national Republican Klan discourse.[85] Klans were informed by northern Republican concepts of the Ku-Klux, which imagined them as focused on national and partisan issues. This frame was available to attackers, who sometimes evoked it explicitly. Similarly, most Ku-Klux victims, before they themselves were attacked, had learned what a Ku-Klux attack was.[86] Some of their ideas of the Ku-Klux came from rumor and other local knowledge, but the understanding of the Ku-Klux even by the illiterate would have been heavily, if indirectly, informed by print media.

Most southern Republicans called to testify would have had a real desire to please, avoid the wrath of, or make use of the Republicans who dominated the Ku-Klux committees. The politically savvy knew what answers these politicians wanted. In the dramatically unbalanced power distribution of the hearing room, all questions rode the force of privilege, and all answers bore the weight of need. Much Ku-Klux testimony was naked in its deference to the committee's needs and interests. One Alabama victim, describing an attack, referred to his attackers only as "they." Asked by committee members to clarify, he responded, "I mean I don't know what I mean. You must take that thing like it fits."[87] Witnesses willingly offered their testimony to assist committee members' purposes.

Where witnesses' testimony did not conform to questioners' expectations, they often expressed their dissatisfaction: voicing skepticism, reminding the witness pointedly that he or she was under oath, telling the witness that the committee was not interested in pursuing that direction, or simply repeating the question, sometimes multiple times, in the (often fulfilled) anticipation of a different answer. As Congressman Luke Poland explained to a particularly confident witness, Judge Augustus R. Wright, "I desire to ask you a very few questions, and only a very few, upon a very few of the subjects that you have talked about, because they are entirely outside of our inquiry; and I want direct answers to my questions."[88] All of these strategies clarified that this was not a forum in which witnesses could introduce the narrative of their choosing; it was not even a forum in which they were welcome to answer congressmen's questions in the way that seemed most true to them. This was a forum in which they could give evidence or interpretation consistent with their questioners' priorities and narratives.

Adding an additional complication for victims was the fact that each subcommittee was politically mixed. Even those victims whose accounts met the expectation of the Republican majority then were questioned, and often insulted, by the Democratic member—Philadelph Van Trump on one committee, and Francis P. Blair on the other. As the *New York Times* put it, "Judge Van Trump subjected all the witnesses called by the majority to the most searching cross-examination."[89]

Southern Republicans may also have complied with narrative expectations out of fear. The committee's perceived coercive authority was perhaps even greater than its real power. Since the committee was a novel type of institution whose own members did not agree on its role and authority, it is not surprising that many freedpeople and white Republicans also did not understand the nature of the committee and the limits of its powers; some feared the practical consequences of displeasing committee members. Freedman Julius Cantrell, confronted by committee members about information he had previously withheld, apologized, explaining, "You see, I was sort of frightened. I never was in a court before in this way." His congressional questioner, playfully evoking minstrelesque stereotypes, asked what had frightened him: "You were not afraid we were Ku Klux?" Cantrell replied, "No sir, but black people is sort of under we have no education and it always frightens us."[90]

Imagine the experience of witnesses like Margaret Blackwell, a twenty-one-year-old white woman from Spartanburg, South Carolina. At the beginning of her testimony, her voice sounded confident: that of a sympathetic victim who had finally found the men who would right her wrongs at the hands of the Ku-Klux. "I am afraid of them," she shared with the committee, "candidly I am."[91] As her testimony progressed, however, it became clear that some committee members, particularly Democratic congressmen Philadelph Van Trump, were responding skeptically. They repeatedly asked her to pin down the date of an attack on her home, reminding her that she was under oath. She became increasingly flustered, saying, "I couldn't tell if I was on my hanging gallows."[92] Van Trump repeatedly insinuated, obviously based on discussions with local informants, that Margaret was a prostitute and that what she described as a Ku-Klux attack was in fact a visit by her customers.[93] When she tried to stop her testimony: "That is all. Now I have answered all your questions. I can't answer any more questions at all," the Republican committee chairman told her coldly that she would answer all the questions put to her.[94] By the end, she was repeatedly evoking her older brother Jason (Jacin in the 1860 census), who, she insisted, could answer questions about the attack much better than she could; she hoped to hide behind his painfully meager patriarchal power as protector of her identity and reputation.[95] The opportunity to testify before the committee seemed full of possibility, but it was also fraught with peril for those who did not or could not fit northern Republicans' image of the Ku-Klux victim.

Republican congressmen were not asking witnesses not to say things that were untrue, but to emphasize certain aspects and interpretations of their own experiences over others. They needed witnesses to negotiate the tension between local meanings of the violent events they had experienced and the relevance of those events to national politics. Witnesses became translators, narrating their attacks in terms that a national audience could understand. It is difficult to read past this nationalizing bias of Ku-Klux descriptions. The easiest way to do so is to turn back to Democratic critiques, which were, for very different reasons, focused on debunking nationalizing claims in favor of local ones. For example, when a witness claimed that Aaron Biggerstaff had been attacked by Ku-Klux for his Republican politics, Democratic committee member Francis Blair pointed out another pressing reason that someone might have wanted to attack him: since he had been "implicated in the murder of one of their friends, and in firing into the house of another," was that not "the most probable cause [of the Ku-Klux attack] rather than his political sentiments?"[96] This attempt to push back against Republican emphasis on southern Democratic organization and frame Klan events as local events was the substance of the minority report Democratic committee members issued after the Ku-Klux committees' investigations.

Despite Democratic objections and occasional witness resistance, the Republicans who dominated the investigative committees were interested in telling a streamlined story about Klan violence. It was about the national politics rather that about personal or local disputes. Victims were moral, defenseless, and in need of their protection and guidance. Using their considerable authority, committee members worked to shape an image of the Klan that would most efficiently serve their pragmatic political needs, even when that image stood in tension with the messier realities on the ground.

Ku-Klux Victims Imagine a Postwar Racial Order

Even the most oppressed historical figure possesses the subjective capacity to assign meanings to the events around him or her. As Michel-Rolph Trouillot has observed, "Human beings participate in history both as actors and narrators."[97] Contemporaries tend to listen much more readily to the stories told by the powerful than to those told by the victimized, but the American public has rarely been as interested in hearing rural black southerners' narrations as they were during the Ku-Klux period. It is hard to think of a time when the words of rural black Americans appeared as frequently in the newspapers as they did in 1871, as the congressional committees took victim testimony.[98] Telling Klan stories gave Klan victims and witnesses an almost unique opportunity to contribute substantially to nineteenth-century public discourse.

Excellent recent work has focused on finding the authentic voice of victims of racial violence, including Klan violence, in the decades after the Civil War.[99] Kidada Williams, Hannah Rosen, and Carole Emberton have all recovered from Klan testimony freedpeople's "vernacular history" of the meanings of Klan violence.[100] Such thorough work has been done in spelling out these dominant strains of testimony that it is possible to tighten the focus: to take dominant strains of testimony as a given and dig into discordant moments, instances in which freedpeople (and occasionally white Republicans) serving as witnesses were either not able or not willing to give their questioners what they wanted. These moments pointed to competing, or potentially collaborative, discourses about Ku-Klux attacks coming not from the national press or political elites but from rural victims themselves. Representations of Klan violence by victims were perhaps not as influential as those by the Pulaski founders, newspaper editors, producers of popular culture, and politicians, but they found their way into the popular discourse.

Since evidence of victims' behavior during attacks comes almost entirely from the later testimony of those same victims, we cannot reliably distinguish between what they did, or refused to do, and what they later determined to represent themselves as having done or not done. Some, like white Klan victim Major Everson, declared themselves to be in a "tight place," constrained by Ku-Klux and Congress alike.[101] It is impossible to know what Klan victims successfully silenced: how many chose not to tell the stories of their attacks at all despite the obvious intentions of their attackers that it be circulated; how many chose not to convey details of their attackers' behavior, or their own, that their attackers would have wanted conveyed; and how many assumed even greater control of their own attack stories, using their brief moment of discursive power to tell the story in a way that reflected their own best interests rather than allowing themselves to be again constrained by the situation created by the attacker. Victims sometimes worked, against the intentions of Ku-Klux and even against the intentions of interrogators, to maintain their civic dignity and autonomous agency. They disputed Ku-Klux's intimidations and congressmen's interpretations alike, and refused to fit their testimony to the narratives pushed by these groups.

Some southern Republican victims and witnesses were willing, even eager, to tell their stories to congressional committees, despite the dangers inherent in testifying. One witness, John Childers of Alabama, apologized that he would have to be vague in some of his testimony to protect himself: "Well, gentlemen, I am delicate in expressing myself. I feel myself in great risk in doing these things. I have no support in the State of Alabama. I am a citizen here, bred and born; and have been here forty-two years. If I report these things I can't stay at home." Yet he continued: "I wish to give you gentlemen all the satisfaction I can."[102]

Through testimony, they sought redress for the injuries done by the Ku-Klux.[103] Their testimony could potentially elicit federal intervention, and represented perhaps the only chance that their attackers would be punished. But even if no help would be forthcoming, witnesses understood it as a rare opportunity to be heard. Whenever northern Republicans made themselves available to hear the stories of Ku-Klux victims, survivors came forward in droves, sometime staying in town for days in hopes of being called. South Carolina Ku-Klux victim Isham McCrary explained why he had decided to testify: "I was aiming to stand up to them. I thought maybe there was a chance for me to get what was justice what was right."[104] Elderly freedwoman Charlotte Fowler, whose weeping during her testimony about the Klan's recent killing of her husband was duly recorded by the stenographer, found some consolation in being part of the national discourse. "I just tell you the whole truth," she explained. "I do not want to put a finger on anybody, but they have ruined me. But his name is published to the whole United States. If you ever get a newspaper and read of Wallace Fowler, that is my husband." Charlotte Fowler had given up seeking justice for her husband's death locally, but she was proud to have a role in a national conversation. Ku-Klux were strong enough in her community that she dared not name her husband's killers, but his name and an account of his death, at least, had escaped their grasp.[105]

Victims testifying before northern Republicans had little room to maneuver. It is impossible to know how much space there was between victims' hushed and private conversation and what they chose to say in formal testimony.[106] Yet Ku-Klux victims resisted the meanings imposed upon their attacks first by Ku-Klux, and then by congressional committee members. Testimony reveals victims rescripting their attacks to work against their attackers' ends. It also exposes powerful moments of tension between witnesses and interrogators—moments when witnesses refused to say what the interrogator wanted to hear or when interrogators did not want to hear what the witnesses were saying.[107]

Some witnesses' refusals to abide by the narratives of Ku-Klux and committeeman were personal and apparently idiosyncratic, but others recur frequently enough that they suggest common elements of Ku-Klux victims' local discourses of resistance. Together these reveal a counternarrative. Freedpeople collaborated on their "hidden transcript" or resistance in the privacy of their homes, and religious meetings, picnics, dances, school-building associations, and in some places militia gatherings or Fourth of July celebrations enabled them to communicate their readings of Klan violence within their community.[108] Sometimes victims approached black community or religious leaders, some of whom were compiling evidence about Klan attacks; these leaders sometimes had the wherewithal to convey their evidence even beyond the borders of the county and to the ears of federal authorities. The boldest of the victims took their complaints to political leaders like state representatives, who were in a position to convey their accounts to the state government, or to representatives of the federal government like military officers and, where they happened to be present, congressional committees. The more public a forum a victim found, however, the more likely he or she was to experience retribution; it is very likely that, for that reason, most victim narratives circulated only within local communities.

Constrained by low literacy rates, many Ku-Klux victims could not rely on written texts to construct their own counternarratives of their attacks.[109] Even the literate, who might subscribe to a newspaper sponsored by northern Republicans, rarely had access to their own presses.[110] While Republican presses were established around the South at the end of the war, almost all were written by and for white Republicans. Of the few black papers that were established after the war, almost all had gone out of business by 1868. Other black-run papers made brief appearances, but with a few exceptions, such as the *New Orleans Tribune*, the *Maryville (Tenn.) Republican*, and the *Charleston Missionary Record*, they did not last long enough to become established parts of a national exchange.[111]

Except when they might have access to the pages of Republican papers or tap into a discursive language with which freedpeople across the South would have been familiar, victim-constructed and -controlled accounts of Ku-Klux violence would circulate orally or occasionally through personal written communication. Scott Nelson traces black communications networks in Spartanburg, showing how drovers and traders became "secular pilgrims" tying communities together.[112] Yet despite these innovations, black discursive communities would fundamentally be more localized than white communities with meaningful access to print media. The similarities that occur in resistant witness testimony across the South, then, likely do not reflect a cohesive regional discursive community: rather, victims facing the same demeaning and dangerous narratives of Klan violence within the context of Reconstruction-era southern culture often developed similar responses to it.

The lack of good means of coordination makes the appearance of common themes across the testimony all the more striking. Freedpeople testifying across the South frequently (though not universally) expressed lack of interest in claims that the Ku-Klux was a formal, organized political entity. If both Ku-Klux themselves, and congressmen taking testimony were deeply invested in establishing the organizational qualities, formal identity, and political intentions of Ku-Klux, testifying victims reminded congressmen that what mattered about the Ku-Klux was not who they claimed to be, not their claims to some broad political purpose, but the raw fact of their violence. As twenty-one-year-old widow Tilda Walthall said when asked why costumed men killed her husband, "Lord knows; I don't."[113] Freedman Robert Fullerlove, asked what he thought had motivated whites to attack him, responded, "I can't tell; really I can't tell." Only when pressed ("Has anyone ever told you what the cause was?") did he say that he had heard that it was on account of Radical politics and his own influence with his neighbors.[114]

Freedpeople also often frustrated congressmen by refusing to describe the Klan as a formal, extensive, organized entity. Again, such claims to organization were strategically crucial to the northern Republican project. Congressmen nudged witnesses to reframe their accounts of local social relationships as though they were more institutionalized. William Burnside Anderson, for instance, reported having been attacked by three men. Two of these had since left the county, and the other had been arrested. Anderson was afraid to return home, and Van Trump asked why:

> QUESTION: But [you had been attacked by] these three individuals only.
> ANSWER: But I believe there were others.
> QUESTION: What reasons have you for thinking so?
> ANSWER: I don't swear to it positively because I don't know, but there are others were very thick with and intimate.
> QUESTION: Name the others you are afraid of in that county.
> ANSWER: I don't know who they would be. This thing is got up so we don't know who they are.
> QUESTION: You say you believe there is an organization in that county?

ANSWER: Yes, sir I believe so.

QUESTION: Do you mean Ku Klux?

ANSWER: I don't know what it is. It does such as was done to me.[115]

There are two nudges here. First, when Anderson describes those he fears, he initially says that he fears those whom his attackers "were very thick with and intimate," presumably their family and friends. Had he not known their identities prior to the attack, he very likely would have had enough incentive to learn them afterward. Only when he is called on to name them, and is understandably reluctant to do so, does he retreat into framing those he fears as an organized body of men ("this thing") who deliberately obscure their identities. He is translating his local situation to outsiders. Telling him their specific names, he seemed to realize, would do the committee little good, and him much potential harm. Second, once Anderson has defined his opponents as an organization, Van Trump pushes him, this time unsuccessfully, to provide it with a formal name.

Like William Burnside Anderson, some other freedpeople and white Republicans chose not to use the term "Ku-Klux" even with the prompting of the committee. Instead they spoke of their attackers as if they were a less formal group. By failing to call them "Ku-Klux," they were also undermining the idea that they were part of a national association. Norwegian Union veteran Henry Anderson consented to use the term "Ku-Klux" but drew attention to its constructed nature in his testimony: "I don't know what they may be, sir. They were drunk with whisky. They were something; you may call them Ku-Klux; I would call them Ku-Klux."[116]

When assigning a "Ku-Klux" identity to their attackers, freedmen victims were also more likely than northern Republicans to emphasize the constructed nature of the label "Ku-Klux." When asked, "Did you ever see the Ku-Klux," Major Gardiner responded, "O, yes, sir; I saw what they call Ku-Klux many a time."[117] When asked who had whipped her, Lydia Anderson replied, "It is what they call the Ku-Klux." When asked if a neighbor had been whipped by the Ku-Klux, she replied, "They said they were Ku-Klux." Asked the same about another neighbor's attackers, she said, "They didn't know who else it was but them." Her daughter simply referred to the Ku-Klux as "them nasty things."[118] Twenty-five-year-old Betty Kinney testified, "I do not know whether they were called Ku-Klux or not, but they were talking about what they had done to Mr. Holliday."[119]

Consistently, though, freedpeople were most interested in redefining their own roles in Klan attacks, correcting the negative assessments both Ku-Klux and white northern Republicans made of their behavior. Testifying victims regularly, and in similar ways, responded to their negative portrayals by southern Democrats, even when their northern Republican questioners' own prejudices placed them more on the side of the Ku-Klux. Most witnesses took a deferential tone in their interactions with congressmen or other governmental officials listening to testimony. Few had the boldness of Hampton Hicklin, of Yorkville, who laughed at the attempts of Democrat Philadelph Van Trump to undermine his testimony. When Van Trump asked, "What amuses you so?" he responded first by pointing to the gulf between himself and his interrogator, "I don't know as I can tell you," and then directly equated the authority of his lived experience to the judge's elite education: "I just consider that you thought I didn't know these men, and want to trip me up on that. I know them better than you can make figures on that paper."[120]

Usually in more subtle ways, other witnesses asserted themselves in testimony. They did so despite congressional interrogators' mostly consistent lack of interest in their own actions, responses, and mental states. For instance, while Ku-Klux worked to portray freedpeople as incapable of association and loyalty, and while congressmen generally were not interested in steps freedpeople had taken to defend one another, some witness testimony emphasized the extent to which they and other victims had looked out for their family and allies. Sent into his house to bring his friend out to the Klan, Edmund Gray recalled, "I thought to screen Jim Hicks and made out I didn't see him."[121] Daughters recounted having falsely claimed to Ku-Klux that their fathers were away. Husbands remembered pleading that their pregnant wives were in no condition to be abused. Female family members recounted meeting Ku-Klux at the front door while husbands and sons leapt out the back window. Concealed men told of coming out of hiding to protect their wives from violence: "I was not in when they came and they went there on my wife. She was in there by herself and struck her to make her tell where I was, but she was asleep and didn't know where I was. I had got up and went out at the time that they went in. He drew a piece of iron on my wife and I went in then."[122] Family members offered to accept violence for one another: "I told him he had better not kill the child. He had better kill me."[123] Wives often testified to their distress standing in the doorway, watching their husbands be dragged away from them. Fathers asked to be spared for the sake of their children.[124]

When Ku-klux arrived at the home of freedman John L. Coley and demanded that he bring out his grandson, whom they believed to be hiding there, he recalled, "I caught up a torch and I went around with them and searched the house but not very particularly, and could not find him. I called to him with all the faithfulness a man could do and with the honest expectation that he would answer me, but he did not."[125] Coley here intends his white northern audience to understand his doublespeak. The key is "not very particularly." Coley wanted the committee to know that he had successfully protected his wife's grandson under threat of violence. The doublespeak describes and rejects the man Coley is not, the one who would be unmanned enough to honestly and faithfully assist the Ku-Klux in finding his own kin. Victims' solidarity during the attack, and their own intentional representations of it to investigative committees, could subvert Ku-Klux's apparent intentions of representing the black man, and black association more generally, as failed, making it instead a demonstration of the depth of the victims' ties with one another. How else could contemporaries have understood the attack on Matt and Maria Nichols, and their son, Matt? "They carried the son and father first and then the wife went after them [and] they killed them all."[126]

Just as frequently, victims used their committee testimony to undermine Ku-Klux's claims of their social isolation and to emphasize the existence and significance of their relationships to others in their community beyond their families. They used time in their testimony to insist that they were good citizens. They claimed that their employer gave them "a good face," or that no man in the community had a grievance against them.[127] "I stood in such a way I didn't think anybody had anything against me."[128] "I was raised there, and they never could put a scratch of a pen against me."[129] They were not afraid of the Ku-Klux, some maintained, because they knew that the Ku-Klux only attacked bad and disruptive men, whereas they were stable, hard-working, honest men and women, and good neighbors. Even outside their descriptions of the attacks themselves, freedpeople often emphasized their robust interpersonal ties with those around them.

Freedpeople also emphasized their integrity as community members and citizens. Georgian freedman Abram Colby recounted that after his attackers "took me to the woods and whipped me three hours or more and left me in the woods for dead," they asked him if he would "vote another damned radical ticket?' I said 'I will not tell you a lie.' . . . I thought I would not tell a lie. I supposed they would kill me anyhow. I said, 'If there was an election to-morrow, I would vote the radical ticket.' They set in and whipped me a thousand licks more, I suppose."[130] James Hicks of Lowndes County, Mississippi, stuck to his denial of having insulted a white woman, even after a whipping, until "at last one of them said he reckoned that I didn't say it, and there was no use to try to beat me to own what I didn't say," and the men left.[131] Others proudly told stories of friends who had successfully stood up in the face of Klan intimidation. Henry Giles discussed a freedman who had chosen to be shot rather than help Ku-Klux burn down a school.[132]

When John Coley was called to testify about having been whipped by a large group of Ku-Klux, he chose to recount several details: Ku-Klux treated him with levity and disrespect and asked him to find his step-grandson. As he elaborated, the chairman, losing patience, inter-jected, "Can you not state more what they did, and less what they said?" (In fact, the committee was often quite interested in "what they said," so long as it had to do with formally political matters.) Coley obliged: "Very well, you simply want to understand the abuse they gave me?" and headed to an account of the whipping.[133] After whipping him, Coley explained, Ku-Klux immediately began asking him about his role in a dispute that had occurred between his step- grandson and another young man. Once again, the chair intervened: "I do not know that that has any connection with the matter we are inquiring about."[134] Coley's step-grandson appears to have been what mattered to the Ku-Klux in this incident. He was also what Coley thought was most important to talk about. But the committee did not what to hear about him. In this way, committee members let wit-nesses know that their words would be heard only to the extent that they fell within certain guidelines. One of those guidelines was that Ku-Klux attacks be described as about matters relating to formal politics rather than local affairs.

Occasionally a witness went a step further, actively constructing a role for himself as Ku-Klux victim so distinct from the story they were telling as to be subversive. Very rarely, the committee almost seemed to listen and be unsettled. The testimony of John Lewis was one of these moments. Lewis—a young black man, "going on twenty-three years," working at Colonel Sam Snoddy's plantation in Spartanburg, South Carolina—testified that Ku-Klux had whipped him. They had threatened to kill him if he should reveal the whipping, yet he claimed not to be afraid of reprisal. "Sir, I just go on and take it as it comes. I hold that if they kill me they kill me on a wrong thing."[135] This was a very unusual response from a Ku-Klux victim. Ku-Klux victims almost universally understood that aspect of their role within the discourse; despite their assertions of personal dignity, despite eliding whatever fearful behavior they may have exhibited within the attack, they soberly acknowledged fear of future attack and desire for the government's protection. Lewis's testimony was closely echoed in the testimony of his close neighbor, young Willis Butler, who had been whipped during the same raid: "I am not afraid of them. I am not thinking about them. I do not know whether they will come any more or not."[136] The distinctive tone of these two men's testimony makes it nearly certain that they based their uniquely empowered, practically stoic understanding of their relationship to Ku-Klux in their relationships with one another or perhaps with a larger local group. They had engaged in some substantial private discussion and in that negotiation had found courage and resistance.[137]

These moments of resistance mattered. Lewis, early in his testimony, mentioned having followed his master loyally to war. Ohio congressman Job Stevenson followed up later:

> QUESTION: Are not you afraid [Ku-Klux] will kill you?
> ANSWER: No sir. I know one thing; when they kill me, I will be dead.
> QUESTION: You do not seem to put a very high price on your life.
> ANSWER: I just know that if they overpower me, I can't help it.
> QUESTION: Were you under fire in the army?
> ANSWER: No, sir. I just went to wait on my master.
> QUESTION: You did not go into battle?
> ANSWER: No, sir.
> QUESTION: Suppose you vote the radical ticket next time?
> ANSWER: I will vote just as I did at first. They will whip me for it anyhow but I will vote again.[138]

No doubt Stevenson, who himself had not fought, is asking about the war in part out of curiosity about the roles of slaves in the Confederate army. But he is also visibly startled and impressed by Lewis's impressive embodiment of contemporary elite northerners' ideal of manhood. Just for a moment, he seems almost tempted to admit him to the fraternity.

Ku-Klux victims, through their acts of discursive resistance, may well have made a difference in the cultural idea of the Ku-Klux. As a movement, the Ku-Klux were always dependent on their own victims to define them.

Often victims chose to silence or subvert the messages Ku-Klux wanted to send. The sweat of Ku-Klux who kept whipping until they temporarily broke the will of their victims, the elaborate work some of them spent on constructing their costumes and plotting out minstrelesque scenarios, fulfilled many of Ku-Klux's local intentions: to threaten individual victims' self-conceptions as rights-bearing citizens, to cause them to cease whatever assertions of those rights were interfering with the Ku-Klux's own strategies for building their postwar lives. But they were of little weight in the national discussion if victims refused to publicly acknowledge their effectiveness. Ku-Klux victims had little enough discursive power, but in this important way they did have the power to refuse to serve as agents in the process of translating this aspect of local violence into the terms of a national racist discussion.

FOUR

The Ku-Klux in the National Press

THOMAS J. PRICE: I joined the Klan because I thought I was obliged
to; I was told, I would get into a hobble if I didn't, and, perhaps, get a
whipping if I didn't join them; they told me that I had to obey orders, or
I'd get into trouble . . .
JUDGE BOND: I think there ought to be another proclamation of
emancipation.

—Testimony of Thomas J. Price, South Carolina, *Testimony Taken by the Joint
Select Committee on the Condition of Affairs in the Late Insurrectionary States*

Northern and southern audiences alike had a powerful taste for accounts
of the Klan. If it cannot accurately said that the Klan spread "like wildfire"
through the South in 1867, stories about the Klan did indeed seem to take
over the national newspaper press in early to mid-1868. At a time when
many northerners were sated with stories from the defeated South and
many white southerners were sick of hearing accounts of the suffering of
freedpeople, articles about the Klan were often eagerly taken up by both
northern and southern presses. This phenomenon was not incidental to
the growth of the Ku-Klux. Though stories of the Klan began with attackers and victims that were then shaped by elites gathering the testimony
of victims and witnesses, the evolution of ideas about the Ku-Klux would
never have progressed without the cooperation of the national press.
Thus this chapter and the next take on the question of what motivated
those who reprinted and read Klan accounts.

The Klan idea held many attractions to northern readers. Among other
things, it offered a simplified social map of complex race, class, and partisan dynamics in the South, and between southerners and the federal
government. The Ku-Klux served, in Stephen Prince's words, as a synecdoche for the untidy mass of white Democratic southerners.[1] But it also
positioned them in relation to other major groups in the South. To discuss

the Klan was to discuss, quite directly, who wielded power over whom in the Reconstruction South. Ambitious freedpeople, freedpeople loyal to their former masters, white Republicans, elite whites, poor whites, northern soldiers, carpetbaggers, and Freedmen's Bureau agents each had a role in the heavily stylized and oft-repeated newspaper accounts of the Klan. Democratic whites, imagined as unifying across class in the figure of the Ku-Klux, were using terror, intimidation, and violence to suppress black southerners and their local white supporters and to resist what they understood as their own suppression by the Republican-controlled federal government. Wherever a particular reader's sympathy lay, the Klan narrative was useful.

Even so, the terms of the schematic offered by the Klan would be contested during national debates from 1868 through 1872. Northerners and southerners, Democrats and Republicans, debated whether the Klan represented both elite and low-class whites, or just one or the other; whether accounts of Klan violence were accurate, exaggerated, or fabricated; whether freedmen's behavior warranted or even necessitated such violent suppression; and whether southern whites' support of the Klan warranted or even necessitated the federal government's violent suppression. The debates circulating around the Klan offered a vocabulary through which Americans engaged these difficult issues regarding the state of the postwar South.

Newspaper readers found this construction compelling, particularly as they began to doubt the effectiveness of Reconstruction. The figure of the Ku-Klux assigned blame for Reconstruction's failures to an "innately depraved," unreasonable, and violent white South rather than to an incompetent and corrupt North.[2] Thinking of southern racial violence as organized lent a potentially reassuring order to the stories of southern violence that appeared regularly in northern papers. Anyone concerned about freedmen's prospects in the South found plenty of evidence in newspapers in 1866 and 1867 that former Confederates were using violence to dominate, oppress, and dispossess them, and plenty of reasons to suspect that the federal response was lacking.[3] Where federal troops were already stationed, they could sometimes intervene, though they were thinly spread at the best of times and usually could act only when they received distant orders. Local Republicans could request troops, but troops could hardly be deployed to every scene even of endemic violence against freedmen. Because collective, deadly violence was by no means unique to the South, it was controversial to claim that a given instance of violence was a political rather than a regular criminal matter, and to reach a consensus that troops were appropriate. With the crude record-keeping and analysis available in the 1860s and 1870s, it was difficult even to make an evidentiary argument that this violence had a meaningful pattern: that it was occurring disproportionately in the South or disproportionately against freedpeople. The Ku-Klux label provided an effective means through which accounts of individual acts of the violent oppression of freedpeople could become more than anecdotes, aggregating into a systematic, and therefore potentially political issue.

The cultural preference for framing southern violence as Klan violence reflected a tendency toward conspiracy theories. Imputing a hidden centralized structure to a body of seemingly disconnected events did for mid-nineteenth-century Americans some of the social synthesis and analysis that would soon be done by the social sciences. As society had become more integrated and organized, as print and commercial culture had become more national, and as the federal government had begun to exercise more centralized power, similar social behaviors cropped up across large regions in ways that suggested some common cause. One way to understand and respond to this coalescence of behaviors was to see it as the result of an intentional conspiracy.

Ian Hacking has pointed out that in this period "categories had to be invented into which people could conveniently fall in order to be counted." Hacking was referring to census categories, but the Ku-Klux also served as such an organizing category, making instances of antifreedman violence legible not only to the state but to a national newspaper readership.[4] The framework that Michael Walsh offered had offered made the January 1868 attack in Pulaski readable not just as another story of sensational violence, but also as a story that invited a large-scale political response.

This chapter traces the circulation of ideas about the Ku-Klux Klan primarily as it appeared in four major urban northern newspapers—the *Chicago Times* (Democratic), the *Milwaukee Daily Sentinel* (Republican, supported Grant in 1872), the *New York Times* (moderate Republican, supported Grant in 1872), and the *New York Tribune* (Republican, supported its editor, Greeley, in 1872) from 1867 through 1872 (it omits the *Chicago Times* of 1872). Together these papers published more than three thousand articles mentioning the Ku-Klux by name before 1873. Considering when and how northern papers chose to tell stories about the Klan unpacks the interest of the Klan story to northerners. Far from passive observers, northern papers played a crucial role in the shaping and proliferation of the idea of the Klan.

WHEN THE IDEA of the Ku-Klux migrated from central Tennessee to a national context, it changed as much as any person moving from small-town Tennessee to northern urban cultural centers would have done. No longer monolithic or shaped by a single group of friends, in the national press the Ku-Klux idea found itself part of many new contexts and relations. Men and women of different political orientations, histories, and interests competed with one another to define it, and it emerged as a complex and inconsistent product of all of these influences. Over the next few years, the thing Frank and Luther McCord and their associates had made would be fought over bitterly, and would bring, in large and small ways, figures as diverse as famed Civil War generals Benjamin Butler, Ulysses S. Grant, William T. Sherman, and Nathan Bedford Forrest, cultural figures like Harriet Beecher Stowe and Thomas Nast, and politicians like Carl Schurz and Alexander Stephens. It even traveled abroad, arousing particular interest in Great Britain, making it onto their popular stage, and ultimately inspiring a Sherlock Holmes story.[5]

Aside from a few scattered mentions in 1867, the Ku-Klux's long run of frequent coverage in the national press began with an article about the killing of Orange Rhodes in the *New York Tribune* on January 18, 1868. The writer of the *Tribune* piece had likely encountered the story through reporting of the event in Nashville papers, probably the *Nashville Press and Times*. The Pulaski riot had all of the elements necessary to catch the eye of an editor: on January 18, 1868, the *Tribune* reprinted Michael Walsh's letter under the headline "The Pulaski Riots: Tennessee Chivalry Fighting for Miscegenation." The next few days saw a new attack, this time in Linnville, just outside Pulaski, in which white men whipped three black men on a Saturday night. The *Tribune* picked this up, and on January 20 ran a story, which replaced the "riot" frame with a "gang" frame, "The 'Ku-klux' Gang Again." Events might have unfolded quite differently if nineteenth-century Americans had categorized violent rural antiblack, anti-Republican southern groups together with urban street toughs, but it was not to be. The same day, the *New York Times* published its first Ku-Klux story, this time using the term "organization," which would prove to be much more persistent than "riot" or "gang": "The Ku-Klux Klan. The Rebel Organization in Tennessee—Its Outrages upon Unoffending Men." This story was on the Linnville whippings, and was sourced from the *Press and Times*. The next day, the *Milwaukee Daily Sentinel* also published a version of the *Press and Times* piece titled "A Dangerous Organization."[6]

"Organization" would be the category that stuck. Descriptions of the Klan in the national press would consistently emphasize the Klan's coordination and discipline over, say, the thuggish nature of its members (which the term "gang" might invite) or the savage frenzy of their violence (which would be evoked by the term "riot"). The Ku-Klux was born into the national press fully formed: the article reprinted in the *Milwaukee Sentinel* and the *New York Times* had the Ku-Klux embracing "nearly all the young men of rebel proclivities" in Maury and Giles Counties and fulfilling its plans of "terrorizing the whole region, and rendering the lives and the property of Union Men unsafe."[7] The newspapers emphasized their paramilitary nature; the men of the Giles and Marshall Ku-Klux were armed with navy revolvers and "were commanded by a major and lieutenant, the men obeying their leaders as though they were in a regular military organization."[8]

These earliest stories outlined the Ku-Klux as Americans would come to understand it. They emphasized what would remain the two essential qualities of the Ku-Klux idea: it was violent, and it was organized. Already present in many of the earliest narratives was the theme that the Klan's power rested on a dangerous combination of physical violence and a hidden but highly effective infrastructure. It was one of the insights of the mid-nineteenth century to appreciate that the danger of such actors lay more in the latter than the former. The men who shot Orange Rhodes and his companions had committed acts of violence, and it was important that they be arrested, but they also had a secret organization that had been orchestrating violence behind the scenes; this larger entity is what Walsh had called to the serious attention of his superiors, and what had merited national coverage. The acts of violence were as much maps to or signals from the underlying structures as they were problems in themselves. The Ku-Klux, "a mysterious organization . . . whose members prowl at night in close disguise," was fueled by frustrated southern nationalism, "a latent fire, ever ready to burst forth in all its native violence."[9] Reporting on the Klan over the next few years would continue to toggle between accounts of acts of violence and ambitious claims about and explorations of the nature of the underlying conspiracy.

The small flurry of introductory Ku-Klux coverage in January was followed by nine days of silence; the idea of the Ku-Klux could simply have disappeared then. But in February it began to metastasize. Beyond whatever internal impetus for growth may have been operating in and around Giles, northern newspaper coverage promised national attention, providing a powerful incentive for the Ku-Klux to become even more active. In making anti-Republican violence a more powerful, consequential act, national coverage encouraged locals to label violent acts "Ku-Klux" acts and motivated some to commit violence against freedmen or white Republicans rather than using their energies and resources in other ways. For a young former Confederate in Giles or Maury County lacking in empathy, morally flexible, and inclined to violence and risk-taking, committing a Ku-Klux attack would have become a very interesting opportunity. As northern urban papers turned their attention to the South, enterprising Middle Tennessee editors searched vigorously for Ku-Klux stories. Local officials kept a sharp lookout for Ku-Klux violence. Tennessee politicians within a few weeks began to evoke the Ku-Klux in speeches: it was appropriate that they should do so in the face of government and newspaper reports, but it was also an opportunity for relevance, and a promising practical angle from which to approach these previously inchoate acts of violence. The discussion of the Ku-Klux in the Tennessee legislature generated still more coverage through the month, which likely inspired more Ku-Klux acts and made these acts more visible.

The new round of coverage began on January 31, when the *Milwaukee Daily Sentinel* picked up a *Press and Times* story that Ku-Klux were harassing and threatening black people along the Shelbyville Pike to vote the Democratic ticket.[10] The following day, the *Sentinel* published another *Press and Times* story about Ku-Klux attacks on freedmen in adjoining Marshall County.[11] The Ku-Klux's reported geographic extent began to increase in the following weeks as Ku-Klux violence occurred in and near Nashville and in other Middle Tennessee counties. Even Democratic newspapers, which had ignored the Ku-Klux during the first two months of national Republican coverage, relented and began to cover it lightly in March. While the *Chicago Times*, *New York Times*, *New York Tribune*, and *Milwaukee Daily Sentinel* together published only five stories mentioning the Ku-Klux in January, they published ten in February, thirty-one in March, and seventy-six in April.[12]

While the idea of the Ku-Klux gained ground in the papers, the Klan was also coming to the attention of local, state, and national governments. In April 1868, Hiram C. Whitley, just then in the early stages of transforming his wartime clandestine operations into the Secret Service, received orders to get to the bottom of this newly threatening Ku-Klux.[13] That same month, federal troops took note of and began to take practical measures intended to inhibit the Ku-Klux.[14] State governments also

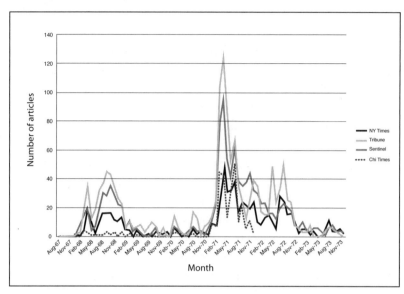

FIGURE 1. The number of articles in which "ku-klux," "kuklux," or "klan" appeared per month in four major newspapers, 1868–1873.

sprang into action. In July 1868 Tennessee became the first state to hold a public hearing on the matter.[15] Alabama followed in November 1868.[16] This high-level response lent the incipient Klan a new significance. As governments responded, Ku-Klux press mentions continued their dramatic increase.

Four Themes in Northern Ku-Klux Stories

While editors wrote in different places for different audiences and interpreted the Ku-Klux through their own experiences and commitments, they also regularly reprinted and responded to pieces from the papers of their political allies and opponents. Heavily interconnected, despite the quirks of their editors, newspapers participated in the same conversation, a single complex narrative with its own timing, emergent themes, and arc. Ku-Klux articles shared a distinctive chronology and regularly returned to the same four themes: the nature of Klan attacks, Klan organization and scope, the role of the Klan in partisan politics, and the government's efforts to suppress the Klan.

Newspaper interest in each of these four themes varied dramatically over time, and was not always as one would expect. Of the 3,356 articles in the database through the end of 1872, under a third (only 899) described or mentioned a specific activity of a Klan, whether an attack or another form of public display. Almost half of the articles (1,629), however, discussed the Klan in explicit relationship to either partisanship or federal or state government (that is, they discussed congressional or legislative debates or lawmaking related to the Klan, the merits of the laws proposed or passed, or the Klan's relationship to partisan conflict). When articles about arrests, trials, imprisonments, or pardons of Ku-Klux are included in the category of stories about the Ku-Klux's relationship to the government, the total rises to 1991, well over half of all articles. Articles about the Klan were, on the whole, much more likely to be talking about the Klan's relationship to the government than the Klan's relationship to freedpeople.

The most dramatic result of breaking down newspaper Ku-Klux mentions thematically is that Klan victims took up surprisingly little real estate. The bulk of articles mentioning the Ku-Klux, even in these first months of national attention, neither described nor even directly mentioned acts of Ku-Klux violence or their victims. A substantial minority of them did, of course, and even where they did not, violence was at the logical center of concerns about the Klan, implicit where it was not explicit. Of the forty-six stories that appeared in those first three months of 1868, sixteen included a narrative of an act or acts of Ku-Klux violence. The others focused on state response or on the question of the Klan's nature and extent.

These "outrage stories" largely conformed to a generic pattern.[17] They briefly named and described victims, gave a brief and sensationalist description of the violence, and usually stated that perpetrators were unknown. For instance, a mid-February article in the *Milwaukee Daily Sentinel* reprinted from the *Nashville Press and Times* reported that a "desperado guerilla" and "rebel soldier" named Aiken had killed an "inoffensive negro man" named Hogg in Marshall County.[18] The *Sentinel* described the attack as "politically motivated," and both the *Sentinel* and *Tribune* asserted that the Ku-Klux would protect Aiken from arrest. On March 10, the *Milwaukee Daily Sentinel* (now reprinting stories from the *Nashville Banner*) reported that the Ku-Klux had captured and lynched a man as the murderer of a presumed Ku-Klux member named John Bicknell; a week later, the *Tribune* gave the lynching victim's name, Walker, and added that he had confessed to the murders of Bicknell and another man before Ku-Klux killed him.[19] Stories in the *Sentinel* and *Times* reported an attack outside Memphis in which a costumed young white man named Henry C. Blair and two others attacked a freedman named Bob Brenner at his home. Brenner shot and killed Blair in self-defense.[20]

Sometimes, particularly where they were drawing from trial transcripts or testimony, news stories gave lengthy accounts of acts of Klan violence, written in the convention of sensational crime reporting.[21]

> They . . . jumped in upon him and beat his head with a pistol, cutting a gash half an inch wide, four inches long, and to the skull. They asked him for fire arms, which he said he had not. They then took him into a field and whipped him so badly that they nearly killed him. They also tore up everything in the house, and then went to his son's house, took him from his bed, smashed a large looking glass over the head of his sick wife who was in bed. They whipped the man with stirrup straps and buckles, which cut long and deep gashes into the flesh. . . . They called him a liar and threatened to hang him. . . . His wife, who was in a critical condition, screamed and pleaded for him, and begged them to spare him on her account. . . . One of them caught him by the hair, jerked him in the face in a most shocking manner, at the same time holding a pistol to his head and threatening to shoot him. Then they left him in an almost insensible condition, scarcely able to crawl to his house.

These articles usually gave details about the violence itself, rather than about attackers or victims, or the social context in which the attack occurred. They rarely described victims of Ku-Klux violence beyond giving their names, locality, gender, race, often their political orientation, and perhaps a shorthand term for their local reputation, such as "inoffensive" or "industrious." They described perpetrators in even less detail: the corporate identity "Ku-Klux" made further inquiry into the individual identities of attackers not only apparently impossible but seemingly irrelevant within the context of the story. All the above story tells us about the attackers is that they were Ku-Klux. It went on to explain that the victim, Joshua Ferrell, was an old and quiet man, had no firearms, and described himself as "a big feeling nigger, votes for Brownlow, and belonged to the Union League, a Union man, and always had been."[22]

Similarly, readers learned little about Freedmen's Bureau agent Colonel Allen Huggins, who was "assaulted by 120 Ku-klux, severely whipped, left in a half-killed condition, and ordered to leave the county."[23] Nor did they learn much about victims in reports like this: "Another band of Ku-klux prowled about till daybreak, committing numerous outrages on colored people. They beat eleven freedmen almost to death, fractured the arm of one, and shot another quite dead. They also beat most cruelly a bright mulatto girl, sixteen years old, and when insensible and almost dead, four of the fiends in succession outraged her person." The story reveals nothing of the attackers except that they were Ku-Klux, and nothing of the victims but their race, gender, and previous condition of slavery, and the age and skin tone of the girl beaten and raped.[24]

This sparseness was generic to newspaper accounts of violent attacks, particularly those in urban papers: stories circulating translocally could not carry much local context. But such stories closed the door to competing interpretations of Ku-Klux attacks. If the only information known about a victim was race, gender, party, and inoffensiveness, the reader would be unable to consider the possible relevance of religious, economic, personal, or other potential factors in shaping Ku-Klux violence. Structurally embedded in most descriptions of Ku-Klux attacks was the assumption that their meanings were fundamentally related to national, partisan politics.

When articles gave little space to descriptions of the attacks themselves, they sometimes focused on issues like the Ku-Klux's organization. Interest in the Ku-Klux's organizational structure was part of a larger intellectual fascination with secret organizations and conspiracies that had begun in antebellum years. David Brion Davis and others appropriated Richard Hofstadter's "paranoid style" to describe the Civil War era several decades ago. Newspapers and other popular texts had for decades described how crimes in the city, diligently investigated, revealed a robust underworld.[25] Secession, it was widely believed, had been the product of the manipulation and coercion of southern popular opinion by organized and secret bands.[26] As visible organizations, from businesses to voluntary societies, were expanding and becoming more sophisticated, many believed that the criminal and antisocial were doing likewise. Ku-Klux members, in producing the Prescript and making great claims to the press, eagerly asked to be understood in that way. From the beginning, newspapers approached the Ku-Klux largely as an organizational puzzle.

Arguing over the nature and extent of the Ku-Klux's organization was crucial to the national partisan divide on the Ku-Klux. As stories of the Ku-Klux percolated up from local communities and offered themselves for inclusion in the national discourse, Democrats grabbed at those that suggested an organization less robust and political and Republicans at those that suggested one more robust and political. While both Democrats and Republicans generally acknowledged that rural southern Republicans suffered violence at the hands of their white

Democratic neighbors, they disagreed about whether and how that violence was organized. Democrats often simply denied reported instances of Ku-Klux violence, but they were as likely to claim that the violence was a criminal or personal matter unconnected to any "Ku-Klux." Republican newspaper articles, in contrast, exposed and elaborated the Ku-Klux's associational qualities: its organization, leadership, membership, and extent. This could take the form of reports that the Ku-Klux had spread to a given place; estimates of the Ku-Klux's numbers; assertions that the Ku-Klux had a centralized leadership; names of leaders; or claims that they secretly controlled certain presses or certain politicians or that they were using the Democratic Party as an organizational structure. Both Democratic and Republican papers frequently came back to the question of Ku-Klux organization: Democratic papers to deny or trivialize it, Republican to establish and describe it.

In previous chapters we have seen how Ku-Klux groups emphasized their own organization and the relative solitude of their immediate victims during attacks—indeed, organization was one of the key qualities that differentiated "Ku-Klux" violence from other acts of violence in popular consciousness. Conventionally, federal political officials and the national press used the "Ku-Klux" label only for violence that was committed by groups structured in a certain way. With few exceptions, a Ku-Klux attack could not be committed by a lone sniper, by two partners in crime, by a public assembly of individuals informed through the local newspapers to gather, or by a spontaneous group of neighbors brought together in response to an alleged atrocity. The national press, like federal officials, Ku-Klux supporters, and Ku-Klux victims, consistently portrayed Klans as private groups, continuous over time, with a leadership structure and with members who were bound to one another by ties of friendship and loyalty.

Stories stressing organization were important from the beginning of coverage. The *New York Times* in February 1868 described the Ku-Klux as supported by the Conservative Party, "number[ing] in the thousands," and, in some places, "having a complete and thorough organization" and having "already commenced operations."[27] A March *Richmond Whig* story reprinted in the *New York Times* introduced a "band of armed men who are styled 'Ku-Klux'" and noted, "it appears that the organization is wide spread and the civil authorities powerless."[28] Newspapers had a particular fascination with secret organizational elements, like rituals, handshakes, distress signals, and the titles of officers. More dramatic than simply stopping a Ku-Klux attack was capturing a copy of a membership list.

Many Republican newspaper accounts of Ku-Klux's structure, organization, and extent were patent exaggerations. Later accounts of Ku-Klux organization, like early ones in Pulaski, often stretched the limits of plausibility in their accounts of Klan organization, size, and discipline. For instance, an 1871 *New York Tribune* article recounted claims that at least 2,100 of the 2,300 white voters in York County were Ku-Klux members, at least 1,000 of whom could be mobilized by their chief within twenty-four hours, uniformed and mounted, and "as thoroughly obedient to his command as disciplined soldiers." These men were organized into at least forty-five dens, each with its own chief, lieutenant, and two or three nighthawks (communications officers). There was reason to believe that they were armed with Winchester repeating rifles from New York, purchased "with funds raised there for the purpose." The chiefs maintained tight discipline over them through "severe" physical punishment. The article's source, Major Lewis Merrill, claimed that Spartanburg had a similar Ku-Klux organization and that they had gone so far as to establish a public whipping post for disobedient Ku-Klux. So effective was York County's disciplinary regime, according to Merrill, that when five hundred armed and mounted men assembled in the nearby town of Unionville, raided the jail, and executed ten men, "citizens who were not Ku-klux had no knowledge of the presence of this great body of armed men in the little village."[29]

This account of the Klan in the South Carolina Upcountry imagines an intensity and effectiveness of social organization arguably without historical parallel. It is in even more striking tension with historians' understandings of the particularly limited capacity for social organization of early postwar southerners. While this article was one of the more dramatically overimagined, it was not unique. Even articles that did not describe impossibly ambitious organizational elements directly often imputed a startling level of centralization and effectiveness to Ku-Klux groups, claiming that Ku-Klux could do things like secretly control the Associated Press wire service or the national Democratic Party.[30]

The irony of newspapers' orientation away from directly describing acts of violence and toward organizational infrastructure is that, while there was plenty of antifreedman violence to be explained and the idea of the Ku-Klux was a pragmatic way to set about explaining it, there never was much Ku-Klux organizational infrastructure to reveal and understand. While there were more ambitious efforts to organize in Pulaski (as chapter 1 discusses) and in parts of the Carolinas (we will see more about this in chapters 6 and 7), journalists and investigators then and historians since have failed to find substantial evidence that Ku-Klux groups had anything approaching the elaborate organization these more ambitious accounts suggest. In looking through the acts of violence to the reality beneath it, contemporaries were pushing aside what demanded explanation to get to what could only elude.

Just as they articulated the Klan's organization, these stories also explored, and generously represented, the geographic extent of the Ku-Klux. For the first few weeks of national coverage, accounts consistently placed the Ku-Klux in Tennessee. Other than the scattered mentions in December referred to earlier, the first report I have found of the Ku-Klux's spread out of Tennessee was on March 24, 1868, when the *New York Times* reported that Ku-Klux notices had appeared in Wilmington, North Carolina.[31] The following day, the Ku-Klux made an appearance in central Mississippi.[32] In the next two weeks, a spate of articles established the presence of the Ku-Klux in Georgia.[33] By mid-March the Ku-Klux, refracted through northern newspapers, was spreading through the South, both as a concept and in the form of actual bodies of violent men. The *Tribune* reprinted an article from the *Mobile Register* that described the Ku-Klux as a southern uprising. This would be followed a week later by a *Chicago Times* reprint of a Ku-Klux article from the *Louisville Courier*.[34]

The Klan did not circulate generally through southern papers any earlier than through northern. The vast bulk of southern papers introduced it to their readers only in mid-March. The *New Orleans Sentinel*, for instance, announced on March 12, 1868, that "there seems to be a new political and social organization in Tennessee, known by the queer name of the Ku-Klux-Klan."[35] A few days later, the *Yorkville (S.C.) Enquirer* informed its readers that "Kuklux Klan is the name of a secret organization which is extending rapidly throughout the north and west, and is striking terror into the Loyal Leaguers."[36]

Soon after stories reported the Ku-Klux's spread to other parts of the South, they noted its proliferation in the North. At the end of March 1868, the *Tribune* reported the creation of a Ku-Klux in Phillipsburg, New Jersey.[37] This would be the first of many claims that the Ku-Klux had spread not only to border states like Missouri and Kentucky, but to the heart of the North. An article in April speculated that the Ku-Klux had actually been founded by a southerner in New York City.[38] The *Milwaukee Daily Sentinel* similarly claimed that the Ku-Klux had been started in Washington, D.C., and had been spreading through the South and some parts of the North.[39]

A young Democratic "Ku-Klux" assaulted a wounded Republican veteran in Milwaukee.[40] Another outraged a colored citizen of Little Falls, New York.[41] Ku-Klux in hideous black masks with terrifying fake voices attacked a Republican in Long Island and rode him out of town on a rail.[42] Even the *Columbia (S.C.) Daily Phoenix* chimed in, introducing the Ku-Klux to its readers in mid-March as "a conservative secret organization which is extending rapidly throughout the North and West."[43] Nor were reports of Klan violence limited to the United States: the *New York Tribune* jokingly reported that with a lull in Ku-Klux violence, the "Southern Chivalry" might well have turned to supporting a filibustering expedition in Cuba.[44] Surely some of the stories of specific Ku-Klux attacks and appearances in the North were true: given northerners' fascination with the Ku-Klux, it would be surprising to hear that no one had chosen to emulate violent deeds as well as costume. The larger claims about established and expansive organization, however, were deliberate fabrications, creative misreadings, and eager exaggerations.

These generous representations of Ku-Klux organization and extent together suggested that it was, indeed, an "invisible empire," as northern newspapers liked to remind their readers.[45] It comprised a skeletal parastate reaching across the continent, but also beyond. It was a bureaucracy run stealthily but perfectly by powerful and distant men. Normal citizens could neither control nor even understand its complex, opaque, and highly centralized operation. Even Ku-Klux themselves had vanishingly little control over the group they belonged to: newspapers reported that arrested Ku-Klux often claimed no knowledge of the translocal structure of their own organization.[46] The Ku-Klux was imagined to be an expansive and sophisticated entity.

EVEN MORE ARTICLES explored the relationship of this shadowy organization to partisan conflict. Newspaper articles mentioned the Ku-Klux frequently as part of their coverage of partisan competition, citing congressmen's (and, less frequently, state legislators') Ku-Klux-related motions and legislation, and speeches on the floor of Congress and to the public. Republicans, in response to the novel nature of the Ku-Klux's organization, were calling for new structures and tactics in the government itself.[47] Since, as a *New York Times* article about proposed anti-Klan legislation quoted a Republican congressman, "outrages and violence prevail[ed]" and state governments "were powerless to restrain assassination and murder," new means, such as the expansion of federal police power, would have to be employed.[48] Democrats frequently and passionately objected to these proposed new federal projects. When articles focused on Washington, of course, accounts of violence on the ground in the South were pushed out of the story. Many such articles never mentioned violence or victims directly; having framed the debate, the scene of violence receded into the background. For instance, a September 1869 *New York Times* piece, "The Conventions," mentioned that a Republican speaker had given a speech titled "The Klan Is the Rule of Misrule."[49] The Klan, in articles like this, was an idea or a problem available to or hindering politicians attempting to govern, seeking legislative victory, or vying for public support. Set not in the midnight rural South but in the halls of Congress or at political rallies, these stories portrayed the Ku-Klux principally as an occasion for another round of an ongoing power struggle.

Where violence found its way into these Washington-focused accounts, it was usually the barely subdued violence between Republican and Democratic leaders. Papers reported political rhetoric relating to the Ku-Klux as particularly heated; talking about partisan discussion of the Ku-Klux became an important way of talking about the unhealed nation. Readers following Congress would have learned particularly from Ku-Klux coverage about the nuts and bolts of partisan power in postwar Washington: these stories led readers through contentious subcommittee meetings, the scrambles for political alliances before election season, the process of amending bills, and the creative use of arcane parliamentary procedures. They also would have learned that the working of power in Washington was nonconsensual and embedded in threats of personal violence from both sides. Because the Ku-Klux issue was so divisive, it provided a particularly clear view into the tactics of partisan conflict, serving as a distressing civics lesson for newspaper readers.

But when the word "Ku-Klux" appeared in an article between 1868 and 1872, the article most frequently referred to it in the context of broader discussions of the postwar state. The Ku-Klux and responses to it served as a synecdoche for power relations in the postwar South and the broader nation.[50] So when the *Chicago Times* published an article on congressional debate over how to respond to Klan violence, it used the headline "The New Federal System." It titled an article on Klan hearings "The Condition of the South."[51] The Joint Select Committee to Inquire into Affairs in the Late Insurrectionary States came to be popularly referred to as the "Ku-Klux Committee." The Enforcement Acts became "Ku-Klux Acts," and so forth. The term "Ku-Klux," coined in 1866 in small-town

Tennessee, by 1868 had come to frame the behavior of the federal government toward the former Confederacy generally.

Discussing the nature and capacity of the government from the angle of the Ku-Klux Klan opened up new channels of analysis and critique. Articles on the Ku-Klux's relationship to the government discussed its efforts to suppress the Ku-Klux, while highlighting the novelty of some of its tactics and functions. These articles explored the apparent novelty of governmental response to the Ku-Klux threat. The government, these articles repeatedly noted, was growing in size, pervasiveness, capability, and scope. This growth was characterized, in particular, by a dramatic increase in two capacities: the use of force, and the gathering of information (by means both visible and clandestine).

Southern Democratic papers began a constant cycle of complaint about the excesses of federal response to the Klan as early as April 1868.[52] These critiques first coalesced around opposition to North Carolina governor William Woods Holden's anti-Klan strategies. Beginning in late 1869, when papers showed bemusement at Holden's decision to set out to arm "negro militias" to suppress the Klan, national critique, largely in Republican papers, grew to a storm by mid-1870, when he brought in George W. Kirk to lead his efforts.[53] Kirk, who had been a Union cavalry leader during the war, had a particular reputation for violence; to call him to action was seemingly to import wartime tactics to peacetime.[54] The *Chicago Times* chose not to jump into the Kirk-Holden controversy, saying very little about the Klan or government suppression of it through 1869 and 1870 except to suggest that black and white Radicals were committing violence in their name, including the violence that justified Holden's response.[55]

National Klan suppression efforts were facing opposition by 1870 and 1871 as well. The term the Democrats applied to the Enforcement Acts was "the Force Bill." Southern Democrats made shocking allegations about the federal government's use of power. A speech by William S. Groesbeck of Ohio reprinted in the *Chicago Times* in September 1871 was one of countless suggesting that federal initiatives against the Klan were in fact intended to institute permanent martial law in place of our Democratic government, first in the South, then in the North.[56] The outrage would reach a peak with the campaign of 1872, as Greeley made Grant's alleged overreaching central to his campaign. In mid-1872 the *Tribune* reprinted a lengthy and passionate letter about the oppression of the southern people at the hands of the federal government: "This is the use now made of the U.S. army . . . to break into houses in the dead of night, drag from their beds to jail unsuspecting citizens, frighten women and children, and break up labor."[57] A few months later, the *Tribune* referred to the acts of revenue officials in southern counties as "terrorism."[58]

NEWSPAPER KU-KLUX coverage was likely to cover the government's tactics of investigation as their new uses of violence. As the government developed strategies to tear the mask off private covert groups, papers noted that the government's investigative apparatus was itself covert. The Klan was the subject of several innovative tactics in state-sponsored detection. Some of this was at the state level. Kentucky and Mississippi, for instance, made news with their plans to create a secret police to counter the Ku-Klux. A J. J. Gainey, who had gained experience in this capacity in Mississippi, sent a letter to South Carolina's governor asking for a detective position: "I am aware that you are suffering from the misdeeds of a certain clan known as Ku Klux, an organization that I detest and have sworn to eliminate and which I have assisted in exterminating in this state."[59] Among the many controversial moves of North Carolina governor Holden was his employment of detectives.[60] And as chapter 7 discusses, detectives were very much in use in South Carolina as well. But more newspaper coverage related to the federal government's use of detectives, incognito marshals, and "Secret Government Agents." This was a story well worth telling: when Hiram Whitley was asked to use his emerging agency to get to the bottom of the Ku-Klux, it was one of the first major peacetime assignments for the group that would become the Secret Service. The idea of the Ku-Klux shaped and encouraged the rise of the Secret Service, providing it a purpose.[61] Stories about federal secret agents abounded in the newspaper coverage. Federal marshals in North Carolina disguised themselves as tobacco merchants to infiltrate a Klan in Moore County. The most famous of the detective stories was that of the disappearance and presumed murder, in 1868, of Detective Barmore in Tennessee, allegedly killed by the Klan group he was sent to infiltrate.[62] In general, the new Department of Justice, the *Tribune* claimed, had an information-gathering system that was startling in its efficiency.[63]

Others of the federal government's experiments in information-gathering were not clandestine. Congress's controversial decision in 1871 to appoint bipartisan subcommittees to travel to Klan-afflicted areas to investigate in person was quite public, though there was debate about when and whether to release testimony transcripts. In sending out committees, the federal government mirrored recent state innovations: the Alabama legislature, for instance, had sent out committees to gather Ku-Klux information in 1868.[64] Yet this was a novel exercise of federal power and served as a concrete symbol of the federal government's entry into local communities, not with guns but with stenographers.

Republican newspapers were basically supportive of state anti-Klan information-gathering measures. The *New York Times* was most firm in supporting the legality and appropriateness of government sleuthing, having little patience for Democrats' "noisy professions of solicitude for the ancient liberties guaranteed by the organic law" while they supported Ku-Klux, "aggressors against all legitimate authority."[65] Yet even Republicans took claims of government overreach seriously enough that they invested considerable space in addressing them. They published Attorney General Akerman's scrupulous explanation of the legality of the anti-Klan proceedings he presided over: "Care was taken to clear the proceedings, which were unavoidably summary and severe, of every touch of cruelty, or indeed harshness."[66]

The Ku-Klux in the Democratic Press

Democratic papers chose to discuss the Klan considerably less frequently than Republican papers did. Of the articles that mentioned the Klan in the *Chicago Times* from 1868 to 1871, only 43 mentioned or described a Klan act. Republican papers generally began to report on the Klan two months before their Democratic peers, and they would publish stories with much greater frequency throughout. From 1868 to 1871, for instance, the *Chicago Times* published only 287 stories mentioning the Ku-Klux; during the same period, the *Milwaukee Daily Sentinel* published 862, the *New York Times* 465, and the *New York Tribune* 1,068. The *Times* did, however, increase its coverage of the Klan dramatically during the enhanced coverage beginning after the 1870 elections. If the strategy of the Democratic papers during the first burst of Klan coverage in 1868 was to ride it out in relative silence, the *Times*, at least, chose to participate substantially in the second, part of a broader pattern on the part of Democratic papers. By 1871 Democratic newspapers chose to talk with much greater frequency about the Klan.

When they did mention the Ku-Klux, Democratic and Republican papers had different emphases and often different conclusions. While

Republican newspapers sometimes allowed themselves to express cautious concern that governmental efforts to suppress the Ku-Klux were excessive or that the Ku-Klux were worthy of pity, Democrats' criticism and empathy were naturally more pointed and direct. Democratic papers were particularly critical of investigations by the traveling congressional committee.[67] The *Chicago Times*, like other Democratic papers, complained that Ku-Klux testimony had been gathered and was being used primarily for partisan purposes. After the Ku-Klux Committee sent off their two thousand pages of testimony to the press, the *Chicago Times* sarcastically claimed, they carefully preserved the stereotypes for use in campaign documents.[68]

In 1871, Horace Greeley left the mainstream Republican Party to run against Grant with Democratic support. His Liberal Republican *Tribune*, around the time of his move, dramatically shifted its posture toward state suppression of the Klan, which it had previously defended. The *Chicago Times* throughout, and, beginning in late 1871, the *New York Tribune*, were filled with stories condemning Grant's imposition of "military rule." The *Chicago Times* reprinted and glossed Democratic political speeches that claimed that the Ku-Klux bill was part of a larger program to subordinate civil to military law, first in the South and then in the North.[69] It described a state of terror that had descended on southern communities: families desperately fled, it claimed, as federal officials roamed the county making mass Enforcement Act arrests.[70] A November 1871 article in the *New York Tribune* contrasted Major Merrill's policy of immediately releasing low-level Ku-Klux to the policy, in Spartanburg, of jailing them: "The latter is hard upon men who were forced into the order, or who joined it solely to save themselves from apprehended violence or death. Not a few Republicans, despairing of protection from the Government, became Ku-klux." The article deplored the poor conditions of the "disgustingly filthy" prison, and the poverty and ignorance of the prisoners. It quoted one "feeble old man": "It's mighty hard for a rheumatic old man like me to lie on the hard floor these cold nights with nothing but a blanket under me." It sympathetically quoted another Ku-Klux arrestee complaining that the hardest part of the ordeal was being forced into association with the criminals in the prison.[71] As the election of 1872 approached, the rhetoric got fiercer: Democratic and Liberal Republican papers accused Grant of using forces in the South to control the election.[72]

Stories of Klan attacks in the *Chicago Times* differed from those told in the *New York Times*, *New York Tribune*, and *Milwaukee Daily Sentinel* in several ways. Most strikingly, the *Chicago Times* rarely mentioned or described any attack of a white Democrat on a Republican. When the *Chicago Times* mentioned a specific act of violence, it was typically in order to refer to it as a hoax or to claim that the disguised attackers were actually black men or white Republicans.[73] When the paper did describe a violent attack by Democratic Ku-Klux, it often claimed the attack had been justified by the victim's vicious behavior. For instance, in July 1868 it reprinted a story from the *Nashville Banner* that described a group of three hundred uniformed Ku-Klux killing a black man named William Gustine who allegedly had raped a white girl, and another from the *Richmond (Ky.) Register* claiming that the Ku-Klux was avenging Civil War–era murders.[74] Democratic papers were also much more likely to include stories of Klan failure and ineptitude. The first Klan attack the *Chicago Times* covered was the attack by Ku-Klux Henry Blair on freedman Bob Brenner, during which Brenner killed Blair in self-defense. Similarly, it published a story of a Klan group captured by its would-be victims, forced to give up its costumes and horses, and left in the awkward position of trying to ask for their horses back.[75] The *Chicago Times*, that is, frequently either denied Ku-Klux violence or published stories about it that interrupted key Republican claims: Ku-Klux were not threatening, not Democrats, not white. Victims were neither worthy nor helpless. Moreover, because they were denying the existence of an organized and structured Klan, Democratic papers did not themselves describe Ku-Klux structure, organization, or extent.

Democratic papers sometimes found themselves not only refuting Republican Ku-Klux narratives, but reproducing them. Particularly when a story reached some level of saturation in the public consciousness or when the federal government was closely involved in eliciting and publicizing it, the *Chicago Times* did include accounts of conventional Ku-Klux attacks in its pages. For instance, it reprinted at great length the *New York Tribune*'s account of the Union County jail abductions and other attacks in South Carolina. Though for much of 1871 the *Tribune*'s position on the Ku-Klux was still radically different from Democrats', the *Tribune* had reporters in the area and therefore had privileged access to a story that had gained considerable public attention because of its enormous scale and bloodiness.[76] The *Chicago Times* also was more likely to mention conventional Ku-Klux attacks in the context of its coverage of the federal government. This sort of Washington-driven Klan reporting would become most substantial beginning in 1871, when suppressing the Ku-Klux became central to the daily concerns of the federal government. The *Chicago Times*,

like the *New York Times*, the *Sentinel*, and the *Tribune*, regularly printed partial daily summaries of congressional business that it received through
an exchange service, and sometimes these summaries included accounts
of specific acts of Ku-Klux violence. For example, as part of their coverage of congressional debates, the *Chicago Times* reprinted Butler's claim
that Ku-Klux had taken seven black men from jail in Georgia and cut off
their ears.[77] Once the congressional Ku-Klux committees began taking
and publishing vast quantities of Klan-related testimony in mid-1871,
the *Chicago Times* took regular note of it. It published far less of it than
the Republican papers did, and it covered the testimony of Democratic
Ku-Klux deniers far more than that of alleged Klan victims, yet the paper
did include and summarize testimony of victims. Thus, largely through
the congressional hearings, conventional Ku-Klux attack narratives regularly made it into the Democratic partisan press.[78]

Analogy

Newspaper articles frequently analogized the Klan to entities of the state
and federal governments. Examples of this can be found as early as March
1868, when the *New York Tribune* suggested that the Ohio Democratic
leadership, in its parliamentary maneuvering, was acting like Ku-Klux.[79]
As this first example anticipates, one of the most common Ku-Klux/
government analogies compared the Klan to the Democratic Party. The
authors of these analogies intended to delegitimize Democrats and
therefore to legitimize the Republican-dominated federal government. In
August 1868 the *New York Times* referred to the Ku-Klux as the Democratic
Party's "right hand."[80] In November 1871, it reprinted a speech describing the Democratic Party as "a corpse with two living arms: Tammany in
North and Klan in South."[81] Most of these claims suggested, in essence,
that the Democratic Party was willing to use violence to gain its political ends—that it used "Ku-klux tactics" to gain and maintain political power.[82] The party was ready to appeal to force in Kentucky, seeing
it as their only hope.[83] To the Democrats, Ku-Kluxing was politics as
usual.[84] Newspapers gleefully reprinted Republican accusations that
Democrats Hampton, Kershaw, and Butler were on an "advisory board"
to the South Carolina Ku-Klux.[85] The connection between Ku-Klux and
the Democratic Party often slipped between figurative analogies, indirect
associations, and literal claims of a supportive relationship or even identity. The Wisconsin Democratic Party was the "Ku-Klux" party because

their interests depended on the suppression of southern black voters; the Alabama Democratic Party was the "Ku-Klux" because the leaders of the party and the Klan were one and the same.[86] While some such claims were extensive and well-articulated, others were simple unsubstantiated slurs. This phrase "Ku-Klux Democracy" became so common, particularly in election seasons, that it must have come to feel natural to readers. Yet this strategy could backfire on Republicans. Democrats, though the minority party, had significant power in the federal government. They were also structurally equivalent to the Republican Party. If they were Ku-Klux-like, it cast a shadow on the government itself. Newspapers yield hundreds of examples of this broader analogy.

In April 1868, the *New York Tribune* reported that four congressional pages had dressed as Ku-Klux to scare a black man who sold cakes and pies in the basement of the Capitol. They succeeded in terrifying him, going so far as putting a rope around his neck.[87] Whether one chooses to read their act as simply a cruel prank or as indistinguishable from an actual Ku-Klux attack, the pages thought it was a fitting thing to do, and a major urban newspaper found it interesting enough to cover. In a complex but persistent way, the Ku-Klux and the federal government were tethered together in the popular mind.

The *New York Tribune*, in an article about a dispute over election results in Ohio in March 1868, described Republican senators as behaving like bloodthirsty Ku-Klux.[88] In September 1868 the *Sentinel* reprinted a story that Kentucky governor Thomas E. Bramlette was the "chief of the Ku-klux."[89] Quite frequently, when papers connected the Klan to a state or local government, they evoked New York City's notoriously corrupt and back-room-dealing Tammany Hall. The *Tribune* referred to New York City government, particularly the Democrats who dominated it, as "the kk gang who rule this city" or the "domestic Ku-klux."[90] The *Milwaukee Daily Sentinel* referred to the New York City government as the "Tammany Ku-klux."[91]

Papers sometimes approached the analogy from the other direction, describing the Ku-Klux as though it were equivalent to or operating as formal government or government entity. Representative Job Stevenson made a widely quoted speech in which he described the Ku-Klux as "the most powerful political machine ever invented."[92] An article in the *Milwaukee Daily Sentinel* argued that the South was not a republic but a despotism because Ku-Klux violence oppressed the people and deprived them of their civil rights.[93] Even if it was not yet acting like a government, the Ku-Klux was positioning itself in direct competition with formal government.[94] In 1868 the Ku-Klux was supposedly plotting to seize power from the federal government; in later years, state governments were its purported targets. The *New York Tribune* reprinted a piece from the *Little Rock Republican* worrying that attempts to impeach the governor of Arkansas were "for the avowed purpose of . . . turning the state over to the . . . old Ku-Klux Klan and White Chameleons [sic]."[95] Similarly, Republican papers regularly defined those who were working to impeach Holden as "the Ku-klux."[96]

THE LOGICAL CONCLUSION of this mass of rhetoric associating the Klan with governmental entities was that the federal government was itself like the Ku-Klux. This analogy was often, but by no means always, a Democratic (or, by late 1871, a Liberal Republican) insult. It emerged in the earliest days of Klan discourse: the *National Intelligencer*, in the spring of 1868, suggested an interpretation of some of the earliest Ku-Klux notices circulating through the press. The "Den of Skulls," it reasoned, must represent the "slaughter" of the Radicals in recent elections. Supreme Cyclops, it reasoned, must mean the Supreme Court, "Wolf's Hole" Thaddeus Stevens's Reconstruction Committee room, and the "Great Past Grand Giant" an unflattering but accurate name for General Grant.[97] Significantly, the period during which the federal government was most frequently equated with the Ku-Klux coincided with the federal government's most aggressive attempts to suppress the Ku-Klux: papers analogized the federal government to the Ku-Klux most often during the fraught years of 1871 and 1872, as the government began to take concerted anti-Klan actions. For instance, when Senator John Scott insisted that the Congressional Joint Select Committee would prove that an organization existed whose goal was to control the 1872 presidential election, the *Chicago Times* replied wryly that such an organization did exist and that it was the Joint Select Committee itself.[98] The *Chicago Times* in March 1871 described Grant as "the chief of a Ku Klux Klan more powerful than that of the South."[99] A few weeks later, in an article titled "Thugs in Congress," it analogized Republican congressmen to Ku-Klux, in that they were willing to violate the law for abstract principle.[100] Northern Radicals, it reiterated, were the real Ku-Klux, because they oppressed southern whites.[101] In 1871, the *Tribune* reprinted a speech by Democrat S. F. Carey asking voters to "rid the country of that great KK operation of which Gen. Grant is the head."[102] Papers of all political stripes covered a speech on the floor of Congress by Democratic senator Francis P. Blair, in March 1871, as Congress prepared to pass the Enforcement Act: "Congress is the original Ku-klux."[103]

The analogy between the Ku-Klux and the federal government that gained the most attention during this period occurred on the floor of Congress in March 1871, when Charles Sumner referred to Grant as the "head of the Ku-klux" because of his efforts to annex San Domingo and his alliance with its leader, Buenaventura Baez, and accused him of imperial ambitions. The press vigorously debated and covered this insult.[104] Of course, Sumner was not accusing Grant of leading the Ku-Klux Klan: he was likening Baez's inappropriate violence in San Domingo to that of the Ku-Klux Klan, and Grant's support of Baez to support of the Klan. But the dramatic accusation spread rapidly and traveled light, shed of much of its contextualization.[105] The New York Times cited the claim.[106] The Milwaukee Daily Sentinel reprinted the speech fully and sympathetically. The Chicago Times sat back and enjoyed the fray.[107]

The choice to call the Republican Grant a Ku-Klux leader, when he was the public face of federal efforts to quash the Ku-Klux, gestures to the plasticity of Klan discourse. The fact that the insult circulated so widely suggested that it struck a chord. And it is not coincidental that the label "Ku-Klux" was paired with an accusation that Grant was engaged in empire building. White southerners, and sometimes their northern Democratic allies, liked to complain about the "new and magnificent empire proposed to be erected by the radicals upon the ruins of Republican liberty in the United States."[108] But supporters and members of the Klan itself sometimes claimed the name "invisible empire," and their means of attempting to control their black neighbors through violence was hardly meant to appear democratic. Sumner, at that moment, was arguably equally hostile to the Klan and to what he saw as Grant's illegitimate grasps at power. (He would soon support Greeley and concur with his claims that Grant was overplaying the Klan threat.) His insult, then, suggested that two sides which appeared to be opposed were in fact as one. The multivalence of the term "Ku-Klux" made it possible to use the term against Grant himself.

And papers analogized the Klan to the military. At first, Republican papers frequently used the Klan as a foil for the current government's appropriate, manly violence, or for the violence of Union and Confederate soldiers alike in the recent war. While the soldier or other government representative was manly, the Ku-Klux was skulking. The Ku-Klux arrested in South Carolina, for instance, contrasted dramatically in their physiognomy with the men so recently seen in the Confederate army. Ku-Klux supporters and detractors both, however, often noted how much Ku-Klux resembled soldiers and the Klan an army. Trial testimony described Ku-Klux attackers who raided the jail and executed prisoners in Union County as "the soldiers."[109] An 1872 sensationalist account insisted that the Klan "is formed the same as an army, and the common members are compelled to obey the orders of the officers as a soldier in the army, or any military organization is obliged to do."[110] Those taking testimony in 1869 on the Tennessee Ku-Klux asked a witness if he believed the Ku-Klux "possessed a mind of military character."[111] Representative Charles Porter of Virginia dramatically claimed that "Ku Klux troops are marching from one point to another, and from one state to another."[112] Occasionally newspapers reported that Klan groups had engaged in open combat with soldiers. Often they used the adjective "military" to describe their behavior.

Just as newspapers (and other public voices) portrayed Ku-Klux as mimicking the role of the military, so the government's armed representatives on the ground in the South kept taking on characteristics frequently attributed to Ku-Klux. We have already discussed the importance of clandestine governmental operations in newspaper accounts of Ku-Klux suppression. The army, exemplary of bold physical force, was apparently adjusting itself to this new, more furtive era. The press celebrated Major Lewis Merrill, responsible for suppressing the Ku-Klux in York County, South Carolina, as one of the foremost leaders of the government's fight against the Ku-Klux. Merrill came to be the public face of the military presence in the South. The Tribune's doting profile of him revealed how closely the state had come to resemble the Ku-Klux in popular perception. With the "head, face, and spectacles of a German professor and the frame of an athlete," Merrill personally embodied both the physical power and the tactical prowess of the state. As soon as he arrived in York, he "went quietly at work studying . . . and familiarizing himself with all the details obtainable." At his encouragement, black people stole into his quarters at night to tell him of Ku-Klux atrocities. He induced some in the Ku-Klux to secretly confess and divulge the names of members and leaders, descriptions of their deeds, and the structure of the order. By the time Merrill received the president's authorization to use force, then, he had covertly readied his own infrastructure and was prepared. Ku-Klux were "astonished and terri-fied" by "this intelligence that seemed to know every crime committed by the midnight rangers, and to have penetrated the horned masks and disguises." Merrill, with hardly any use of force, "crushed [the Klan] as easily as a man would an egg-shell."[113]

The Transfiguration of the Ku-Klux: Attacker to Victim

The frequency of mentions of the Klan varied dramatically from 1868 to 1872.[114] There were two distinct national conversations about the Klan, separated by a period of national lack of interest. During the first, January 1868–March 1869, the four papers I surveyed together mentioned the Ku-Klux by name approximately fifty times per month. In the second, from January 1871 to November 1872, they mentioned the Ku-Klux by name over one hundred times per month (since the *Chicago Times* of 1872 was not included in this study, we can confidently assume that the total for that period is artificially low). Between these two periods was a trough: from April 1, 1869, through December 31, 1870, the papers discussed the Ku-Klux at a rate of only slightly over twelve total mentions per month. The timing of interest in the Ku-Klux does not seem to track the frequency of actual Ku-Klux violence. While historians lack even a rough estimate of how many Ku-Klux attacks occurred nationally per month, few would disagree, for instance, that the end of the Ku-Klux's activity, mid-1871 through 1872, saw substantially less Ku-Klux violence than 1870, when the Klan was particularly active in North Carolina, among other places. Yet Klan mentions were at their height from mid-1871 through 1872, and were near their lowest in 1870. What newspaper interest in the Klan does track is the intensity of the struggle over the character and limits of governmental, and particularly federal, power. As Richard Zuczek put it, "Oddly enough, while hostilities . . . seemed to be on the decline, activity in Washington was on the rise."[115]

The nature of the articles mentioning the Ku-Klux also changed over time. The first period of intensive Klan coverage, in 1868, was substan-tially more oriented toward giving accounts of Ku-Klux acting upon victims than would be the case in later periods. The second, from 1871 through 1872, was decisively more oriented toward accounts of the Ku-Klux being acted upon by government. Looking just at Klan coverage in the Republican papers in the first period, up to March 1, 1869, 121 of the 744, or about a sixth, of the pieces mentioned governmental actions.

Almost half, 352, mentioned Klan acts. But the second period of heightened national interest in the Klan—from November 1, 1871, to November 30, 1872—is very different. Only 448 of these 2,122 articles, or a bit under a quarter, mention Klan acts, while 1,142, or a little more than half, refer to governmental acts.

The first period of national interest in the Ku-Klux peaked at the time of the Johnson impeachment, declined briefly over the summer, then hit a second peak before, during, and after the 1868 election. The second, and much more pronounced, period of press attention corresponded to the passage and implementation of the third Enforcement Act (March–April 1871), the South Carolina Klan trials (by far the biggest effort to use the federal courts to try accused Ku-Klux, late November 1871–January 1872), and the Congressional Investigative Committees (1870–1871). The Klan came to be powerfully connected to Johnson's impeachment in the popular mind, and the fact that interest in the Klan peaked during the proceedings was no coincidence. Johnson was impeached on February 24, 1868. His trial began on March 30 and lasted through May 6. The votes occurred on May 16 and May 26. Newspaper coverage of the impeachment repeatedly returned to two themes relevant to the Klan: force and secrecy. George Rable has influentially explored the importance of the "conspiracy" theme to the impeachment. Americans became deeply concerned that the impeachment indicated that power in Washington had become dangerously covert and invisible. Impeachment managers and their supporters accused Johnson of a conspiracy to gain full possession, by force, of the military to strengthen his position relative to the legislative branch. Part of the trial focused on the question of whether Johnson had met with various military leaders (notably General Lorenzo Thomas, whom he had selected as a temporary replacement for Secretary of War Edwin Stanton) to gain their loyalty in support of a planned illegal takeover of the War Department. Johnson's opponents also carefully mobilized the terminology of conspiracy against him, describing Johnson's supporters' efforts to defend him as "cunning devices." But they also proclaimed it directly: Thaddeus Stevens, for example, accused him of engaging in a "daring and bold conspiracy" to mobilize the state's force against the will of Congress.[116]

Though the Klan was evoked by name only a few times in the hearings, some came not only to understand the impeachment crisis in terms of a "conspiracy" against democracy but also to relate this conspiracy to the Ku-Klux Klan. Charles Sumner depicted Johnson as having "patronized massacre and bloodshed and [given] a license to the Ku-Klux-Klan," and proclaimed that only removing Johnson could save the republic and stop the Ku-Klux's "orgy of blood."[117] But the Ku-Klux was not only a distant object of federal policy: during the proceedings, three impeachment managers claimed to have received written death threats from the Ku-Klux.[118] In what appears to have been an unfortunate coincidence, accused Johnson conspirator Lorenzo Thomas had attended a masquerade ball the evening Edwin Stanton had him arrested. One Johnson opponent used this to justify Stanton's controversial decision to arrest Thomas in the middle of the night: Stanton "did not know at what hour [Thomas] might bring his masqueraders upon him, and thereupon he took care to protect himself at the earliest possible hour."[119]

Johnson supporters claimed that anti-Johnson conspirators were evoking the specter of the Ku-Klux to "frighten" citizens and other senators into supporting the impeachment. But they went further: one Johnson supporter, during the hearings, suggested that "nine tenths of the murders and assassinations that have been reported in the newspapers and talked about here in Congress are made to order, got up for political effect, with a view of keeping up agitation and excitement." Republicans, some claimed, were not simply exaggerating or fabricating stories about Ku-Klux atrocities, but were themselves the Ku-Klux and were committing atrocities against their own supporters to frame Democrats.[120]

It is a testament to the importance of the Johnson impeachment hearings in shaping a popular response to the Klan that early popular texts about the Klan, such as sensationalist pamphlets, consistently emphasized the connection between the Klan and the hearings.[121] Indeed, it is difficult to find a popular text about the Klan of more than a few pages that does not thematize the impeachment. The 1868 detective story *Masked Lady of the White House* develops the idea, advanced in the hearings, that the Ku-Klux was a devious conspiracy on the part of Radical Republicans to build up a fraudulent case for the impeachment of Johnson by framing him for atrocities that they themselves had committed against freedpeople. E. C. Buell's 1868 comic song "The Ku Klux Klan" depicts the Klan gleefully and gorily killing important figures involved in the impeachment trial. D. A. Warden's 1868 Klan song features curious and disloyal northerners winning the Klan's approval by insulting impeachment manager Benjamin Butler. The narrator of *Terrible Mysteries*, forcibly inducted into the Ku-Klux, is revealed to be a spy working for William Seward, who is implied to be a political ally of the Ku-Klux, perhaps along with Benjamin

Butler and Thaddeus Stevens. To complicate matters further, the text suggests that the Klan is scheming to reelect Johnson in 1868.[122] A sensationalist pamphlet titled "The Oaths, Signs, Ceremonies, and Objects" warns that the Klan would find the impeachment proceeding or, alternatively, the next presidential election the perfect opportunity to stage a unified uprising.[123] An 1868 newspaper parody of sensational depictions of the Klan, "A. Head Exposes the Ku Klux Klan," ends with an involuntary initiate eagerly awaiting the results of the impeachment hearings.[124]

The New York Tribune, which had been most aggressive in following the Ku-Klux during the first months of 1868, was quick to latch on to this broader association. A May 16, 1868, article, "By the Bullet and the Bowl," noted that many impeachment supporters had been experiencing ill health and asked, "How do we explain these 'Ku-klux coincidences'?" The Tribune also printed two stories covering a speech by Frederick Douglass which, among other things, expressed his hope that impeaching Johnson would end the Klan.[125] When Johnson was not convicted, the Tribune claimed the news was met by the cheers of a crowd of Ku-Klux.[126] A March 28, 1868, article in the Milwaukee Daily Sentinel discussing a Ku-Klux threat received by a Republican impeachment supporter was titled "A Missive from One of Andrew Johnson's Friends."[127]

Interest in the Klan, of course, continued long after the impeachment trails had ended. The Klan remained relevant in the national press through the elections of 1868. That coverage was largely in the form of reports of Ku-Klux violence by Democrats in the South. Articles in the New York Tribune described intimidating Ku-Klux displays in Alabama and reported on concerns that Nathan Bedford Forrest was plotting outright rebellion in Tennessee.[128] There was an uptick in reports of specific violent acts everywhere from Texas, where 125 masked men killed a white Republican leader, to Louisiana, where Ku-Klux destroyed a Republican newspaper office, to Arkansas, where Ku-Klux ambushed and murdered two men, including a Freedmen's Bureau agent.[129] Several articles used the idea of the Ku-Klux in their coverage of northern elections as well, attributing acts of election violence and vandalism in Milwaukee (a Republican in Milwaukee was hit in the head with a rock, and a venue where a Republican meeting was going to take place was set afire) to Ku-Klux.[130] An article claimed that "Ku-Klux" in Iowa had attempted to kill thirty-six Republican girls by upsetting their carriage.[131]

Republicans in the 1868 election also gleefully appropriated the "Ku-Klux" image as damaging to the Democratic cause. A group of

Republican paraders in Madison, Wisconsin, mocked Democrats by dressing as Ku-Klux, riding about on fiery steeds led by "Wade Hampton," and cheering lustily for Seymour and Blair.[132] Paraders in the Catskills apparently did much the same.[133] The *Milwaukee Sentinel* offered some free campaign advice to their Democratic opponents, recommending that Andrew Johnson try to help Seymour out by taking a new "swing around the circle," but this time wearing a Ku-Klux costume.[134] Interest in the Klan dwindled rapidly after the election, however. The *Chicago Times* sarcastically noted that the Republican papers would likely have little more use for the Ku-Klux, but since much of the violence they were describing was election-related, the decrease is not hard to explain.[135]

For a year and a half, from the spring of 1869 to the fall of 1870, the Klan almost entirely fell out of the national discourse. The publication of Klan-themed songs, sensational fiction, and ads all but ceased. Everyone seemingly lost interest in naming their teams and societies after the Klan or wearing Klan costumes to public events. The second revival of interest in the Klan, beginning after the 1870 elections and extending through the elections of 1872, would have a very different character and focus than the first. It had to do with the government's information-gathering efforts (through the traveling congressional committees) and increased use of force (through the Enforcement Acts). Articles published during this second period were most likely to portray the government as equivalent to the Ku-Klux: a perpetrator of violence invisibly guided by privileged access to and secretive control over social information.

The second wave of interest in the Klan would see an increase in the number of stories portraying Ku-Klux as victims of federal force, and a decrease in the number of stories depicting black victimization. This increase coincided exactly with the federal government's decision finally to invest substantial resources into suppressing the Ku-Klux. This timing makes intuitive sense: when the government finally went after the Ku-Klux, newspapers started expressing interest in whether it was doing so appropriately. Yet it was also problematic: just as the federal government was beginning to take more effective steps to suppress the Klan, the public began to see Ku-Klux more often as helpless, overpowered victims, less often as perpetrators of violence; it became more common to express sympathy for Ku-Klux and question the justice of the government's initiative.

Between the decreasing mention of Klan violence against freedpeople and the increasing focus on federal efforts to suppress the Klan, Ku-Klux migrated from the role of the attacker to the role of the victim. There was nothing new about the story of the unjust and unduly forceful government pursuit of the Ku-Klux. The *Pulaski Citizen*, after all, had begun to claim as early as August 1867 that the Tennessee government was using the Ku-Klux to justify its militia.[136] The increasingly popular story of the helpless Ku-Klux relentlessly pursued by the federal government mirrored and replaced the earlier story of the freedman helpless before the Ku-Klux.

Even pro-administration papers reflected this change. In these stories, the direct victims and proper objects of pity were the accused Ku-Klux. These stories began to roll in with the rising criticism of federal power around the Kirk-Holden war. Kirk's critics claimed that his severe tactics for arresting suspected Ku-Klux, eliciting their confessions, and gathering information from them were beyond the rule of law.[137] Several articles claimed that Kirk not only extended the reach of state government, but used his state-sanctioned violence in new and disturbing ways. The *Milwaukee Daily Sentinel* and other papers repeated accounts that Kirk frequently arrested people not because he had any evidence of their guilt, but as hostages to force the community to disclose the identities of the real Ku-Klux.[138] Some newspapers claimed that his tactics in interrogating his prisoners amounted to torture. Kirk was said to have hanged accused Ku-Klux "by the neck until life was nearly extinct," or, as several articles reported and others denied, by the thumbs, "in order to force from them the confession that they belonged to the Ku-Klux Klan."[139]

The passage of the federal Enforcement Acts, and the declaration of martial law under them, generated several more stories either anticipating or reporting excessive, extralegal use of violence by the federal government. As news of an upsurge of violence spread in early 1871 and Republican newspapers described it using terms like "insurrection" and "rebellion," many agreed that urgent governmental action was necessary.[140] Congress passed the Enforcement Act on April 20, 1871; by early October, Grant had suspended the writ of habeas corpus in parts of South Carolina.[141] As the papers covered the turbulent popular and legislative debate over and passage of the Enforcement Acts, and then the preparation for and declaration of martial law in several South Carolina counties, Democrats began to refer to Grant's treatment of the South as "bayonet rule."[142] An article in the *Columbia (S.C.) Daily Phoenix* in March 1872 which claimed that "there is a perfect reign of terror throughout [Union] County" might look like evidence Klan activity persisted there long after federal intervention. A second read, though, reveals that the terror confronting residents of Unionville was that of being arrested under the Enforcement

Acts. The *Phoenix* had never recognized black terror as valid but was more than willing to appropriate and invert national tropes of Klan coverage to make accused Ku-Klux the victims and federal troops the attackers.[143]

Grant, aware of broad concern about the potential that the federal government would overuse its powers, described his governments' acts carefully: "Great caution has been exercised in making these arrests. Notwithstanding the large number, it is believed that no innocent person is now in custody."[144] Newspapers across the political spectrum expressed extreme concern about expanded governmental power; the *New York Tribune* would quote a Democratic speech, on the eve of the 1872 election, claiming that cries of "Ku-Klux" were the pretext for the imposition of federal dictatorship.[145]

Newspaper stories of convicted Ku-Klux tugged at readers' heart-strings. One story in the *New York Tribune* gave an account of a seventeen-year-old Wake Forest College student who had ridden along with the Klan once "in a spirit of frolic or desire for adventure" and now found himself wasting away in the Albany Penitentiary.[146] The *New York Times* also reported on the arrival of a group of prisoners in Albany. "They were all apparently white men, but a more forlorn, woe-begone, haggard-looking crew could scarcely be found. . . . With one or two exceptions they bore upon their faces the stolid look of utter ignorance. . . . Only one or two could read or write." One was an old man, "the head of a large family."[147]

The Ku-Klux served as an interpretive key to the changing postwar federal government. Papers repeatedly analogized the Ku-Klux and government, precisely at the moment of widespread popular anxiety about the perceived opaque and threatening machinations surrounding the Johnson impeachment. The very large percentage of discussions of the Klan that were about anti-Klan policy rather than antifreedmen attacks resulted in part from how the Klan was absorbed into the structure and generic conventions of newspapers. Many mentions of the Klan in the context of congressional debate were not discretionary choices by editors: all of these papers summarized or transcribed congressional debates, so when Congress chose to discuss the Klan, it would generate a mention of the Klan that I would code as pertaining to government action because it would be in the context of debating congressional legislation. I would also code it as mentioning Ku-Klux violence if descriptions or mentions of Klan violence came up in the summary or transcript. This raises the question, however, of why the Klan came to be a substantial part of the coverage of national politics, particularly of congressional debates, but failed to make such a dramatic inroads into, say, sensational crime coverage. And the impact on the reader is the same regardless of whether an editor had specifically sought to publish a story about congressional Klan policy: newspaper readers were substantially more likely to encounter a mention of the Klan in the context of an article about the federal government's efforts to suppress it than they were to encounter an article that made any mention of an action by a Klan.[148] Between 1868 and 1872, when Americans substantially interested themselves in the Ku-Klux Klan, then, the Ku-Klux came to be an important lens through which to observe white violence against black people, but it served much more frequently as a lens through which to observe postwar state power exercised on white people. During these years, the Ku-Klux, as the target of government force, gradually became an object of sympathetic identification even for many newspaper readers deeply opposed to the suppression of freedpeople. The discourse on the Ku-Klux serves as a microcosm for the rapid shift from postwar enmity to reunion.

The Ku-Klux, in 1871–1872 stories, had become more oppressed than oppressing. The federal government had as much as stepped into the group's former role. The causes of this discursive change were broader than the Klan debate itself. Heather Richardson has explored the striking decrease in sympathetic portrayals of freedpeople around 1870 and 1871, pointing out that at the same time, "northern Republicans were increasingly anxious about the attributes of American workers in general, a concern highlighted by the escalated organization of labour" and the menacing daily news reports of the Paris Commune that were pouring through the transatlantic cable.[149] By mid-1871, moderate northern Republicans were viewing black South Carolinians with increasing skepticism, as forces of labor radicalism and threats to the security of property.[150]

But the seed of this reversal in Ku-Klux reporting had been planted at the beginning and cultivated by the generic qualities of the national news story. It was the practice of the press to efface the local, to present particular experiences as universal, to assure its relatively educated and prosperous readers that they were capable of comprehending distant and strange events, and to do so within the space of an article. Newspaper articles produced this comprehension effect by analogizing the strange with the familiar, by placing new events into already-articulated generic forms, and by using vivid, moral, and emotive language to invite readers to imagine themselves in the scene, identify with participants, evoking his or her own personal experience of oppression or coercion. This practice, most directly, encouraged readers to imaginatively identify with, the victims of Ku-Klux violence when they read about Ku-Klux attacks.

Yet these representations were also normalizing. Analogizing the Ku-Klux to familiar institutions and experiences detracted from both its exceptional nature and its threat. If the Ku-Klux was like familiar things (however unpleasant), or like other threatening things from the past and present (which had already been managed), then while newspaper readers might feel victims' pain, they would be less likely to see it as evidence of a distinct and intolerable state of affairs. Instead, the victims' story would become available to them as one powerful expression of a more general problem that they themselves had suffered from or could suffer from. The Ku-Klux, then, was made available not so much as a way to discuss a specific postwar southern crisis as a subject through which to discuss power and oppression much more generally.

It was this generic nature of the discourse surrounding Ku-Klux violence that made it possible for Ku-Klux to change their location within the discourse from aggressor to victim. This transformation began toward the end of 1870 and developed through 1871. By 1872, more than twice as many newspaper articles in the New York Tribune, New York Times, and Milwaukee Daily Sentinel referred to the arrest, trail, or imprisonment of Ku-Klux (187) than to any act attributed to the Ku-Klux (92).

When postwar northern American newspaper readers looked at the government through its relationship to the Ku-Klux, they saw it as wielding unprecedented power and understood that power to be both increasingly violent and increasingly covert. Even those who agreed that these new powers were necessary in order to suppress the Ku-Klux experienced them as new, and usually as potentially dangerous. To the substantial extent that the discourse on the Ku-Klux was "about" the federal government, it was specifically about exploring the extent, limits, and nature of its powers. The federal government, like the Ku-Klux itself, was a mixture of force and secrecy. Klan-themed articles on the federal government interrogated the combination of these two forms of power. The Ku-Klux Klan, as discussed in the national press, embodied many of the very qualities that they detected and feared in the Reconstruction-era government. In an 1872 review of the Klan's sins, Ulysses S. Grant himself chose to highlight the Ku-Klux's use of "systematic spying" as one of its evils demanding suppression—this at a moment in which it would be very difficult to claim that anyone but the federal government itself was developing "systematic spying."[151] Terms like "coercion," "secret," "torture," and "conspiracy," with all of the elaborated bodies of meaning and context each carried, appeared regularly in descriptions of both the Ku-Klux and the government. The Ku-Klux became, among many other things, a displaced location for expressing, sharing, and working toward solutions to these concerns about the postwar state.

The most obvious explanation for newspaper stories' shift toward using the Ku-Klux to explain the nature of the state and away from examining the Klan's aggressions against southern Republicans was that Klan violence had dramatically decreased by late 1871. But if Klan discourse and events produced one another, an end to the practice of Klan violence should be not only reflected but also embedded in discursive change. Such a change is apparent in a noticeable shift in the weight of newspaper narratives: even articles that mentioned the Klan tended to avoid referring to scenes of Klan violence. Rather, despite the enormously low rate of prosecution, conviction, and imprisonment of Ku-Klux, newspapers focused heavily on the plight of Ku-Klux pursued, captured, convicted, and imprisoned by the federal government. While national newspaper coverage of the Klan began in 1868 with stories of attacks by Ku-Klux on helpless and sympathetic southern Republicans, it ended in 1872 and 1873 with accounts of the unjust arrest and cruel imprisonment and release of helpless and sympathetic Ku-Klux, and with widespread demands of clemency for them.

Several newspapers, most frequently but not exclusively the Democratic papers, had begun in early 1871 to focus on the oppression of Ku-Klux by the federal government. In May 1872 the Columbia (S.C.) Daily Phoenix referred to the men making arrests of suspected Ku-Klux under the Enforcement Acts as "Grant's 'night riders,' terrorizing the population."[152] The Tribune claimed in July that "a crowd of special deputy marshals have gone into the interior counties [of North Carolina] to overawe doubtful voters with warrants for Ku-klux arrests."[153] A few weeks later, it published a letter claiming that the Secret Service agents who had spread through the South allegedly to stop the Ku-Klux would be playing active roles in manipulating and intimidating the citizenry into supporting Grant's reelection, and a second article suggesting that Secret Service agents had deliberately spread misinformation to support Grant.[154] Newspaper readers following Ku-Klux-related news, whatever their own politics, were well aware that the federal government had developed a rather extensive, and largely clandestine, network to counter it.

The Chicago Times described in some detail the "Reign of Terror" imposed by the federal government on rural Upcountry South Carolinians when they began their mass Ku-Klux arrests. Stories described desperate men and fleeing families, helpless before the government's indiscriminate exercise of power.[155] The *New York Tribune*, like many other Democratic and Liberal Republican papers, in late 1872 and early 1873 featured stories about Ku-Klux prisoners with titles like "Grant's Prisoner's [sic] in Town. The Arrival of Twenty-Three South Carolinians Consigned to the Albany Penitentiary—Sentenced to Rot to Death." This story describes the convicted Ku-Klux on their way to federal prison: they ranged from beardless youth to gray-haired age. Their "sunburned faces and hardened hands" proved them to be farmers. Some of the "poor wretches" had been coerced into false confessions. All had been tried illegally. Taken from their home communities and friends, they had been placed on a ship to the North. The *New York Sun* claimed that they had been "stowed away between decks in the fore part of the ship" in 98-degree heat with no air circulation. Having lived through that ordeal, some were slowly dying in their dank Albany jail cells.[156] A similar story, reprinted from the *Hartford Times*, referred to convicted Ku-Klux as "cargoes of men sent north, to long years of life or death in Northern dungeons."[157]

Thus the *Sun* and the *Tribune* substituted Ku-Klux for slaves in an overt echo of antebellum abolitionist rhetoric about the horrors of the Middle Passage. This was not as anomalous as it would seem. Greeley himself, of course, was a former slavery opponent, and several, though not most, of his peers had joined his defection from the Republican Party in the 1872 campaign.[158] Even some of those who remained Grant Republicans showed a striking level of concern in later 1872 for the well-being of Ku-Klux. Famed abolitionist Gerrit Smith was concerned enough about convicted Ku-Klux that he visited them in jail. Discovering three whom he believed to be in ill health or mentally incompetent, he wrote a letter asking the federal government to consider clemency toward them. When Alexander Stephens and others gleefully welcomed Smith, on the strength of this intervention, as a fellow Klan-denier, he decisively clarified that he did not believe them to be innocent and was completely unsympathetic to Ku-Klux generally. Still, in a world filled with injustice, advocacy for convicted Ku-Klux had found its way into Smith's busy reformist schedule.[159]

A few days after receiving Smith's letter, President Grant sent Secret Service director Hiram C. Whitley to "make a thorough investigation into the condition of those persons, and report to the Department my views as to the expediency of exercising Executive clemency in regard to any of them." Whitley, of course, had begun his dealings with the Ku-Klux by leading a clandestine federal effort to infiltrate them, with the aim of stopping their anti-Republican violence. In his new capacity he was to investigate each individual's guilt and present condition, functionally retrying him, in order to protect innocent or sympathetic convicted Ku-Klux from persecution by the federal government.

Whitley found the Ku-Klux prisoners compelling. They were "manly, frank, and communicative" (a fascinating compliment by the Secret Service director) but also worthy of pity and sympathy. Many were poor and ignorant and had left large hungry families at home. They had been tricked into joining and coerced by leaders (who had themselves evaded arrest) into committing acts of violence, which they now deeply regretted. To Whitley, all of these factors "appeal strongly for mercy."[160] He urged Grant to pardon those among them who seemed to be struggling most in prison. It is not surprising that Whitley's investigation occurred just months before the 1872 election: pardoning the Ku-Klux became an important issue in the presidential election. Greeley ran largely on a platform of amnesty; the Tribune claimed that even Grant recognized that freeing "these wretched men" was the right thing to do but was unwilling to do it before the election for political reasons.[161] Yet Grant proposed immediately issuing four pardons in response to the report (in a sign of the political sensitivity of this issue, he then quickly announced that he would delay them), and the New York Times, his organ, broadly suggested that more would be forthcoming.[162] Victims of Klan violence had entirely fallen out of this part of the discourse about the Klan. They were rarely even mentioned in accounts of Ku-Klux's appeals for clemency.

William Gillette has characterized the results of the Enforcement Act as "pitiable indeed." By the beginning of 1873, of the 1,355 people indicted as Ku-Klux in South Carolina, only 27 had been convicted and 75 had pled guilty. The rest had not been prosecuted. By January 1873 papers were filled with accounts of Ku-Klux pardons, and by July the federal government had officially announced and substantially executed its policy of clemency, the suspension of prosecution, and near-universal pardons of convicted Ku-Klux except in extraordinary circumstances.[163] Newspapers had first encountered the idea of the Ku-Klux as a way to think about the violent coercion of freedpeople. Within four years, they had turned it into a problem that could be solved only by sympathy with and pardon of their persecutors.

FIVE

Ku-Klux Skepticism and Denial in Reconstruction-Era Public Discourse

Mrs. [Harriet Beecher] Stowe thinks that since she and a lady friend have been able to make the trip to Florida and return without being eaten up by the Kuklux, that such clans do not exist in the South at all, and that all we read about them is bosh.

—*Milwaukee Sentinel*, June 10, 1871

It has long been and is yet a question of doubt with most people whether there is or ever was any real, organized clan . . . but the conclusion has forced itself upon us that Ku-kluxism isn't all a myth.

—*Pulaski Citizen*, April 3, 1868

As fixated as the national press was on the Ku-Klux, Americans seemed to have remarkable difficulty coming to the most basic consensus about its nature. Major newspapers poured unprecedented resources into investigating it, and the government took extraordinary measures to suppress it, yet the most fundamental question about the Ku-Klux—whether it existed at all—remained unsettled even in mainstream public discourse.[1]

The heartiest and most consistent Ku-Klux denial came from those who had clear political motivations: Democrats and, during the 1872 election season, Horace Greeley's Liberal Republicans. Even Republicans before 1872 and Grant Republicans in 1872, however, also expressed basic doubts about the information they received about the Ku-Klux. While Ku-Klux and their Democratic political allies deliberately spread doubt about Ku-Klux reports, they could not have succeeded as thoroughly as they did without the substantial, if intermittent, collaboration of their Republican opponents.

The violence committed by the Ku-Klux had pragmatic utility primarily to those who were committing and supporting it. The idea of the Ku-Klux, in contrast, had practical utility at various times and in various ways to the Ku-Klux themselves, to white southerners who supported them, to a broad northern audience, to Republican partisans, and even to victims of southern racial or political violence. The potential utility of the Ku-Klux label was not lost on contemporaries. Rather, the nature of the relationship between the representation and reality of "Ku-Klux" violence was itself central to Ku-Klux discourse. The Ku-Klux name would be mobilized frequently by Republicans, North and South, as a figure of oppression and cruelty effective in rallying their supporters. Yet the Ku-Klux designation also came in handy for those who had an interest in downplaying the significance of anti-Republican violence. Democrats came to understand that the very act of calling a violent act a Ku-Klux attack cast doubt upon its legitimacy. Throughout the period, but particularly by the period leading up to the second wave of national interest in the Klan in 1871–72, Democrats found the Klan to be an effective frame for press accounts of racial violence.

Just as discussing the Ku-Klux became a way for Americans to critique the expanding federal government, so discussing the unconfirmed nature of information about the Ku-Klux became a way for Americans to critique governmental information-gathering mechanisms and the postwar press as unreliable. Ku-Klux violence occurred at a time of profound transition in how Americans received political information. Postwar Americans enjoyed a volume of published news substantially greater than they had access to a decade earlier. Moreover, news reached readers more quickly; national news now appeared in print within twenty-four hours.[2] Editors were making new assertions about the significance of their writings: they maintained partisan affiliations, but began to make claims of neutrality in choosing which of this vast tide of available stories to publish. These innovations radically changed the experience of reading the news. Readers had to determine how much confidence to put into newspaper editors' selection and presentation of news, and how to deal with the phenomenon of stories rapidly continuing to unfold as new information arrived from one edition to the next.

At the same time, through the circulation of news about the Klan, Americans collectively encountered an incipient national popular culture. News had long circulated nationally, but national trends of interest now emerged in a more coordinated way. As the rapidity of communication created the possibility of feedback loops in which the reception of the story shaped its unfolding, certain events and ideas began to take on a life of their own. Ku-Klux violence was one of these ideas, and in declaring such coverage reliable or unreliable, Americans were implicitly evaluating changes in the circulation of the news.

Throughout this period, the debate over the Ku-Klux never effectively silenced those who argued that the Klan did not exist at all. Despite massive and productive public and private efforts to gather, circulate, and evaluate information about the Ku-Klux Klan, and despite the federal government's devoting attention and resources to the Klan as though it were a real threat, the national debate over the Ku-Klux failed to move beyond the simple question of whether the Ku-Klux existed. The idea of the Ku-Klux as a fundamental threat to the nation always coexisted in tension with the idea that it was simply the product of overheated imaginations. Often the same individual or newspaper would toggle between a passionate conviction that the Klan's threat was real and a real skepticism about its existence or nature—a position resembling the psychological phenomenon of "knowing and not-knowing" associated with trauma.[3] Skepticism about the Ku-Klux even in the face of abundant proof of the Ku-Klux's existence endured and thrived, perhaps because people on all sides of the era's partisan conflicts at times found ambiguity about the Ku-Klux desirable and productive.

Credible evidence of widespread and deadly Ku-Klux violence was never in short supply. Men who called themselves Ku-Klux and were labeled as such by their communities attacked thousands of freedpeople and white Republicans, prominent and humble, leaving a gruesome trail of physical evidence in the form of corpses as well as "scarified backs, gun-shot wounds, maimed ears, and other proofs of the violence they had suffered."[4] They threatened and attacked not only thousands of rural freedpeople, whose voices were too easy to ignore, but also scores of white Republican officeholders, schoolteachers, and other representatives of northern authority, often leaving the objects of their threats (often well-connected and credible northerners) to bear witness. Sometimes their threats were written and later served as evidence. They paraded by the dozens, or even hundreds, down the streets of southern cities and towns, alerting citizens in advance to be present, and often inviting newspaper coverage. They produced organizational documents and statements of their purpose, and sometimes published them in sympathetic newspapers. At times they even engaged in combat with state militias or armed U.S. agents, including marshals and military units, generating a trail of official reports.[5] Sometimes Ku-Klux suffered casualties in their attacks and authorities were left with their dead bodies, or with costumed Ku-Klux prisoners.[6] Federal agents circulated photographs of these captured costumes and sometimes sent the costumes themselves to be displayed in the North and in southern cities.[7]

Some of the most influential people of the day put daunting energy and resources into keeping this, and other, evidence of Klan activities constantly before the public. Newspaper writers, along with federal, state, and local government officials, aggregated and circulated an extraordinary, perhaps even unprecedented, amount of evidence of the Ku-Klux's existence and of the details of its deeds and nature. A few major newspapers that during the Civil War had begun to aspire to national scope and coverage invested heavily in unearthing and publishing a robust body of information on the Ku-Klux. As chapter 2 has discussed, Horace Greeley's New York Tribune published more than fourteen hundred articles mentioning the Ku-Klux between 1868 and 1872. At first the Tribune relied on exchanges and on a network of informal correspondents located in southern cities. From 1869 through 1872, the newspaper supplemented these sources with the correspondences of leading writers, including James S. Pike and Greeley's close friend Nathan C. Meeker, in hopes of "let[ting] in such light upon this tangled web of charges and denials, that ignorance of the true state of affairs will no longer be excusable to Congress or the country."[8] Greeley himself even traveled to New Orleans, and then on to Texas, in 1871, hoping to gather still more information about the nature of the Ku-Klux.[9]

The emerging rival New York Times also sent journalists, including Henry W. Raymond, son of the newspaper's founder, Henry J. Raymond.[10] Though the Times was no match for the Tribune in Ku-Klux coverage, it would publish more than six hundred articles mentioning the Ku-Klux between 1868 and 1872. The reporters sent down by these papers stationed themselves in local groceries, rode through the countryside on mail hacks, interviewed local Democratic elites, met with Klan victims and witnesses, visited military command posts to sit in on Ku-Klux confessions, and dug through courthouse records.[11]

The federal government, boasting a much stronger infrastructure in the wake of the war, also set to work investigating the Ku-Klux. The federal government and, to a smaller extent, state governments devoted substantial resources to determining the nature of Ku-Klux violence.[12]

The Secret Service (established in 1865) and the Justice Department (established in 1870 and given control of the U.S. Marshals) created new capacity not only to enforce federal law but also to investigate violations of it; both would focus on gathering information on the Ku-Klux in their early years. Given broad authority to intervene to protect voting rights by the three Enforcement Acts passed between 1870 and 1872, these federal officials represented a significant expansion of effective federal power.[13] Additionally, the 1870 and 1871 Enforcement Acts' authorization of the president to use military force, where necessary, and to protect voting rights allowed for the enhancement of the federal government's investigative capacity. While the troops President Grant posted in several states mainly served to support U.S. Marshals making arrests, local commanders often considered it part of their duty to learn about the local Ku-Klux, and the more ambitious among them, like Major Lewis Merrill in Yorkville, South Carolina, took on extensive investigative functions.[14]

Expected to gather information about the nature of the Ku-Klux in the rural South, these representatives of federal authority found themselves in an unprecedented role, often with little supervision and little understanding of how they were expected to carry out their tasks or of the limits of their authority. Some allied with local Republicans, compiling and authorizing their complaints and reports. Others attempted to befriend elite Democrats, hoping that they would be alarmed by Ku-Klux excesses or would come to see Ku-Klux violence as opposed to their interests and would thus cooperate in suppressing it. Some raided suspected dens for incriminating documents and costumes.[15] Others paid Ku-Klux members for information or offered them immunity in exchange for it.[16] Still others hired detectives or themselves clandestinely infiltrated local Ku-Klux groups.[17] Information on the Ku-Klux cascaded to Washington in torrents, though hardly methodically. Those looking to Washington for more specific guidance were disappointed: the new attorney general, Amos T. Akerman, was dedicated enough but was looking back at them for inspiration, even spending two precious weeks of his term in Yorkville, South Carolina, observing the practical workings of federal Klan suppression on the ground.[18]

The evidence of Ku-Klux violence was substantial by the end of 1868 and positively formidable by mid-1871. From mid-1871 to early 1872, however, the federal government produced and circulated two bodies of evidence so large that they would seem impossible to ignore. The first of these was the transcript of the South Carolina Ku-Klux trials, mainly heard in the winter of 1871.[19] These trials, presided over by some of the most prominent men in the country, included the testimony of several confessed Ku-Klux about the details of the local organization and its attacks on freedpeople and appeared to definitively settle the question of whether the Ku-Klux existed. The most imposing body of evidence about Ku-Klux atrocities, however, was the testimony taken by Congress, which was discussed in the previous chapter. Newspapers around the country published extracts from this testimony as it was given. All of it together, however, was published in the spring of 1872. Printed with committee members' reports, this daunting collection of evidence filled thirteen large and closely printed volumes.

In their study of the historical development of the idea of scientific objectivity in the nineteenth century, Lorraine Daston and Peter Galison evoke the idea of the "working object," a standardized, agreed-upon representative of the thing under investigation that could be replicated and circulated. This "working object" in scientific fields provided a common ground from which scientists began their analysis, allowing them to be in conversation with one another and holding out the promise that they might reach the same conclusion. "Working objects" preceded the rise of objectivity and provided a precondition for it—a body of evidence which, if objectively interpreted, might yield a defensible truth. This thirteen-volume work was such a working object, holding out the possibility of a national consensus around facts too copious and too visible to be ignored. In fact, the volumes were far from comprehensive: congressmen's time and tolerance for the rural South were limited, and they visited only a few locations. They did not explain the logic of their choice of these locations, though they selected those which had been featured most frequently in the national news. On their arrival, both Republican and Democratic committee members called some witnesses (relying on local informants to provide them names), but others also came forward to volunteer their testimony. They relied quite disproportionately on white witnesses. Tennessee, Texas, Florida, and Louisiana were relatively neglected by these investigations, and Kentucky and Missouri were not within the committee's purview. Yet it was possible to read this massive multivolume series as a comprehensive and authoritative treatment of the Ku-Klux.[20]

Thus Americans received a wealth of information and evidence about Ku-Klux Klan violence from a wide variety of sources, unearthed through the use of powerful new tools and often gathered and verified with a great deal of care and due process. The American public had access to more information about the Ku-Klux than about almost any other person, event, phenomenon, or movement in the nation: to maintain a posture of skepticism about the nature of the Ku-Klux was to fundamentally question the reliability of both the government and the press. Yet many did just this, consistently claiming that they knew almost nothing about the Ku-Klux.

In part, the persistence of skepticism about the Ku-Klux represented the success of a deliberate strategy on the part of perpetrators of Ku-Klux violence. One of the characteristics that distinguished "Ku-Klux" from other violence was its mysterious and bizarre presentation. Though they could not make the government's accumulation of corpses, captured documents, and witness reports disappear, members of the "Invisible" Empire did as much as they could to keep it invisible. Those familiar with the Ku-Klux denied they knew anything about it. Ku-Klux groups themselves rarely kept written records, pledged members to secrecy, and required them to perjure themselves. Ku-Klux usually committed their violence in isolated areas, in disguise, and at nighttime, and often threatened victims and witnesses not to report the incident.

Yet one goal of Ku-Klux violence, like any form of terrorism, was to influence the broader society beyond their immediate victims. Even while taking measures to ensure secrecy, participants in Ku-Klux violence courted publicity, appearing in public processions or publishing accounts of their own actions. The tension between their deliberate secrecy and their aggressive self-publicizing often gave the Ku-Klux an air of mystery. Ku-Klux would deliberately leave clues of their existence and nature, but in an indirect manner intended to be coy. All the way back to their Pulaski origins, Ku-Klux had embraced prevarication. Baldly stating ridiculous falsehoods about the Ku-Klux to the press remained common to those involved in or supportive of Ku-Klux violence. The boisterously humorous tall-tale editorial so standard in Pulaski would become a smaller part of public discourse about the Klan as the body count increased, and extravagantly dishonest claims would shift toward false denials and attributions of guilt. But this culture of secrecy, indirect speech, and dishonesty made certain important types of evidence about the Ku-Klux—all of that spread by the Ku-Klux itself and perhaps its supporters—problematic. What, after all, was a serious reporter to do when he learned that a Ku-Klux "what-you-may-call-it" had been issued, threatening, "Dream as you sleep in the inmost recesses of your houses, and hovering over your beds we gather your sleeping thoughts while our daggers are at your throats"?[21] It was hard to determine whether this was a serious threat, a bugbear or hoax, or some combination of the two. Ku-Klux violence was deliberately made difficult to pin down.

Texts produced by Democrats who supported the Ku-Klux toggled between playfully speculative accounts of the Ku-Klux and denials of the Klan's very existence. On the one hand, Democratic papers might periodically reprint, with an air of bewilderment, a "supposed" notice from a Grand Titan that had mysteriously appeared on the editor's desk. At the same time, the same papers dismissed serious accounts of the Klan as ridiculous. Savannah's *Daily News and Herald*, in a column entitled "The Kuklux Humbug," explained that a threatening Ku-Klux placard recently found in town was a youthful prank and that "the Ku Klux Klan . . . has no actual existence." The *Edgefield (S.C.) Advertiser* gleefully recounted that a group of men arrested for parading through the streets of Augusta, Georgia, carrying a coffin had turned out to be representing not the KKK but a parodic group calling themselves the QQQ.[22] Nevertheless, "our northern enemies . . . eagerly believe anything to our prejudice," such papers argued, and will capitalize on it.[23] Northern Democratic papers, such as the *New York World*, similarly took the position that the Klan did not exist. For the most part, Democratic politicians, North and South, did the same.[24] Senator Willard Saulsbury of Delaware sarcastically commented on the floor of the Senate in the spring of 1870 that it was his dearest wish to see an actual Ku-Klux (that "convenient class") before he died.[25] Denial of the existence of a real and violent Ku-Klux was a common (though not universal) position of Democratic papers and politicians, northern and southern, during the entire period of the Klan's existence.

The Ku-Klux skepticism used to deny or belittle the plight of southern Republicans took many forms. In his work on cultural responses to atrocities, Stanley Cohen analyzes mechanisms that enable members of a society to deny collectively the horrors they have participated in or witnessed. The most common expressions of Ku-Klux skepticism fit into his category of "counteroffensive" (that is, "rejecting all allegations as lies [or] propaganda"): a crude claim that all stories about the Ku-Klux were deliberately made up for political purposes. Ku-Klux denial took more subtle forms as well. Cohen also describes the phenomenon of "partial acknowledgment" ("Yes, the alleged event happened, but is 'only an isolated incident' ").[26] For instance, a Ku-Klux skeptic could concede that a certain reported Ku-Klux attack had occurred, yet maintain that it was a prank or a personal conflict misrepresented by excitable or manipulative

Republicans. Adherents to this more sophisticated form of Ku-Klux skepticism acknowledged that whites sometimes committed violence against freedpeople, perhaps even collectively, but that these were simply sporadic incidents of criminality that could be found in any time or place. Such a Ku-Klux skeptic might even concede that, in the aftermath of the war, collective violence in the South was rather high, but argue that it lacked any organization or political intent and that it therefore should not be seen as a single entity or phenomenon and did not merit federal involvement. While these different claims represented different levels of subtlety, those making them all agreed that stories circulating about the Ku-Klux were a product of the northern mind, deliberately misrepresented by Republican partisans, rather than a description of a real entity.

In practice even the most sophisticated Ku-Klux skepticism could slip into crude denial. Consider, for instance, the typical "intelligent southern Gentlemen's" views of the Ku-Klux relayed by a sympathetic Eunice Beecher (wife of Henry Ward Beecher) from her vacation home in Florida, where she was staying with Harriet Beecher Stowe. The first of these gentlemen claimed that "fearful stories are told, daily, of the Ku-klux—of southern violence and inhumanity. Should these sad occurrences, even when the reports are not at all exaggerated, be taken as a fair interpretation of [southerners'] real character any more than" a recent sensational murder in the North should be taken to apply to the entire North? The second argued: "This talk of Ku Klux is all a blind for political maneuvering. There is no such thing here, any more than you have in New York." He continued to describe crime in the North and then declared, "before God, that if the ruling powers will keep 'carpet-baggers' away from us and refrain from sending politicians down here . . . there will be no trouble with the Ku Klux. . . . These stories are false—cruelly false."[27] The first of these gentlemen cannot fairly be described as a Ku-Klux denier but is skeptical of the veracity of claims about the Ku-Klux and about "southern violence and inhumanity." He leaves open the possibility that some "sad occurrences" attributed to the Ku-Klux were not exaggerated and never denies that the Ku-Klux exists. Yet by describing the reports as "fearful stories" and claiming that some of them have been exaggerated, he takes a stance of skepticism toward accounts of Ku-Klux attacks. The second begins with that same position—there is crime in the South, but it is not fundamentally different than in the North—and then uses it as the basis for his declaration that the stories of the Klan are "false, cruelly false" and that the Ku-Klux is simply a pretext for Republicans to assume more power. He ultimately undermines his denial of organized, political violence by claiming that, by reining in the carpetbaggers, the North could cause it to go away.

The slippage between such subtle expressions of skepticism and cruder denial is apparent in the newspaper response to Eunice Beecher's letter. The Democratic *Daily Arkansas Gazette*, perhaps confusing Eunice and Harriet, crowed, "And now Mrs. Harriet Beecher Stowe takes sides with General Sherman and Horace Greeley about the non-existence of the Ku-klux. In a recent letter from the south to the *Christian Union*, she utterly explodes all the Ku-klux stories that have found their way into northern print."[28]

These more nuanced accounts shared with the crudest denials of the Ku-Klux's existence not only a skepticism about news stories, but also a positive claim that a coordinated Republican effort to spread false stories was under way. Ku-Klux skepticism was not simply a negation of the dominant account of the Ku-Klux or a denial of the existence of a Ku-Klux; always implicit (and often explicit) in Ku-Klux skepticism was an account of dishonesty and gullibility on the part of those spreading the tale. In Ku-Klux skeptics' view, southern whites attempting to rebuild a functioning society and reclaim their political rights had been stymied by northerners driven by greed and the desire for power. The Ku-Klux scare had emerged when freedpeople and their northern allies, out of constitutional nervousness, dramatically overreacted to some youthful pranks by white southerners, and Republican leaders had deliberately stoked these initial fears because they found the stories of Ku-Klux atrocities politically useful.

Though it is not too surprising to find Democrats embracing Ku-Klux skepticism, it is remarkable that their position took such a hold on American culture as a whole. Republicans enjoyed a definitive majority of popular support and controlled both the federal government and a lion's share of popular media organs. They should have made short work of Democrats' narrative of Ku-Klux denial, or at least limited it to a core of the Democratic faithful. Yet Republicans frequently assisted in circulating and giving credibility to the narrative of Ku-Klux denial, regularly expressing doubt about individual Ku-Klux reports as well as public perceptions of Ku-Klux violence more generally. They did this even while themselves involved in a massive effort to produce credible evidence about the Ku-Klux. Even as they published countless serious reports detailing Ku-Klux outrages, they regularly interspersed them with articles questioning their veracity. Part of this was a manifestation of a budding commitment to objective journalism: in truth, there was a good deal of exaggerated information about the Ku-Klux in circulation.[29] But the position of Klan skepticism was embraced with such enthusiasm that it is necessary to seek further motivations.

Take, for instance, coverage of the Ku-Klux in the *New York Times*. In April 1868, the *Times* printed, without comment or framing, a letter from a southern correspondent who claimed that there was no Ku-Klux in South Carolina; rather, it was "banter and practical joking, conducted by that style of persons at the expense of those overnervous parties who are constitutionally sensational."[30] By mid-May, as the Ku-Klux coverage surrounding the Johnson impeachment was on the wane, the *Times* mused, "There is no doubt whatever that a great part of the uproar we had a short time ago about the Kuklux Klan, was without cause. The order had a queer name, was secret, mysterious, and horrible. . . . No sooner had one or two outrages been brought to their door, than myriads of outrages were imputed to their mystic devilment."[31] In October 1870, as the second period of popular interest in the Klan was beginning, the *Times* ran a story headlined "The Kuklux Bugbear," asserting that "when the Kuklux ha[s] not been good enough to do enough whipping and slaughtering . . . the matter was put into the hands of literary gentlemen, who thereupon started armed bands in all directions through the newspaper woods, dragged out newspaper negroes from newspaper homes and, tying them up to trees of the mind, lashed their newspaper backs till the blood ran down, awful to behold."[32] The *Times*' disdain for Ku-Klux reports would only increase in 1871 as its competition with its rival, the *Tribune*, became more explicit. It would maintain its precarious position through the beginning of 1872, frequently describing and deploring Ku-Klux outrages, but also regularly publishing articles expressing deep skepticism about Ku-Klux reports generally. It was not until the campaign of 1872 heated up, with the *Times* serving as the flagship paper for the Stalwarts, that such skeptical articles disappeared from its pages.

The *Tribune* followed a rather different chronology. From the beginning, its writers took allegations of Ku-Klux violence more seriously, and talked about the Klan more frequently, than did those of any other major newspaper. Yet *Tribune* articles, like articles in other papers, regularly signaled that information about Ku-Klux violence was not reliable. As early as March 1868, an article giving an overview of Ku-Klux violence in Tennessee began apologetically, "Rejecting a great deal of exaggeration, and a little pure invention in the reports sent to us from Tennessee."[33] An article a few weeks later began, "We have been slow to put faith in the curious stories [but there seems to be] a solid reality under the stuff and nonsense with which the South-Western papers mask this rapidly-spreading organization."[34]

These early concerns about the reliability of sources grew over time. In 1870, the *Tribune* became a forum for an embarrassing dispute after it printed a letter written by Albion Tourgée that included several implausibly exaggerated accounts of Ku-Klux violence in North Carolina. Tourgée claimed that the letter had not been printed as written and had perhaps been deliberately doctored by North Carolina's embattled Republican governor, William Holden, who had passed it from him to the paper.[35] In mid-1871 (after the vast bulk of Ku-Klux violence had occurred), the paper deplored the fact that "a dense cloud of misrepresentation" obscured the truth about the Ku-Klux, both because of Democrats' stubborn claims that "stories of Kuklux outrages are a mere invention" and because "in some cases the passions of the hour may sometimes have led refugees and Unionists into exaggerated statements."[36] It was at this moment that Greeley further increased his Ku-Klux investigations. The resulting extensive series of *Tribune* articles concluded that Ku-Klux violence did exist, it was a real problem, and federal intervention was justified, but also that it had often been misrepresented by the northern press. When Greeley traveled briefly to Louisiana and Texas in the early summer of 1871, his publications during the trip insisted that the Ku-Klux were real: "The Kuklux are no myth, although they shroud themselves in darkness. They are no flitting ghosts. They are a baneful reality." Or, "But I have been asked, 'Are there any Ku-klux down South?' Yes, gentlemen, there are. They didn't come up to me and tell me they were Ku-klux very often. They didn't undertake to perform their delicate operations upon me. I should have had very much more respect for them if they had. [Great laughter.]"[37] Yet he expressed increasing sympathy for the plight of white southerners and made richly connotative comments like "Not as much violence occurs in Texas as in New York city. . . . There are more desperadoes in that city than in Texas, and it is harder work to manage them."[38] Ku-Klux skeptics, reading between the lines (Greeley's statement was "mildly put, but to the point"), detected a potential ally. Some began immediately to claim him as a fellow Ku-Klux denier, and some Republicans later came to see the trip as having been instrumental to Greeley's undeniable 1872 conversion to a position of Ku-Klux skepticism.[39]

By the first half of 1872, as the presidential campaign began, local reports of Ku-Klux violence had almost entirely stopped. Greeley would base his campaign against Grant largely on the idea that the Klan had been suppressed and it was time for reconciliation and amnesty. His *Tribune*, however, anticipated that Grant would attempt to thwart this effort and make the Ku-Klux peril central to the campaign: "We do not doubt that before three weeks are over, the Grant press will teem daily with reports of murderous Ku-klux assassinations."[40] Greeley was not precisely a Ku-Klux denier: he reminded readers that he and his paper had sounded the alarm first and loudest while the Ku-Klux still existed; but he claimed that it was now utterly gone. In assuming, however, that he could reliably predict a coming increase in coverage of Ku-Klux atrocities, consisting purely of politically motivated lies and distortions, Greeley adopted the rhetorical position of Ku-Klux denial. Like it or not, by taking the position that Grant's allies could and would use the government and newspapers to create and circulate fraudulent Ku-Klux reports, he gave credibility to Democrats' earlier claims of such fabrications. For the rest of 1872, the *Tribune*'s dismissal and mockery of reports of Ku-Klux attacks was indistinguishable from those that had long populated Democratic papers. Grant Republicans, the *Tribune* claimed, knew that the Ku-Klux was dead, but they had "captured its hideous mask and gown, which they guard as jealously as the Israelites did the ark of the Lord," using it to frighten voters into supporting them.[41]

At the same time that they expressed their own periodic doubts about Ku-Klux reports, Republican papers helped to circulate and lend credibility to denials made by Democratic papers and politicians. Usually they did so in order to counter the denials or point to the bad faith behind them. Yet the frequent notice of the position of Ku-Klux denial in Republican papers, even when presented with a tone of exasperation, reminded readers that it was a viable and popular position. So the *Tribune* chastised northern Democratic papers for "attempt[ing] to create the impression" that it was "manufactur[ing]" Ku-Klux atrocities "to order."[42] The *Times* elaborated on the ways in which the Democratic *New York World* "whitewash[ed] the Klan."[43] The *Milwaukee Daily Sentinel* printed a letter from a northerner in South Carolina frustrated that his fellow northerners simply would not believe that reports of Klan violence were true and another article describing the claims of Ku-Klux deniers at length and in detail, in order to point out their inconsistencies.[44]

At the same time, Republican papers treated Ku-Klux denial as though it were a position that could be held by a reasonable person. Writers repeatedly trumpeted that the newest evidence to come to light, or the investigation that would soon be concluded, should finally put the question of the Klan's existence to rest.[45] But the question never was put to rest. The debate never progressed to the point where the basic facts of the Klan's existence could be taken as given, even in Republican papers' own pages. In spring of 1871, at the very height of Ku-Klux violence, the Milwaukee Daily Sentinel still found itself publishing articles condemning Ku-Klux deniers who would not see the truth and insisting that the Ku-Klux Klan was not "a myth, but a dark, horrible reality."[46] That fall, after publishing mountains of evidence about the nature of Klan violence, the New York Times printed an article, "Some Light on the Kuklux Question," pondering why so little was known about the Ku-Klux Klan.[47] The Sentinel, a week later, swore vengeance on those who had until that point "deceived both the people and the government administration" and "blinded the minds of loyal men" by convincing them that Ku-Klux were but "myths . . . springing from a disorderly political brain."[48] Newspaper readers—whether Democrats, Liberal Republicans, or Stalwarts—would have been imbued with a substantial dose of skepticism regarding the information they were consuming about the Ku-Klux.

Though they passionately disagreed about many things, Ku-Klux, Democrats, Liberal Republicans, and Stalwarts all kept viable the premise that evidence about Ku-Klux atrocities, and about the nature of the Ku-Klux itself, was at best inconclusive. One reason they all agreed on the unreliability of Ku-Klux narratives was that so many of them were transparently, even deliberately, unreliable. It is not surprising that papers thematized this unreliability. But papers of all political orientations at times allowed the confusion planted by those stories which were bizarre falsehoods to obscure the abundant evidence readily available about many other Ku-Klux attacks. It was quite reasonable to claim that some stories about Ku-Klux violence circulating in the paper were exaggerations or outright falsehoods; it was entirely unreasonable to entertain the possibility that there was no Ku-Klux.

Enabling widespread Ku-Klux denial to persist in the face of such strong evidence of its existence was a feat. It rested on two strategies: globally denying the credibility of all evidence, and trivializing potentially powerful Ku-Klux narratives through comic or sensationalist framing. The first was the claim that all of the information circulating about the Ku-Klux was the product of deliberate invention and distortion on the part of Republican partisans. Republicans undeniably controlled most public and private mechanisms for investigating and circulating information about the Ku-Klux. Republicans generally, and, after 1871, Stalwart Republicans specifically, benefited from heightened public concern about the Ku-Klux. There is no doubt that many fanned the flames of the Ku-Klux narrative for political reasons.

In part because of this incentive, and in part because of the exaggerated and carnivalesque nature of the Ku-Klux's self-presentation, demonstrably false and exaggerated stories about the Klan circulated even at high levels. The difficulty that contemporaries faced—and, for that matter, historians still face—in assessing the validity of even fairly straightforward evidence about the Ku-Klux is illustrated by a much-publicized fall 1868 interview by former General Nathan Bedford Forrest, a widely condemned war criminal who was widely suspected of being a leader of the Ku-Klux Klan. In this free-ranging interview by a reporter from the Cincinnati Commercial, Forrest apparently confirmed the Ku-Klux's existence and influence and winkingly acknowledged his own role in it. Upon the interview's publication, Forrest simply denied the accuracy of the transcript, insisting that much of what he was quoted as saying was "the fabrications of [the reporter's] own brain."[49] And doubtless the reporter would have benefited from such fabrication. It is quite likely, however, that Forrest, nothing if not impulsive and self-aggrandizing, had bragged about the Ku-Klux, deliberately inviting the reporter to imagine that he was the head of a vast and powerful organization. His later blanket denial of the interview fit perfectly into the play of opposites so important to public talk about the Ku-Klux. For those looking for a way to deny the growing body of evidence about the Ku-Klux, making the bold claim that it was a tissue of lies was an attractive approach.

Ku-Klux skeptics imagined a vast conspiracy between the government and the press to construct the Ku-Klux wholesale. Freedpeople's testimony, which formed the backbone of the evidence, was either simply the product of fearful ignorance or had been bought or coerced by party leaders.[50] Corroborating reports by military and other government officials demonstrated their willful obtuseness and subservience to their politically oriented commanders. Confessions by those who committed the violence had been coerced through the threat of harsh sentences or use of force.[51] One of the many consequences of this wholesale rejection of claims made by government officials or newspapers about the Ku-Klux is that it left skeptics with no alternative source of information they could consider authoritative, and thus with no evidentiary basis for political decision-making.

The most pronounced Ku-Klux skeptics felt no compulsion to take any source of information about the group seriously: they simply presumed that someone in the process could have manipulated or contrived the evidence. When Republican senator Morton, on the floor of the Senate in 1871, read "an official list" of Ku-Klux atrocities that had occurred in Kentucky, Democratic senator Stevenson "inquired what official list he meant." When Morton replied that the information came from the Freedmen's Bureau, he was met with what the *Tribune* described as "derisive laughter" from the Democratic side. Stevenson explained that he did not recognize the Freedmen's Bureau as an authority.[52] Republican representative George Frisbee Hoar tried to get around conservative skepticism about Ku-Klux evidence by citing figures from the 1870 census showing that illiteracy rates were high in areas said to have active Ku-Klux; Democratic representative James B. Beck dismissively replied that the census was "taken by fellows who tried to make it as bad as possible."[53]

One of the most dramatic illustrations of the power of Ku-Klux skepticism occurred with the publication of the transcripts of the massive congressional Ku-Klux hearings: one volume containing a report, accompanied by twelve volumes of testimony. Unable to agree on the results of their investigation, Republicans and Democrats issued contradictory majority and minority reports. The majority report asserted that the reality and fundamentally political and conspiratorial nature of the Ku-Klux was now, finally, undeniable. The minority report, in contrast, claimed that the entire investigation was without value. Minority committee members' Ku-Klux skepticism was quite sophisticated. Indeed, it was not technically a blanket denial, as they conceded up front that some costumed men had committed some acts of violence. Yet not only did they proceed to deny that Ku-Klux violence was widespread, organized, or political; they also consistently expressed extreme skepticism about each individual act of violence described to them. Very rarely, during the testimony or in the report, was there an acknowledgment on the part of Democratic members that any given violent incident was a Ku-Klux act.

Representative Philadelph Van Trump of Ohio, the minority member of the Klan subcommittee that had visited South Carolina, immediately on his return to the North issued a statement describing the "recent publication of the results of their work as untrue . . . colored for the purpose of producing partisan and false impressions."[54] In this way he summarily rejected, in its entirety, what was arguably the federal legislature's most ambitious, expensive, time-consuming, and carefully bipartisan investigative effort up to that point. It is hard to imagine what possible body of evidence might have stood up to such dismissal.

Rejection of Ku-Klux evidence by Democrats and members of Republican factions hoping to play down southern violence remained bold and thorough through the Ku-Klux period, even as denial was increasingly implausible. It was one thing to dismiss the Klan in 1868 as "a mythical maggot of distempered Republican brains," but Ku-Klux deniers gave little ground as evidence accumulated.[55] Democratic newspapers printed blanket denials of the existence of the Ku-Klux during and after its most active period of violence. A Georgia paper screeched in November 1871 that the Klan "has existence only in the imaginations of President Grant and the vile politicians who have poisoned his ears with false and malicious reports. . . . The reports of collisions between armed bands of Ku-klux and federal troops are utterly false, base, and slanderous fabrication, uttered for a purpose."[56] Rather than retreat and regroup as more evidence slammed their position, those who were invested in believing that there was not a pattern of extreme violence against southern Republicans stood firm. As the *Daily Augustus Gazette* reported summing up the Ku-Klux trials, "And now, after all this has been done, and after the expenditure of a vast amount of the public money, a skeptical public are less disposed than ever to believe in the existence of a Ku-Klux organization. True, numbers of prisoners when brought to trial have confessed . . . and there has been an unlimited supply of evidence to the same effect taken, but it could not deceive anyone who desired to know the truth of the matter."[57]

Since Ku-Klux skeptics' position rested on the idea that the Ku-Klux was a product of the fertile imaginations of freedpeople and Republican politicians, one way to mark Ku-Klux stories as false was to introduce generically fictive elements into them. Ku-Klux skeptics, then, worked to frame evidence about Ku-Klux violence as comedy or sensationalism. Ku-Klux sometimes did some of this work themselves. As chapter 2 discussed, Ku-Klux attackers sometimes committed violence in a comic mode, self-consciously wearing costumes or employing formulas from the minstrel stage not only to confuse, frighten, and demean victims but also to obscure accounts of their deeds.[58]

Newspaper reporters, producers of popular performances, and individuals circulating in the public sphere often contributed to this comic frame, sometimes by producing and circulating comic parodies of Ku-Klux-related evidence. Take, for instance "Pompey Squash's Trilogy: A Drama of Yorkville, S.C.," which begins with the testimony of freedman Pompey Squash before Major Merrill (referred to only as "the Major"). After asking Merrill to feel the "whulks" on his back, recounting seeing "dem ghosts a marchin' behind de floatin' lamp," and naming names, Pompey returns to his home and laughs at how he fooled Merrill with his lies and got some money out of it too.[59] The *Savannah Daily News and Herald* reprinted from the *Richmond Dispatch* a lengthy Ku-Klux order parody written in comic consonance: "The Ku-Klux Klan are kalled upon to kastigate or kill any kullered kusses."[60] It later reprinted a parody of a Ku-Klux atrocity tale from the *New Orleans Crescent*, "A. Head Exposes the Ku Klux Klan," concluding with a forced initiate, having withstood various tortures, "clothed with the habiliments of woe" and comforting himself with "Mrs. Winslow's Soothing Syrup."[61] The *Bristol (Tenn.) News* reported a terrible Ku-Klux attack at a Grant rally: it claimed that an Irishman calling for Grant to "say more" was misheard as yelling for "Seymour" and almost killed by fellow Republicans.[62] The Ku-Klux-friendly *Memphis Avalanche*, in another widely reprinted parodic Ku-Klux story, begins with "The Ku-Klux Klan is said to number seventy-five thousand members in Alabama" and works its way up to "The Ku-klux troops are very fond of n___ meat, and the Great Grant Beef major has just issued ten days' rations of Union Leagues."[63] Another newspaper made a comic Ku-Klux threat to those who were behind in paying their subscriptions.[64] An 1869 business directory lists a comic newspaper called the *Ku-klux Kaleidescope* in Wayne County, North Carolina.[65]

Comic Ku-Klux parody was not confined to newspapers: E. C. Buell's 1868 comic song "The Ku Klux Klan" recounts witnessing a scene of gothic Ku-Klux horror, only to find that he has been asleep and dreaming on a barstool. As he blithely concludes, "You can be sure I was glad to find that I had / And had not seen the horrible Klan."[66] D. A. Warden composed "K.K. K.: Ku Klux Klan: Comic Song" the same year, with a chorus beginning "Hokee, Pokee, Kluxee Klan!" The Bryant Minstrels performed a number called the "Ku Klogs Klan" in New York City, a Nashville publisher issued a polka called "K. K. K. Bloody Moon," and a Louisville stage hosted a burlesque performance titled *Little Bo Peep*, which parodied the Klan and whiskey runners.[67] Celebrated children's author

Oliver Optic's paper, *Our Boys and Girls*, joked in July 1868 that a certain "Komikal Komposition upon the Ku Klux Klan is a kurious komplikation of confused konsonants."[68] Ku-Klux comic parody even reached the floor of the Congress, when Representative William E. Niblack, Democrat of Indiana, dramatically read an affidavit he had supposedly received as evidence of Ku-Klux outrages, in which the witness claimed he was being persecuted by "naked and shameful" twenty-five-foot-high demons who fed on human flesh.[69]

Private individuals and voluntary associations also played a role in this comic framing of the Klan by adopting the designation "Ku-Klux" for their nonserious activities. This too was a form of parody, though it was more a parody of Ku-Klux themselves than of stories about Ku-Klux. Baseball teams from Georgia's Emory College, to Virginia's Washington and Lee, to Bangor, Maine, named themselves after the Klan. (Not to be left out, a newspaper in Milwaukee quipped with a callousness remarkable even in the context of the times that two local baseball teams *ought* to be named the "Cu Clux Clan" because of "the way they slaughter the other clubs with which they play.")[70] A young man named W. H. Bishop wore a Klan costume to a masquerade ball in Maine during the 1872 election season.[71] A March 1872 tournament in Aiken, South Carolina, featured a Ku-Klux contestant alongside Humpty Dumpty and a "wild Irishman."[72] The use of the Ku-Klux in advertisements for everything from cigars to quilts and the reported popularity of "Ku Klux Eucre" would have contributed to the same effect. Significantly, these comic representations were not confined to Democrats. The callous Milwaukee paper was the stalwart Republican *Milwaukee Sentinel*, and Greeley's *New York Tribune* approvingly reprinted the threat to newspaper subscribers.[73]

It is possible to parody texts without completely undermining them, and these light-hearted assumptions of the Ku-Klux identity were complex. Those assuming a comic Ku-Klux identity might have been claiming the virile, amoral mystique of vigilantism, mocking those who feared Ku-Klux, or perhaps endeavoring to mock Ku-Klux themselves. However, in emphasizing the minstrel, literary quality of the Klan, these parodies fed into the idea of the Ku-Klux as a literary construct. There was a slippage between parodic or comic accounts of Klan violence and those that were intended to be serious but gestured to comic elements. Parodic humor, as a literary form, played on the tension between reality and comic exaggeration. As Constance Rourke once said of American folk humor, it starts with realism, "but at the moment of humor it breaks into fantasy."[74]

The Library of Congress identifies the men pictured here as members of the Watertown, New York, Division 289 of the Ku-Klux Klan, c. 1870. Marian S. Carson Collection, Library of Congress.

With Ku-Klux deliberately introducing comic elements into their acts of violence and the widespread practice of reducing the Ku-Klux to a comic parody, readers may well have approached reports of Ku-Klux violence with an expectation of comic exaggeration.[75] For instance, when the *Little Rock Morning Republican* quoted the (Republican) *Memphis Post*'s claim that Ku-Klux "have evidently learned their language in the school of the Black Crook," a contemporary hit burlesque production, neither paper may have desired to trivialize violence against freedpeople.[76] Yet when a Savannah Democratic paper, the *Daily News and Herald*, similarly analogized the Ku-Klux to the *Black Crook* a few days later, it easily took the logic further, calling the Klan as a whole "a capital joke—a 'sell.'"[77] Similarly, when a piece of seemingly incontrovertible evidence of the existence of the Ku-Klux emerged, it could be neutralized by translation into farce. Days after the *Daily National Intelligencer* (Washington, D.C.) reported that a costumed Ku-Klux had been killed by his would-be victim, it clarified it had all been a tragic misunderstanding. According to this follow-up story, a young white man, probably inspired by his belief in "the universal terror of blacks" (that is, black people's "constitutional timidity"), had decided to scare a black man by donning a mask and sheet, approaching his house at night, and threatening to kill everyone in it. Unfortunately for the prankster, the freedman he targeted had not known that this was a joke.[78] Similarly, when three congressmen claimed to have received Ku-Klux threats during the impeachment hearings, Democrats dismissed it as a "hoax" or even an April Fools' Day joke.[79] Southern humorist Brick Pomeroy published a book in 1871 in which a worthless northern man headed south, acted obnoxious there ("Plowin', are ye?" Why ain't ye in a grocery, hurrahin' for Grant? Is this the way you spit upon your benefactors!"), and then accused those who gave him a quite reasonable "bouncing" of being Ku-Klux.[80] It was common for newspapers to write about racial violence using sensationalist or min-strelesque tropes (the bullet "passed near the head of a 'school marm' present, who is said to have jumped over three benches at one jump in her excitement").[81] It was difficult for contemporaries to locate the "solid reality" beneath the Klan's "stuff and nonsense."[82]

Framing Ku-Klux violence in a sensationalist mode worked in much the same way as framing it in the comic mode. Like comedy, sensationalism worked by presenting accounts of Ku-Klux violence so grotesque and exaggerated that it was impossible to take them seriously. Sensationalist writing was intended to evoke horror or fear rather than laughter, yet the two were often so entangled as to be indistinguishable from one another. The *Tribune* article "Horrible Disclosures" was a comic parody of sensationalist writing: it lampooned Stalwart accusations against Greeley during the campaign, confessing that Greeley "committed Ku-klux outrages in nearly all the southern States. . . . At present he is . . . compassing the murder of Senator Conkling and the Hon. Mat. Carpenter."[83]

Just as perpetrators of Ku-Klux violence themselves deliberately embraced comedy, too many also employed sensationalist tropes. One *New York Times* correspondent, after noting that a Ku-Klux group had left a human skull on a doorstep, joked that the Ku-Klux "published a card of thanks to the publisher of Beadle's Dime Novels for valuable and telling phrases for their numerous advertisements."[84] Particularly in the spring of 1868, Ku-Klux did make substantial use of the language of sen-sationalism, circulating darkly cryptic coded notices, leaving daggers and empty coffins at the doors of potential victims, attaching horns to their costumes, claiming to be the ghosts of dead soldiers, publishing cards featuring phrases like "Blood! Blood! Blood!," and evoking full moons and dismal caves. One typical Ku-Klux notice asserted: "When the black cat is gliding under the shadows of darkness and the death watch ticks at the lone hour of midnight, then we, the pale riders, are abroad."[85] Another, dated from the "Den of Skulls, Day of Retribution," threatened, "The guilty are free to commit dark deeds that mortal eyes do not see."[86]

Ku-Klux's own use of the literary language of sensationalism made even precisely accurate accounts of them seem manufactured; yet as more accounts of this deliberately sensationalist violence circulated and more evidence to support these accounts emerged, sensationalist Ku-Klux accounts became more plausible. Ku-Klux intending to present an account of their doings recognizable as sensationalized had to go to extremes. Frequently they found themselves evoking cannibalism. Ku-Klux in a midnight procession in Rome, Georgia, carried a banner describing various Ku-Klux atrocities against freedpeople and "Leaguers": "We catch 'em alive and roast em whole, then hand them around with a sharpened pole."[87] The *Charleston Courier* reprinted a Klan notice first published in the *Marion (S.C.) Star*: "Bring a full supply of blood and rations. Bloody work will be done. Skeletons are needed and must be on hand."[88] A notice which, according to the *Little Rock Republican*, was left in a Republican officeholder's yard and threatened that his life would be in danger if he barred certain people from registering to vote also included references to Ku-Klux dining on "pickled negroes," "Republican stew," and sandwiches made of Thaddeus Stevens and Benjamin Butler.[89] The Ku-Klux's use of sensationalism gave even the most scrupulously accurate reports of their actions a fictive and unserious quality.

Producers of popular cultural texts took the opportunity presented to them by the Ku-Klux and came out with a slew of sensationalist accounts of the Ku-Klux. Several full-length pieces of Ku-Klux-themed sensationalist fiction were published, particularly in the earliest months of the Ku-Klux's existence. Authors of these sensationalist texts, like Ku-Klux themselves, faced the substantial task of describing the Ku-Klux in ways that contemporaries would recognize as sensationalist even given the sometimes bizarre nature of actual Klan violence. They rose to the challenge, finding creative ways to exaggerate the perversity of individual acts of Klan violence to the point of implausibility. Accounts included more tales of cannibalism (initiates forced to drink blood from human skulls), claims that beneath innocent-looking towns there were Ku-Klux chambers where victims were tried by immense bodies of Ku-Klux and then tortured by horned beasts, or descriptions of Ku-Klux able to control lightning bolts.[90]

Popular texts also sensationalized the Klan by portraying it as a vast conspiracy. Historians have found no significant evidence that Ku-Klux organizations coordinated with each other beyond the level of a few adjoining counties: most dens were short-lived local groups without any meaningful organizational connections to one another. As the last chapter has discussed, straight newspaper accounts and even government reports sometimes included elements of exaggeration. Writers of self-consciously sensationalist texts dramatically exaggerated the Klan's scale and centralization, presenting it as an unbelievably vast conspiracy secretly controlling the fate of the nation. They portrayed the Ku-Klux, variously, as running the mechanisms of government, as a hidden army poised for a military uprising, or as a finely tuned organization with agents spread throughout the country ready to do the leaders' bidding. As The Oaths, Signs, Ceremonies, and Objects of the Ku Klux Klan (1868) claimed, "Brothers have already been in every northern city of any prominence and accessibility. The 'pestilence' will go broadcast over the whole North." Those fleeing the Ku-Klux were pursued "with hound-like pertinacity" by Klan enforcers supported by an invisible nationwide network of sympathizers and collaborators.[91] Naturally, the most extreme and marginal conspiracy thinkers eagerly integrated the Ku-Klux into their theories. An 1869 book by conspiracy theorist Robert Parrish, for example, claimed that the emergence of the Klan, the consolidation of the telegraph service, the Fenian Brotherhood, the Golden Circle, John Brown, and Harriet Beecher Stowe's Uncle Tom's Cabin were all part of a European plot (spearheaded by Jews and Roman Catholics, of course) to destabilize the United States.[92]

In insisting that Ku-Klux had expansive national networks of supporters and secretly controlled the levers of power, popular writers unceremoniously plugged them into already well-articulated roles in conspiracy fiction and sensationalist genre fiction. For instance, descriptions of Ku-Klux conspiracies in sensationalist fiction closely resembled those of Jesuits, Masons, or wealthy urban rakes. Charles Wesley Alexander, who had previously authored Poor Ellen Stuart's Fate, or, Victim of the Free Love Institute in Oneida, N.Y.: A True and Thrilling Account of Miss Ellen Stuart's Captivity in a Free Love Institute, and Her Tragic Escape and Sufferings transitioned quite naturally to Masked Lady of the White House, yet another story of evil-intended conspirators torturing and coercing the helpless.[93] Sometimes authors evoked these parallels with other popular subjects of sensationalist fiction explicitly, as when Horrible Disclosures: A Full and Authentic Exposé of the Ku Klux Klan referred to the Klan as "Jesuitical."[94]

The frontispiece of the Klan-themed sensationalist novel *The Masked Lady of the White House* (1868) depicting the "Frightful Punishment of Traitors to the Ku-Klux-Klan by the Grand Central Lodge."

It was problem enough that Ku-Klux sensationalized their own deeds, and that popular cultural texts enthusiastically joined them, but when apparently serious reports of the Ku-Klux by government officials and the press echoed some of their language and ideas, the result cast all evidence of the Ku-Klux in a dubious light. Several individual important in spreading Ku-Klux accounts to a national audience, such as William Gannaway Brownlow, Horace Greeley, and Benjamin Butler, were masters of extravagant partisan rhetoric. Nor did they rein in their usual dramatic style when referring to the Klan. Brownlow claimed in early 1868 that the Ku-Klux ramified into almost every part of the eleven Confederate states "hatching plots to scatter anarchy and permanent disorder wherever it may have an existence."[95] Butler, stumping for Grant in 1872, brought a man dressed in a Ku-Klux uniform to display on stage with him during his speeches. (Greeley, by then in full Ku-Klux-skeptic mode, sarcastically referred to Butler's stump speeches as "The Great Modern Ku Klux Show, Benjamin F. Butler, Manager.")[96] The framing of the Ku-Klux as a massive conspiracy, discussed in the last chapter, coexisted in productive tension with Klan skepticism. An 1872 *North American Review* article asserted, quite typically, that, Ku-Klux violence was "terribly far from being sporadic, but bore, on the contrary, every evidence of a gigantic political conspiracy."[97] The subtitle of the joint congressional committee's thirteen-volume report on Ku-Klux violence, *The Kuklux Conspiracy*, echoed, though in a more restrained way, this central sensationalist trope.

Republican discourse took on Ku-Klux sensationalism in other ways as well. Take, for example, the extraordinarily offensive "timely rhyme," to the tune of "Baa Baa Black Sheep," printed by the *Lansing Republican* and reprinted by the *New York Tribune*, describing 1868 Democratic candidate Frank Blair with a bag of "N__ Scalps from Georgia / Kuklux got them all."[98] This was a Republican-produced, explicitly political text, apparently intended to associate Blair with Ku-Klux violence. At the same time, the central image—Blair holding a bag of freedpeople's scalps—loudly declared its own fictive nature, as a deliberately implausible grotesque exaggeration of both the perversity of Ku-Klux violence and the Klan's complicity with mainstream Democratic politicians. Further, setting it to the tune of a nursery rhyme borrowed a then-popular burlesque practice. So the song simultaneously presented Democrats' complicity with Ku-Klux violence as a serious political issue and trivialized Ku-Klux violence through obviously fictive presentation.

Contemporaries often dismissed Klan stories that seemed too sensationalist. For instance, the *Savannah Daily News and Herald* published a piece of Ku-Klux skepticism that accused newspaper writers of seriously exaggerating and misrepresenting the existence of violence in the South, titling it "Working Up a Sensation."[99] Representative Fernando Wood of New York dismissed accounts of Ku-Klux violence on the floor of House, characterizing them as "inflammatory appeals . . . [a] rehearsal of . . . imaginary cruelties with the 'raw head and bloody bones' . . . presented in all their hideousness, and . . . reproduced with proper dramatic trappings."[100] A short-lived journal of political satire apparently funded by Tammany Hall, *Punchinello*, mocked an anti-Ku-Klux speech by Missouri senator Charles Drake, claiming that he "has been studying elocution under a graduate of the old Bowery, and has acquired a most tragic croak," and summarizing his speech as follows: "The soil of the south was clotted with blood by fiends in human shape. . . . In his own state, the Ku-klux ranged together with the fierce whang-doodle."[101] Those arguing the Klan should be taken seriously sometimes realized that the use of the sensational mode, even when it accurately reflected the deliberately sensationalist reality of Klan violence, could undermine their effort to convince Americans of the Ku-Klux's real existence. "These statements may seem extravagant," the *Lowell Daily Citizen and News* acknowledged defensively, then followed up unhelpfully, "[but] so it was said of the 'Golden Circle' movement."[102] After portraying Ku-Klux butchering women and children while "dancing around their bleeding victims and performing their horrid rites" and suggesting that the Spanish Inquisition could have benefited from their innovations of torture, a *Milwaukee Daily Sentinel* writer insisted, "This is not a fancy sketch." The Ku-Klux's "blackness cannot be portrayed in language. Its criminality staggers credulity."[103]

The Ku-Klux occupied a ghostly space in American political and popular culture.[104] It was either unnaturally fierce and terrifying, or it was nothing at all. It was very much before the public eye: people were constantly looking at it, looking for it, fearing it, wondering about its nature. At the same time, many were not sure it was there. Those who gathered and circulated evidence were constantly frustrated in the failure of their extensive efforts. The Ku-Klux was a looming but always-obscured presence in American political discourse. Americans refused either to look away from the Ku-Klux or to acknowledge with certainty that they had finally seen it. The image of the ghostly and metaphors of ghostliness were central to both Ku-Klux self-presentation and to its representation by politicians and by newspaper and other popular media. As a *New York Times* correspondent put it, the Ku-Klux was "a Phantom of diseased imagination."[105]

One example of how the Klan could be simultaneously represented and denied was the Memphis Mardi Gras parade of 1872. This southern event structurally paralleled the national Klan discourse. The parade occurred well after substantial Ku-Klux violence had ceased in Tennessee and had declined precipitously throughout the South. The extensive parade coverage in the *Memphis Avalanche*, a Democratic paper edited by prominent Ku-Klux supporter Matthew Galloway, both described and enacted violence against freedpeople: "Those mythical terrors to negroes, the Ku-Klux were well represented. . . . In every instance they were in black, with high hats of a conical shape. Each hat bore the skull and cross bones and the terrible letters K. K. K. in white. As they marched along, the Negroes [moved] back. Many of the K. K.'s had rope lassos, and it was a favorite bit of pleasantry to lasso a Negro. No violence was offered, but the contortions and grimaces of the captives were highly amusing."[106] Later the *Avalanche* portrayed the Ku-Klux as "arrayed under a transparency bearing a skull and cross-bones and 'K.K.K. Deadbeats.' In their black dominos and hideous masks, they were not a party calculated to inspire confidence in the minds of the loyal. They were peaceable enough, though, as they amused themselves by blowing upon tin horns and beating miniature drums."[107] The equally pro-Klan *Memphis Appeal* described a tableau in the same parade featuring "representatives of the Ku-Klux from all the states of the South. All the terrible scenes alleged to have been enacted for years past in the Carolinas were presented. The Ku-Klux appeared in full regalia. One of their number personated a living ace of spades, the veritable butt-end of midnight, the impersonation of loyal leaguism. The negro was executed according to all the forms made familiar by Nast's pictures, and by the trustworthy correspondents of the Cincinnati press."[108] This account of representations of the Ku-Klux in the parade shows all of the chief elements of Ku-Klux skepticism I have discussed: a proliferation of both comic and sensationalist Klan narratives and an explicit dismissal of the reliability of Ku-Klux narratives influenced by Republicans.

That these Ku-Klux denials were taking place not only in the South, however, but in one of the epicenters of Klan support makes their complexity even starker. On the one hand, audiences simply saw men representing Ku-Klux committing atrocities. But they were told that these paraders were not actually representing Ku-Klux; rather, they were depicting the "false" representations of Ku-Klux in the northern press. At the same time, it is likely that many of the men representing Ku-Klux were, or had been, actual Ku-Klux. Officially the Memphis Klan had voluntarily disbanded three years before the parade, but they never had been prosecuted, and they continued to maintain their contacts with one another through legal organizations like Democratic clubs, Masonic lodges, and probably (as has been shown in the case of New Orleans) carnival societies. So presumably the parade presents the bizarre spectacle of actual Ku-Klux marching in Klan uniforms, attacking both blackfaced white performers and actual black onlookers, to make the point that Ku-Klux violence was a figment of the northern imagination.[109]

The same Memphis carnival also featured "fine gentlemen sitting familiarly in barouches beside cotton-field negro girls."[110] Both of the inhabitants of these carriages were likely white men, one of them in "wench" disguise, though it is also possible that they were two white female prostitutes, one with her gender inverted, and the other her race.[111] This carnivalesque representation of miscegenation attacked interracial relations as absurd to the point of impossibility. Yet Memphis citizens were well aware of the real prevalence of miscegenation, which could not be discussed publicly but was nonetheless apparent. This starkly public representation of miscegenation invited viewers to look at one another self-consciously and to collectively laugh off this undeniable truth in a paradoxical display of denial.

Whites who attended this and other, similar parades must have experienced an odd sense of double vision.[112] Maintaining two logically contradictory positions simultaneously, whether simultaneously acknowledging and denying the existence of miscegenation or of the Ku-Klux, required a certain self-deceit on the part of cultural producers and consumers alike. It is complicated to consider how self-deceit works even on an individual level. If a society represents an untruth consistently enough and with enough conviction, do people begin to believe it? Perhaps, as Max Black has suggested of self-deceiving individuals, people are aware of materials they have suppressed only "in a twilight way."[113] Nor have such suppressions been uncommon in political life: as Michael Milburn and Sheree Conrad have put it, "Our official life as a nation is built on a shared denial of painful realities and the sufferings they engender."[114] Part of the allure of misrepresentations is that they can help individuals or societies gloss over their own inconsistencies and develop more robust and appealing self-understandings.

Part of the impulse behind Ku-Klux skepticism must have been the collective desire to avoid thinking about the plight of freedpeople and their allies and to avoid taking responsibility for protecting them. Yet nineteenth-century Americans rejected the most convenient way to achieve that end: discussing neither the Ku-Klux nor southern violence by any other name. Rather, they showed a stubborn collective determination to debate incessantly about, yet resist a final consensus on, the nature of Ku-Klux violence in the South. The Ku-Klux was a convenient and disposable container in which to place evidence of southern violence against freedpeople and their allies. Many nineteenth-century Americans neither ignored nor denied the Ku-Klux; rather, they chose to maintain an internal tension between their knowledge and their skepticism about the Ku-Klux.

There are several explanations of why "knowing and not-knowing" the Ku-Klux might have been desirable to nineteenth-century cultural producers and consumers. The first, and most obvious, is that even though it was often in the political interest of a given group to deny Klan atrocities, the conviction that Ku-Klux violence was real was so widespread in the culture as to be difficult to ignore. So denial or trivialization of Klan violence by Ku-Klux and their Democratic political allies, by Grant administration defenders in 1871 and by Greeleyite Republicans during the 1872 campaign, made strategic sense. Reports of Klan violence inspired and justified federal intervention, allowing the Republicans who controlled the federal government to strengthen their position while simultaneously showing Democrats in a very bad light. As internal Republican tensions grew, however, Grant supporters began to worry more about attacks from Radicals who claimed the administration was not going far enough to suppress the Ku-Klux. Trivializing or denying Klan violence was a tactical measure used to counter this criticism. Then, in 1872, Greeley's Liberal Republicans bolted from the party and determined to ally with Democrats. This alliance worked only because the Liberal Republicans reversed course and agreed that federal intervention in the South had gone too far. The denial of Ku-Klux violence was, for pragmatic reasons, crucial to their campaign.

Another explanation for Americans' interest in maintaining a robustly ambiguous position on the Ku-Klux is that it served to illustrate their own canniness as consumers of political texts, their awareness of the processes through which information was created and distributed. Postwar Americans were experiencing a radically altered structure of information circulation. To a significant extent, the debate about the existence of the Ku-Klux was also about the reliability of this new system. Klan skeptics wondered whether stories about the Klan circulating in the newspaper, as well as those conveyed by politicians and government, could be accepted as genuine, and, if so, to what extent they had been corrupted, shaped, and manipulated.

Like the dominant story of a powerful and coordinated Ku-Klux, the claim that the idea of the Ku-Klux had been manufactured by Republicans for political gain was a conspiracy theory. Mark Summers has described the Reconstruction period as an age of conspiracy thinking.[115] Indeed, to the extent they contemplated the possibility that many, or all, stories about the Ku-Klux had been manufactured and circulated for political purposes by a massive league of freedpeople, white southern Republicans, government officials, and newspapers, those skeptical of the dominant account of the Ku-Klux were engaging in a rather lavish exercise in conspiracy thought. It is perhaps not too surprising that conspiracy thought should have thrived during this period, when the actual operations of power were so complex, unstable, and opaque. Conspiracy theories provided accounts of how power actually worked, often distressing in their practical implications but at the same time reassuring in their coherence and detail. Indeed, as Ed White has argued, conspiracy theories had certain

advantages as a way for average citizens to process the political information they received about their complex society. Rather than encouraging
passive acceptance of political information, conspiracy thought "asserted
agendas not accessible to public or 'surface discourse'" and "posited
dishonest or ironic forms of cultural expression used by conspirators to
achieve those agendas."[116] That is, in entertaining basic suspicion about
the dominant accounts of the Klan found in authoritative forums like government reports and major newspapers, nineteenth-century Americans
marked themselves as knowing insiders, "accustomed to sift and weigh
evidence."[117]

The fear of being a "dupe" pervaded mid-nineteenth-century culture.
The antebellum figure of the "confidence man" discussed by Karen
Halttunen has recently been further explored by Walter Johnson,
who understands him as produced by, and posing a great danger to,
the constantly expanding and fundamentally speculative economic
form of cotton slavery.[118] If there ever was a society that was inherently speculative, it was the South as it sought to recover after the Civil
War and, to a lesser extent, the new and healing nation. As Americans
became increasingly aware of the produced and circulating nature of
information in midcentury, they fretted about protecting themselves
from deliberate deceit.

The more Klan stories circulated by newspapers and politicians
appeared to take on characteristics of sensationalism or comedy, the
more tempting it was for skeptical insiders to reject them. Informed late
nineteenth-century readers were sensitive to the various ways literary
forms could evoke emotional rather than rational responses. The posture of skepticism emerging in this period would ultimately lead to the
rise of a preference for "realism" and to distaste for apparently stylistic,
artistic, or formal elements.[119] To the extent that representations of the
Klan resembled comedy or sensationalism, they aroused the suspicion of
self-consciously sophisticated Reconstruction-era readers.

Reconstruction-era newspaper writers and editors shared their readers' emergent posture of skepticism, though they naturally defended
their own neutrality. They asserted their own independence and reliability, continuing their transition from explicitly partisan to ostensibly
professional and objective journalism. The *Tribune*, for instance, regularly alleged that Ku-Klux accounts given by other papers were shaped
by partisan interest, even while defending itself against allegations of
partisanship. The paper insisted, in one representative passage, that

its sole goal in Ku-Klux coverage was "to ascertain the truth and report it with perfect fairness and in a spirit of impartial justice."[120] It denied "partisan bias" and complained of rival newspapers' failure to maintain a posture of impartiality: "Is that journalism?"[121] The *Tribune* and other papers prided themselves on their willingness to print stories and make editorial judgments independently of their partisan interests.[122] By publicly assuming an attitude of skeptical discrimination toward Ku-Klux reports, even at the cost of undermining their own usual editorial position on the Ku-Klux, they enhanced this image.

At the same time, the maintenance of a posture of Klan skepticism in newspapers and among politicians filled the important function of creating a new way to differentiate between "insiders" and "outsiders." The war had ended the "slave/free" dichotomy that had loomed so large until then, replacing it provisionally with "rebel/loyal." Ku-Klux rejected that new understanding of citizenship. The idea of an indeterminate Ku-Klux helped to enable the emergence of a new dichotomy. Sociologists interested in the cultural dynamics of group formation have suggested that the consensual construction of collective political stories is central to the process. As Ann Mische argues, "Potential meanings [of political events] . . . can be activated or deactivated, made visible or invisible, by individuals and groups within the constraints of a social setting."[123] This is very much like the process of collective memory construction that has been so important in recent studies of the legacy of the Civil War.[124] The process of tacitly agreeing to accept a particular version of events, present or past, was crucial to forming a group bond.

Neither of the two positions described here—either insisting on the reality, political nature, and danger of the Ku-Klux or believing that evidence of Ku-Klux atrocities was manufactured for political ends—had become so entrenched as to be clearly dominant. Bruce Baker, focusing on the later part of Reconstruction, differentiates between official memory and "countermemory" and between "public" and "private" memory, but during the early years of Reconstruction, no version of the Ku-Klux had achieved hegemonic status.[125] The process of building a collective story of Reconstruction and the process of building a new body politic were in many ways one and the same.

Ku-Klux-themed texts worked in part by challenging the reader (or audience member) to locate the line between truth and exaggeration. The ability to determine whether laughter or anxiety was an appropriate response to a particular claim (or a particular embodied threat) worked as a test not only of character, but also of inclusion. Ku-Klux tested freed-people and their southern allies in precisely this way. Ku-Klux frequently emphasized their victims' gullibility as a justification for attacks on them, a way to frame the attacks as comedy, or a reason for discounting their testimony. Historians have interpreted this emphasis as a simple expression of racism or a pragmatic effort to protect themselves from punishment, but it also served an important exclusive function.[126] Ku-Klux were claiming that the way freedpeople and their allies responded to the specter of the Ku-Klux proved they were terrified and superstitious people who could be manipulated by absurd theatrical displays and would therefore make poor citizens.

Northerners who accepted without question the accounts of Ku-Klux violence percolating up from the South were in grave danger of being placed in the same category as freedpeople, carpetbaggers, and scalawags. For instance, a New York Times correspondent expressed the suspicion, in 1869, that the Ku-Klux did not really commit atrocities and that, to the extent it had an existence, it only served to scare "negroes and fools generally." The writer of the piece desired to "throw light" on "rumors" about the Ku-Klux that had been taken seriously by "over-credulous hunter[s] after political sensations."[127] Or, as the Daily Arkansas Gazette put it on the conclusion of the South Carolina Ku-Klux trials in 1872, "Perhaps the credulous inhabitants of some thriving settlement on the banks of the Skoodoowabskookois . . . may believe it, but in the states, where civilization triumphs, and the people are too intelligent to be imposed upon by clumsy fabrications, anyone who calls up the kuklux bugbear for political effect will be laughed from the hustings for his pains."[128] Eunice Beecher carefully asserted early in her 1871 letter expressing skepticism about the existence of the Klan that she and her traveling companion in Florida, presumably Harriet Beecher Stowe, "are not naturally timid."[129] Comic and sensationalist representations of the Klan proposed a new test to determine inclusion in or exclusion from the American body politic to replace the previous screening mechanism based on condition of servitude. Ku-Klux observers, both Democratic and Republican, found themselves intrigued by the idea of response to the Ku-Klux as a test. Whether Ku-Klux sensationalized their own actions or Republican newspapermen did it for them, it was incumbent on the reader to recognize the story as sensational rather than serious.

By deliberately imposing a framework of perverse, bizarre self-presentation, Ku-Klux and their supporters stylized what would otherwise have been all-too-predictable postwar acts of oppression of freedpeople and their allies. In doing so, they exploited a rift in northern culture. They extended an invitation to those northerners who believed themselves to be too "intelligent to be imposed upon" by fantastic stories and mysterious terrors. By rejecting these accounts, they could imagine themselves living again in a familiar, and comfortably sober, political landscape rather than a world that had unaccountably taken the form of a dime novel. Many Liberal Republicans accepted that invitation, choosing, like the throngs lining the street of the Memphis parade, to adopt what was, to them, a more utilitarian account of the situation in the South.

In the wake of several important works on the politics of memory has come a good deal of scholarly consideration of the political importance of forgetting.[130] Most notably, David Blight has influentially written about the calls, even among Republicans, to forget the recent war.[131] Greeley and his *Tribune* were very much a part of this effort, having frequently pled for the pragmatically motivated willed forgetting of wartime atrocities.[132] Greeley was the standard-bearer in this cause, calling for political amnesty and also more generally for "oblivion for offenses long bygone."[133]

Historians of Reconstruction have carefully analyzed the ways in which sectional reconciliation depended on a process of reimagining the Civil War, emphasizing some things and forgetting others.[134] This process no doubt flourished on the battlefields, as individual soldiers contemplated the meanings of their individual horrors, but by the Reconstruction era, Americans worked collectively to deny or reimagine violence and injustice in the contemporary South. Denying the existence of the Ku-Klux or leaving the question deliberately ambiguous worked in much the same way as retrospective forgetting. Societies develop "unwritten agreements about what can be publicly remembered and acknowledged" and "collude" with one another in denying brutal facts, sometimes "using techniques like minimization, euphemism and joking."[135] Resisting a public consensus about the existence of the Klan and relegating Klan reports to sensationalist and comic forms assisted in the process of cultural forgetting and allowed for the reunion of northern and southern elites.

Beneath the thin cloth of sensationalism in which Ku-Klux were cloaked, there was nothing bizarre or comic. Defeated white southerners, insufficiently controlled by the North, competed with each other and with their often extremely vulnerable black neighbors for political power, economic resources, and social position in the new order. It was a particularly ugly display of human nature, and the worst thing about it was precisely that it was not in the least mysterious. Ku-Klux and their suffering victims were all too human and all too plainly visible to anyone who had the fortitude to look. Folding Reconstruction-era violence into the Ku-Klux, imagining it as spectral, ambiguous, and indeterminate, enabled Americans to turn away from that unjust reality and all of the political implications and obligations it entailed.

SIX

Race and Violence in Union County, South Carolina

The men who went into Unionville for the jail raid were probably more respectable than other Klansmen. From the manner in which they conducted that thing. It was done by order and system. There was some evidence of management and skill in the transaction that I thought would not have come from common, stupid, ignorant men. For instance, they dressed a fellow in white clothes—that is the story I was told about it—and they set him at the door, and brought the negroes out one at a time. He was standing at the door, and they would call him Stevens—that was the name of the man whom these prisoners had murdered. They would say to him, "Was this one of your murderers, Stevens?" They would say that to the man who personated Stevens's ghost, and he would say, "Yes." And they would say, "Well, take him off," and another would be brought out and he would answer, "Yes" and they would take him off. And in that crowd were two that this man said were not his murderers. The prisoners were in there for murder, and true bills found against them, but the jury acquitted these two men. This proved that these parties had taken pains to look into that thing with great care. As one of the citizens told me, some of the citizens went there to shield one of the men at one time. He was satisfied that that fellow was innocent; and although they came there determined to kill them, he thought possibly he might, by his being a prominent man, control them.

—Testimony of Simpson Bobo, South Carolina, *Testimony Taken by the Joint Select Committee on the Condition of Affairs in the Late Insurrectionary States*

The preceding chapters have shown the post-Pulaski idea of the Ku-Klux developing in the ether of popular culture, untethered from a local context. Yet the abstract idea of the Ku-Klux could take root in specific southern communities only if some group there found it a desirable identity and tool. It could grow only if a larger community learned of it and chose to recognize its participants as Ku-Klux.

The story of racial violence in the South Carolina Upcountry generally, and in Union County specifically, already has been well told. Newspapers and political leaders gave substantial attention to Klan terror in Union as it unfolded. Local historians since, drawing on white community memory, have provided their own thorough, though sometimes strikingly racist, treatment. As the standard story goes, Union's "slickers" became a "Klan" when James G. Long sent his courier, Dr. Charles Sims of Union, to get information on the organization from Grand Cyclops J. Bank Lyles. Long had established the Den 500 Klan in Union in early 1866 to deal with Republican misgovernment and black lawlessness. On December 31, 1870, Long came to believe that Union League leaders were planning to kill him and other white conservative leaders, so he armed himself and hid in a forest. Instead, black militiamen killed an industrious one-armed drayman named Matterson Stevens. Many of the accused perpetrators were arrested in the following days, though one black group killed a white man who was attempting to make an arrest. After consulting with the Grand Cyclops, the Klan staged two massive raids on the jail, took out and killed first two, then ten more of the perpetrators. Academic historians, relying upon but also supplementing and contextualizing local histories, have produced more detailed and thoughtful accounts of events in that county than we have for almost any other.[1]

The Klan has been such a dominant frame for understanding postwar southern racial violence that any other history of racial violence or conflict has been drowned out. And this flattening of the understanding of racial violence was true for contemporaries as well, particularly in places like Union County that had an active and notorious Klan. The national and nationalizing idea of the Ku-Klux powerfully shaped, and continues to shape, the interpretation of events in Union County, to the near exclusion of other contexts.

The next chapter discusses how insiders and outsiders in Union came to label its violence as Ku-Klux violence, and what the racial violence in Union County looked like to the state and federal government and to the national media. This chapter, in contrast, reads the "Ku-Klux" movement as one of many aspects of the system of racial violence that developed in postwar Union. It digs beneath the term "Ku-Klux" to discover the local contexts and meanings of the racial violence in the county. The conventional Klan narrative is so robust a framework for violent events in postwar Union that it is hard, in retrospect, to tell the story of the county in any other way.

This chapter may be boring. The term "Klan" was manufactured to defeat boredom, after all. The "Ku-Klux" label streamlines and simplifies, giving small actions a large ethical meaning and transfiguring the petty everyday tyranny of forgotten men into epic events on the national stage. Describing the endless power struggles and oppressions within some rural community in the South inevitably feels like a dead end. The human dynamics were always messy, and people refused to fit into clear explanatory schemes. Yet this sloppy and dissatisfying everyday oppression is what will always be found beneath the Ku-Klux's flashy costume.

This chapter turns to historical network analysis to tell the story of violence in Union County. Network analysis is a structural approach to the study of a group of actors. By labeling each person in the community as a "node" and creating a connection or "edge" between two nodes each time they are related to one another in a historical record, it is possible to map structures of relationships in a community. Creating this map reveals qualities of the network too complex to detect through informal methods. The network I created for Union County, which has 5,414 nodes and 36,139 edges, maps how victims and suspected perpetrators of Klan violence fit into the county's broader social structure. This is not a complete map of interactions, of course: it only reflects the particular dataset—in this case, every name appearing on the county's criminal indictments from 1852 to 1878 as accuser, accused, bondsman, or witness. Each time two individuals occurred together in a given indictment, in any relationship to one another, I created an edge between them. The network produced by this data, then, is not a map of the county as a whole, but one that captures the county at its moments of dysfunction—that shows relationships only in situations of tension. Once I have entered the information for this map, I can use various network mapping systems (I used Pajek and Gephi) to create and manipulate visualizations of it.

The graph can only reflect the data it is based on. Where a person wrongly or falsely accused someone, the two will be related in the database just as surely as if the accused did indeed commit the crime. Where someone got away undetected, where a victim was paid off or too intimidated to make a formal charge, or where neighbors intervened to settle the matter informally, the events are not reflected in the database. And the map reflects only the fact that two people appeared together on an indictment, not whether, on that occasion, they were allies, enemies, or neither. But whenever a group of Union Countians found themselves jostling uncomfortably together at the Unionville courthouse while the sheriff's deputy wrote up his sheaf of subpoenas, allegations, and bonds after an allegation of wrongdoing, they are connected in this network. Two men who appeared together repeatedly, or a group whose members kept turning up together, were socially proximate to one another. Determining the nature of their relationship often requires going beyond the network and considering their roles in the indictments in more detail.

One truth about the nature of Klan violence in Union County has long been hidden in plain sight: The two massive and deadly jail raids that form the core of Klan activity in the county were responses to a black militia attack on a bootlegger attempting to deliver liquor to the town's hotel. Formal analysis of the Union County criminal/victim network, together with informal analysis aided by the clarity that the network visualization can provide, suggests that these were not just a single incidents but a basic dynamic of racial violence in the county: the threat of black leaders interfering with a working relationship between elite Union Countians and those involved in illegal vice provoked Klan violence. Patterns of violence during the Klan period were both continuous and discontinuous with what Union County violence looked like before the emergence of the Klan. In Union, Ku-Klux violence not only had a national significance but also fit several local purposes. Klan violence emerged at a time when an emerging group of black leaders challenged a long-standing but unacknowledged working relationship between certain wealthy Union Countians and a group of lower-class socially marginal whites who supported vice-related businesses in the county. Klan violence, which in Union was largely a collaboration between these elite and marginal whites, incapacitated black leaders (who were troubling largely because they were too competent at certain aspects of their job) but also represented a shift in the relationship between the two white groups: some elites found themselves no longer simply using the services of, but actually working to satisfy the interests of, members of a white criminal underclass.

The Klan worked differently in different counties, and while this pattern was probably not unique to Union County, there is no reason to think that the primary motivation for Klan participation more generally was a desire to retain illicit relationships between the elite and the vicious. Yet the national Klan narrative fit the lived experiences of other counties as poorly as it did the lived reality of Union. The national Klan narrative was never about explaining events on the ground. It was always about sorting and interpreting these events in ways useful to northern whites.

Race and Violence in Union County before the Ku-Klux

Union was a modest-sized county in the South Carolina Upcountry with a moderate black majority. According to the 1870 census (which probably undercounted), the county's total population was 19,248, of which 9,554 were black, 947 mulatto, and 8,718 white. During the Reconstruction era, Union still had a cotton-centric economy, though some were growing winter wheat, Indian corn, and sweet potatoes, and many were raising pigs and sheep.[2] Union was also an insular community: only 252 people on the 1870 census claimed to have been born outside South Carolina, just under half of them from North Carolina.[3]

Like many Upcountry counties, Union's wealth was heavily concentrated in the hands of a small elite. In the 1870 census, 1,761 householders declared any property, real or personal. Of that number, only 786 had $500 or more, 318 had $2,000 or more, 140 had $5,000 or more, and 48 had $10,000 or more. The wealthiest was worth $56,000. Only 19 of the 1,761 householders claiming property were black: the wealthiest was thirty-year-old Hattie McMahan, with $950; hers was among the wealthiest third of Union County households. The county's small mulatto population, many of whom had been free before the war, did much better: 62 mulatto heads of household reported property, a much higher rate of property ownership than that of their much more numerous black neighbors. Thirty-year-old mulatto Gilbert Peeler of Gowdeysville was wealthiest, with $1,500.

Even as Union Countians worked to get what share they could of the county's prosperity, it was impossible to be innocent about racial violence in Union. The specter of inconceivable violence had long loomed terribly over the county: on June 26, 1848, twenty enslaved children had been sleeping in a house on Governor David Johnson's plantation when a fire started for reasons never certain. All of them burned to death. The fact that this case was filed with later indictments suggests that it was still very much alive in postwar memory. (Among the 1874 indictments there are several earlier murder cases from the postwar years, mainly those involving white-on-black or white-on-white Republican violence. This case is filed with them.)[4]

Like every county, Union had its own local traditions of violence, shaped both by structural factors and by countless choices made by Union Countians over decades. Perhaps the geographic stability of its population meant that even more than in many other places, violence in

Union was often intimate among people embedded in intricate webs of obligation and conflict. It fell into familiar patterns: since the antebellum period and doubtless beyond, groups of men had visited homes at night and verbally threatened, harassed, thrown rocks at or shot at those inside.[5] Men had waylaid people traveling along thinly populated roads at night to rob, harass, or harm them. Men had confronted other men with whom they were in conflict in bars and groceries, at sales, or on the street, insulting them by calling them damned liars and sometimes declaring a desire to cut out their guts.

Most relevant to what was to come, Union County, like other counties, also had a long history of specifically white-on-black collective violence. Because antebellum black Union Countians, whether slave or free, lacked many of the rights and much of the access to the courts that whites enjoyed, such violence only occasionally found its way into the historical record in the antebellum period. In 1855, Asbury Garner, Charles Garner, Levi Davis, James Fowler Jr., Calhoun Vinson, and Thomas Comer attacked Giles, a slave of William Cole, and also threatened and menaced white Hezekiah McKissick with clubs and knives. That same summer Mary Dupree, William Dupree, and Napoleon Dupree assaulted Cansada Martin, a free person of color, throwing rocks at her house and beating her with a stick.[6] In November 1857, William F. McCullough, J. Reese Parker Jr., William R. Parker, and Walton Parker assaulted Jery, a slave owned by James Corry.[7] James J. Jeter, Thomas B. Jeter, Thomas R. Jeter, James Hudspeth, Davis Watkins, Christopher Sartor, and Thomas J. Comer were charged in September 1860 with unlawfully beating Peter, the slave of Reuben Thomas.[8] We cannot be sure of the race of these attackers, but as they are unlabeled, they are all likely white. Some of these groups likely were patrols who were authorized to regulate slave populations but who overreached the limits of their authority.[9]

Collective white-on-black violence was reported more frequently after the war, though it is difficult to know how much of that increase in reported violence was due to an increase in its frequency and how much to freedpeople's formal access to the court and new optimism that they might find assistance there. Surely there was an unusual level of white-on-black violence in the postwar Upcountry, even by the quite violent standards of the time. Officers stationed in the South Carolina Upcountry echoed the astonishment of their brethren in postwar Tennessee when they discussed local racial violence. One officer in Edgefield County, South Carolina, wrote in March 1866:

Two men (white) had killed a negro + cut an Ear off another the Evening before about 5 miles left of my Encampment, it is presumed they belong to a regular Organized band of Guerillas which infests that country. . . . It is practiced among these monsters either to kill or mutilate any colored people who unluckily falls into their power [sic]. . . . none of the colored people dared to sleep in their houses at night, but had to take refuge in the surrounding country. Some part of the peaceful loyal white population are well acquainted with the haunts of these depredators, but dread them would they betray them, as there is no protective power in the country. . . . They are a terror to the loyal population at night these ruffians besotted with drink rave and tear, like Prarie indians, through the Streets of the city. The civil law is powerless to protect against such desperados.[10]

In Edgefield and Newberry in March 1866, "a band of outlaws . . . infest[ed] the District." This group apparently whipped those attempting to leave their old plantations to find other work and those who employed them. Adelbert Ames reported that freedpeople were being taken from their homes and sometimes killed, because they were searching for work, or demonstrated "the faintest disrespect" or the "slightest show of resistance." It was, he believed, "an attempt to keep them in the same state of subordination as when slaves." An assistant provost marshal reported that this group had killed five freedmen and one white man.[11] A similar group in Union called the "Slickers" (or " 'Slick,' as they style themselves") emerged in Union at the same time. "Slickers" was a generic term that had been applied to vigilante and guerrilla groups across the mid-South since the 1840s. Henry Augustus Storey, an army captain in the Maine Fifteenth, stationed in and around Union County from early November 1865 through June 1866, claimed in 1890 in a military history that the Union County Slickers closely anticipated the Ku-Klux. He described them as having been "thoroughly organized, armed and mounted," riding at night for the purpose of intimidating blacks into remaining in the employ of their old masters and recounted how he and his men had tracked and killed Slicker leader James G. Fernandez. Local Union County historians maintain that the Slickers would later feed into the Klan, and name its members as Jim and Harry Fernandez, Asa, Billy, and Elipas Smith, Sam Sumner, Dolphus Gregory, and D. C. Gist.[12]

Not everyone agreed that Union's condition was dire. Lieutenant F. H. Whitter, commanding the military post in March 1866, took a sunny view:

"The citizens are orderly and well behaved," and no troops were necessary. Freedmen's Bureau acting assistant commander A. P. Caraher saw a very different situation when he arrived at his post a few months later. Reporting back to Charleston, he described a recent murder of a veteran freedman named Mac, and continued, "If the troops were withdrawn from this district the freedmen could not live here. Many of the planters after getting their wheat crop gathered find that one or two freedmen and their families can be dispensed with and set to work at once to run them from the plantations."[13]

Union County whites also had some rather pointed anxieties about black organization. Antebellum white southerners everywhere had feared slave insurrections, but Union Countians had come closer than most to experiencing one. In October 1861, a barkeeper and community leader named William Keenan had charged a slave named Sax with planning a slave rebellion. A fellow slave testified that Sax had been reading the papers of Governor Gist (who had been largely governing the state out of his home in Union) and was trying to convince his fellow slaves that the Confederacy did not have enough fighting men to win the war and that the time was therefore ripe for insurrection. Whites had long known that Sax often kept the lights in his carpentry shop burning into the evening and that it had become a gathering place for slaves. This had generated concern, and one white man had even snuck up to eavesdrop but had discovered nothing untoward. After the allegation, searchers found damning evidence at Sax's home: a large empty weapon box, lined in green felt like a box for dueling pistols, and a volume of *Hardee's Military Tactics*. Other slaves testified that Sax had attempted to recruit them. Yet Sax was a remarkably charismatic figure: several elite white men testified to his character, praising his submissiveness. One white elite said he was more like a white man than any Negro he had ever known.[14] Sax also had a defense: he acknowledged that he was organizing a military unit among slaves, but claimed that he had been planning to surprise local whites by offering it to them for the Confederate cause. Remarkably, Sax had been found innocent and released.[15]

Four years later a white Union County mob tried to lynch Sax. As nearby Columbia burned and Union Countians awaited their fate, Sax had been arrested on February 19, 1865, for writing a letter to a young white woman, Susan Baldwin. The letter read: "Miss Sue, I take the liberty saying to you that you be perfectly easy. I have a plan provided for you and you must keep silent as possible. Dont you fret at all." He was brought before Justice of the Peace Moses C. Hughes, who found Sax guilty of "grossly insulting proposals" to a white woman and sentenced him to eight hundred lashes on his bare back, to be delivered in four installments. A mob led by James Keenan, the brother and housemate of the man who had four years earlier unsuccessfully charged Sax with insurrection, broke into the jail to extract Sax.[16] Dr. James P. Thompson confronted the mob and called on them to wait for the law to take its course. Keenan, who had earlier warned that he would "kill the first damned rascal that tried to protect the negro," shot Thompson, inflicting a serious but nonfatal wound. Thompson then shot and killed Keenan. It was not until March 15 that a mob, this time wearing disguises and Confederate uniforms, assembled once again and killed Sax.[17]

William Faucett and Union's Vicious Whites

Much of Union County's prewar violence had centered around an effective and persistent group of white criminal actors who had a long-standing pattern of short-term collaborations with community elites. At the heart of Union County's violent subculture from the 1850s up through the Ku-Klux period was a group of men who met in the grocery of a white man named Robert Greer, thirty-eight years old in the 1870 census. The most violent and active of these men was William Faucett, aged sixty at the time of the 1870 census.

Faucett dominated Union County's criminal records at least from 1852 until his death in 1874. From 1852 to 1878 Faucett appeared in the criminal records on forty-seven occasions, more than all but one man, John Skelton, who appears to have served as some sort of professional bondsman.[18] Faucett not only appears second most frequently in criminal indictments in the county; he also emerges at or near the top of other calculations of an individual's structural importance in a network. In terms of network math, his "betweenness centrality," at .0246, was higher than that of anyone else in the county (Skelton was one behind him). This means that the shortest path between any two other people in the network was more likely to be through him than through any other person, hypothetically giving him some control over the spread of resources and information. "Degree centrality" describes the proportion of all other people in the network a given person is connected to.[19] There Faucett's score, .291, was second to that of Skelton, but was still near the top within the county. It is all the more remarkable that Faucett's metrics are so high on this network, given that he died in 1874 and therefore appeared on no indictments in the last four years of the period calculated. These calculations do not mean that Faucett was the most prominent man in the county (there are better ways to gain popularity and influence than frequent trips to the courthouse), but it does mean that, wherever things in Union became contentious enough that they reached the ear of the sheriff, William Faucett was by some margin more likely than anyone else (besides Skelton, in his role as bondsman) to be involved.

Faucett appeared in these indictments in every possible role. Sometimes he was accused of assault, sometimes he was a witness, sometimes he was a bondsman, and sometimes he was claiming to be the victim of an assault or other crime. Most frequently, when he was accused of criminal acts himself, it was for assaults and barroom brawls, though in April 1858 he was also accused of cattle theft.[20] In July 1861, for instance, he was accused of beating twenty-nine-year-old Elizabeth "Lizzie" Willard in her home "in a most barbarous manner" while two other men who had accompanied him to her home encouraged him.[21] As an antebellum witness, he had often testified against people for allegedly stealing from him or others. As a bondsman, he tended to defend socially marginal whites, particularly those indicted for running vice businesses like houses of prostitution and illegal bars.[22]

Faucett had a regular group of associates who congregated with him at Greer's bar: Charles Garner, a propertied white man, sixty-six years old in 1870, who resided in Pinkney; H. Thompson Hughes, a white man in Union, twenty-eight in 1870, with a small amount of property; Thomas Jefferson Greer (brother of Robert Greer), thirty years old in 1870, a propertyless white man in Union, who had lost a leg at the Battle of the Crater;[23] George Matterson "Mat" Stevens, twenty-five, propertyless, who lived in Union in 1870 and had lost an arm; Edward Hawkins, a twenty-four-year-old white man who lived beside Jefferson Greer; and others.

Faucett and his friends were socially marginal. Their frequent appearance in the indictments suggest that they had ongoing tensions with their neighbors and that either they or their neighbors chose to draw in the state to resolve them. The sorts of charges that were brought against them, often for assault or riot, underlined their marginal status. There were other indications: H. Thomas Hughes in late November 1870 was indicted for assaulting a sheriff's deputy, fifty-year-old white man B. Frank Gregory Jr. His friends, including Faucett and Mat Stevens, went

FIGURE 2. A visualization of the connections among William Faucett and his closest associates in Union, S.C. It is a dense subnetwork of all individuals who co-occur with at least thirty-four other members of the network. The k-core was derived in Pajek, and the visualization was rendered in Gephi, using the Fruchterman-Reingold algorithm followed by the Label Adjust algorithm for clarity.

his bond, but he was required to do something that there is no evidence any other person in the county had ever been required to do: sign a pledge not to drink at all for the following year, and never again to drink to intoxication.[24] Other indications abound: when John Sanders shot Thomas Jefferson Greer in his brother's grocery, the citizens of Union did not pay Greer's doctor's bill, which Greer had expected them to do. To (literally) add insult to injury, in early 1871 several of his neighbors got up a petition requesting leniency for Sanders.[25]

Faucett and his associates had many feuds among themselves and with others in the community, but they also had a particular history of conflict with black men, stretching back to the antebellum years. Faucett and his friends seem to have associated regularly with black men. These associations were not always negative. Faucett went bond for Benjamin Whitehead when he was accused of trading with a slave in 1854, and for William Littlefield when he was charged with gaming with a slave in 1857.[26] Faucett's friend Levi Davis was accused of selling spirits to a slave in 1859.[27] But most recorded instances of interactions between Faucett and his friends and black men were contentious. Charles Garner and Levi Davis, for instance, were indicted for beating a slave in 1855.[28]

Faucett and his friends would continue this pattern of interactions with freedpeople. Because so many individuals named in indictments cannot be confidently matched with census records, it is impossible to quantify the frequency of Faucett's friends' interaction with freedpeople in the same way as with (easily identifiably) slaves, but it is apparent that the interaction between Faucett's group and freedpeople continued to be more frequent than between most other whites and freedpeople. When Faucett in 1869 allegedly threatened John Powell, a small white man, "not very active," whose feet were not straight, with an axe, Powell stabbed him several times. In Faucett's indictment of Powell, he claimed that Powell should not be allowed to testify in his own defense as he had been "convicted of an infamous crime: gambling with a slave."[29] Given Faucett's own history of support for those who had fraternized with slaves, this claim was hypocritical. Yet it was consistent with the complex and adversarial relationship Faucett and his friends continued to have with black Union Countians after the war.

Faucett's close ally H. Thomas "Tom" Hughes is an example of this. A Saturday night in February 1868 apparently found Hughes beating on the door of Lydia Skelton in search of freedwoman Mary Davis (likely the Mary Davis of Bogansville who at that time was seventeen years old). When Skelton told him that Davis was not in, he beat in the door and rushed at Skelton with a knife. When "she evad[ed] him," according to a witness, "he made several other attempts, cutting her bonnet. The noise awoke her husband, who went immediately for assistance. Hughes then released her and ran away. Her husband declined applying to the civil authorities, fearing they might not be justly dealt with."[30]

Or take Charles Garner. As Charles Garner and William Faucett were walking away from a polling place in May 1869, they passed two black men or boys wrestling. Faucett and Garner were around sixty years old. Garner, like Faucett, had been repeatedly indicted for assault over the decades, mainly for fights with whites, once for illegally beating a slave. Though he did not know the black fighters, he bet one of them, Billy Gist (probably fifteen years old), twenty-five dollars that he could throw him down. Gist gamely replied that he could throw Garner down. Garner suddenly hit him on the head with his horn-tipped cane. Although those around him could hear the impact of the stick on the Gist's head, witnesses made a point of noting that it did not knock him down. Garner then walked off with Faucett. Displaying impressive self-control for a fifteen-year-old, Billy apparently refrained from responding to the assault physically or verbally, but he had the wherewithal in this brief window of Republican control to bring an indictment. Those who testified seemed sympathetic to Gist, aside from Faucett, who alone denied that Garner had hit Gist ("I hear the little negro say to Garner that he could thrown him down. I never saw any lick struck").[31] Garner, even as a man in his sixties, had a desire to compete with black men, to jump into their games—a confident racial privilege paired with a sense of familiarity.

After the war, Faucett's interactions with freedpeople were mostly adversarial. He served several times as a prosecutor or witness in cases where freedpeople were accused of larceny. In 1868, he accused a freedman of stealing some bread and dried beef from him. The man died (starvation?) before the case came to trial.[32] His friends frequently served as witnesses and bondsmen for him in these cases. For instance, in February 1868 Tom Hughes brought a case on Faucett's behalf accusing freedwoman Charlotte Miller of stealing a bonnet and a pair of socks. Mat Stevens served as a witness.[33] Faucett's involvement may suggest that he frequently interacted with marginal and desperate black people, owned property particularly irresistible to larcenous freedpeople, or that he offered himself as a false accuser or witness as a way to harass freedpeople with whom he was in conflict. On taking charge of Unionville in November 1866, A. P. Caraher noted, "There are a number of Freedmen confined in this Dist Jail, by the Civil Authorities, on charges which are frivolous, and in some cases made by irresponsible parties."[34] For Faucett and his friends, violence against black people was more likely to be personal than abstract.

Faucett and his friends were socially stigmatized, but they had their role. Some of Union's wealthiest elites appear to have had an understanding with him. Figure 3 shows that William Faucett was very much tied to the elite community in Union. The figure is the central part of a graph that I made in Gephi by extracting Faucett and the wealthiest Union citizens from the network, and then using a Fruchterman-Reingold algorithm, followed by a Label Adjust algorithm for visual clarity. Fruchterman-Reingold is a force-directed algorithm that places each node (in this case, the name of an individual) closer to those nodes with which it is most connected and farthest from those with which it is least directly connected. The "wealthy" on this graph are those Union County heads of household who claimed over $5,000 on the 1870 census. There were 140 such individuals in the census, and 108 of them could be reliably identified in the network. A tie does not prove that Faucett and the elite man in question were allies (though in many cases they were); it merely shows that the two had co-occurred on the same criminal indictment. That is, the two likely knew each other and had some common ground or interest, even if they were on competing sides of that interest. The size of each person's name ("node") indicates his "degree," or the number of connections he had to other people. The intensity of the line (or "edge") connecting the names indicates the number of connections that existed between those people. William Faucett's degree, and his geographic placement within the network, reflect the fact that many of Union's wealthy men *within the criminal indictments* had more connections with him than they had with one another. No doubt they had more social and business relationships with one another, but when they came before the law in any role, they found themselves frequently involved in the same incident as Faucett.

An algorithm applied to a group of Faucett's closest associates combined with the partition of wealthy elites connected to Faucett intermingles them in interesting ways.[35] Elite James Steadman is grouped with Faucett associates Edward Hawkins and Thomas Jefferson Greer. Faucett, Stevens, and Hughes are grouped with ultrawealthy John Cotton and James Rogers. Caution is required here: this merely indicates that they co-occurred in several cases. In part this might simply reflect Faucett's ubiquity and his inability to resolve matters of concern outside the court system in a way that tensions between two elites might have been resolved. Be that as it may, when John Cotton went to court, he was more likely to be there with Faucett and his friends Stevens and Hughes than with fellow elite Steadman.

One way that Faucett and his companions were tied to wealthy men was their participation in the county's underground economy. Some of Union County's wealthy men had substantial ties to the underground economy. James Rice Rogers, for instance, seventy-four years old and boasting a hefty $6,000 in property on the 1870 census, was indicted

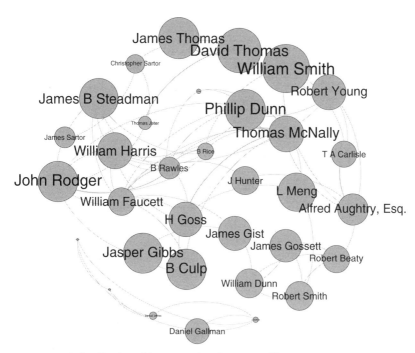

James Thomas
Christopher Sartor
David Thomas
William Smith
James B Steadman
Thomas Jeter
James Sartor
Robert Young
Phillip Dunn
Thomas McNally
T A Carlisle
B Rice
William Harris
B Rawles
John Rodger
J Hunter
L Meng
Alfred Aughtry, Esq.
William Faucett
H Goss
James Gist
James Gossett
Jasper Gibbs
Robert Beaty
B Culp
William Dunn
Robert Smith
Daniel Gallman

FIGURE 3. A visualization of the connections between William Faucett and identifiable Union County residents claiming at least $5,000 total property on the 1870 census.

in 1870 for retailing spirituous liquors without a license.[36] Rogers and Faucett intimate Robert Greer seem to have had a close relationship. They served together as bondsmen and witnesses on several indictments. Rogers would be serving as sheriff during the first Ku-Klux jail raid and would later be arrested under the Enforcement Acts.

It seems that Faucett and his friends served the interests of those running Union's underground economy. Before the war, both Faucett and his friend Samuel Sumner (local histories name him as one of the members of the Slickers) had bailed out and served as witnesses for those accused of running houses of prostitution and illegally selling liquor, a pattern that would continue after the war.[37] These connections to respectability may help to explain why such lawless men as Faucett and H. Thompson Hughes continued to be tolerated in Union. Men accused of cattle theft or men who made a practice of beating down seventeen-year-old freedwomen's doors on Saturday nights or beating unprotected women with sticks might risk being run out of town, or at least jailed. Flipping through Faucett's and his friends' records, however, reveals a sea of *nol pros* decisions.

The Threat of Black Organization

Republicanism in Union County basically meant black Republicanism. The very few white Republicans in Union were targeted so relentlessly by social ostracism and by Klan and other violence that they either left Union, were killed, or changed their partisan affiliation. Hyman Rubin III, drawing on gubernatorial correspondence, identifies only nineteen white men in Union who, at some point during Reconstruction, identified themselves as Republicans. These Republican whites were few and far between. They were important transitional figures, but the power they were working to usher in would be black.[38]

There is little doubt that white Union Countians felt threatened by black Union Countians, but there may have been more to their fear than they represented. They claimed they feared that black Union Countians, supported by an armed black militia, would rise up en masse against white people and that they would use their powers to oppress white people as a class. Although nearly all of the collective violence reported in the Upcountry in the few years after the war was committed by whites upon blacks, whites in South Carolina generally, and in Union County specifically, spoke frequently about the potential for black violence, and particularly of the potential for organized black violence. Federal officials recognized southern fears and asked officers, in their monthly or biweekly reports, to list both outrages committed by whites against blacks and those committed by blacks against whites.

These fears were exacerbated by the advent of Radical Reconstruction and the dramatic power shift it represented. Under its terms, the federal army established an outpost in Union in 1867. The Union League began to organize that summer.[39] The new South Carolina constitution, enfranchising black voters, was passed in March 1868. Robert K. Scott, formerly a strong voice for racial justice in the Freedmen's Bureau, took office as governor on July 9. During these busy months, Union County sent delegates to the constitutional convention, organized local Union Leagues, and overwhelmingly supported the election of the governor. Scott Nelson has described the broad and important function of the Union Leagues in black community organization: "The Union and York County leagues resembled institutions as diverse as Masonic clubs, evangelical churches, and modern trade unions." They engaged in and facilitated economic cooperation.[40] By late July, Union County Republicans were organized enough to plan a large barbecue, likely the first large public gathering in the county since Scott's election.

Republicans in Union were in a position of unprecedented influence, but they were afraid of Democratic violence. Scott received streams of fearful letters from Republicans, white and black, in Union and the rest of the Upcountry, particularly in the late summer of 1868. White Republican Sebastian Kraft, who clarified that his letter was "neither radical nor democratic sensation"—and did not mention the Ku-Klux— wrote that although he had lived in Union for more than three decades, he was facing public insult by powerful men and "lay[s] himself lyable [sic] to be killed without any chance of protection." The extreme level of anxiety produced by the Republican barbecue points to the persistence of the antebellum "psychopathic fear of negro insurrection inherited from slavery days" augmented by the new federal commitment to enforce black rights.[41] When local black Republican leaders Hiram W. Duncan and Robert Martin began to write a letter to Governor Scott a few days before it, they claimed they expected a race war in the county to commence soon: "Tha preparing and we are redey. When tha start with us we are going to try to meet them righ and all that want to see the Negars and Rebels fight can com up here tha say that war has to start and it had jest as well start now as aney time."[42] According to newspaper reports, the barbecue was well attended. Even if the number given in one Democratic newspaper, fifteen hundred, was seriously inflated, it was presumably a large gathering. Some of those present carried weapons.[43]

A group of armed white Democrats confronted and violently dispersed the barbecue. Duncan and Martin reported that the white attackers killed a man, though the death did not generate a murder indictment.[44] Democrats' anxiety about the barbecue was transparently about the capacity of local Republican organization that it expressed. According to an article reprinted in the *Edgefield Advertiser*, Republican leader John Bates had "invited the negroes to organize and promised arms and music for them at an early day, and encouraged preparations of a military character on the part of the negroes."[45] Bates was a "Major of Battalion" of the local Union League.[46] It is impossible to know how much military organization did in fact occur at the barbecue. Militias were informally organizing in the Upcountry in this period, though black militias would not be officially organized and armed for two more years. But whites feared that the road from picnic to militia was a short one.

Whites were likely attributing more organizational capacity to Union's freedpeople than they possessed. A *Union Times* article justifying the attack claimed that black Union Countians had used the barbecue to plan an assault on the county jail in order to release a prisoner named Sam Glenn. Glenn was facing a charge of assault and battery for dangerously injuring a man named James Dineson in a knife attack a few months earlier.[47] It is not clear why whites suspected black Union Countians of this plan, but the *Union Times* breathlessly claimed that only white vigilance had narrowly averted the attack: "This Broad River battalion [Union County men] were to have been reinforced by similar bands from Spartanburg, Chester, and Newberry. We know that the Newberry party crossed Tyger River, well armed, on Friday night. . . . We feel certain that they intended to attempt the release of Sam Glenn, and that many of them were determined to rob the stores. We are sure that two thousand negroes would have been here." While "the threatened riot did not come off," Union Democratic whites feared there would be more such attempts.[48]

Despite Duncan and Martin's bold claim in their letter to the governor, freedpeople in the county were far from ready for a race war. Whites only recently returned from a real war must have understood the distance between even the loudest and most confident call to arms and a coordinated multi-thousand-person campaign. They must have grasped that organizing new freedpeople in a hostile countryside would pose substantial challenge and delay. Yet South Carolinians' recent wartime experience likely also contributed to their irrational fear. Military invasions of southern civilian spaces would have felt plausible. No doubt Union Countians, like civilians in war zones everywhere, had developed mental images of streets teeming with enemy soldiers. Scott's plan to organize black men into militias would have reawakened these wartime fantasies.

A month after the barbecue, there was another large and violent racial confrontation. On August 26, John Bates, a black delegate to the constitutional convention, a local organizer of the Union League, and a correspondent of Governor Scott, was returning by rail to Union County, presumably from Columbia. Fearing ambush, a significant group of Bates's supporters, some armed, were waiting at the depot to serve as guards. Several young and middle-aged black Republican men were present, and likely at least two women: Amy Mobley, wife of emerging black political leader Junius Mobley, and an unidentifiable woman named Callista Gist.[49] In a telling demonstration that black Union Countians were developing effective informal associations by the summer of 1868, they had begun to provide a guard for Republican leaders, including Bates and Junius Mobley, who had taken office in July as their new state representative. Whites attempted to disperse the armed group before Bates's arrival, promising they would ensure Bates's safety. The guard refused to disband. When Bates arrived, shots were fired between the groups.[50] Bates later named a white man named John Harrison Sartor as having shot him. A freedman named Moses Whites also shot Hawkins in the thigh. Sartor, on his part, accused Bates, along with freedman Frank Hobson, of shooting at him, along with whites W. J. Vaughan, J. C. S. Vaughan, "and others," with a double-barreled shotgun.[51]

The aftermath of these shootings suggests that black Union Countians were developing meaningful organizations: Bates and Hobson turned to a network of propertied black men rather than white patrons to provide their bonds.[52] Their bondsmen were Peter Jeter, a twenty-two-year-old black man in Fishdam who would boast $200 in property on the 1870 census; Charles Jenkins, a fifty-four-year-old black man from Union; Randell Dawkis, a forty-three-year-old black man from Fishdam with $40 in property; Anderson Jeter, a twenty-two-year-old black man from Pinkney; Mark Hampton, a twenty-six-year-old black man from Union; and Giles West, a fifty-six-year-old black man from Union with $175 in property. The other five men listed as contributing to their bonds—George Walton, William Barnes, L. B. Jeter, Henry Cabeen, and Ephram Hobson—could not be identified reliably on the census. The novelty of freedmen providing bonds is shown by the note written on the indictment: "Note. These three boys have three horses Ephraim Holson, Randal Dawkins and Adison Jeter. I think they will do very well."[53] Most of the identified bondsmen lived in Unionville, and two lived in outlying townships. While the necessity of eleven bondsmen (usually two sufficed) points to prejudicial treatment and lack of financial resources, black Union Countians in 1868 were able to pool their resources together to protect their leaders.

The coordination of black Union Countians on the ground anticipated one of the central elements of Governor Scott's strategy for destabilizing white Democratic control of the Upcountry: since the first days of his administration, Scott had discussed organizing and arming Republican militias. It was not until June 13, 1870, that the state officially recognized three companies, all in the Thirteenth Regiment: Company D, under the command of J. Alexander Walker; Company E, under the command of L. Dow Reid; and Company F, under the command of M. Wallace, with

R. S. Cannon and Aaron Lyles as lieutenants.[54] On August 18, 1870, Dow Reid received eighty-two rifles, and Alex Walker received ninety-eight.[55]

The organization of the militia system increased the visibility and influence of certain black leaders in Union. Most notable was J. Alexander "Alex" Walker, a militia captain who would also be elected a trial justice. Walker appears on the 1870 census as a twenty-five-year-old propertyless black man residing in Unionville with a fifty-year-old black woman, presumably his mother, and three black children, ages four, two, and one. Walker, a "schoolteacher and a magistrate," had lived in Union County his entire life. Literate, analytical, political, connected to powerful leaders outside the community and commanding the respect of several other high-status black leaders in Union County, Walker, like John Bates or Sax Joiner, was the sort of man who could preside over the building of a postwar Union County in which black people meaningfully shared power.

Walker accepted the role of militia leader and would soon prove himself to have more than his share of personal courage. Even so, he had a strong sense of the limitations of force in the struggle for black rights. He believed instead in a careful negotiation of terms of alliance with white leaders. In his correspondence with Governor Scott, he assumed a posture of dignified dependence, a pragmatic appeal to patronalism no different from that taken by Union County whites in their correspondence with the governor.[56] He also strove to run his militia with minimal provocation to whites: unlike other militia leaders in Union, he refused to allow his men to bring their arms home, keeping them in a central storehouse. As he wrote to the governor in September 1870, "I would have let the company taken ther Guns home with them but I have been looking for [large-scale racial violence] and I new what they would do if they had their guns with them at ther houses." He had just witnessed "great croads of Democrats" amass to go support the white riots in Laurens, "would beg your information what to do if the same commenses in Union County." These men, he told the governor, were threatening to take his locked but unguarded weapons, but still he did not distribute them to the militiamen; instead he turned to the governor for counsel.[57] The approach taken by Walker, a reasonable man in unreasonable times, proved disastrous. Perhaps his competence made Democratic whites as nervous as guns in the hands of his men would have done. As W. E. B. Du Bois noted in *Black Reconstruction*, "If there was one thing South Carolina feared more than bad Negro government, it was good Negro government."[58]

As Walker's ascension to militia leader showed, black Union Countians increasingly did have access to some meaningful formal power, through their connections to state and federal officials and, particularly by 1870, through their access to militia weapons. White Union Countians complained about this power bitterly, claiming that it put them in fear for their lives and safety, as well as their property. Yet there is little evidence to substantiate whites' stated fears that black Union Countians used their power to violently coerce or injure white citizens generally. There is, however, substantially more evidence that black Union Countians were using their new power in another way damaging to the interests and well-being of certain whites: Alex Walker and other emerging black leaders threatened to unsettle the productive working relationship between white elites and Faucett's friends by disrupting the illegal activities that both profited from and by revealing the unsavory relationship to prying eyes.

Black Union Countians were not as ready to ignore William Faucett's and his friends' frequent violations of the law as white elites had been. Recall H. Thompson Hughes's assault on Lydia Skelton in his pursuit of Mary Davis in 1868. While the Freedmen's Bureau agent had walked away from Skelton convinced that she and her husband were too intimidated to bring a charge against this very dangerous Faucett ally, indictments reveal that somehow they changed their minds and brought it. We cannot know what led to this change of heart: perhaps it was simply that they found their own courage. But perhaps they were visited by local black leaders after the white officials left.[59] And they were not alone in standing up against these violent men.

Twenty-two-year-old mulatto militia leader and state representative Junius Mobley bravely took out a peace warrant against William Faucett himself in 1868. Taking out such a warrant was a real, and often an intentional, irritation to its object. It forced Faucett to come once again into the courthouse, sign a bond for his good behavior toward Mobley, and find a man willing to put money on it (given his history, this could not have been a simple task). Elite gentleman John Rogers must have had his doubts as he posted that bond, but he must have found it in his interest to do so. Faucett, in what may well have been a calculated insult, then took out a peace warrant claiming to fear physical attack by Amy Mobley, Junius's twenty-nine-year-old mulatto wife.[60] In June of the next year, Joseph Hix brought an indictment of assault against Faucett. He was enabled to do so because freedman Ellison Scott was willing and able to post the bond for Hix's appearance to prosecute the case.

Another Union elite, hotel owner William Steen (who, as we will see, relied on Faucett's friends' bootlegging services), came forward with a bond for Faucett.[61]

Faucett and his friends were, of course, quite familiar with the courthouse. Not only did Faucett himself frequently initiate indictments during this period; he and his friends had frequently been indicted by whites as well, and had reliably managed to use their local influence to get the indictments *nol prossed*. But in this brief window of Republican control in Union, these indictments had more teeth behind them. Lydia Skelton's, for instance, had gotten the serious attention (though not the effective action) of the Freedmen's Bureau. And when, in July 1870, William Faucett found himself facing the trial judge, it was none other than J. Alexander Walker. Walker did in July 1870 what white trial justices had conspicuously avoided doing for decades: sentenced "Bill Fossit" to serve twenty days in jail.[62] The gauntlet had now been thrown down.

The counteroffensive against black Republican efforts to govern Union would come together most brutally in the fall and winter of 1870–71. Faucett and his friends had long brought frequent charges of petty theft against their black neighbors, but Faucett's warrant against Amy Mobley was an early indicator of a new strategy. These men began to claim to be physically intimidated by politically assertive freedpeople. So it was that, on October 29, 1870, Tom Hughes accused young freedman Joe Vanlew for assaulting him by placing his hands on his collar.[63] Later in 1870, Hughes and Faucett both breathlessly claimed that the black militia were now threatening their lives. An article in the *Daily Phoenix* interested itself sympathetically in the well-being of these normally unsavory, violent men. It wrote in mid-November that some men presumed to be militia had thrown rocks at both Hughes's and Faucett's homes. Faucett claimed to have fled his home for safety, only to learn that the men had planned to set it on fire had he been present.[64] A local elite, Robert Shand, later testified that a black militia had also driven Hughes out of his home on one occasion that fall.[65] Rising black leaders, then, were in persistent tension with Union's criminal underclass, and several elite whites were stepping forward to defend Faucett and his allies.

It was in the context of this strife and these stratagems that one of the most violent and organized Klans of the Reconstruction era took shape in Union County.

Klan Violence

Evidence about the organization of a Klan in Union is as spotty as it is about the organization of the Klan in Pulaski. It is largely based on much later memoirs and local histories, which range from the convincing to the implausible. Mr. Charley Jeff Harvey later remembered that the Union County Klan built a twenty-five-foot boat to carry freedmen down the Broad River, where "they would take the negroes own guns, most of them had two guns, and tie the guns around the negro's neck. . . . When the captain would say : 'A-M-E-N,' over the side of the boat the negro went, with his guns and bullets taking him to a watery grave." Accounts like these may have some basis in the period they describe, but have also been profoundly shaped by the twentieth-century tellers' sadistic romanticization of racial violence.[66] William Rice Feaster names J. C. Long as having "sent his Knight Hawk (courier) Dr. Charles Sims of Cowpens" to get information from J. Banks Lyles, the Grand Cyclops of South Carolina, then organized the first den in the county, "Den 500."[67] He occasionally refers to the earlier "Slickers" as Klansmen and imagines them as a highly organized and political group, responding to the army, militia, and Union Leagues. Allen D. Charles claims that there were sixteen dens in the county and that most white men were members.[68]

Historians continue to debate the level of Klan organization in the Upcountry. Most agree that the Upcountry was among the most highly organized of Klan regions. Joel Williamson says, "There was no conspiracy above the very local level, and often none existed there. There were local organizations of South Carolina in 1870 and 1871, but it is highly doubtful that any of these were organized before this time and it is a virtual certainty that no statewide or even widespread organization of the order ever existed."[69] Richard Zuczek lets Chief Constable John B. Hubbard explain the extent of organization. Hubbard had been informed by his own travels and correspondence, and from reports by his agents, that "a complete organization exists from the Savanna river to Chester . . . and its object is to intimidate Republican voters on election day and if necessary murder leading Rebublicans."[70] Bruce Baker says, "Existing collectivities long familiar with the use of violence and various other social networks merged with political activists opposed to the Republican Party . . . to ride through the night under the banner of the Ku Klux Klan"; he names "a set of young merchants and professionals from Unionville and the railroad town of Jonesville" as leaders, including teacher J. Banks Lyle, clerk James Gideon Long, and perhaps prominent lawyers William H. Wallace and Isaac G. McKissick. According to Baker, they became active within the county in the summer of 1868.[71]

The chief difficulty in doing a local analysis of Ku-Klux violence has always been, of course, that Ku-Klux actors were never reliably identified and tried. This holds true in Union County. While we have the names of 102 men the federal government arrested under the Enforcement Act, the number arrested may have been substantially higher, and the government lacked the reliable local information it would need to consistently arrest the right men. Some arrestees, like Republican loyalist William F. M. Williams, may have falsely confessed as Ku-Klux in order to testify against and convict others. Yet many of those arrested do make sense, and the list of those known to have been arrested is useful as a guide. We have a much more reliable list of the Ku-Klux victims. The list of victims of deadly violence is close to definitive, though even there accounts sometimes slightly vary. Names of victims of nonfatal attacks are available through congressional testimony and newspapers, and again have to be approached with care.

Union County racial violence had first became substantial in the fall of 1868, as the federal election approached. Chapter 7 will discuss in more detail whether this first round of violence was "Ku-Klux" violence. Collective violence in Union in 1868 was political, targeted at Republicans, effective, and brief. Yet records leave us no leads about who might have been committing it and give only a handful of specific names of those victimized by it. Those who tried to vote at the township of Santuc in 1868 were turned away. No one could get ballots at Goshen Hill, Cross Keys, or Cedar Bluffs. Fifty-four-year-old Jed P. Porter, a white Republican from Pinkney attempting to bring Republican ballots to a polling place, had the ballots taken from him, was forced to leave the polling place, and was followed from town by his neighbors: Edward Lindsey, a wealthy thirty-three-year-old; Thomas Foster, fifty-two; Jno. H. Foster, fifty-three; Richard Page, fifty-nine; Joseph Kelly, forty-three years old and propertied; Simion Kelly; and Lemuel Sprouse, forty-eight. These men knocked Porter from his horse, stomped his prostrate body, threatened to finish him off by hitting him with a rail, then left him for dead. The attack was not generally called a Ku-Klux attack.[72] The most committed and able potential Republican voters took the long trip to the county seat, Unionville, where they were once more prevented from voting, either by groups of armed white Democrats or by claims that their names could not be found on the books.[73] Some accused the Democrats of fraud: Richard Kinyon testified to having personally witnessed Sheriff J. Rice Rogers stuffing ballots into the box in Union.[74] These tactics were very effective in suppressing Republican votes. The result in this Republican-majority county was 1,725 votes for Democrat W. D. Simpson and 866 for Republican A. S. Wallace, with James H. Goss, running independently, receiving 89.[75] Simpson won the election, though it would be overturned after a federal inquiry in 1870.

After the elections of 1868, there was a period of relative quiet in Union, with no reports of Klan violence for some time. "Everyday" white-on-black violence continued, of course. D. D. Going, for instance, wrote to the governor about a terrible shooting of a fifteen-year-old black boy named Alfred Gist by white man James M. Askew in January of 1869.[76] The second, much more intense round of increased racial violence would begin in November 1870 and continue through spring 1871. As the election of October 19, 1870, approached, tensions ramped up through the Upcountry, though the real explosion of violence would not occur until just after the election.

In October, large numbers of Union County men for the first time joined with white Democrats in surrounding counties to commit acts of collective violence. When word arrived from Laurens County the day after the election that a large armed conflict was in progress between militias and white Democrats, David Gist, the son of the former governor, led a group of Union County men to Laurens to support the county's whites. Alex Walker described the group mobilized to go from Union to Laurens as "great cro[w]ds," but other sources have it at less than twenty.[77] This group would not have included Faucett and his friends. They probably did not own horses, and they did not socialize with Gist, even in strange times. H. H. Wilson, sent to Laurens to investigate, reported that eight hundred to one thousand men had gathered there, having arrived in "organized bands" from Union and the rest of the Upcountry.[78] In addition to mustering such a large force, he reported that Upcountry whites had run their assault in a military manner, picketing all roads to and from the railroad and all stations within twenty-five miles of Laurens.[79] Caution and generous discounting is called for in reading this impressive organizational claim, but at the very least it was a large and menacing gathering, and many people within and beyond the Upcountry believed that such impressive organizational mechanisms were in place and operative around them.

Back in Union, nighttime raids by groups of armed men against black and white Republicans began in November 1870. The men targeted for attack showed several common characteristics: they were generally politically assertive, seem to have been particularly prosperous for Republicans, and lived in the northeastern part of the county, particularly in Pinkney, where William Faucett and many of his closest connections lived. Some of them also had histories of social tensions. White trial justice Alfred B. Owens, a forty-seven-year-old white man living in Gowdeysville (near Pinkney), had served as a witness to the apparent attack, on July 16, 1860, of a slave, Jerry (described in the indictment as "deceased"), who was indicted for "resisting and hitting pattrol with his fist."[80] A few days later, he had been accused together with seven other men (including those who had apparently been assaulted by Jerry days before) of assaulting a (presumably white) man on the public highway in 1860 by setting a dog on him.[81] Likely, then, he had been a member of a brutal slave patrol. Two years later, during the war, he had been a witness when one of the men who had allegedly released the dog with him was deliberately run down by another man's buggy. The buggy driver had then thrown a large stone at his victim.[82] In addition to probably participating in violence against slaves and factional violence against other whites, Owens shows signs of close proximity to slaves: he had been indicted, in 1861, for trading with a slave, and had been a witness in a slander trial in which a slave had accused a marginal white man of theft.[83]

Owens would be the first person killed in a Klan attack. The inquest for his November 8, 1870, murder merely said that he had been killed by unknown parties, but a later indictment specified that he, along with his son and daughter, had been staying at a neighbor's home. Twenty-five costumed men "dressed in black with read around the eyes and other colors" had forced them from the home by threatening to set fire to it. The men then killed Owens. Republican trial justice Drury D. Going, a fifty-nine-year-old Pinkney resident, wrote to Scott that he was likely to be attacked next by "these outlaws and Ku Klux," and indeed he was.[84] Going had less of a presence in earlier criminal indictments than Owens had. In 1844, Amasa Going had been accused of "Negro Stealing" in what looks like assistance in the attempted escape of a slave named Andy. Drury had served as a witness, and since Going was not at all a common name in the county, it is safe to assume they were close kin.[85] Drury had been assaulted by the contentious James Millwood—beaten around the shoulders—a year later, in 1855. Interestingly, J. P. Porter, who would later be assaulted by his neighbors while attempting to deliver Republican ballots, went Millwood's bond.[86] When costumed men attacked Goings on December 1, 1870, he was dangerously wounded, but survived.

That same day, a Ku-Klux group attacked and whipped a sixty-year-old freedman named Giles White. Like Owens, Going, and even Porter before him, White resided in Pinkney. In fact, he had the misfortune of living only a few households away from Faucett intimate Charles Garner. The fact that White had an eleven-year-old son named (or possibly renamed) "Abraham Lincoln White" suggests that the two would not have been on easy terms.[87]

On December 10, Ku-Klux arrived at the Gowdeysville home of fifty-year-old mulatto blacksmith and farmer Alfred Wright. A witty and confident man, Wright must also have been quite industrious: he employed hands and had planted the experimental crop of peanuts in 1870. When Ku-Klux came to attack him, proclaiming that they had come from hell to carry Alfred Wright back there, he hid and they departed. He claims to have tracked them and discovered their identity by following the path of peanut shells they left behind. On Christmas, a large Ku-Klux group came to the home of thirty-two-year-old white Republican farmer W. F. M. "Bud" Williams in Jonesville (just south of Gowdeysville and Pinkney) and took his firearm.[88] Williams had a history of participation in collective violence. He had been accused, along with ten other men, of a Christmas Eve 1856 nighttime attack on the home of prosperous white Pinkney planter T. J. Whitlock.[89] A few years later, he was accused of violating the peace warrant he had signed promising not to harm white farmers Samuel and Willis Ward of Jonesville.[90] He was accused of assault in 1868.[91] He also had some contact with Faucett's friends. In 1867, he and Mat Stevens both served as witnesses in the case of a freedman accused of larceny.[92]

The five attacks on Owens, Going, Wright, White, and Williams in November and December 1870 would be the attacks most widely recognized as "Ku-Klux" before the large raids to come. But a good deal of collective violence, much of it political and racial, was occurring around Union in the final days of 1870, and it was uncertain whom should be credited. White Republican farmer Jesse Mabry claimed that just after the election, in November 1870, he had been approached by seven costumed men and told to stop allowing Republicans to speak on his property.[93] He apparently ignored them, but when they returned he called them thieves and threatened to shoot them. His neighbors, he claimed, came to his defense: "If he is going to be hung, we are going to protect him, for he is an honest man."[94]

On December 28, a "general melee" ensued at William Barnett's estate sale in Cross Keys. The Alexander and Bishop families, both white, lived a few households away from one another in Cross Keys and were involved in a long-term feud.[95] On December 28, Ross Bishop, a middle-aged man, got in a fistfight. Seeing the fight, Ross Alexander, sixty-five, approached, held a stick over his head and urged the man fighting Bishop to "kill him, kill him, kill him." Ross Bishop's son, twenty-five-year-old Clough Bishop, then attacked Ross Alexander, "kick[ing], stamp[ing], [and] rais[ing] [a]stick to strike" him. Ross Alexander's twenty-one-year-old son Robert rushed to defend him, at which point either Clough or his twenty-one-year-old brother Rufus shot at Robert two times, missing him. Nothing in the indictment brought by Robert suggests that anyone thought of it as having political or racial significance. The politics of the Bishops and Alexanders are not known. But federal marshals arrested Clough Bishop under the Enforcement Acts in 1872.[96]

That same evening saw a murder of a freedman by costumed men that many doubted amounted to a true Ku-Klux attack. The victim was twenty-two-year-old John Mills of Draytonville. Mills had been convicted of stealing a small quantity of seed cotton in 1868 from his landlord, John P. Dawkins, sixty-eight and one of the wealthiest men in the county, and from thirty-year-old John Tench, probably Dawkins's overseer or tenant. He had served time in jail, had been pardoned by Governor Scott in May 1870, and had returned home.[97] On his return, he testified on behalf of Dawkins and Tench that the white men to whom he had sold the cotton, Noah and William Webster, had been aware that the cotton was stolen. In response, the Websters, as was conventional in these cases, had put up a long series of witnesses to testify to their good character and the bad character of their accusers; they also brought in a series of witnesses who testified that Tench had paid Mills to give the testimony. If the Websters were not themselves Republicans, they had close Republican allies. Jesse Mabry of Draytonsville, a farmer in his fifties who was one of Union County's few white Republicans and served as a constable for the governor, testified on the Websters' behalf.[98] But while this conflict may have had a political element, alliances were not exclusively along political lines. Democrat J. Rice Rogers had also been pulled in to the case on behalf of the Websters, testifying that he had heard Mills brag about the bribe in jail.[99] On multiple occasions during the early Reconstruction Tench had been indicted for assaulting freedmen and -women who lived on or near his land, perhaps because he believed they were stealing his cotton (he brought periodic larceny charges against them as well). At the height of the first bout of Ku-Klux violence in the summer of 1868, for instance, Tench had been indicted for entering the home of his near neighbors, freedwomen Henrietta and Rhoda Dawkins, pointing a pistol at them, and threatening to kill them.[100] Yet when John Mills was killed on December 28, 1870, by costumed men who slit his throat and perhaps shot him as well, a local elite suggested that the group of men who killed Mills were not the "regular" Ku-Klux.[101] John Wesley Scott, a twenty-four-year-old white man and a close neighbor of the Websters, was indicted for his murder.[102] There is no evidence that Tench, Dawkins, or Scott was ever arrested as a Ku-Klux, though Mills's killing was brought up in congressional hearings. The killing of a freedman by a costumed group of whites in itself did not necessarily count as Ku-Klux activity within or without the county.

A final violent event that week was the fatal attack on a freedman named Wade Johnson or Wade Hawkins on the day of the Stevens shooting. This attack, like that on John Mills, had a backstory. In August, a young black man named Albert Martin claimed he had been assaulted by a group of partisan Republicans, including nineteen-year-old mulatto man James Hawkins and twenty-one-year-old black man Silas Hawkins. Martin claimed that the group had told him they intended to stop him from making Democratic speeches and threatened to kill him, but he managed to escape them.[103] Martin's charge fit closely with allegations made by Democratic congressional candidate Isaac McKissick, who would soon challenge Republican A. S. Wallace's victory on the grounds that black Republicans coerced black Democratic voters.[104] It was also an attack on the militias, which had begun to receive arms less than a month before the incident. Silas Hawkins and another member of the accused group, Monro Long, were both well-connected black Republicans. When they were charged, Republicans leaders rallied to their aid. Hiram W. Duncan, a state senator, and Junius Mobley, a member of the state House of Representatives, both went bond for the accused men. When they were found guilty by the local jury, Governor Scott pardoned them.

On December 31, 1870, two men attacked Wade Johnson/Hawkins. First a black man named Sam Harris struck him with a shoemaker's hammer, debilitating him and confining him to his bed. Later Albert Martin entered his home and shot him fatally in his thigh.[105] Wade Johnson/Hawkins had not himself been a member of the group that Martin had named as having attacked him in May, and his specific relationship with Silas and James Hawkins is unclear, but James Hawkins prosecuted the charges against Martin when Wade Hawkins was killed, suggesting that he was a close family member. Wade Hawkins's family was a political one; he lived with his father, Moses Hawkins, who had been shot defending John Bates in 1868.

Harris and Martin's killing of Johnson/Hawkins appears to have been another chapter in heated feud between Republican and Democratic freedmen: freedman Sylvanus Wright, who would be a Klan victim within days, had been accused of shooting Harris in the knee during the violent period of 1868. Another freedman who would soon be killed by the Klan, Barrett Edward, aka Burt Woodson, had been listed as a witness to that event.[106] There are also close connections between this attack and the violence that would transpire that evening and the next day: appearing in court that very day to give bond for James Hawkins's appearance to prosecute at the trial was Thomas Vanlew, who lived at Silas Hawkins's house and would the following day find himself shooting at Robert Greer, among others, as they attempted to search his home following the shooting of Mat Stevens. In 1872, when Samuel Harris ended up in jail for another assault (this time on twenty-two-year-old mulatto John McBeth), Faucett ally Thomas Jefferson Greer would write a letter to the governor attesting to his peaceable character and asking that he receive a pardon.[107] That is, there is suggestive, though not definitive, evidence of alignment between the black Democrats involved in this case with the Greer gang, and of a similarity or even an identity in the choice of Republican targets of each. And indeed, Albert Martin would be one of the handful of black men whom we know to have been arrested by federal marshals as a Ku-Klux.[108] Sam Martin does not appear on the list of arrestees by name, though we do know that an unnamed mulatto shoemaker was among those arrested.[109]

Sometime before 11 P.M. on December 31, 1870, a series of events began that would see at least fifteen deaths and bring small, rural Union County into national attention as an epicenter of organized, political Ku-Klux violence. Two propertyless white friends of Faucett, twenty-five-year-old Mat Stevens and his forty-two-year-old neighbor Benjamin Robinson, set off to drive a barrel of whiskey from "Balau's house," five or six miles out of town, to Steen's hotel in Unionville.[110] Driving at night was perilous, partly because of the poor visibility and bad roads but mainly because of the elevated violence Union and surrounding counties were suffering, which included nighttime ambushes along roads. Stevens and

Robinson's cargo, however, was illegal and so best transported at night. Stevens took out a flask and lay in the back of the cart with the barrel while Robinson drove.

After some time Robinson came upon a group of black militiamen picketing the road. The men were members of two militia companies. Only some of them were armed (the unarmed militiamen were likely members of Walker's company). They had set up the informal picket because they had heard a rumor that the Democrats were planning to attack either black Republican Junius Mobley or white Republican W. F. M. Williams, who lived about seven miles out of town. Some have plausibly suggested that setting up a picket on a major road into town on New Year's Eve was also part of their efforts to suppress the vice trade.[111] Since Williams had been visited and disarmed by a masked band a few days earlier, and since Wade Johnson/Hawkins, the son of an active black Republican, had been assaulted and killed that very day by black Democrat Albert Martin and his associates, it is not surprising they were on alert. Possibly they were anticipating Martin's group, though it may have been Faucett's they expected all along. When Robinson and Stevens tried to pass, the men stopped the wagon. Discovering its illegal cargo, which would have been very hard, under the circumstances, for Stevens and Robinson to report stolen, they demanded that he give it to them. According to Robertson, Stevens filled up a flask for them from the bottle he had with him in the wagon but refused to give them any from the barrel. Sylvanus Wright claimed that no whiskey was given: "Robertson said it ain't my whisky and Stevens said the same." Stevens told Robinson to drive on. As the men pulled away, some members of the company shot at the wagon. This shot would be a crucial link in a terrible chain of events, and it is hard to understand what motivated it. Perhaps it was important to the pickets (or those who fired) that white men not dismiss their armed demands and drive breezily by. Such pickets were part of how power operated in Union, and to mobilize the resources to set one up, only to have it dismissed, might have serious consequences.[112] Perhaps the shots were not about the whiskey at all. There is some reason to suspect that Stevens, having passed through the organized group, would have headed straight to Faucett, which might well have led to trouble not unlike that which was caused by shooting him.

When the shots rang out, Stevens and Robinson stopped the wagon and ran in separate directions into the woods. Robinson got away, but Stevens ran into a nearby home inhabited by forty-two-year-old mulatto man Ben Parr, twenty-three-year-old Dele Parr, a woman named Fanny Davis, and three children. Ben Parr was outside with the militia, but apparently the women in the home tried to shield Stevens from the militiamen, who came after him in pursuit. (It is possible, of course, that one or more of the women was complicit in, or encouraged, the killing. All of the descriptions of this event come from militiamen's testimony, and they might have protected them.) Parr, Jim Hardy, and some other militia members following on the heels of the pursuers later testified that they too attempted to protect Stevens and were ignored. They may have been up for a defensive picket, or even an attack on Albert Martin, and considerably more wary about one on Faucett's friends. Three other militiamen—Henry Cannon, Taylor Palmer, and Isaiah Noland—allegedly pulled Stevens out from under a bed. Stevens asked to see Hardy, but Hardy had prudently left as soon as he realized that his objections were to no avail. Stevens pleaded with the men, using that typical mid-nineteenth-century plea of inoffensiveness: "Don't hurt me boys, I'm all right." Cannon, Palmer, and Noland then allegedly took him back to his wagon and drove him into the woods, where they fatally shot him. They, or perhaps other militiamen surveying the scene after the killing, propped up his head on his hat, and laid his jacket over his body.[113]

The attack (dragging a man from a house into an isolated place in the woods and executing him ceremonially) mirrored the Ku-Klux attacks that Republicans had been suffering, some in Union likely (as we will see) at the hands of Stevens and his friends. Cannon, Palmer, and Noland reported to those militiamen who remained by the road that they had killed Stevens. The men then dispersed, leaving the body where it lay.[114]

The black militia here was replicating the subculture of collective violence with which Union Countians were familiar. Picketing a road to defend one of their own from attack was conventional Union County behavior, as, probably, was the shakedown of Stevens. Even shooting after the retreating figures of Stevens and Robinson as they ran their picket would perhaps not have been particularly abnormal in as gun-happy a culture as Union County's. The killing of Stevens made it a much more serious matter, of course. Militiamen, however, might have miscalibrated elites' willingness to support Faucett's marginal men. Given Stevens's liminal status, had the militia been composed of white members, it seems likely that the whole affair would have blown over. Indeed, when Stevens's peer Thomas Jefferson Greer had been shot just months earlier, his assailant, John Sanders, had enjoyed widespread public support.[115]

Ben Robinson, in the meantime, had run into Unionville to the home of Mat Stevens's brother-in-law, H. Thomas Hughes, twenty-eight, who lived a few houses away from Robinson and Stevens (and who had lost a leg). There he found three white men: Hughes, William Faucett, and William Powell. The question of why these three violent men were burning the midnight oil that evening is worth considering: perhaps other plans were in the works. The three men launched a search for the wagon and Stevens. Ultimately they found the wagon, with the whiskey barrel, they claimed, partially empty and Stevens's body not far away. The following morning, whites in town mobilized. The sheriff deputized Greer and several other whites and issued open-ended search warrants. The response to the Stevens shooting, among other things, made it clear that black militias would not be absorbed into Union County's dysfunctional culture of violence. Indeed, the speed and force of the response makes it apparent that whites had been waiting for a provocation. Faucett's friends sprung to action. Faucett fell back on his professional skills, measuring the whiskey remaining in the barrel to determine how much had been taken by the militia, and tasting whiskey found in freedmen's homes to determine whether it had the peculiar "musky" taste characteristic of the particular batch of whiskey in the barrel (it did). Robert Greer recognized a bottle found in a freedman's home as one that Stevens had bought from his bar the day of his death.[116]

Despite Steven's questionable social status, townsmen, including several local elites, sprang into action to find his killers. Groups went through the streets taking militia weapons from black homes and arresting dozens of men as accomplices to the Stevens murder. Most black men yielded their weapons and allowed themselves to be arrested without resistance. As night fell, however, one group determined to take their stand in a boardinghouse in town that locals called either the "Yellow House" or "Silas Hawkins's house." Hawkins was a twenty-five-year-old black man who had been one of the group of black Republicans who had allegedly attacked black Democrat Sam Harris. Hawkins, however, was not present. Instead, brothers Joseph Vanlew (nineteen), Thomas Vanlew (twenty), Alfred Vanlew, Charley Vanlew (twelve), their cousin Major Palmer, and several other people, including their mother, Eliza Chalk (a forty-year-old mulatto woman), were living there when the white deputies came around on the evening of New Year's Day. Joe Vanlew was a member of Alex Walker's militia company but had not been present at the fatal picket the night before. Earlier in the day, he had expressed his willingness to give up his gun "if they don't pester me." As night fell, however, and probably having been apprised of the enormity of the white response by a recent conversation through his window with thirty-four-year-old mulatto James Ray, the brothers and Palmer determined not to give up their guns or yield to potential arrest. These young men refused when Daniel Smith and Robert Greer demanded that they open the door, telling them that they would be "g-d d-mned if [they did]." As Joe Vanlew put it, presciently, "If you arrest me, you will kill me."[117]

While there is conflicting testimony about who shot first, a gunfight ensued between the young black men at the upstairs windows of the house and an increasing collection of white men outside. Thomas Vanlew was shot nonfatally, and Daniel Smith was shot in the groin. The injury would be fatal, though he would linger for several days. Robert Greer took him, bleeding heavily, to the hotel to convalesce, and returned. The mob of white men around the house argued about what to do next. Eliza Chalk testified that she heard a man outside call for breaking down the door and killing everyone in the house. She heard another voice, however, saying, "That will not do."[118] Ultimately, prominent white Democrats H. L. Goss and Isaac G. McKissick convinced Chalk to let them into the house to negotiate. McKissick was a former lieutenant colonel of the Seventh Calvary Regiment and the Democratic candidate (defeated) in the recent House elections.[119] He presented himself as a moral leader: just before the war, he had been one of the founders of a YMCA chapter in Unionville.[120] Chalk's son (probably twelve-year-old Charlie) had nursed McKissick's son (he had both a one- and a two-year-old boy on the 1870 census) when he was sick the year before, perhaps with a contagious disease that precluded less expendable nurses, and McKissick told Eliza from the street that he wanted to be sure her son had not been hurt. "He said 'Liza, you know me. I am not after any harm.'" Either she or her son let him and Goss enter. During the conversation that followed, Chalk remembered, McKissick said little, but Goss expressed his bewilderment at the extreme response to Stevens's killing.[121]

While they were inside the house discussing the terms of their surrender, Robert Greer and others snuck in by the back door. Surprising the group, they arrested Joseph Vanlew, Alfred Vanlew, and Major Palmer. According to Eliza, who was "standing there crying," "Mr. Bob Greer . . . caught hold of Joseph and said 'Come out of here, God Damn you. You are my man.'" The injured Thomas Vanlew was not arrested until the following week. Goss and McKissick, apparently embarrassed by this violation of their terms of truce, insisted to Greer that they had sworn to the men that they would not be harmed. Seemingly reluctantly, but immediately, they turned over the men to the care of saloon keeper, whom they did not trust to keep their word. For the time being, he brought them to the jail as promised.[122]

The arrests at the Yellow House are a synecdoche for how the Ku-Klux worked in Union. The capture of Joseph Vanlew combined the efforts of respectable elites like McKissick and Goss and violent, marginal men like Greer. The presence of seeming moderates like McKissick weakened Republican defenses. Greer then did the dirty work while McKissick wrung his hands. It is possible that McKissick and Goss planned the entire thing out with Greer beforehand, but they were likely unhappy about how things had transpired: their public false promise to Eliza Chalk represented a loss of credibility and reputation to them. It was, in fact, a classic challenge to their honor. Yet they did not challenge Greer. They did not challenge him in the house as he led Vanlew away, or in any way that produced a paper trail in the following days and weeks, as it became increasingly clear that Greer had no intention of protecting Joseph Vanlew. They could tell themselves, perhaps accurately, that they were helpless against Faucett's friends.

It is worth bearing in mind what did not happen the day after Stevens's shooting, which must have been on the minds of all involved. The conditions in the town were ripe for a riot, as had recently occurred in neighboring Chester and Laurens. As Chalk, Vanlew, McKissick, and Goss entered their negotiations, preventing a riot was an important goal. A voice in the angry mob outside wanted to storm the house and kill its inhabitants. Would they have stopped there, or spilled out into the street seeking more victims from the freshly disarmed black population? But in Union, the voice that said, "That will not do," like Dr. Thompson confronting Sax's first lynch mob, could still barely prevail. In fact, the Ku-Klux death toll in Union would ultimately be commensurate with that of a riot. But rather than being selected by angry mobs on the street, the black men who would be lynched in Union would first have their names negotiated over by some group of powerful (whether the wealthy or the criminal elite) Union Countians.

A few days later, Alex Walker was arrested just after having boarded a train to Columbia with Representative Junius Mobley. The two were going to alert the governor to events, including the fact that white Democrats had taken possession of Walker's company's stored militia guns. Although no one claimed that Walker had been present at Stevens's killing, and no one would have argued that the militia was anticipating Stevens's arrival, Walker was arrested as an accessory to Stevens's murder. A large group of armed black men rushed to the scene ready to fight for Walker's freedom. Walker, always a voice of moderation, counseled them not to interfere with the arrest and allowed the white men to take him away on a railroad handcart, promising his supporters that he would be freed soon.[123]

He wasn't. On January 5, a large group of Ku-Klux wearing "big gowns" raided the Union County jail, extracting five black Republican men they considered implicated in the deaths of Stevens and Smith.[124] Their jail raid would have evoked several precedents for them: the killing of Sax six years before, their vivid fears of a black militia doing the same two years before, previous Ku-Klux jail raids they had read about in newspapers. It is not possible to name many of the members of the costumed group, but because many (though not all) of the men were on horseback and were costumed, we can imagine that many of the group's members were elites. From the size of the group, even if it we accept only a cautious estimate, it seems likely that they came from adjoining counties. This would imply an elite group like the one that had just traveled to Laurens, perhaps a return of the favor. Yet there is a good deal of evidence that some of Faucett's friends were present, and in a leadership role, at this event. The death of their comrade Stevens perhaps gave them a status they would not have had before. Perhaps someone was generous enough to provide funding for their costumes. In any event, Alfred Vanlew and Eliza Chalk later testified that the survivors said they knew all of the men who were most centrally involved in the shooting. They only gave a few names: Bob Greer, Tom Hughes, Barby Hawkins, Dan Black, and Mr. Rogers.[125]

"Mr. Rogers" is Sheriff Rice Rogers. Rogers would ultimately be arrested as a Ku-Klux, and, as has been discussed, he had long-standing ties to Faucett and his friends. He himself had once engaged in liquor sales and perhaps used Faucett's services. He had served as a bondsman to Hughes less than two months earlier, in November 1870. Yet in his account, he was himself victimized by the January 5 attack. He claimed that he was sitting at a hotel in town having a drink with his deputy and other "gentlemen" and that on seeing the Ku-Klux come through town he ran to the jail to protect the prisoners but found himself so outnumbered that resistance was futile. He refused to hand over the keys, forcing the men to break down the door.[126] Dr. A. W. Thompson testified to having witnessed him overpowered by the Ku-Klux. If his resistance was merely performative, it was rather an extensive performance. However, is quite possible that Rice both was present to ceremonially resist the turning over of the keys and then donned a costume, as victims claimed, to join the Ku-Klux and engage in the violence.

Dr. A. W. Thomson tried to intervene. Though warned away from the jail by Robert Greer, who was out on a nearby street (structurally serving as a picket, though no contemporary made note of that), he continued on, and apparently came up in time to see Rogers "walking backward [verbally] parlying with some men." Rogers was asking them to let him go sit down and telling them, "I don't mean to see what you do." Finally, Thompson testified, the sheriff sat down on a pile of rocks.[127]

When J. Rice Rogers apparently would not give the attackers the key, they broke into the jail with an axe and called seven names: Joe Vanlew, Charner Gordon, Andy Thompson, Sylvanus Wright, Alex Walker, James Hardy, and Sam Byers. The earliest moments of the attack included a coerced minstrel performance: Joe Vanlew testified that before they took him out of the jail, a Ku-Klux asked him if he liked whiskey: "I said, yes first rate."[128] Their own comment was likely intentionally intended to evoke minstrelsy, though it was also a specific reference to the whiskey barrel at the center of the story, which so readily lent itself to a racist framing of the Stevens shooting. However intentional the minstrel framing was, Vanlew read their comment as demanding a minstrelesque response: "Yes, first rate." His use of a response that indicated both informality and enthusiasm to this question posed by the men whom he knew to be likely to kill him could only have been a put-on. The phrase "first rate," or "fust rate," which had emerged in the 1820s, was a colloquialism common on the midcentury minstrel stage. Vanlew does not appear to have been a submissive young man. Months earlier, he had been accused of putting his hand on Greer ally H. Thompson Hughes's collar.[129] Vanlew and his brother and cousin on January 1 had not walked into town to hand over their guns, as many militiamen had done. When whites came for the guns, they had chosen an audacious direct confrontation while they still had their arms rather than trusting their treatment by a nighttime crowd once they were disarmed. If they had done so with the expectation of armed assistance that did not materialize (and there is some evidence that they had), they took that information with them to the grave. They were bold, and they were strategic. If they had been white and had lived in less desperate times, they would have been called the "active young men" of the county. Joe Vanlew's options were distinctly limited. When he adopted a minstrel tone, he was donning the mask to save his skin.

In another evocation of minstrelsy, the Ku-Klux had a man in their group pose as Mat Stevens:

> They dressed a fellow in white clothes—that is the story I was told about it—and they set him at the door, and brought the negroes out one at a time. He was standing at the door, and they would call him Stevens. . . . They would say to him, "Was this one of your murderers, Stevens?" They would say that to the man who personated Stevens's ghost, and he would say, "Yes." And they would say, "Well, take him off."

Whether this ghost was intended to actually play on freedmen's supposed superstition, or whether it was intended to render as irrational these men's quite natural terror at the imminent mortal danger they faced from armed whites, is hard to say, but these men were being asked to perform minstrelesque superstitious terror.[130]

Two of the men initially called, James Hardy and Sam Byers, were not taken from the jail. It is unknown why Byers was not taken, but he is likely the "Tom Byers" who would soon be killed by the Ku-Klux. According to later testimony, Jim Hardy was saved by the intervention of Dr. A. W. Thompson. Thompson claimed that he tried to convince the Ku-Klux to stop, but succeeded only in winning the release of Hardy, "a yellow boy who worked in the blacksmith's shop." Hardy was broadly popular with white Democrats and, according to the coroner's inquest at which Thomson had also testified as the medical witness, had been present at the shooting but had tried to save Stevens.

After taking Alex Walker, Charner Gordon, Sylvanus Wright, Joseph Vanlew, and Andy Thomas from the jail, Ku-Klux forced them to walk to a place half a mile distant and just outside the town limits. They then called out Walker, whom Andy Thomas referred to as "Captain Walker" and "Squire Walker." A man issued an order for ten Ku-Klux, whom he identified without using their names, to kill him. "Gentlemen, whip me," Walker pleaded. He had charted his course as a politician based on the assumption that whites would respond best to blacks if they demanded their rights, but in as conciliatory a way as possible. He had been reluctant to allow his men to keep their arms. It was no coincidence that he was not present the night the militia shot Stevens, and Stevens was likely shot by members of the other militia, who had their firearms with them. He had insisted that his armed defenders allow him to be unjustly arrested rather than engage the white deputies. It was fitting, then, that his last words were a call for moderation. The men shot. Two bullets apparently killed him immediately.[131]

Next they called out Sylvanus Wright, a thirty-year-old mulatto man who had been a lesser militia officer. We can't know much about Wright, but the small evidence that remains of his life puts him in a good light as a generous community leader. Besides agreeing to serve in the dangerous role of a militia officer, and going bond for fellow black Union Countians in need, he had distinguished himself in his testimony after the Stevens shooting.[132] While some militiamen desperately named others in an attempt to escape blame, Wright denied that he participated in the shooting; but he resolutely refused to finger others beyond the three who had fled, naming men as having opposed the shooting but repeating that he did not recall who had called for, supported, or committed the violence. In any event, six men shot him and he fell to the ground, badly though not fatally injured. He would wait until the men had left and seek help. They then called twenty-two-year-old Andy Thomas to where the bodies lay. The six men who were meant to shoot him "were looking like they were slow in coming" and were prodded to come forward, which they did. As they backed away to fire at him, "he run off as fast as he could." Though two men ran after him "yelling 'halt, halt,'" and he was shot in his arm, he got away. Giving up on him, they told Joseph Vanlew to go out. "When they told me turn around I put out as hard as I could." He received six gunshot wounds, which he claimed were from H. T. Hughes's shotgun, but he, too, would escape death that evening. "I left Charner Gordon standing to be shot and begging for his life." Gordon's body was found the next morning.[133]

The three men who managed to escape sought refuge with friends, but the reign of terror was so complete in Union that no one was able or willing to conceal them effectively or spirit them out of town. Sylvanus Wright made it to the home of William Prater and his daughter Emma. They had heard the shots but had not gone to investigate. They knew Wright: when Emma had been accused of stealing a hundred-dollar bill in 1867, Wright had come together with her father and four other black men to go her bond.[134] But, according to their testimony, they were unwilling to make Wright's trouble their own. Prater recalled, "He called me 'Bill Prater' about a dozen times before I answered." Wright called out for water, telling them through the walls that two were dead and that he was dangerously shot. Emma recalled, "His voice trembled as if he were scared." But William Prater testified that he "never got up. I said I want you to move on."[135] It is possible that they were more helpful than they admitted: he would have had no hope for safety at their house, so close to the scene of the shooting, and somehow the severely wounded Wright reached a more plausible person to take him in. The day after the shooting, T. J. Greer indicted "Ed Meng" for harboring Wright. This could possibly have been a black sixteen-year-old of that name in Unionville. It is more likely, however, that the "Ed Meng" referred to here is J. Edward Meng, a wealthy white man living one household down from the other Ed Meng, and no doubt his former master. The fact that substantial white property owner Thomas McNally went Meng's bond suggests this, together with the fact that the body of one of the men ultimately killed by the Ku-Klux, likely Wright himself, would be taken to Meng's plantation for burial.[136] A much later memoir of the Klan in Union, housed in the Union County Historical Society, refers to Sylvanus Wright as "Sylvannus Meng," which would suggest that Meng had been his master.[137] Meng was no friend to Republicans. He was a partisan Democrat and one of the men who had "found" the circular on the courthouse steps. If he not only harbored Wright but also angered Greer enough that Greer brought an indictment against him, it would seem that he thought the Ku-Klux had gone too far, or at the very least took pity on Wright. Neither the Praters nor Ed Meng, however, gave Wright the assistance he would have needed to survive: concealment until his wounds healed enough to travel, then transport out of town. With whites easily able to observe and control access to the depot and with the town deeply embedded in hostile countryside, it would have been a very difficult task to spirit an injured fugitive out of town. With potential supporters unable or unwilling to harbor them, the three men who had escaped the Ku-Klux were back in prison by the next day.

For a few weeks, Union seemed to draw its breath. Several freedpeople fled, many to Columbia.[138] The day after the raid, Isaac McKissick and William H. Wallace held a public meeting in which town elites requested troops to calm the county. General C. L. Anderson, the state's militia head, came to Union and had a satisfying meeting with them.[139] Sheriff Rogers was replaced by Republican Phillip Dunn, who had been elected the previous year and who immediately appointed Tom Hughes, a Faucett intimate, a likely a participant in the first raid, and Stevens's brother-in-law, to run the jail. Republican leader W. F. M. Williams wrote a letter to Scott on January 14, nine days after the attack. While it was the letter of a worried man, unsure how he had escaped Ku-Klux violence, Williams said that things had quieted and reminded Scott of his promised appointment as auditor. The governor, on his part, was increasingly funneling appointments to Democrats, including those involved in Ku-Klux violence. T. J. Greer claimed to have gotten Drury Going's support to replace him as probate judge, instead of "that hat-headed reformer" Joseph Gist, who also wanted the job.[140]

Eliza Chalk later reported that her son Joe, though he named Hughes as one of their attackers, considered him "mighty kind to him and mighty good" as a jailer.[141] In the general community, crime rates were low during this period. The records indicate only one domestic assault and one public assault—a low rate for Union, particularly in light of the violent activity over the previous two months. But as in the period between the explosions of racial violence in 1868 and 1870, much was going on behind the scenes. It was a time of organization: men who later that year would confess to being Ku-Klux claimed that it was after this raid that they joined the group. It was also a fraught cultural time in Union. A "negro clown" called Porte Faust came through Unionville on January 24 as part of a circus. It is hard to imagine how the presumably mixed audience would, at that moment, have responded to the minstrel genre, which both thematized black vulnerability, immorality, and incompetence and evoked empathy for the black man. They knew the genre well, of course, but perhaps they saw it through new eyes.[142] At some point between Christmas and Ash Wednesday, which fell on February 22, J. N. Herndon threw his annual costume ball, attended by elite white Union Countians. Several Union elites had costumes made for the ball, dominos in multiple colors. Colonel Joseph F. Gist, suspected of being a Ku-Klux, would testify a few months later, "I know nothing of the Ku-klux. I have never seen a man disguised in my life except at a fancy ball."[143] A black seamstress, Christine Page, a close neighbor to the recently murdered Alex Walker, believed that the costumes she had made for the ball were similar to those the Ku-Klux would wear in the second raid. A local Republican white, William Bolt, claimed they were precisely the same.[144]

On February 9, fifty-seven-year-old black man John Tinsley, who sold cakes on the train, ran up from the depot to hand the new sheriff, Democrat Phillip Dunn, a confidential message from Governor Scott. It was a prison transport order. Those being held in the Union County prison as suspects or accessories in the Stevens and Smith cases were to be immediately put on the train to Columbia.[145] Dunn hesitated to comply. Consulting a group of Unionville elites, he came to doubt the legality of the form in which the request was made. He did not put the prisoners on the next train. They would wait until Monday to be transported to Columbia. In the meantime, someone spread word of the confidential order.

On Sunday, February 12, a massive group of mounted horsemen, reported in the Union Times as from five hundred to seven hundred people wearing "black gowns with masks fitting tight to their faces," raided the jail again.[146] It was dark and pouring rain; one of the few witnesses to testify to seeing the Ku-Klux pass was J. P. McKissick, who claimed, likely with an eye to sensational fiction, to have seen the Ku-Klux by the flash of lightning.[147] Reports on the number of attackers range widely, from eighty to fifteen hundred.[148] By most accounts, it was considerably larger than the January 5 attack. These men apparently overpowered Tom Hughes and his assistant Lunney B. Hill, bound them to a post, secured the keys from Hughes's wife by threatening to shoot her in the head, and abducted ten men, probably Sylvanus Wright, Andy Thomas (aka Andy Thompson), Barret Edwards (aka Burt Woodson), William "Bill" Fincher, Ellison Scott, Benjamin Simmons, Thomas Byers (aka Innes Green), and perhaps Aaron Thompson (aka Aaron Estes), and Amos McKissick, all of whom had been implicated in the Stevens killing. They also took Joe Vanlew, probably a man named Mac Bobo, who had been charged with burning a cotton gin, and possibly a second accused arsonist (thought this second accused arsonist may be Aaron Estes). The Ku-Klux marched them out of town to the old muster grounds or "hanging grounds." Allegedly they forced a bound Tom Hughes and Lunney Hill to march with them for most of the way, insulting them as "nigger-protectors," before sending them scurrying home. They hung Sylvanus Wright and Andy Thompson (who they had failed to kill with bullets earlier) and fatally shot Tom Byers, Joe Vanlew, Barret Edwards, and Aaron Thompson. The bodies of the others were never found. No substantial accounts of the scene of the killing have ever surfaced, though Damon Mosely later confessed to having tied the rope used for one of the hangings.[149] By one account, they then proceeded to kill two men who had been indicted for arson at the scenes of their crimes.

There seem to have been at least two very different entities who were broadly granted the name "Ku-Klux Klan": a local one, which went out in relatively small numbers and made individual attacks on successful and influential black men and white Republicans, and a translocal one, composed of wealthy elites from the region. As Simpson Bobo, a white elite in nearby Spartanburg, explained, the Klan was "generally of the lower class of men," but he believed those who participated in the jail raids were "men in disguise, and were respectable men."[150] It is hard enough to get a solid sense of who the local Klan might have been, even for the locals themselves. In the fall of 1870, more than one Union County group seems to have offered themselves up for the role of "Ku-Klux." Robert Shand, a local elite, said in his later memoir, "Incidents in the Life of a Private Soldier," "Throughout the County there were several Klans, and each Klan could make its own raid. They undertook to govern all things at their own sweet will."[151] Some men's attempts to call themselves the Klan were summarily rejected. For instance, a young white man named Mullins who was believed to have constituted such a band was apparently whipped by another band claiming to be the true Ku-Klux.[152] In December 1870, Shand testified of the costumed killers of a black man, John Mills, "I heard that it was suspected that it was not the regular band of Ku Klux but some private parties who did it."[153] There was also a group of Democratic-aligned black men engaging in collective attacks on black Republicans. Some of these black Democrats and those believed to be the costumed killers of Mills would ultimately be arrested by the federal government under the Enforcement Act, but at least some Union Countians apparently believed that the title "Ku-Klux" belonged elsewhere.

The local group most broadly considered to be "the Ku-Klux" was very likely William Faucett and his friends. Assigning Ku-Klux identity is rarely definitive because evidence tends to conflict and because "being a Kuklux" was inherently such a slippery category. While there is a surprising amount of evidence about who various groups of contemporaries understood to be the Union County Ku-Klux, witnesses testifying before Congress, whether Union County elites, confessed Ku-Klux, or victims, gave contradictory lists. Later family and local histories proudly named ancestors and local elites as having been Ku-Klux and Ku-Klux leaders. Some Union Countians themselves confessed to being Ku-Klux. The most substantial sources of names of Ku-Klux are lists of arrestees found in newspapers, and a list of forty-eight men who brought a suit for false arrest because they had been denied the right of habeus corpus.[154] This list, and the supplemental names, might be considered superior to the other sources because while the others are simply individuals accusing or confessing, all of the men on this list had gone through some investigation and procedure before being arrested and held. But the list is not complete: it contains only 102 names, and the federal government likely arrested at least twice that many. It is also not at all clear that the federal government would have arrested the right men. Few of those who were arrested were ever tried and convicted. Any armed force faced substantial problems when policing an area with which they were unfamiliar and relying on some combination of local informants and a hastily constructed overview of the situation. And since, despite the widespread intention that these acts were to target Ku-Klux, the actual arrests were not for "being Ku-Klux" but for violations of the Enforcement Act, so the fact of being arrested under the Enforcement Act did not necessarily label one as a Ku-Klux.

Among those indicted for vice crimes up through 1870, wealthy Union elites, and those who would ultimately be arrested under the Enforcement Acts in 1871 (suspected Ku-Klux), Faucett is central. While he is a member of none of the groups (never indicted for vice, not known to have been arrested as a Ku-Klux, not wealthy), his "degree" within that induced network (that is, the number of times he co-occurs in criminal indictments with the people in those three categories) is by far the highest, at thirty-eight. Second to Faucett, at twenty-seven, are James "Rice" Rogers, the sheriff at the time of the first Ku-Klux attack—whose number is (arguably) artificially inflated by the number of times that, in his official capacity of sheriff, he served as a witness—and John Sanders, an associate of Faucett who showed up in several illegal distilling cases.

Still, this evidence points to Faucett's friends as the core of what the bulk of contemporaries recognized as the Union County Ku-Klux. Many of the men in Faucett's clique—T. Jefferson Greer, Robert Greer, H. Thomas Hughes, Edward Hawkins, and several of their acquaintances, though not Faucett himself—were among those known to have been arrested under the Enforcement Act. Survivors of Ku-Klux violence apparently named several Faucett associates as their attackers. Contextual evidence also supports the idea that Faucett's friends participated in, and in part directed the actions of, the Ku-Klux. It would have made a lot of sense for them to take on that role. They were "experts in violence," with a set of skills, practices, and tolerances that would be useful to them as Ku-Klux. They would have found the Ku-Klux structure, practices, and ideology comfortable. They had little compunction or embarrassment about committing intense personal violence against individuals unable to defend themselves. They were at ease perjuring themselves in the courtroom and could rely on one another's cooperation. There was no clear reason for them to pass up the opportunity to rebrand themselves as Ku-Klux.[155] This was an opportunity for a group of marginal men to become indispensable.

And there is some indication that these men received concrete benefits from allying their own interests with those of Democratic elites. It was a truism in the Klan period that Ku-Klux had no problem finding wealthy men to go their bond, and this appears to have been true in Union County.[156] For instance, Rice Rogers went H. T. Hughes's bond in late November 1870, and in the wake of the Stevens attack, local elite John P. McKissick went bootlegger Benjamin Robinson's bond, and Union elites Thomas McNally and John E. Cotton went H. T. Hughes's.[157] These men were not previously accustomed to such august supporters. There could also be more substantial benefits: T. J. Greer was tapped to fill D. D. Going's job as probate judge while he was incapacitated by his severe whipping by masked men, and H. T. Hughes became jail keeper after the jail changed hands in the wake of the first raid.[158]

It is undeniable that, whatever else they may have been, Klan victims in Union were quite disproportionately active and influential Republicans. This congruence between active Republicans and enemies of Faucett and his friends could be explained in various ways: perhaps Faucett's friends, though not themselves politicians, were interested enough in politics to take offense at active Republicans. Perhaps they hated assertive black men, and most of those men were active Republicans. But it seems most likely that Faucett's men exercised some choice in which active Republicans to attack. On their end, it appears that elites were willing to accommodate Faucett's friends' preferences and align their interests with those of Faucett's companions. Not all black Republican leaders or militia members, or even all of the most assertive or important among them, would be targeted by the Ku-Klux. Those who were victimized appear to have been those whom, informally, elites and Faucett's friends could agree to target.

As a group, the victims of the jail raid executions had telling previous network connections with those groups who should be considered candidates for having been their attackers. While no jail raid victim had a high node value within the network (the men in the group had never or rarely previously been named as accusers or accused; they showed up more often as witnesses and, especially, bondsmen) and thus the group in fact had remarkably few connections within the network, they were disproportionately connected, in the years immediately preceding their deaths, to all of the following: wealthy elites, those later arrested under the Enforcement Acts, those indicted for vice offenses, and William Faucett himself. While these prior connections do not prove that all of these entities were involved in the killing (and it is worth noting that a minority of these connections were positive ones), it does illustrate how the jail raid executions served the interests of several factions in the county, particularly of certain elites and certain of the criminally inclined.

It is quite possible to imagine Faucett informally drumming up a few dozen men. The militias had come up with a similar-sized group on the night of Stevens's killing. They had their militia structure to draw on, of course, but they had largely assembled by word of mouth, as neighbors traveled by foot to mobilize their neighbors. The large number of mounted, costumed attackers involved even in the first raid, and even more dramatically in the second, however, even taking the lowest estimates, must have included men from other counties. The speed with which the second attack must have been organized (the clay roads and hilly terrain in the area made the thirty-mile distance between county seats a "good day's travel") suggest that many of the men had cavalry experience. A messenger could not have gotten from Union to nearby county seats until Friday evening, and the Ku-Klux was in Union County by Sunday evening, giving them not much more than a day to organize. Those familiar with military mobilization later commented that such quick movement would be "good discipline for a military force."[159] Federal investigators indicted forty-four men for the attack, including Faucett friends T. Jefferson Greer, Robert Greer, and H. T. Hughes, but also elites like J. Rice Rogers and Isaac McKissick, and David Gist, and even one black man, John Dawkins.

There is testimony to suggest that Faucett and his friends participated along with elites in the smaller first attack. Yet elites were seemingly becoming less enthusiastic about working with Faucett's friends. Shand's sarcastic tone in his later memoir—"They undertook to govern all things at their own sweet will"—conveys clearly his disgust at the pretensions of these nonelite men who refused to accept the guidance of their betters.[160]

This second raid was perhaps less kind to Faucett and his men. The press, and Hughes himself in later testimony, claimed that they tied Hughes and Hill up, apparently forced them to accompany them some distance on foot, mocked them as Radicals and "n___r protectors," then gave them a written message claiming that the lynching was necessary given the failure of the Republican government to fairly punish black offenders, and sent them, still tied together, running back to the jail. Perhaps, as was likely the case with Rogers in the earlier attack, the performance of adversary treatment of the men was an attempt to provide them with protection from prosecution. But they could not have been happy about how they were mocked in the local paper in the wake of the attack. The February 17 issue of the *Union Times* (the original is lost, but it appears to be reprinted verbatim in a local history book) made much of Hughes and Hill's inglorious rush back to the jail ("on reaching town [they] were completely exhausted, but truly thankful, even to the Ku Klux, for letting them off with no greater punishment than a terrible fright. Poor fellows, we learn they looked more like ghosts than human beings") and claimed that some of the Ku-Klux "appeared to take delight in insulting and tantalizing" them.[161] This too could have been an (unsuccessful) effort to protect Hughes and Hill from arrest as Ku-Klux, but it could also mark a fracture in the cross-class coalition that the Ku-Klux had briefly represented. Isaac McKissick and men like him had their resources and were coming to realize that it was not only black Union Countians and their allies who were paying a terrible price for Faucett's empowerment.

The final bloodshed directly related to the Stevens killing was the conviction and execution of two men for themselves shooting Stevens. Three men were tried on March 17, a bit more than a month after the second Ku-Klux raid executions.[162] Henry Cannon and Taylor Palmer were found guilty and slated for execution. Significantly, the third, Fed Green, was acquitted, as though a fig leaf to cover the legal system's shame. The jury was half black and half white, and surely all jurors had an eye to their personal safety as they made their decisions. When the presiding judge—a Democrat now that Alex Walker and A. B. Owens had been gotten out of the way—addressed the condemned men, he took the opportunity to explain to them that black men's inadequacy as citizens was to blame not only for Stevens's death and their own, but also for the thirteen killings that occurred between them: "To place power in the hands of the weak and unskillful has always been dangerous and resulted in ruin. . . . To have placed guns in your hands, and have you take the law in your hands was worse than madness. . . . What did you, or your officers know of their use?"[163]

Ku-Klux violence did not end with the Stevens executions. In March, Union County elite Joseph Gist would lead a band of men to participate in a race riot in Chester County.[164] And back at home, over the next few months, all of those Republican county officials who had managed to retain their jobs were threatened by Ku-Klux notices and forced to resign; their offices were almost immediately requested by and quickly granted to local Democrats.[165] The arrival of a cavalry unit in Unionville in March had a dampening effect, but more grotesque local violence was still to come. By Richard Zuczek's count, Klan violence in the Upcountry peaked in May 1871. In Union, Reverend Lewis Thompson, a newly appointed Methodist minister and an influential Republican, was warned not to preach to his new congregation at Goshen Hill in June. He defied that order. According to testimony he was taken by costumed Ku-Klux, castrated, and executed, with a notice on his body warning anyone against cutting it down. Only the arrival of the congressional committee, and its offer to arrange for armed men to provide a guard for his brother, enabled his family to recover his body. His brother, Peter Thompson, told the story of the killing. Thompson had been taken from his home by masked men. He had not been allowed to dress, but had been taken in his underclothing. The mangled body that Peter was finally allowed to recover had been subjected to abuse "befitting and characteristic of some of the worst Indian practices."[166]

Union County elite James B. Steadman, asked by the congressional committee to make sense of the Ku-Klux attacks a few months later, insisted, "There is not the slightest evidence that political feeling had anything to do with these two riots at Union Court-House. It was just one of those spontaneous outbreaks of human passion and vengeance which occasionally occur in any community."[167] This was a deliberate falsehood that contained a larger kernel of truth. Ku-Klux violence in Union had everything to do with the political. Attacks closely followed the rhythms of elections and worked efficiently to destroy black political power by targeting leaders and functionaries who enabled it. Bruce Baker's explanation of the attacks Union County largely in reference to the political is entirely convincing. Ku-Klux violence of the early Reconstruction-era Union was a tragically effective assault on Union's rather promising black leadership. In its wake, "the Republican political leadership that had been developing in Union County for the four years between the passage of the Reconstruction Acts in March 1867 and the coup d'etat in March 1871 were dead, fled or cowed."[168]

But the political account too flattens the lived reality of Union. When a man from Union chose to support the Democratic Party, he embraced a set of abstract principles that included white supremacy and the dangers of governmental overreaching. But he embraced it as a shorthand for his immediate experiences and relationships in Union, or even as a strategic rescripting of them. As he navigated complex local issues like how much to tolerate or even profit from the local vice business supported by men like Faucett, whether to be willing to deal with emerging leaders of freedmen like Alex Walker, and what to do about the violence so endemic to the county at all levels, he found that the Democratic framework, and then the Ku-Klux framework, smoothed the rough edges of his disjointed situation.

There was also truth in Steadman's claim. The abstract political commitments represented by the high Klan could function only in relationship to the grungy reality of coalitions on the ground. "Human passion and vengeance" was as crucial in causing Union's jail raid executions as elites' desire to regain political power: in this case, the more passionate, rather than the more political, held the reins. Just as taking Joe Vanlew required both that McKissick talk his way through the front door and that Greer sneak in through the back, so the jail raid executions, together with the many smaller local Ku-Klux raids, were a pincer movement between political elites and the criminal underclass to eliminate a group of emerging black leaders who posed a threat that was not only ideological but also practical.

SEVEN

The Union County Ku-Klux
in National Discourse

Union C. H. . . . has been the theatre of great excitement for some weeks.

—"Editorial Correspondence," *Anderson Intelligencer*, February 16, 1871

Contemporaries did not like to wade into the messy, hopeless, and dissatisfying realities of violence in Union County any more than later historians do. It was perhaps partly for that reason that, by late 1870, Union Countians themselves, whether Republican or Democrat, frequently chose to understand their local racial violence in terms of the national Ku-Klux idea, whether by describing others' acts as Ku-Klux acts or by themselves becoming Ku-Klux. Many Union Countians, marginal and elite alike, declared themselves Ku-Klux beginning in November 1870. They may have felt that tapping into the broad network of cultural and political meaning the Ku-Klux had taken on would allow them to rid the county of its too-able black leaders and the few white Republicans who supported them.

There could have been other violent solutions to the challenge of black empowerment. The most obvious choice would have been to have Alexander Walker, Joseph Vanlew, Sylvanus Wright, and whoever else threatened them, killed by smaller groups, costumed or not. Surely it would not have been difficult for elites to convince Faucett and his friends to kill these men, or even just to drive them away, particularly after they were implicated in the killing of Stevens. It might have been difficult to convince them to refrain.

Instead, Union County's whites did everything in their power to send a message to the national media and to the state and federal government that there was a Klan in Union, that it was highly organized, that it was led by elites, and that its intention was to challenge Republican rule.

264

They went so far as to leave notes that stated all of those things, in case anyone misunderstood their entirely obvious performative meanings, and to write follow-up letters to local papers as well. Their jail raids would have the effect of bringing a great deal of federal attention, in the form of various bodies of armed men, congressional committees, and reporters, into their county over the course of the next year or so. While Union County's white elites would complain bitterly about these arrivals, there is no way around the fact that they brought them there deliberately. In the fall of 1870, the same moment that the national Democratic press began to vigorously join in the conversation about that Klan rather than avoiding its mention, Union's elites felt they would benefit from publicly declaring that they led a massive, violent, political Klan.

Union County and places like it, then, fed back into the national discourse as Klan victims, witnesses, suspected Ku-Klux, and prominent men from Union were called on to narrate their local Klan story to a national audience. Union Countians became experts on the Klan, the controllers of knowledge necessary for the interpretation of this national phenomenon. The emergence of the Klan in the community marked the breaching of the borders of the community. It made certain the arrival of uninvited visitors asking questions and carrying weapons. At the same time, it gave locals potential extralocal power.

Yet little about any Ku-Klux attack was obvious even to locals who had a much richer idea of the background and context of the violence. Even the basic question of whether to label a person a "Ku-Klux" or an act of violence against a Republican a "Ku-Klux attack" was contested. Many Union Countians experienced the word "Ku-Klux" as imposed on them from outside; it never came to seem like their own. Scholars working on the Klan in the Upcountry have disagreed about whether to consider the 1868 political violence that afflicted the county "Klan" violence. It is an interpretive choice: until late 1870, there is very little evidence that anyone in the county applied the term "Ku-Klux" to himself (of course men did not incriminate themselves by claiming to be Ku-Klux, but even in disguise they often did not identify themselves to their victims as Ku-Klux). Victims, too, were reticent about using the term. The word both empowered and endangered those it labeled. Its application translated local events into a translocal context and, in so doing, awakened a sense of solidarity, and often practical support too, among many Democratic whites in Union and beyond. It also mobilized the Republican press and the investigative, violent, and judicial power of the state and federal governments. Those outside Union applied it to events in the county before there is any evidence of Union County residents applying it to themselves.

Union Countians probably learned the term "Ku-Klux" in the spring or summer of 1868 through newspaper stories. Union County's paper, the *Union Times*, is not extant, but its articles (including many relating to Ku-Klux violence) were frequently reprinted in other papers, and there is every reason to imagine that its content closely resembled that of other Upcountry counties and of the major nearby paper, the *Columbia Daily Phoenix*. Two major impulses were at work in South Carolina coverage of the Ku-Klux, both consistent with national news patterns: a fascination with what looked like promising political, organizational, and violent energy on the part of southern Democrats, and a simultaneous and incongruous denial of the Ku-Klux's existence and mockery of those who believed Ku-Klux stories. At first, these papers located the Ku-Klux outside South Carolina. The *Columbia Daily Phoenix* named the Ku-Klux as early as mid-March 1868, calling it a "conservative secret organization."[1] The *Charleston Daily News* did likewise a week later in an article perfectly combining both a celebration of the effective violence of the Ku-Klux ("Its errands of vengeance are always performed in the dead of night") and a mockery of those who feared it ("and with such weird accessories as to invest them in the eyes of the superstitious with peculiar horror. . . . The terror which it has everywhere inspired among the southern radicals is something ludicrous").[2] Articles in the next weeks said that the Ku-Klux was growing and that it frightened freedpeople and northerners alike. By mid-April, the *Phoenix* was claiming that the Ku-Klux had proliferated through the entire South.[3] On April 18, the *Phoenix* dismissively reported the first apparent Ku-Klux action within South Carolina—the leaving of a threatening miniature coffin at a door.[4] In July the *Phoenix* could perhaps be read as tacitly acknowledging a Ku-Klux attack in South Carolina when it reported that the state legislature had offered condolence to the family of a Ku-Klux victim in Kershaw without explicitly criticizing the legislature or arguing that the attack had not occurred.[5] Articles into the summer of 1868 continued this early pattern, delivering local stories with a tone of dismissal and disbelief, but also regularly noting the Klan's increasing scope and function.

South Carolina Democratic papers responded approvingly to the idea of the Ku-Klux, emphasizing its potential as a response to new black forms of organized power. As the *Columbia Daily Phoenix* proclaimed in April 1868, "We now have two intensely hostile elements organized and organizing, and facing each other—the Ku Klux Klan, or secret society of white men, on the one hand, and the loyal league association, or secret society of negroes, on the other, each struggling for supremacy, and each of a race alien in civilization and ideas to the other."[6] The *Edgefield Advertiser* similarly enthused, "If we mistake not, this mysterious order originated lately in the North, and has already sprung as if by magic into gigantic proportions. Its numbers and influence are said to be extending with the rapidity of the wind. . . . Beware Loyal Leaguers! Your machinations are to be no longer unopposed or tamely suffered."[7] The *Anderson Intelligencer* in April included two lengthy introductions to the Klan, one of which was reprinted from a circular from the *New York Herald*, as "a great and unconquerable organization" consisting of all white men, northern and southern alike, who resisted tyranny and believed in constitutional liberties.[8]

South Carolina papers in the spring and summer of 1868 rarely recounted individual Klan victims or individual attacks; instead they broadly described the Klan as punishing Radicals and wrongdoers in nighttime visits.[9] An article published on August 12, 1868, in the Upcountry *Edgefield Examiner* suggests how depictions of Ku-Klux violence were absorbed into and shaped local ideas of violence. It was one of the few early articles that described specific attacks, and the one it described was not a small attack on an individual home, but a massive Ku-Klux mobilization against a jail: the mid-July jailhouse abduction and lynching of a black man named William Gustine in Franklin, Tennessee. The article claimed that Gustine had outraged a white girl and been jailed:

> At the striking of the midnight bell the well known signal of the
> Klan was sounded throughout the town as a body of horsemen, in
> the Uniform of the Klan, apparently three hundred strong, rode
> into the place. The corner of every street was strictly guarded by
> the sentinels, and no one was allowed to pass out of their lines. A
> number of the Klan immediately proceeded to the jail, obtained the
> keys from the reluctant jailor, took out the prisoner, carried him
> to Douglass church, four miles and a half from Franklin, on the
> Lewisburg turnpike, shot him twice through the head and left him
> lying dead near the roadside. The Ku Klux soon after dispersed, but
> at what exact time and to what locality is not known. They were all
> mounted.[10]

Articles like this had a rich resonance to Upcountry South Carolinians. In Union, readers would have thought of the county's recent past: the lynching of Sax a mere three years earlier. But it also had a chronolog-ically immediate referent: this story had been appearing around South Carolina since the end of July and therefore was in circulation at exactly the time that white Union Countians claimed to have uncovered evidence that freedpeople planned to converge to break into their jail to free a black comrade.[11] It is impossible to prove a causal relationship between the two stories: the Tennessee story might have been suggestive to Union's Democratic whites, who would prove quite eager, on other occasions, to claim an equivalence between white and black organized violence. Union Countians would not have realized it at the time, but this story most closely modeled their own dark future: the abduction, the hundreds of armed men, the pickets, the reluctant jailor, the carrying of the victim some distance, and the mysterious arrival and departure of the perpetra-tors anticipate their own 1871 jail raid executions. This and other stories of the Ku-Klux renamed and reframed past and potential acts of collective racial violence, providing a new justification for them by paralleling them to stories of black organizations, and offered a template of action that felt new, appropriate, and perhaps even inevitable.

Even as they breathlessly explained the purpose, spread, and actions of Ku-Klux groups, these Democratic papers continued to weave Ku-Klux denial and skepticism into their coverage. The *Phoenix* in April addressed those "excitable mortals" who feared the Ku-Klux, assuring them that it did not exist and attributing menacing notices supposedly written by them to the class of people who like to make April Fools jokes.[12] Doz-ens of stories in the *Phoenix*, the Charleston papers, and Upcountry papers like the *Edgefield Advertiser* and the *Newberry Herald* did likewise. The *Charleston Daily News*, in September 1869, complained of northern-ers' use of "Ku-klux and Bug-a-Boo" and published two brief sketches mocking Ku-Klux narratives.[13] An article published in late October 1870 insisted that it was obvious to the knowledgeable that "all the hue and cry about Ku-klux-Klan and sanguinary rebels is only intended to deceive the outside world, and to enable Governor Scott" to continue to main-tain his unjust political power through the support of the "strong arm of the United States."[14] The *Newberry Herald* in April reprinted a humorous piece from the *Richmond Dispatch*, parodying exaggerated Klan depictions: "Whenever konvened, they must kerrectly give four kountersigns. These are: Kill the kullered kuss; klean out the karpetbaggers; krush the kon-vention; karry konservatism; konfusion of kongress; konfederates will konquer. Of kourse the Klan kreates konsiderable konsternation among the Kongos."[15] In July, it mocked freedpeople's fear of the Klan in an article titled "De Large Negro Scare."[16]

While Union Countians likely got most of their ideas about the Ku-klux from newspapers, they had other sources too. Some of the popular cultural representations—the ads, songs, and plays discussed in chapter 3—must have made their way to Union County. John Robinson's circus traveled through South Carolina in the fall of 1868, featuring "The Ku-klux-Klan[:] one of the richest and most amusing farces that has ever appeared on sawdust."[17] There is no evidence that Robinson made it to Unionville that year, but these ideas of the Ku-Klux were in the air and accessible to Union Countians.

The ideas they encountered about the Ku-Klux left Democratic Union County residents in a strange position. On the one hand, the idea of encouraging Ku-Klux violence had an apparent utility to outnumbered Union County whites. Union County Democratic whites had long been committing violence, often collective violence, against the county's black population and their white allies. Formalizing or centralizing this, and directing it more specifically to a political purpose, must have appealed to Democratic elites, and perhaps to their less elite allies as well. Yet they were keenly aware that evidence of the presence of the Ku-Klux in Union would be of political utility to Republicans. Like South Carolina Democrats generally, many whites likely wanted to make use of unifying power and the cultural meanings of the Ku-Klux, while maintaining to those outside their locality that it was a fiction. So some elite Union Countians deliberately played with the Ku-Klux idea as an idea, without taking any apparent steps to form a physical Ku-Klux. Unionville elite Robert Shand claimed that a gambler from another county had convinced "an old man from the lower part of this county" named Shelton (perhaps D. H. Sheldon of Cross Keys, a wealthy man yet actually a youthful fifty-one years old in the 1870 census) to surreptitiously place orders for feed and stabling for fifteen hundred horses in Columbia on an upcoming date, then tipped off the state's chief detective that these mysterious orders signaled an imminent Ku-Klux attack, throwing the state government into chaos.[18] The widely practiced Ku-Klux strategy of outright lying and highly selective recounting was a deliberate and comfortable practice for many in Union, and at least some Democratic elites understood the power to control narration as crucial to their future.

Democratic elites worked to maintain control over the story of their county. As Vernon Burton said of Edgefield County, black citizens of

Union were at a tremendous disadvantage in communicating with one another. With the illiteracy rate hovering around 90 percent, "communications . . . were conveyed through personal contact in political, educational, religious and military institutions. For news of events beyond Edgefield, blacks relied upon their leaders."[19] In contrast, some elite Democratic Union Countians, like Robert Shand, had relationships with major papers in Columbia and Charleston, which would publish their accounts and interpretations of events pseudonymously. Union Times reporting was often picked up by papers around South Carolina and beyond as an authoritative account of events in Union.[20] Black Union Countians would begin to gain communications access with the dislocations and migrations of the early Reconstruction era and with the arrival of relatively influential northerners: soldiers, missionaries, Freedmen's Bureau agents, journalists, and entrepreneurs were more likely to be willing to hear and repeat freedpeople's stories. But the clearest challenge to Democratic elites' ability to control the story of Union County was in the new state constitution and state government established in 1868. When new black voters gained the power to send representatives to Columbia for the constitutional convention and then to serve in the legislature, they represented them not only with their votes, but also with their voices. Hovering above the violent struggles occurring throughout the state in the next few years would be the discursive struggle between legislators finally playing a role in building a narrative of Union County outside of its borders and old Democratic elites trying to silence them through intimidation and mockery.

Suppressing the voices of their black neighbors and their marginal white allies became become more complicated in 1868 not only because of the presence of outsiders and black enfranchisement, but also because well-resourced institutions began to put impressive effort into hearing them. The state and federal government both established investigative mechanisms in Union to expose local violence to extralocal scrutiny, analysis, and labeling. Newspapers and government entities developed and circulated narratives of Union County violence. Some of the information-gathering innovations that arose during the Civil War would be brought to bear on the Union County Ku-Klux.

Despite white South Carolinians' fears that a "large sum of secret-service money was sent down to South Carolina, and a small army of paid spies and informers" have been "hiding behind doors, lurking under windows, violating the privacy of private conversation and the sacredness of social intercourse," there is no evidence that any of these federal detectives made it to Union County.[21] But South Carolina's state government was doing much the same thing as the federal authorities and did not neglect Union. Governor Robert K. Scott put impressive resources and effort into creating an information-gathering mechanism. At the center of Scott's plans was John B. Hubbard. Hubbard had been serving in Columbia as a detective under Generals Sickles and Canby; almost immediately after becoming governor, Scott named him chief constable, with a generous budget and extensive powers.[22] By September, Hubbard had selected at least one deputy constable from each county based on recommendations from newly elected state senators and representatives.[23] He appointed other constables who were meant to travel from place to place as need arose, for a total of 151 constables. By January 1869, 4 of these were stationed in Union.[24] These men were charged with writing regular reports beck to Columbia, always at least monthly, but sometimes weekly or daily. Hubbard would aggregate them and present them to Scott.[25] As with any patronage position in these tight times, the role of detective was likely a desirable one that people lobbied to get. Enoch Cannon wrote to Scott from Union in December of 1870, recommending the employment of more detectives and suggesting, "I think I can devise plans. By which the most of the K. K. K.s can be detected."[26]

Freedman John Bates, a delegate to the constitutional convention, was likely one of first of these constables: the Union Times skeptically recounted his claim that "Gov. Scott conferred upon him the high office of detective."[27] If in fact it is the constable position he was claiming, it is noteworthy that he described his role just as Hubbard sometimes described his own, as that of a "detective." We also know that other black Union Countians like Junius Mobley and J. Alexander Walker were in personal contact with the governor and reported to him about events in the county, though it is not clear whether they did so as formal constables. By 1870, five men were listed as having been paid for their duties as deputy constables in Union: all four whose race could be identified were white Republicans. They were J. C. Bonsall (a thirty-year-old unmarried white man, almost certainly from elsewhere, with $500 in property), W. F. M. "Bud" Williams (native, described by lawyer Robert Shand as "a radical—a republican, a white man"), Jesse J. Mabry (similarly a native active white Republican), C. C. Baker (a white New Yorker superintending gold mining, of whom more will be said later), and Samuel Loblic (he does not appear on the 1860 or 1870 census or in the criminal/victim database). The seeming absence of black constables suggests either that black informants were informal and unpaid or that Scott's informant base was whitening over time, which would map onto his gradual abandonment of core Republicans and his move to accommodation and collaboration with Democrats. An embittered John Hubbard later testified that "ostensibly, the object of the constabulatory force was for the preservation of the peace, but in reality it was organized and used for political purposes and ends."[28]

Some examples of these deputies' communication with Hubbard and Scott remain. On September 28, 1870, for instance, just as Union was heading into its period of peak racial violence, Bonsall wrote:

Have nothing to report to-day. Has been quite a number of people in town from the County; considerable drinking. A white man assaulted a colored man; was arrested by the Town Marshal and placed under bonds. The excited feelings of the people are becoming more quiet, although they say they are determined to protect themselves against Scott's militia, and that when the fight commences it will be a hard one. Some do not think the difficulty in Laurens is settled. A mass meeting will be held here to-morrow; expect a large turnout. No news from the [gold]mines to-day. Will I send you the names of those who were on the raid?[29]

The lack of detail in this correspondence may reflect Bonsall's outsider status. But it also may reveal what sorts of information Scott was looking for. Bonsall gives a general description. He is not sure whether Scott wants specific names. Unlike Lewis Merrill, who would be over in York County busily compiling specific information about local residents, Scott seems to be looking for a more holistic mood of the community. Bonsall also believes that Hubbard and Scott have been following several different narrative strains in and around Union (the feeling of the community, events at the mine, the Laurens raid, the response to the militia). Even where his informants were more embedded in the community, they had their limitations: outsiders could be vulnerable because they lacked local allies, of course, but truly local informants could be particularly vulnerable because their lives were so tied to the place. John Bates, for instance, had brought an assault charge against fifty-two-year-old white Santuc resident W. K. Thomas in May 1870, claiming that Thomas had threatened to shoot him if he dared say a word.[30]

On at least two occasions, Hubbard himself headed to Union to gather information. The first was just after his appointment, in the late summer of 1868. In what must have been one of the first trips he took as chief constable, he spent time in Union in August 1868. If we are to imagine that his reports are accurate, he seems to have joined in informal political conversations to gather information: "When I was in Union . . . they declared openly that they would carry the election their way no matter what occurred. I asked them how and they said 'We have a trick you will see.'" He later revealed that he sometimes failed to reveal his real identity on visits to Upcountry counties: "In York they said that if they had known that I was Hubbard I would never have gotten out alive." Yet he must have used his own name in Union. Apparently he was present at the time of the shooting at the depot between black Republican representative John Bates and his impromptu bodyguard and local white Democrats: he himself brought an indictment for assault with intent to kill against white assailant John Harrison Sartor on behalf of the wounded Bates. Hubbard also wrote a report back to Scott recounting the event. This report, which was widely published, showed substantial sympathy with the county's Democratic whites, blaming the violence on the unreasonable desire of black Republicans to guard Bates and, remarkably, failing to mention that Bates had in fact been shot by one of those whites.[31] This may reflect Hubbard's personal politics, which would emerge in his harsh criticism of Scott's government a few years later; it may suggest that his letter had been edited before publication by Republicans in Columbia who were hoping to mend fences with Democratic elites; or it may suggest that the same elite gentlemen who successfully dominated the narration of Union County beyond its borders had also made themselves available to Hubbard. By late 1870, Hubbard had come to the view that the Klan was extensive and pervasive. Before the 1870 election he wrote, "I am satisfied that a complete organization exists from the Savannah river to Chester, a distance of nearly two hundred miles" and claimed that it aimed to intimidate voters and kill Republican leaders, and to bring in large numbers of North Carolinians and Georgians to illegally vote.[32]

Hubbard would make another visit to the county after the second jail raid on February 12, 1871. Sent by Governor Scott to assess the violence, he reported:

A. B. Owens Trial Justice, Alex Walker, Trial Justice, were killed and D. D. Going, elected Probate Judge, was taken from his house and as badly maltreated and whipped that he died. Five men were taken from the jail and deliberately shot. On the night of the 12th inst, a band [sic] disguised men, numbering about eight hundred, took from the jail ten prisoners, six men shot, two were hung and the remaining two fortunately escaped. About seventy five in this county have also been more or less injured by being barbarously scourged and whipped, and at least one hundred persons have been driven from their homes.[33]

Under the circumstances, it is not surprising that Hubbard has abandoned his earlier posture of sympathy for white-on-black violence. Yet Hubbard again failed to get an accurate picture of events in Union. He missed some earlier attacks by costumed men, including the murder of John Mills. Drury D. Going, the murdered probate judge, showed up a few months later to testify to the congressional committee about his brutal whipping. The mistakes Hubbard made in this second investigation, like those he made in his first, would suggest that he never strayed far from the depot in gathering his information (presumably he would have been afraid to do so), but instead relied on secondary reports by interested parties.

While there is no evidence that the federal government sent any of its anti-Ku-Klux detectives to Union County, it gathered the voices of Union Republicans in other ways. In 1869–70, Congress launched an investigation in support of A. S. Wallace's challenge to the results of the 1868 election. Wallace alleged that Democratic candidate William D. Simpson's supporters had been given firearms in order to intimidate voters and that large parties of them had ridden through the county threatening, shooting, assaulting, and beating potential Republican voters before the election and preventing them from voting on the day of the election.[34] Wallace's charge does not name the Ku-Klux: it alleges a "combination or conspiracy" to prevent him from being elected.[35] The board of state canvassers supported his claims, confirming that there was "a wholesale system of proscription terrorism and assassination prior to the election" in the Upcountry.[36]

The first set of depositions, in February 1869, were taken in Columbia and limited in scope. Witnesses confirmed that Democratic groups had used violence and intimidation to prevent Republican men from casting their votes. Yet like many victims and their allies beyond Union, these witnesses seemed intentionally to avoid labeling any of these attackers as "Ku-Klux." The first set of deponents from Union were victim Richard Kinyon (about whom there is little information), who had been threatened at knifepoint while distributing Republican tickets at Draytonville, and black Republican state legislators Junius Mobley, Simeon Farr, and Samuel Nuckles.[37] Simeon Farr never mentioned the Ku-Klux, describing attackers as "members of the Democratic party."[38] Junius Mobley, asked who had made the threats, first answered, "Them who professed to be Democrats," though he later clarified that "the colored men told me that it was the 'Ku-Klux.'"[39] Nuckles, a Baptist minister, reported that a group of eighteen men "known as Ku-klux, they and their horses dressed in white" rode through town the night before the election, cursing and threatening voters.[40]

Republican witnesses from other counties who testified in 1869 used the term "Ku-Klux" selectively. York County residents used it by far the most regularly and the most confidently. P. J. O'Connell of York County reported that a miniature coffin and threatening note signed "Ku-Klux Klan" were left by his door.[41] York confectioner Nelson Hammond gave the same account.[42] John L. Watson of York testified that men "known as Ku-klux" patrolled the county, and John Wesley Meade of York described "a party of men disguised, calling themselves Ku-klux."[43] They had ridden menacingly around his house, and he "was afterward told that they were the Ku-Klux Klan."[44] Laurens County witness George Tuxberry described attackers as "men representing themselves to be members of the Ku-Klux Klan." Sancho Sanders, a Baptist minister from Chester, recalled "a party calling themselves Ku-klux."[45] Alexander Bryce of Oconee County referred to the violent organization he knew of in his county as "Democratic clubs," though he also noted that his friends had been menaced by members of this club "calling themselves Ku-klux."[46] Another man was asked to join a secret society, and "I think he told me it was called the Ku Klux Klan."[47] The consistency with which these witnesses distanced themselves from the term "Ku-Klux" by putting the name into the mouths of others was remarkable.

In early 1870, Congress commissioned white state legislator Joe Crews, a well-connected white Republican from Laurens County, to take a second round of depositions on the same election violence. This time Crews went into Union, enabling him to interview a wider range of people. He chose John Bates, Alex Walker, Moses Hawkins, Sebastion Kraft, Jed Porter, Jesse Mabry, Drury Going, Alfred Wright, C. C. Baker, and W. F. M. Williams. Crews had a strong understanding of Union County. Hawkins, Bates, and Porter were all obvious choices, as they had themselves been attacked by white Democratic mobs in 1868. The choice of Going, Walker, Williams, and Baker, however, was prophetic: they would play more important roles in the Ku-Klux events of the winter of 1870–1871 than they had in the 1868 election violence. This group, interviewed in the county, and a year later, resembled the first in their consistent confirmation of widespread antirepublican violence, threats, and intimidation. They were even more reluctant than the first group to apply the term "Ku-Klux" to election violence. In fact, the second set of interviewees did not use the term "Ku-Klux" at all. Crews frequently referred to the "Ku-Klux" in his questions, and his deponents generally concurred with his use of it, but they did not use it themselves. Asked whether "armed bands of Ku-klux" had "patrolled" Union at the time of the election, John Bates responded, "They did, and threatened all Republicans. They came to my house disguised, drew their arms upon me, and swore they would kill me. After they left my house I heard a shot fired by them at a colored man by the name of Henry Jeter, who was wounded by them."[48] Militia leader, trial judge, and future Ku-Klux victim Alex Walker confirmed that there was a Ku-Klux in the county that fall, that its organization was general, and that it intimidated voters. He also had witnessed it personally: "They came within five hundred yards of my house the night before the election . . . inquired for Aleck Walker and [Junius Mobley], and said they would kill them before morning."[49] Black Republican Moses Hawkins and white Republican Drury Going both agreed that a Ku-Klux group had ridden through their neighborhoods at nighttime, threatening voters with death. Jed Porter had heard of the Ku-Klux at the time of the election and had known a black man who had been threatened and fled to Columbia. Fifty-five-year-old farmer Isaac Poole agreed that Ku-Klux groups during the weeks prior to the election would "travel in disguise at night all over the county, threatening and spreading terror and dismay among all colored republicans." He had seen them and they had come to his own house. Yet none of these men themselves used the word "Ku-Klux" in their testimony. Sometimes they quite naturally used a pronoun to refer to the "Ku-Klux" term already introduced by their interrogators. But when they did feel a need for a descriptive noun, they said "bushwhackers" or "Hell's terrorists" or, most frequently, just "Democrats."[50]

The length to which some witnesses went to avoid assigning a "Ku-Klux" label to Democratic attackers is striking. Jesse Mabry had the most extensive account of violence of all the witnesses. He was first asked, "By whom were these threats made?" and answered, "By members of the Democratic Party." When he was then asked whether there was a Ku-Klux Klan in Union, he responded:

It was generally understood that there was such an organization, and many outrages were committed on republicans by men in disguise riding after night, who claimed to be members of that organization. Five persons, all of whom were republicans, were murdered within my knowledge; three shot and two hanged. A sixth man had his throat cut so that he died at once. Another republican was caught by such a party of men in disguise, tied hand and foot and thrown into the river, but in struggling he broke the rope and swam out. Several other republicans were taken from their homes and whipped and beaten. These outrages were notorious, and believed all over the county. I am satisfied that they were committed, and I am satisfied that it was done by members of the democratic party for the purpose of intimidating and frightening republicans, and preventing them from voting at the election for President and member of Congress.[51]

Mabry did say here that men "claimed to be members of that organization"—the only evidence to suggest that Union Countians self-identified as Ku-Klux in 1868. He also listed several atrocities documented nowhere else. But equally interesting is his apparent choice to avoid claiming that a Ku-Klux organization existed. He readily admitted that organized groups of Democrats calling themselves Ku-Klux had attacked people, but evaded answering the question put to him. Similarly, when Crews asked fifty-year-old mulatto man Alfred Wright, "Were there any bands of Ku-Klux Klan in your neighborhood?" Wright reframed it: "A crowd of men in disguise came to my house on Saturday night before the election, and fired several guns above the house and halloed: 'Hide out, radicals.' "[52] He elaborated on this, discussing whippings committed by the same band, and the abduction and likely murder of one man by unknown people during the night. But he left the assignment of the name "Ku-Klux" to his questioner.

Those targeted by collective nighttime racial violence in Union might have had several reasons for not enthusiastically applying the term "Ku-Klux." As chapter 2 discussed, Republican witnesses were likely reluctant to appear credulous. They knew that only the gullible and cowardly believed in Ku-Klux, and putting "Ku-Klux" in others' mouths protected them from that degrading representation. They were also likely following the lead of Union's Democrats. Victims' gingerly use of the term suggests that it had been employed only sparingly or inconsistently, if at all, during 1868 in Union, probably less so than in other parts of the Upcountry. Union Republicans shared a common discursive culture with their Democratic neighbors, and avoiding the term was consistent with Democratic discursive strategy. The voices of the 1868 Union County attackers have been lost, but given the ambiguity about the Ku-Klux in Democratic papers, Democrats would have been leery about adopting the name as their own.

Political actors beyond Union County both actively participated in the telling of Union County's story and made efforts to intervene in its unfolding. Union's racial violence had begun to appear in the papers outside Union during the 1868 election season. Hubbard's letter on the Bates conflict was widely reprinted, and papers offered editorial responses in support of Union's whites.[53] Governor Scott issued a proclamation in October noting the many reports he had received of organized anti-Republican violence in the state, and he singled out Union County as among the most violent, noting that Republican leaders had been threatened, Republican supporters had been attacked, and there was a general atmosphere of contempt for the law. The Democratic Club of Union challenged Scott's narration of events in their county, suggesting that Scott relied on ill-chosen informants because he was too cowardly to investigate events in the county himself.[54] Joseph Dogan and E. R. Wallace wrote the response. Their reply, published in the *Columbia Daily Phoenix*, denied Scott's allegations against Union line by line. "*There has not been a single instance* of resistance to the laws in Union County," they insisted, denying that anyone had been forced from their home, that death threats had been made against Republicans, that there was a declared intention to keep Republicans from voting, that Union whites had armed themselves in order to control the election, or that Democrats were picketing and patrolling the highways. Union Democratic elites resolved that copies of their resolution should be sent to the *Phoenix*, the *New York Herald*, the *National Intelligencer*, and (oddly) the *Lacrosse (Wisc.) Democrat*.[55] The dramatically lopsided election results in 1868 seemed clear proof to Republicans of a massive campaign of voter intimidation, but Democratic newspapers cynically shrugged it off. Noting that in the Ninety-Sixth District only eight or ten black men voted, the *Charleston News* explained, "The colored people did not desire to vote, and preferred to stay at home."[56]

The period from December 1868 to July 1870 saw a real dip in newspaper coverage of racial violence in Union. This seems also to have reflected the abatement of collective white violence against black Union Countians: there were no indictments or other evidence that groups of whites assaulted known black or known white Republican victims from January 1868 through July 1870.[57] A group of black men, close neighbors in Bogansville, were accused of riot and assault with attempt to kill their neighbor Louis Gee, a forty-five-year-old black man.[58] Two men, one of whom was mulatto, attacked with a gun and a stick a man named William Fowler, and William Faucett went bond for a female relation of the racially unidentified attacker.[59] Three men, at least one of whom was black, assaulted nineteen-year-old Calvin Briggs in March 1870, and Sheriff Rice Rogers posted their bond.[60] Richard Zuczek's calculation of Klan outrage mentions in South Carolina Klan testimony begins with October 1870 (witnesses were discouraged from reaching back before the passage of the Enforcement Acts), but shows that numbers were relatively low until a dramatic increase in reports in spring of 1871.[61] The county's indictments also do not reflect a change in its overall level of violence. The number of indictments for assaults, attempted murder, and murder remained relatively stable from 1868 to 1870, increasing very slightly. Larceny and arson indictments, perhaps the best bellwether of racial tension, dipped in 1869 but were the same in 1870 as they had been in 1868.[62]

As the 1870 election approached, however, a change was in the air. Both racial tensions as reflected in indictments and news interest in racial violence began to increase. As press attention returned to Union, Democratic elites kept their standard posture of publicly admiring the idea of the Ku-Klux while rigorously denying any local accounts of Ku-Kluxes or Ku-Klux attacks. The dramatic increase in jousting tournaments, for instance, reflected both an increase in the prosperity of some South Carolinians and a (ceremonial) adoption of a costumed and martial self-presentation.[63] For instance, in mid-September a jousting tournament followed by a costume ball was held in Glenn Springs, in Spartanburg County near the border with Union. Several of Union's elites were listed as judges or managers of the tournament, including J. G. McKissick.[64] Other tournaments, some with overlapping managers, were held in Columbia, Charleston, and elsewhere in the following weeks.[65] At a November 8 tournament in Charleston, one knight was costumed as a "Ku-Klux" with a red hood with two black horns and a "black half-mask with a crimson curtain." Unlike many tournament representations of the Ku-Klux, which were carnivalesque, this knight's costume was described as deadly serious. The Ku-Klux served, to those assembled, as a symbol of their lost military dignity.[66]

Ku-Klux denial continued in the fall of 1870. Those conservatives who were hoping to win freedmen's votes that fall made it a point to play down Ku-Klux violence. A letter from North Carolina's Zebulon Vance widely reprinted in South Carolina papers in September, for instance, reassured potential black supporters of a conservative ticket that "reports of the Ku-klux Outrages from two or three counties have been greatly exaggerated."[67] In November, the *Keowee Courier* reprinted an article from the *Carolina Spartan* that attributed supposed Ku-Klux violence to "the radical Ku-klux" (that is, Republican freedmen).[68] Fairly consistently, articles printed in South Carolina papers from June through August 1870 mocked and denied claims of Ku-Klux activity. In the fall of 1870, though, the Klan was creeping back into the papers. An article in the *Columbia Daily Phoenix* on September 11, 1870, joked that the Ku-Klux had given a black politician named Menard a "public position" in the silent tombs.[69] This was significant as a straightforward acknowledgment of Ku-Klux violence. Together with the embrace of the Ku-Klux at South Carolina tournaments at this time, it pointed to the beginnings of a new strategy for South Carolina Democrats, who seem to have determined, at this moment, to claim Klan violence as their own.

Union Democrats Create a Local Fake Ku-Klux

The previous chapter shows that beginning in November 1870, Union saw serious and repeated episodes of Ku-Klux violence, including the murders of John Mills and A. B. Owens, the near-fatal attack on Drury Going, and several raids of the homes of freedmen and white Republicans. Not surprisingly, these attacks were almost completely absent from the Democratic press. But Union County Democrats did not simply work to keep the Klan out of the papers: they began a campaign to produce a fake Radical Ku-Klux in the local press. Believing that Republicans were at work trying to "get up a public impression about the Ku-klux," Union County Democrats complained loudly about what they took to be the deliberate misrepresentation of them by Republican newspapers and political leaders.[70] A *Union Times* article titled "A Newspaper Outrage," reprinted in the November 3, 1870, *Carolina Spartan*, condemned Scott's

Republican press in Spartanburg for falsely accusing white Democrats of Ku-Klux attacks for political gain, when in fact, claimed the *Times*, it was black Republicans who actually had been apprehended committing Ku-Klux violence in Fair Forest and Pacolet (both in Union County): "We have heard of colored people willing to take a whipping for a few dollars, and many could be induced to swear against the white people anything that the leaders of the radical party may tell them."[71]

To respond to what they represented as false claims of local Ku-Klux violence, Union's elites began a campaign to expose these claims. Taking advantage of their control over the local press and their influence with presses farther afield, Union Democrats released a series of stories meant to demonstrate that Republicans were making up Ku-Klux stories. Instead of just working defensively to prevent accounts of white-on-black violence in Union from circulating beyond the county, they moved toward managing their own public impression. This shift may indicate their increasing confidence in their influence over the representation of local events. They realized that, despite the stated intentions of powerful state and national entities to hear freedpeople's voices, freedpeople's ability to frame the discussion of their county was limited. They published specific accounts of local events that could be easily disputed by local freedpeople, confident that freedpeople and the few white Republicans in the county would be unable to make themselves heard.

In mid-September 1870, three prominent Democrats, Andrew McNease, J. Edward Meng, and John P. McKissick, claimed to have found a copy of a secret circular on the ground outside the Central Hotel in Unionville. The circular, they claimed, had been written by Radical leaders: "Comrades: The radical cause is in danger. The Reform party is gaining rapidly. . . . We must save our cause, although we may be called upon to sacrifice the lives of some of our best men to carry the point. Remember Randolph, the martyr of his own party; it was his foul murder being charged to the Democrats that saved the State for General Scott, two years ago. We must win again, if we have to sacrifice the lives of a score of our prominent leaders." The circular then called on Republicans to create a list of those within their counties whose lives they would sacrifice. Democrats claimed that the genuineness of this notice was confirmed when they observed prominent Radicals scouring the ground, seemingly for the lost paper.[72]

In the following days, the *Union Times* and the Democratic papers that drew heavily from it pushed the already preposterous account further.

They suggested that Republicans had actually selected sacrificial victims, as requested in the circular, and that these victims were willingly gathering, but that the plan had been thwarted by their own timely revelation of the content of the dropped circular. In response to this disclosure, Radicals had been forced to shift tactics and had decided to create fake Ku-Kluxes to menace their allies in order to generate anti-Democratic publicity. The paper claimed that Union's Radicals had actually begun to implement this plan, sending "colored men around the country, representing themselves as white Ku-Kluxes, and at night call at the residences of colored people, to frighten and even kill them." Freedmen Gilbert Chalmers (a twenty-one-year-old black man in Bogansville listed in the 1870 census as Gilbert Shelmar), Horace Gregory (possibly this is a thirteen-year-old black male in Santuc, but likely there is an older Horace Gregory, his relation, not listed on the census), Benjamin Parr (the forty-two-year-old black militia member into whose house Mat Stevens would soon flee), Robert Bogan (a seventeen-year-old black man in Bogansville), and Dick Gist (a twenty-three-year-old black man in Bogansville), calling themselves the "Alabama Ku-klux," had allegedly done just that the previous week, visiting and threatening three black Republican men at their homes. The alleged victims were forty-one-year-old July "Red Eyed Jim" Gist of Bogansville (who had himself been accused in 1869 of participating in a riot and attempt at a "false arrest" of forty-five-year-old Bogansville black alleged rapist Louis Gee); his immediate neighbor, fifty-five-year-old Richard "Dick" Sartor (who had served as a bondsman in the rape case); and twenty-one-year-old Frank Chalmers (in the same household as Gilbert, possibly his cousin or twin).[73] The paper further cautioned that the similar parties making Ku-Klux visits around the county "are all freedmen."[74] The attack mentioned in the article finds no parallel in the indictments. This article, in fact, is one of the few reasons to think that there were Ku-Klux attacks in Union in the weeks leading up to the 1870 election: it seems to be explaining away Ku-Klux attacks that had in fact not made any public record. By most accounts, the Upcountry had been unusually quiet until the election, as some elite southern whites hoped they could attract black support through their shift from the Democratic Party to the Reform Party.

These articles combined sensationalism with a wealth of local detail befitting a detective story, providing the names of the men who found and witnessed the finding of the paper, and the precise time, place, and circumstances under which he found it. The note itself was said to be available for scrutiny by the curious. Whites' surveillance of the scene in the hours following the finding of the note revealed (incongruously, unnamed) Republicans' desperate efforts to recover the note. The article on the "negro Ku-klux" visits gave specific names of real Union Countians as attackers and victims, along with details that sounded as though taken from victim testimony, including the precise words uttered by attackers and victims, acknowledging one uncertainty (had the attackers said they intended to "shed" or "take" blood?) in order to underline their care in transcription.

The second article also brought in a heavy dose of generic minstrel elements. When the fake Ku-Klux pointed a stick at the freedwoman as though it were a gun, she exclaimed, "Oh Lord protect us from these white Ku-klux." When the Radical Ku-Klux asked one of the black men they visited about his politics, he replied subserviently (and foreshadowing Mat Stevens) "that he was anything they were—'he was and would be all right.'" And one of the fake Ku-Klux climbed up to the roof of another cabin and dropped a large rock on the fire, which "so alarmed the inmates that they ran out of the house in their night clothes and some of them ran half a mile through the dewy cotton." This all was straight off the minstrel stage, and heavily derivative of other Ku-Klux stories in circulation, but differed from them in that the victims and accused were theoretically available to confirm the account.[75]

Accepting any truth to either the circular or the descriptions of Radical Ku-Klux visits is for today's readers out of the question, and it is difficult to believe that readers were expected to accept it at the time. The specific details, the elite men on the record as having picked up the note, and the quotations specifically attributed to precise people make it clear that these were deliberate lies concocted by several local elites working in concert. Union elites may have believed that some would read the stories as a literal truth. The Democratic press had emphasized for years that Republicans believed even the most patently fraudulent stories about Ku-Klux; they may have decided, cynically, that readers would be likely to believe their ridiculous account as well. More likely, they were adopting the tall-tale tradition so popular in Pulaski: insiders would see what they were up to, and outsiders deserved to be manipulated.

They would not likely have believed, though, that northern elites as a whole would be fooled by their minstrelesque account. To northerners, conservative whites were communicating that violence was the tactic they had been forced to use, and ridiculous stories were what they had been forced to write, in order to manage the ignorant people whom northern elites had allowed to govern them. They probably doubted that northern elites would invest the time and resources necessary to challenge their stories. Union's black majority, despite their many new formal rights, still had precious little ability to be heard beyond the borders of the county. Deputy Constables still in the area who tried to report were socially marginal enough to be easily contradicted and discredited. Politicians sent to Columbia feared for their safety should they spend time back home. After witnessing what had passed for investigation by Hubbard, Union's white elites could not have been very concerned that some intrepid northerner would head out to Bogansville to investigate their false stories.

If Union's Democrats had determined to fight out the racial and political conflicts in their county as though it were sensational fiction, South Carolina's Republican leadership met them and raised them. As early as 1868, Chief Constable Hubbard had considered bringing in a paramilitary force of northerners to send to rebellious counties.[76] In the fall of 1870, Hubbard and Scott finally pursued this idea. They commissioned C. C. Baker, a New York transplant running a gold prospecting company in the county, to travel to New York and hire a few dozen northern men to protect his operations. Baker was a northern Republican and Union veteran who lived in Union at least from 1868 to 1870. He also had testified as a Ku-Klux victim in 1869, had served as a paid constable for Scott, and was sometimes referred to as a "detective."[77]

When he arrived in New York, Baker turned to Colonel James E. Kerrigan to recruit and lead the men. This was a surprising choice. A staunch Democratic political leader and a notorious adventurer, Kerrigan had begun his career as a Bowery Boy and a Tammany Hall thug.[78] He had fought in the Mexican-American War and served as a Nicaraguan filibuster under William Walker in 1856, reportedly with a "band of vagabonds" from New York under his command.[79] He had become a political leader of Tammany and sometimes rival Democratic factions, serving as a councilman and often representing the Sixth Ward at conventions. In 1860 he was elected to the U.S. House of Representatives from New York's Fourth District. The *New York Tribune* sarcastically noted that Kerrigan's "merits have been sung in song and told in story. . . . He is remarkable for his being a strong man to head crowds at political meetings, and may be relied upon for any emergency." It conceded that, should Congress decide to give up on debate and just fight it out on the floor, Kerrigan would be the best man for that job.[80] He had been outspoken in his support for slavery during the secession crisis; in December 1860 he had threatened to form a military organization in New York City to protect the rights of its Democrats against Republican encroachment and the rights of southerners against national encroachment.[81] After the war, he led a military venture to bring arms to Ireland in the ship *Erin's Hope*, was part of a plan in 1868 to invade Cuba, and recruited men the same year to invade Canada in support of Irish independence. The *New York Times* mocked him as "Brig.- Gen. Kerrigan" busy recruiting "several hundred juveniles" into a "brigade of vagrants."[82]

Given Kerrigan's strong Democratic partisanship, he was an unusual choice to protect Republicans from Ku-Klux in Union. Yet he quickly arranged for a group of twenty-five "detectives" from New York to take temporary residence in the county. Hubbard, questioned a few years later after he was estranged from Scott, had a particularly low opinion of the detectives: "I don't think it possible to have found or selected a more dangerous lot of men than they were in any city of the union." The men on November 23, 1870, took a steamer to South Carolina, then a train out to Union County.[83]

Union elites Robert Shand and James Steadman would complain expansively about Kerrigan's detectives: according to Shand, "there was a man up at the gold mines, Kerrigan of New York. It was said he had been employed to come here to murder a dozen or more citizens."[84] Steadman similarly complained of "the importation of men into our community understood to be of desperate character by Governor Scott . . . twenty five or thirty New York roughs . . . armed with Winchester rifles and employed as a special constabulary force."[85] While there is no record of the Kerrigan detectives causing problems during their stay in Union, Scott's decision to bring them to Union only confirmed Democratic whites' fears that the Republicans would use their superior bureaucratic organization and resources to mobilize force from beyond the county. The fact that Kerrigan was a Tammany operative and a lifetime Democrat—as, presumably, were many of his men—only complicated matters. The *New York Herald* reported that when rumor had first spread that Dan Kerrigan's men were headed to South Carolina, people believed they were coming "with the avowed purpose of cleaning out the negro legislature." The paper clarified, however, that this was not the case.[86]

Things did not turn out as Scott and Hubbard had planned. By December 1870 the men had become disgusted, had returned to New York, and Kerrigan, Hubbard, Scott, and Baker were engaged in a bitter public argument about what the arrangements had been. Baker insisted that the detectives had been hired to protect himself and his miners, some of whom were freedmen, from night attacks by Democrats. Kerrigan insinuated that his men had been asked to do political dirty work, and some of the men swore they had been asked to assassinate prominent Union County Democrats.[87] When they had arrived at the mine to ostensibly protect its workforce, they had found it deserted, with no one to protect. Kerrigan's men did very little, generated no indictments, and left within a few days. But the presence of these hired detectives fed dramatically into Democratic Union Countians' sense of lack of local control, and into the encroachment of popular narrative into the unfolding of actual events in Union.

On December 19, after the men were gone, C. C. Baker's fellow gold mine employee Oliver Cornell wrote a letter to the *Union Times*. The letter was endorsed by Alvin Utley, another mine employee. Baker, Utley, and Cornell lived together. Utley was listed in the 1870 census as a thirty-seven-year-old ("Utty") from New York living in Bogansville with Cornell (also thirty-seven, from Connecticut), Baker, and Baker's wife. Utley was also Baker's brother-in-law. Cornell and Utley condemned Baker as a corrupt political operative. They claimed that Baker had fabricated reports of threats to his mining operations and then exhibited a self-inflicted gunshot wound to his hand as though it had been inflicted by violent Democrats. Baker, they insisted, had been collaborating with Radical Republicans in other counties, including Joe Crews, and had, among other things, deliberately orchestrated the events leading up to the deadly riot in Laurens.[88] Hubbard, testifying years later against Scott, was also highly critical of C. C. Baker's role in the matter, "Baker never rendered any service to my knowledge, except to shoot several holes in his own coat and represent that he had been shot at by bushwhackers in Union County. I examined his coat myself, and know that he would have been severely wounded had the balls passed through his coat while on his person."[89]

The arrival and departure of Kerrigan's men coincided precisely with the emergence of Klan violence in the county. On December 29, 1870, two days before the killing of Mat Stevens and while Union generally was spiraling into mass violence, the *Charleston Daily News* printed a lengthy top-of-the-column front-page story, "The Disorders in Union County. The Facts of the Case." The article focused on Baker and on Kerrigan's men and on Baker's fear of "an imaginative Ku-klux." It was largely based on claims of the Radical Ku-Klux earlier made by the *Union Times*.[90] In January, the story from the perspective of Baker's men would be published prominently on the front page of the *New York Sun* and republished in the *Charleston News* as "A Monstrous Story." This story first written for a northern audience recounts how the men were recruited with the promise of easy money at a New York bar, bundled off to South Carolina, put on a train to Union and then a cart to the mines, armed, and told that they would be paid extra for assassinating Union County elites, including Sheriff J. Rice Rogers. They soon realized the false position they were in and demanded to be allowed to leave, which they were, though they complained they were never paid at the rate they had been promised. The article went on to claim that in early January, just as deadly violence in Union reached its peak, Governor Scott and Joe Crews had made a pleasure jaunt to New York City and were attending a popular entertainment at Niblo's Garden when they happened upon Kerrigan and an ugly confrontation ensued.[91]

The Baker story looks like the third fruit of Union Democrats' strategy of placing patently ridiculous stories in the press to undermine the credibility of Republicans and their straight Klan reports. The evidence leaves no doubt that Scott and Hubbard did in fact bring down this ridiculous boatload of off-brand Pinkertons, and that they had to scramble to get them back out very soon after they arrived. But the stories of Baker shooting his own hand and cloak, and of Republican leaders conspiring to have prominent local Democrats assassinated by New York street toughs, feel written by the same hand as the circular story and the Radical Ku-Klux story.

Historians of the Upcountry have noted that Democrats were unusually pacific in the months leading up to the 1870 election, as they worked to sell themselves as moderates and win some black support. Immediately after the resounding defeat of that strategy, the region shifted toward extreme racial violence. In part, this shift may have occurred because the relatively moderate had had their chance, and had lost credibility. But it would have been clear to Democrats that the absence of Ku-Klux in the county in 1869 and 1870 by no means prevented the arrival of external intervention. The militias had been armed, and Kerrigan's men had dramatically materialized. Any idea that adopting the language of the Ku-Klux might evoke extralocal involvement might have seemed less relevant by late 1870.

At the same time, Union's elites must have become less fearful of the consequences of potential Republican intervention in their county. By late 1870, as the tone of Klan coverage in the national press had begun to change, white Democratic elites had reason to hope that they could find some sympathy for their position and forge a working relationship with Republican whites. Those in power in the Republican Party nationally shared with them a firm belief that white men's judgment and intellect was superior to blacks', together with a profoundly conservative commitment to the rights of property owners and employers. As long as they could frame events in Union as a conflict between patient, reasonable whites pushed to violence as a last resort in their efforts to exert control over an ignorant and undisciplined black population, they might find support.

In Columbia, Governor Scott had shown himself strikingly unable to respond effectively to riots in Laurens and Chester Counties. He was rapidly and visibly buckling to Democrats' demands and violence. In an attempt to stabilize, he was by late 1870 reaching out to Democratic elites for alliance. He was, for instance, in the process of making the major and politically debilitating concession of filling county appointments irrespective of party. It was clear that once whites had disarmed their local black militia, Scott would not be arming them again.[92]

Union County elites surely also gained confidence from the Kerrigan debacle. These New York "toughs" were happy enough, in the abstract, to go south to protect a northern company from Ku-Klux attackers, but once they arrived they were uncomfortable with their allegiances. When outside force arrived, whether in the form of Hubbard or Kerrigan's men, Union County elites generally had found that they could capture them effectively. Evoking the Ku-Klux, and therefore involving state and federal force, would have begun to look more palatable to Union's Democrats. From the beginning, they had a defense of Ku-Klux violence worked out, and by 1870 they may have detected that many northerners, even many powerful Republican northerners, were ready to listen.

Along with accounts of fake Ku-Klux and stories of Kerrigan's men, the Democratic press ginned up accounts of militia violence. Although, until Stevens, militias were responsible for no known deaths or serious injuries in Union, newspaper accounts of Union consistently described violent attacks by militias against whites. Repeatedly, these papers accused militias of shooting into private individuals' homes at night and of collective violence against political opponents. Between the circular and false Ku-Klux stories and the relentless accounts of the menacing militias, stories out of Union tracked trends in the national press, flipping the narrative of the white Democratic attacker and the black Republican victim.

IT MUST HAVE been right at this moment, in November or December 1870, that a substantial group of elites from Union and adjoining counties decided to publicly declare themselves as Ku-Klux. Because they chose to do so dramatically, in the form of a massive act of costumed violence (they could not have known as they planned precisely what form it would take), it required some preparation. They would have had to make or commission costumes (though some of these were likely repurposed from costume balls or tournaments) and piece together systems of leadership and communications (perhaps drawing on remnants of beats or military units). The task would have been made easier by the military discipline that most Upcountry elite men of active age already had. In their dress and actions, these Upcountry men would closely mimic newspaper accounts of large Ku-Klux attacks with which they were familiar. They would wear costumes that already had come to be associated with elite Ku-Klux in their area and that also bore some resemblance to the "Ku-Klux" knight described in the Charleston tournament: "With a mass of white red and black on the face . . . ribbon fitted over the face and head and hair covered and large horns on. Some horns were red and some black and some of the tassels were black."[93] Certainly by December the plan was in place, awaiting a provocation.

The killing of Stevens is likely not the provocation Union's elites would have chosen to display their power to a national readership: Mat Stevens was too clearly tied to the white underworld elites he would have rather not to have been publicly associated with. Other types of attacks would have been more suitable: those on allegedly corrupt or incompetent Republican political leaders, on workers lacking discipline, or even on black men accused of having attacked sympathetic white victims (perhaps women) with impunity. Even the *Union Times* may have been genuine when it gave the first attack "our hearty condemnation."[94] And some potential participants may have opted out of the January 5 raid for this reason: the first raid was considerably smaller than the second would be.

Many elites did come out for that first attack. Faucett, Greer, and others had managed to mobilize a substantial segment of the white community on January 1, to draw fire from the Yellow House residents, and to produce a dying white deputy to accompany the corpse of their (more dispensable) one-armed whiskey runner. Far from demonstrating that elites had Union under control, this first attack could too easily be used to demonstrate that Faucett, Robert Greer, Thomas Jefferson Greer, Hughes, and their friends were calling the shots. Perhaps the ties between these men and an important subgroup of elites, like Rogers, were enough to set the plan in motion, even in the face of skepticism or disapproval by other elites.

Several influential Democrats must have been particularly unhappy with the first mass lynchings. Isaac McKissick and H. L. Goss had publicly given their word to protect Joe Vanlew, and may have meant it. Ed Meng seems to have been similarly in serious conflict with Greer and company in the immediate aftermath of the raid. And Union's elites may have anticipated that the first jail raid would have been enough to force Robert Scott to work with Union's Democrats. After Scott sent a military representative to Union to remind whites of the authority of the law, Thomas Jefferson Greer wrote a friendly letter to Scott on January 28, offering himself as a narrator of the current situation in Union: "It has occurred to me that you would perhaps like to have an account from a disinterested observer, of the success of the mission of General Anderson to this refractory (so called) section of the state."[95] Many men in the community, white and black, met and signed a paper pledging to protect the prisoners from further violence and sent a mixed-race committee to Columbia to ask for troops to be dispatched to the county.[96] The state legislature refused to take their community meeting seriously. Quite reasonably, though unhelpfully, they insisted "that the very committee who represented the wealthy, elegant and refined citizens of Union, a few weeks ago, were themselves responsible for the outrages lately committed in their county."[97]

One way to save the first raid from appearing to be a collaboration between elites and criminal whites was to retrospectively redeem to reputations of the whites involved. The apotheosis of Mat Stevens began immediately after he was killed. From a whiskey runner regularly involved with the town's most active criminal group, he became, within a week of his death, a beloved father and community benefactor whose "kindness of heart had, unfortunately, led him to bestow a great portion of his hard earnings upon the poor around him leaving his own household, by his sudden death, unprovided for."[98]

The participants in the first raid made certain that they could be mistaken for nothing other than a substantial group of local elites wearing Ku-Klux costumes. Robert McKnight, the editor of the Union Times, perhaps did not get the memo. In its piece on the first raid, the Times did not identify attackers as Ku-Klux, calling them "disguised armed men" and "mysterious persons."[99] Yet the event—costumes, horses, discipline—showcased both the elite nature and the Ku-Klux identity of the attackers. And indeed, the South Carolina press made little effort to deny that a Ku-Klux attack had occurred. After years of avoiding the designation for local affairs, the *Columbia Daily Phoenix* printed a letter from Union largely justifying the attack (though theoretically condemning Ku-Klux violence) and referring to the attackers as "Ku-klux."[100] The first attack did spur Scott and his state government to increased action: he set the wheels in motion to transport the remaining Union prisoners in the Stevens and Smith cases to Columbia for protection.

Yet the first Ku-Klux attack, with its death toll of two, may not have gained the publicity elites were seeking. If anything, the three escapees suggested that Ku-Klux attempts to gain local mastery were hindered by their own incompetence and by the quick thinking and quick acting of their victims. The second attack was much bigger and substantially bloodier and gained significantly more national publicity. Union County was heavily covered by the major national papers after the second jail raid. On February 15, 1871, the *New York Times*, *Milwaukee Daily Sentinel*, and *New York Tribune* each printed an article on the attack. Indeed, the *Tribune* printed two on that day discussing the Union attack, and followed up with two articles later in the week.[101]

As they committed the second attack, the attackers left a long, performatively literate note identifying themselves as KKK, and explaining their purpose as a political act in response to the incompetence of Judge Thomas:

TO THE PUBLIC: KKK taken by *habeas corpus* In silence and secrecy thought has been working and the benignant efficacies of concealment speak for themselves Once again have we been forced by force to use Force. Justice was lame and she had to lean upon us. Information being obtained that a doubting Thomas the inferior of nothing the superior of nothing and of consequence the equal of nothing who has neither eyes to see the scars of oppression nor ears to hear the cause of humanity even though he wears the judicial silk had ordered some guilty prisoners from Union to the City of Columbia and of Injustice and Prejudice for an unfair trial of life thus clutching at the wheel spokes of Destiny then this thing was created and projected otherwise it would never have been. We yield to the inevitable and inexorable and account this the best. Let not thy right hand know what thy left hand doeth is our motto. We want peace but this cannot be till Justice returns. We want and will have Justice but this cannot be till the bleeding fight of freedom is fought. Until then the Molock of Iniquity will have his victims even if the Michael of Justice must have his martyrs KKK.[102]

Newspapers in South Carolina and nationally again acknowledged the "Ku-Klux" identity of attackers.[103] The *Union Times* began its widely republished editorial on the second attack, "That an organization of desperate and daring men is in existence throughout the South and perhaps in many of the Western States cannot now be doubted," then went on to identify it as the Ku-Klux.[104] This did not mean an end to older denials, however inconsistent the juxtaposition between acknowledgment and denial may have been. The *Phoenix* interspersed these stories with articles like "How Ku-klux Stories Originate," which was yet another account of black Radicals "dressed up like Ku-klux."[105]

Union County, as the *Anderson Intelligencer* proclaimed, had become a "theatre of great excitement." It was impossible not to read these two jail raid massacres as calculated performances of contempt for the supremacy of the government. In making them, Union's elites not only risked federal intervention but demanded it. Word of the massacres made it to Congress through several channels: federal officials heard many accounts of the raids from the press and from South Carolinians Thomas D. Wilkes and Sam Nuckles, who Scott sent to represent the situation to Congress.[106] The event was crucial in pushing through the 1871 Enforcement Act, which, buttressed by the report of Attorney General Amos Akerman, who had been taking an investigative tour of the Upcountry, would soon result in the temporary imposition of martial law in Union and neighboring counties.[107]

The jail raid executions not only strengthened calls for stronger enforcement and helped gain support for the Enforcement Act, which passed on April 20, 1871, but also provoked a second congressional response that Union's elites likely did not anticipate: Congress determined to send a subcommittee to Union and neighboring Spartanburg County to investigate the situation there in person. In July 1871, the Joint Committee to Inquire into the Condition of the Late Insurrectionary States selected a subcommittee of three congressmen—Senator John Scott (Republican of Pennsylvania), Representative Job Stevenson (Republican of Ohio), and Representative Philadeph Van Trump (Democrat of Ohio)—to gather extensive testimony in areas of intensive reported Ku-Klux violence in South Carolina, including Unionville.[108] (James H. Goss had already met on June 12 with the full committee to testify in Washington.) Having just come from a nine-day stop in Spartanburg, much longer than they had anticipated, the congressmen arrived on July 16 or July 17 hoping to make their stay in Union much shorter.

Just as, on closer inspection, descriptions of Klan violence played a rather small role in the newspaper discourse on the Klan, so too most testimony the committee took in Union was contextual, only indirectly tied to accounts of Klan violence. Though one of the ostensible reasons for traveling to afflicted areas in person was to avoid local partisan framing, the committee's schedule of witnesses would suggest that they nevertheless intended to allow Union's elite Democrats to author the county's narrative. The first day of testimony was dominated by the lengthy testimony of Robert Shand and James Steadman (a wealthy thirty-seven-year-old lawyer), and much of the following morning by the testimony of Joseph P. Gist (a fifty-two-year-old lawyer). These three elite white Democrats' testimony would not only be the framing perspective, but the bulk of the information the committee would gather. After Gist, the committee more briefly questioned nine other white witnesses; one of these was another elite white Democrat, John Rodger. Only four of the white witnesses were, or claimed ever to have been, Republicans. These men could not testify to the attacks themselves, of course, but provided background contextual information, mainly in the interest of justifying the violence.

The committee questioned no black witnesses in Union, in part because those closest to the Ku-Klux violence had fled, and for those who remained in the county, testifying was not safe. They then returned to Columbia, where they spent July 20 with ten witnesses, nine of whom were from Union, and eight of whom were black or mulatto. They emerged from their inquiry with 104 printed pages of testimony from elite white Democrats (including supporting documentation related to their testimony), about 30 each from nonelite white Democrats and apparent white Republicans, and 43 from black Republicans.

Union County elites testified strategically. It is surprising neither that they repeatedly claimed to be personally distant from the violence nor that these claims to distance often do not bear scrutiny. There is a good deal of evidence that the men testifying were themselves involved in the violence. Robert Shand was locally suspected of being the author of one of the Ku-Klux warning notices posted in town to demand the resignation of local Republican officials. But Shand had also pseudonymously written a letter to the *Charleston News* giving his view of events in Union and the Ku-Klux more generally in which he had pointed out that the Kerrigan incident had caused "the white race" in Union to fear assassination and that the killing of ten men in this raid in retaliation for the killing of Stevens was poetic, given that Republican leader Junius Mobley had allegedly said ten white men would be killed in retaliation for every black death. This explanation for why the Ku-Klux had killed ten men in the second raid does not seem to have appeared in other published sources: Shand may not have participated in the violence himself, and of course it is possible that Mobley's reported comment had not occurred to attackers at all, but it seems likely that Shand was privy to the meeting where white elites decided to kill ten men.[109]

Elites continued to be careful about their use of the word "Ku-Klux." Even after many men were whipped or killed by smaller bands of Ku-Klux, then hundreds of armed men dressed in elaborate costumes rode into their town and killed a total of twelve men on two occasions, leaving written notices identifying themselves as Ku-Klux, Unionville elite Robert Shand was not completely comfortable identifying the attackers as Ku-Klux: "They were Ku-klux; those to whom that name has been applied."[110] Asked, after both jail raids and after many other threatening notices, whippings, and murders had successfully driven almost all Republicans out of county office, "whether an organized band, commonly known as Ku-klux, exists in this county," Union elite Joseph Gist would only say, "I am morally certain that there are bands of disguised persons in this county."[111]

Their testimony suggests what these Union elites had to gain from this highly visible Klan raid. The Klan's function, for them, was twofold. Locally, historians have long noted that the Klan served a class-smoothing function, and Union County's Klan exemplifies this. The Klan facilitated a shift in local social organization by allowing elites to ally with a crucial group of nonelite whites by embracing their common whiteness, renaming their criminal violence as political, and attacking their common enemies. But the Klan in Union also served a translocal function. It reminded northerners of their own fundamentally racist assumptions, vividly demonstrating to them that whites were meant to lead, blacks to follow. It performed whiteness, organization, power, and competence to a national audience that might have allowed itself temporarily to doubt southern white elites' natural right to mastery.

The Klan in Union could potentially serve both of those ends, but only as long as elites were perceived by outsiders to be calling the shots, exerting authority over the disorderly and assuring that the Klan's function was not, at bottom, savagery, but control. Their testimony deemphasized the violence that Ku-Klux had so publicly committed, suggesting that it had been brief and contained and that elites now had it under control. While denying that they themselves would engage in or countenance extralegal violence, they simultaneously defended elite-led Ku-Klux raids such as the jail raids as a reasonable response to the black criminality, corruption, and ignorance imposed on them by Republican rule. They took care to reinforce the top-down and orderly nature of the two jail raids: Shand described the Ku-Klux who committed the raid as organized, with "sentinels" to prevent local people from interfering.[112] Later he gave his view that the South Carolina Ku-Klux was an "organization that seems to be pretty extensive" and that Klan members are likely "respectable young men."[113]

Yet the important role of Faucett and his friends was not easily reconcilable with that narrative of the Union County Klan. Congressmen's choice to come physically to Union made it impossible for Gist, Shand, and Steadman to write nonelite criminal whites out of the story. Elites in some other counties had chosen to excuse themselves from some Ku-Klux violence and blame it on common criminals, and Union elites did some of this distancing, attributing the murder of John Mills, for instance, to false Ku-Klux, but the Union County elites who planned the two large raids, and then Shand, Gist, and Steadman testifying about them, decidedly rejected that approach, choosing instead to ignore nonelite whites when they could, and aggressively defend their character when they must. As Robert Shand claimed, "Any party which was organized to punish bad men would necessarily punish nine radicals in South Carolina to one Democrat. Certainly in Union County that would be the case."[114]

Whitewashing Union County's criminal whites was no easy task. The fact that a whiskey runner was so central to the Klan raids posed a problem for Union elites. Steadman parried a long series of leading questions from Representative Job Stevenson which suggested that the Ku-Klux in Union was defending illegal distilling. "I will state, as I have had to state all along . . . that this Ku-klux has nothing at all to do with illicit distilling."[115] Steadman implausibly claimed not to know much about the Klan raid, though he had served as a prosecution witness against Stevens's murderers, but he was certain that Mat Stevens had no connection to the whiskey trade.[116] Shand insisted that Stevens was "a very inoffensive young man with one arm, who had given no offense to anybody among those who committed the crime, so far as we knew."[117] Steadman positively effused, "Stevens, as I have said, was . . . one-armed, peaceable, and a favorite in the community . . . a man who was beloved for his excellent character, for his obliging disposition, for his amiable temper. . . . He was not obnoxious in any way, as I have ever heard, on account of politics—an inoffensive, harmless man, who was liked by the whole community for his obliging and kindly temper and disposition, from the pleasure with which he did acts of kindness. He was a favorite for all these reasons in the community."[118] This reflected the stories that were being sent out from Union to the Democratic press. Robert Shand, writing to the *Charleston News* as "Brutus," described Stevens as "a one-armed, inoffensive white man, of good character, who toiled honestly for his daily bread, and did harm to no one."[119]

Perhaps the most blatant part of Stevens's rehabilitation is the occlusion of his assault on white peace officer B. F. Gregory just more than a month before his killing. On November 24, 1870, Gregory had charged Stevens with assaulting him in the line of duty. The indictment reveals little of the context of Stevens's assault on Gregory, but there is every reason to read this assault as part of a confrontation between Stevens's criminal associates and those attempting to maintain order as the county spun out of control in November and December. Gregory must have understood Stevens as representing a larger group: the following day, Gregory took out a peace warrant not against Stevens but against his brother-in-law, H. Thomas Hughes. Stevens, Faucett, and their close allies Thomas McDaniel and W. H. Sanders went Hughes's bond, joined by A. C. White, John R. Smith, and elites John E. Cotton and J. Rice Rogers (under whom Gregory was serving when assaulted).[120] Rogers, then, required Hughes to pledge a year of sobriety, perhaps as a condition of his signing the bond.

Not only did Union elite narrators occlude Stevens's implication in criminal and violent activities; Steadman appears to have claimed that it had been black militia members, rather than Stevens and his friends, who had assaulted Gregory.[121] Though Steadman said repeatedly that his memory of the event was "rather vague," and tried to beg out of discussing it once he brought it up, he testified that Gregory had complained that he had been stopped and menaced by "skulking" militiamen in the line of duty. It is possible, of course, that the unfortunate Gregory had been menacingly confronted by both groups in those violent times and that his attack by the militia never came to indictment, but it seems considerably more likely that Steadman found it easier to mislead congressmen about the nature of the confrontation.

Or take Steadman's testimony about militia attacks on local whites in the months leading to the Stevens killing. A long article published on November 17, 1870, in the *Columbia Daily Phoenix* had reported that H. Thomas Hughes and William Faucett were menaced, threatened, and driven from their homes by black militiamen. Yet while Steadman mentions the attack on Hughes in his testimony, he completely fails to mention the attack on Faucett.[122] Perhaps Faucett's involvement simply escaped Steadman's mind. But Faucett would not have been easy to overlook. And Steadman knew Faucett. Anyone who made a living practicing law in Union County would have been familiar with the man who was the second most frequent participant in the county's indictments. Steadman had also initiated a case for retailing spirituous liquor without a license against Wesley Sanders, in which Faucett's close ally Robert Greer had cooperated with him as a witness.[123] He had testified alongside Faucett in the 1869 case emerging out of John Sanders's shooting of Faucett's friend Thomas Jefferson Greer in Robert Greer's bar.[124] It is difficult to avoid the conclusion that here Steadman was deliberately keeping the unpalatable Faucett out of the story and out of the record.

Visiting congressmen were skeptical of elites' rehabilitation of the white Democratic lower classes in Union. They experienced rural South Carolina as a depraved, impoverished, and uncivilized place and later represented their trip there as dangerous and difficult. While they were in Yorkville a local man had, perhaps deliberately, spilled a pitcher of milk on Senator Stevenson. This "assault," heavily covered in the press, encapsulated the men's disgust with their visit.[125] The congressmen took particular note of the presence of unsavory whites in Unionville. When Steadman made a statement presuming that any larcenous activity in Union was done by freedpeople, Senator John Scott called on his new personal acquaintance with Union to disagree. Steadman asserted that the nocturnal smokehouse thieves who had allegedly been afflicting the community were freedpeople, and Scott asked why he had made that assumption.

> ANSWER: The general impression was . . . that it was by the colored population.
> QUESTION: Had you the same class of white population we see about your hotels now?
> ANSWER: Yes, sir.
> QUESTION: Go on.[126]

Congressmen also were skeptical about the elite witnesses' athletic efforts to rehabilitate Mat Stevens. They did not dig too far into the illicit white subculture of Union, but they appreciated that there was an unseemly connection between the gentlemen before them and the scruffy white men loitering outside their hotel. As Scott asked Steadman, "Let us have an explanation from you of why it is that when Stevens, a white man of good character, and engaged in bringing in illicit whisky, was murdered, the people turned out, but when the probate judge of your county was whipped by disguised men nobody turned out."[127]

Many Union County elites had long had tacit working relationships with these men on the disreputable underbelly of their society. They had tolerated Faucett's presence in the county, and that of his friends, and in so doing countenanced a good deal of behavior that could not be made to appear in a good light. They had for many years presided over a system which consistently refused to prosecute them. But many had done more than that: for years they had occasionally gone bail for Faucett and his men, used their illegal services, and invested in their illegal businesses. The terms of this working relationship may well have changed after the war, which lowered the fortunes, capacity, political power, and access to state violence so central to their status while only enhancing Faucett's livelihood, and causing a real demand for his expertise in informal organized violence. Their symbiotic relationship must at times have been painful to them: remember Isaac McKissick silently watching a crude Robert Greer lead Thomas Vanlew away in violation of a gentleman's promise he had just made to Vanlew's weeping mother. Within Union, these elite men had maintained their reputation as gentlemen without being called on to explain their implication in the violent, commercial, and common.

Congressmen Job Stevenson and John Scott, however, were not so careful of Steadman, Gist, and Shand's reputations as gentlemen. They repeatedly suggested that neither they nor any other men in Union were behaving as gentlemen ought. When Steadman insisted that the town was being policed by Union's "best men" on the night of the second jail raid, Scott was incredulous: "The best men in the town permitted the town to sleep on without arousing them?"[128] Steadman's testimony includes many expressions of his shared class position with his questioners. He explained to them that Republican leader D. D. Going was "not a man of education" but rather "a person of low life."[129] He also gingerly worked to distance himself from less refined events in the county: when he testified that a militia member had said that the group intended to "mug a man," he quickly clarified, "I have no more idea of his meaning than you have, but suppose it was violence."[130] He adamantly denied Scott's implication that the Ku-Klux were the "pets" of Union's elites.[131] Yet the congressmen were not feeling chummy; even the Democratic member, Van Trump, quickly rebuffed any assumption of familiarity between himself and Union elites. "Explain why you use my name," he demanded, when Shand suggested that the witnesses Mr. Van Trump had called would be just as appropriate as any Shand himself might offer.[132]

THE COMMITTEE'S TREATMENT of Union County elites must have stung—and matters would only get worse. On July 28, 1871, Scott issued a proclamation offering two hundred dollars to anyone arresting, with the evidence to convict, a person for violation of the Ku Klux Act. The government appointed Henry H. D. Byron, a U.S. commissioner, to go to Union to examine Ku-Klux cases.[133] The Seventh Cavalry arrived in Union and began to assist in making arrests. From October 1871 through December 1872, post commanders reported sending out detatchments of from six to forty mounted men to assist in issuing arrest warrants on at least forty-five dates. As maddening as it must have been to be led through town to the post by these detachments, it was perhaps most galling that "several colored witnesses arrested by Deputy U. S. Marshalls also accompanied them."[134] The *New York Tribune* on November 6 reprinted a report from Columbia that many people in York and Spartanburg had been arrested, but also five from Union, all of whom were suspects in the jail abduction/executions. Four of these men were a hotelier, a probate judge, and merchants; the last was "a mulatto and a shoemaker."[135] The *Milwaukee Daily Sentinel* on November 13 reprinted a *Yorkville Enquirer* article claiming that many had been arrested in York and Union, some on the strength of the "corrupt testimony" of "worthless" blacks.[136] A few days later, the *Chicago Times* expressed outrage that Union County Ku-Klux prisoners were remanded on the basis of the testimony of "one negro."[137] The *New York Tribune* reported that on November 17, 1871, a company of the Eighteenth Infantry was sent to Unionville to reinforce the garrison there and assist with arrests.[138] About six hundred men had apparently been arrested in Union and surrounding counties by December 1871.[139]

Figure 4 shows William Faucett's relationship to those ninety-six individuals who were identified as arrested under the Enforcement Acts through either being a party to *ex parte Thomas Jefferson Greer* or being named in newspaper accounts of Union County arrests who I could, with some confidence, identify in the network. Although I have found no evidence that Faucett himself was arrested under the act, he was a central figure in the network. Several others who appear in the network have been discussed in this account; H. Hughes is H. T. Hughes and William Williams is Republican leader W. F. M. Williams. The Greer brothers are there, and proximate to Faucett. Elites like Isaac McKissick and David Gist can be found as well. G. Stout Noland and Robert Lamb, who show up in other popular accounts as important in the history of the Union County Klan, are present here, and proximate to Faucett. Some men arrested under the Enforcement Acts were not interconnected to others in the network and

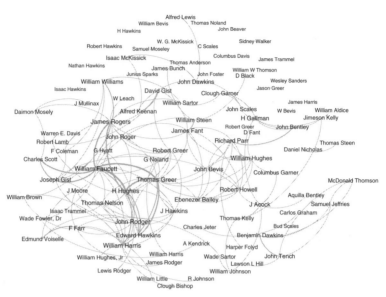

FIGURE 4. A visualization of the connections between William Faucett and identifiable of Union County residents arrested under the Enforcement Acts.

thus would be outside of the frame of the graph. Again, people at the center of the figure were central to the network. Names are not sized by degree.

Those arrested included several associates of William Faucett, though Faucett himself does not appear on the list. They also include people closely associated with victims of Ku-Klux violence. Arrestee Wade Fowler lived close to A. B. Owens. Many of the white men of active age within ten houses of Alex Walker were among those arrested: S. M. Fant, Frank Farr, and Edmund Voiselle were just a few houses down on one side and William C. Harris, D. B. Fant, and B. Frank Gregory on the other. Jason Greer was not much farther. Mac Thompson, Samuel Jeffries, and J. B. Tolleson had been witnesses in the case of theft against Noah and William Webster, tied to the killing of John Mills, and of course John Tench was closely connected to that case as well.[140] Ambrose Adams lived next to J. P. Porter (who had been beaten in 1868 for carrying ballots), and John Bently was a few houses down. Many of the town's conservative elites also faced arrest: D. B. Fant, Joseph Gist, John Rodger, Dr. James Nott Moore, Joseph McKissick, William Steen (the hotelier referred to earlier), and J. Rice Rogers were among those arrested.

Some of the arrests are more difficult to integrate into the story of Union County Ku-Klux. Eight of those reported as having been arrested were black: John Dawkins, forty-five, of Gowdeysville; William Nichols, probably a forty-five-year-old in Gowdysville; a Daniel Nicholas (his brother?), thirty-five, of Jonesville; Wade Sartor (listed as Wade Salter), a twenty-six-year-old black man from Santuc; Alfred Keenan (in the census as Kunan), a twenty-six-year-old black man from Jonesville; William Little, a forty-three-year-old black man from Union; Albert Lewis, who does not appear in the records; and the unnamed mulatto shoemaker (almost certainly Sam Harris, who had debilitated Wade Hawkins with a shoemaker's hammer).

John Dawkins was a Democrat: the Democratic press railed against his arrest as evidence that black men were only to be allowed to vote if they voted Republican. He, together with Sylvanus Wright, had gone bond for Emma Prater when she was accused of stealing a one-hundred-dollar bill (the prosecutor, and presumably the victim, was Freedmen's Bureau agent John N. Andrews), and had done the same when a white man accused her and her father of stealing peaches in the summer of 1870.[141] In October 1871 Alfred Keenan had been given a bond by W. D. Humphries, later arrested as a Ku-Klux, and had been accused, together with Dawkins, of committing larceny against Isaac McKissick.[142] In September 1869, he had been indicted as part of a group of nine other black men who assaulted forty-four-year-old accused rapist Louis Gee of Bogansville. Rice Rogers had gone his bond.[143] Dawkins made a certain amount of sense as a candidate for black Ku-Klux, and perhaps Keenan by association. There is not enough information to say anything very substantial about the others named. And in fact there is reason to believe that more black men than this were arrested: the *Milwaukee Daily Sentinel* reported that on Halloween 1871, troops arrested twenty black and four white Ku-Klux in Union County.[144]

The most unexpected inclusions on the list are the names of some known Republicans, and particularly W. F. M. Williams himself. After his arrest in March, Williams testified in April 1872 that he had in January 1871 (between the two jail raid executions) agreed to be inducted into the Ku-Klux and had become a chief.[145] He was the most important of at least a trio of white Republicans, also including Damon P. Moseley and William Mullinax, who stepped forward, confessed that they consented to become Ku-Klux in order to save their own skin, and provided substantial insider evidence against Democrats accused of Ku-Klux violence. Moseley claimed to have climbed a tree to tie the noose used to hang one of the men taken in the second jail raid.[146] Not only had he been through a formal initiation, enabling him to describe in detail the order's oaths, rituals, and secret signals; he had also been present at a meeting of Ku-Klux chiefs and thus was able to provide a lengthy list of prominent men from Union and surrounding counties. Daniel Black, a thirty-year-old who had been indicted for assaulting a white man in 1868, and then a William Gage, likely black, at the time of the 1868 election violence, also turned state's evidence.[147] He said he had been falsely accused of some things and was in a "ticklish" place, so had to testify. In any rate, he seems to have thrown his lot in with the Republicans. He shows up a few months later as a bondsman in a group of active Republicans.[148]

Newspapers covered Union County arrests selectively. Local Democratic papers printed regular tallies of the names of those arrested. Major Republican papers took a more general view, sometimes mentioning numbers of arrests, and occasionally reporting, as discussed in chapter 4, on the degraded, hapless, or pitiable nature of the arrestees, and on the deprivation of their surroundings.[149] An Atlanta newspaper reported in March that Union County's grand jury had presented to Judge Thomas a statement of the deplorable prison conditions their arrestees suffered, including several wheelbarrows full of "human excrement and other offensive matter" allowed to accumulate in the cells, insufficient and poor-quality rations, and "something in imitation of coffee."[150]

Union's elites faced unpleasant consequences for their choice to form themselves into a Klan. The soldiers were unwelcome, the testimony unpleasant, and the imprisonments brief but decidedly inconvenient. But while all of this dramatic unpleasantness was occurring, Democratic Union Countians were steadily regaining all meaningful positions of power. If Union County's elites had bet that they would not in fact pay a terrible price for bringing down upon themselves the might of the federal government, they were correct. And many of them got the cultural benefits they sought; in later years they took pride in their Klan identity, a sign that their manhood was uncrushed by the hardships of defeat and evidence of their fitness to rule. Their children and grandchildren could be counted on to proudly point to, or perhaps even exaggerate, their role within the Klan for years to come. Those Union freedpeople who had placed their faith in the promises of freedom discovered the bitter truth that the arrival and departure of a seemingly endless array of powerful men claiming to protect their citizenship did not bring about meaningful racial justice.

Conclusion

In her work on the trickster figure in folk culture, Barbara Babcock-Abrahams asks, "What happens when the fool becomes central to the action" while retaining his chaotic power.[1] In the Klan's case, he puts away his jester's cap and becomes once again the gentleman. Though the Reconstruction-era Klan was not the first vigilante movement to assume carnivalesque costume while making their attacks, it marked both the climax and the beginning of the end of this centuries-old tradition in the United States.[2] By 1872 Klan groups had already done a great deal to increase the power and prosperity of white Democratic southerners at the expense of freedpeople and their allies. They had lynched hundreds, shot hundreds who tried to elude them, driven many thousands from their homes, driven hundreds from office and seen to it that they would be replaced by officials more sympathetic to the priorities of white community insiders, intimidated black voters on a massive scale, and taken substantial amount of property from black families not only by stealing their physical possessions small and large but also by forcing them to abandon their crops and livestock and to sell their land cheaply. They had exposed, sexually molested, and raped black girls and women, powerfully proving that these women and those who hoped to protect them were unable to determine who had sexual access to their bodies. They had demonstrated that the federal government and its "pet" state governments' responses to their violence was ineffective and often half-hearted.

The brief life of Klan groups had been particularly hard on those black rural southerners who were particularly able, assertive, and well-connected. Although Klan groups were locally oriented, with each self-appointed group targeting those black men and women (and their white allies) whom they found to be most in tension with their own interests, this often was a quite effective way to target the most powerful and effective black people in a community. Those who came to the negative attention of the type of men who would be most likely to transmogrify into Ku-Klux were people who had not only courage, but also goals and the confidence that they could achieve them. Often these individuals were formal political or religious leaders, and just as often they were the bondsmen, the well-connected, the more affluent, and the promising young people of a community.

In Union County, South Carolina, the Klan had disappeared by the beginning of 1872. In less than a year of activity, these local Klan groups had changed the face and future of Union by killing at least sixteen men (in addition to the two men executed by the state for the killing of Stevens). But they were not just any eighteen men: like Sax Joyner, who had been lynched at the end of the war, these men had emerged as respected leaders of black Union County: J. Alexander Walker, Sylvanus Wright, Thomas Vanlew, and white allies like A. B. Owens. Other prominent leaders, such as Drury Going, had been intimidated into submission, forced to abandon their formal positions. Still others seem to have dropped out of public life after facing physical threats, like John Bates. And who knows what sorts of accommodations men like Junius Mobley, who remained, may have found themselves willing to make in order to survive in the environment or terror created by the Klan. When Congress came to interview black witnesses to Klan violence, they found none to interview in Union; they had to interview them where they had taken refuge, in Columbia. By 1872, the Klan in Union had accomplished what it could. Much the same was true of other Klan-ridden communities.

Nationally, the idea of the Klan had accomplished certain ends as well. In broadcasting accounts of these lynchings and shootings, of families driven from their homes, of terrorized officials and voters, of theft and of bodies violated, newspapers and politicians amplified and, ironically, normalized the acts. When outsiders viewed the South through stories of the Klan, as they frequently did, the personal safety, economic prosperity, political empowerment, and sexual integrity of black southerners was unimaginable. These stories circulated widely through the South as well; while both black and white southerners weighed them alongside their own local knowledge and experience, the more stories of Klan atrocities black southerners read, the more they must have despaired of their safety and prospects. As conservative southerners read them, they saw their futures unfolding before them. During the postwar years, when everyone was forced to develop new categories, schemas, and truisms to approximate the dramatically transformed world, the idea of the Klan marked the inevitability of white dominance and the tragicomic nature of black aspiration. If anyone had briefly wondered what might become of "the black character" after slavery's oppressions and controls, the dominant national narrative of the Klan attack had an answer to that as well.

By the time the state meaningfully stepped in to suppress the Klan, in 1871 and 1872, it had run its course. The Klan's terrorism, after all, depended on its ability to work up a sensation, but the novelty of its costume and violence were wearing off. Its foothold in northern popular culture beyond newspapers had peaked only months into its debut, in 1868, and dwindled ever since; as many northerners came to be aware of the very serious nature of Klan violence, the joke became less funny. And while mentions of the Klan only went up in 1871 and 1872, those later mentions were very much more about the government's suppression of the Klan than about the nature of the Klan itself. Novel entities are fascinating because they force readers to adjust their understandings of the world. But by 1871 and 1872, the Klan had taken its place in the conventional wisdom about the nature of the South and of the characteristics of and relationships among those who lived there. New tactics like the massive raids that occurred in Union County in 1871 could still win national attention, but stories of Klan violence were played out.

Both of the key elements of the Klan identity, carnivalesque performance and racial violence, would continue unabated into the post-Klan South, but they would diverge from one another. Mardi Gras celebrations proliferated, spreading to many major southern cities and even to Washington, D.C. The age of burlesque and of the circus had arrived in South and North alike, but southern costumed racial violence, if it occurred at all, now occurred only in very isolated incidents.

Even when the Klan itself revived in the Progressive Era, it would do so almost entirely without its carnivalesque trappings. The second Klan wore uniforms rather than disguises, though their pointed hats and robes evoked the tradition of their Reconstruction-era predecessors. Though they introduced the sensational cross-burning ceremony and adopted the tradition of the parade, they would retain little memory of their predecessors' grotesque idiosyncrasies. After the Klan, white male supremacy was reestablished on an increasingly regular and institutional footing, and its bizarre performative aspect became just a memory and a symbol. In fact, it came to be a way for Progressive Era historians to imagine white southerners as a "volk" with their own colorful traditions. It remained available to northern and southern whites seeking power and identity in a world of Darwinian savagery, but southern white men no longer needed it to explain their public violence to themselves. The bulls' horns, polka-dots, squirrel-skin masks, burnt cork, and women's dresses fell away, leaving only the even more grotesque sight of confidently civilized white men grinning around a dangling black corpse.

WHAT DID THE Klan's end feel like to the people who survived it? In Unionville, the everyday violence of Reconstruction remained very real. Many white men who preyed on their black neighbors had never been arrested as Ku-Klux, and even those men who had been arrested under the Enforcement Acts drifted back into Union as their cases were dismissed or they were pardoned. Two years or so after Ed Voiselle returned to Union after has arrest, on April 18, 1874, he took issue with a Pat Park, a black man who was sitting in the doorway at Mr. Rogers' store. A confrontation ensued, and Voiselle kicked Park and beat him repeatedly with a large piece of wood, killing him. He continued to kick the dying and limp body, and then he dragged it by the feet around the street for some time. When he stated his intention to "cut his damn throat," the men who had been witnessing the murder from the other side of the road had finally had enough, and interfered.[3]

And Klan survivors continued on as best they could in a world with constricting options for black Union Countians, but in which a man who kept his or her eyes open might have some opportunities to influence fate. As he continued to make his home in Unionville in the years after the jail raids, Silas Hawkins, by 1874 twenty-nine years old, must have reflected at how lucky he was to be alive. He had been among those black Republicans accused of assaulting black Democrat Albert Martin in 1870, the conflict that had fed into the fatal attack on black Republican Wade Hawkins hours before the Mat Stevens killing.[4] He had somehow not been present when the Vanlew brothers fatefully took their stand against the white mobs disarming and arresting black men, but the boardinghouse they were all living in, the "Yellow House," was also frequently referred to as "Silas Hawkins' house." When, soon after the jail raid executions, attempts had been made to pin them on some poor white men at odds with Faucett's friends, Hawkins had gone bond for one of these white-men-on-the-outs, Richard LeMaster.[5] When black Republican leader Hiram Duncan campaigned in Union in September 1872 and was assaulted by a Louis Trumbley, witnesses and bondsmen to the case were a Who's Who of surviving black leaders in Union: Giles West, Junius Mobley, Ben Palmer, Mark Hampton, and Silas Hawkins.[6] Hawkins's family connections and his alliances before and after the jail raid executions suggest that he was an influential and political man: among other things, he was brave enough to serve as a trial justice in 1873. Somehow he had come out of the entire nightmare unscathed.

One February day in 1874, Silas Hawkins had the opportunity to witness to the injuries that led to William Faucett's violent death. After the

Klan suppression, and despite the jailing of many of their number, Faucett and his friends had kept up not only their careers of violence but also their tradition of drunken fighting. In January 1872, forty-five-year-old Pinkney resident Henry Fowler had angered Faucett's friend Levi Davis by declaring himself to be "master of Pea Ridge" (the neighborhood) and stating his intention to "master" Davis "or kill him in the attempt." Davis assaulted Fowler, who charged him with attempted murder.[7] Faucett's old friend Charles Garner may have aged out of fighting, but his relations kept up the old grudges: in June 1873, a thirty-five-year-old James Garner from Pinkney was indicted for striking Henry Fowler on the head with a plank.[8]

It was with another Fowler, George Fowler (a twenty-seven-year-old propertyless man from Pinkney who was almost certainly kin to Henry Fowler), that William Faucett, the man of violence who had been such a central figure to the Klan attacks in Union County, fought his last fight. The later trial of Fowler for Faucett's murder reveals the nature of his death. Faucett (by now sixty-four years old) and Fowler were in Andy McNeace's bar with many of their usual companions, including Levi Davis, Thomas Jefferson Greer, and William Hughes. Fowler and Faucett, described by a witness as "a large man, physically much superior to George Fowler, and . . . a quarrelsome . . . man," began fighting in the bar and moved out of doors. The men in the bar gathered around the yard to witness the long and desperate struggle.

Silas Hawkins later claimed to have been looking through the window for the beginning of the fight. "William Faucett gather George Fowler by the collar or throat, and push him back against the house, and continued choking him for some time," Hawkins recalled. "Fowler seemed to be struggling for breath and requested Faucett two or three times to let him loose. Faucett however still held to his throat or collar. Fowler then threw his hand toward his pocket and then Faucett said 'God dam you, do you draw your knife on me' and thereupon jerked Fowler near to the ground." At this point, Hawkins said, he left and saw no more of the encounter.[9]

Perhaps Hawkins decided it was prudent to move along as tensions escalated, or he was simply apathetic or disgusted at witnessing yet another act of ugly violence: he claimed that he left just before Fowler got the upper hand and did not wait to see Faucett receive the six stab wounds that would ultimately kill him. But perhaps it was not just a coincidence that Hawkins happened to see all the things that would incriminate Faucett and none of those that would incriminate Fowler. Faucett had been stabbed before, and the bad old man always seemed to return ready to fight some more. Perhaps Hawkins had witnessed the entire thing and was only willing to give testimony that would help Fowler's defense. Perhaps Hawkins was not at the window at all. After all of the terror and deaths he and his friends had experienced, after all of his own narrow escapes, Hawkins risked his life again in coming forward to try one more time to make sure that Faucett would not be back to walk the streets.

Despite, or because of, William Faucett's long history of thuggery, newspapers outside Union County noted his wounding and then his death. As the *Orangeburg News* reported on February 7, 1874, "A difficulty occurred in Unionville last Monday afternoon, between a young man named George W. Fowler and William Faucett, an elderly citizen of the county, in which knives were freely used, and Mr. Faucett was badly cut in twelve or thirteen places."[10] But neither the suppression of the Ku-Klux nor the death of Faucett appears to have fundamentally changed power relations in Union. The end of the Klan was a good thing for men like Silas Hawkins, of course, but it did not radically change their still-vulnerable existence. Having largely dispatched the black men who hoped to displace them, men like Faucett, and the higher-bred white men who hated to acknowledge their connection to them, could return to fighting among themselves for what was safely theirs to divide. Both in the national press and on the streets of Union County, the Ku-Klux had done, and done well, the terrible work of reinscribing white dominance and black hopelessness.

Acknowledgments

So many people have supported and inspired me as I wrote this book. This book benefited a great deal from the work of my research assistants at Duquesne University. I have always been surprised at my good fortune in so consistently working with research assistance with such great talent and dedication. Aaron Gallogly, Bill McGovern, Teresa Madden, Aaron O'Data, and Cassandra Parsons provided endless assistance, largely in the form of building databases and helping me impose organization on my research notes and data.

Many of my colleagues have generously taken time to read the manuscript in part or in whole. Special appreciation goes to Bruce Baker, Michael Fitzgerald, Mark Summers, and Amy Wood, who read it in its entirety. The book is far better for their insights. Many others have read and commented on chapters or on the two articles that formed part of the basis of the book: Aaron Astor, Jim Bailey, Greg Barnhisel, Ed Blum, Gregory Borchard, Tsekani Browne, Bob Brugger, Greg Downs, Carole Emberton, Brian Fonken, Carl Frantz, Carolyn Frantz, Janet Frantz, Kathy Glass, Lesley Gordon, Mara Keire, Stephen Kercher, Tom Kinnahan, Caleb McDaniel, Rob McDougall, Bill McGovern, Jeff Mullins, Rob Nelson, Scott Nelson, Steve Prince, Scott Romine, Dorothy Ross, Brooks Simpson, Barbara Straumann, Tim Tangherlini, Brook Thomas, Michael Trotti, Frank Uekoetter, Ron Walters, Daniel Weinfeld, Colin Wilder, Gregory Wilson, Natalie Zacek, and the anonymous readers of the *Journal of American History*, the *American Quarterly*, and the *Journal of Southern History*.

Others still have provided me with valuable ideas in response to conference papers and in informal conversations. Gregory Borchard, Sundiata Cha-Jua, Song Chen, Doug Eckberg, Laura Edwards, Ian Finseth, Michael Fitzgerald, Elisa Grande, Max Grivno, Anne Helmreich, Julia Irwin, Stephen Kantrowitz, Franklin Knight, Chandra Manning, Susan O'Donovan, Heather Cox Richardson, Hannah Rosen, Diane Miller Sommerville, Margaret Storey, Mark Summers, Frank Towers, Kidada Williams, and Lou Falkner Williams most readily come to mind.

One pleasure of any research project is having the opportunity to work with archivists and librarians. My research took me to many public and private libraries and archives. I could have navigated none of them successfully without the dedicated professionalism of the archivists and librarians who staffed them, who many times led me to material I never would have located through printed guides. My thanks to the David M. Rubenstein Rare Books and Special Collections Library at Duke University, the Southern Historical Collection at the Louis Round Wilson Special Collections Library of the University of North Carolina at Chapel Hill, the Memphis Public Library, the South Caroliniana Library, the Historic New Orleans Collection, the New Orleans Public Library, the Tulane University Special Collections Library, the University of Tennessee at Knoxville, the Museum of Mobile, the Missouri History Museum Archives, the Library of Congress Rare Books Room, National Archives I, the Tennessee State Library and Archives, the Alabama Department of Archives and History, the South Carolina Department of Archives and History, the North Carolina State Archives, the Filson Society, the Auburn University Special Collections and Library, the Louisiana Room at the Edith Garland Dupré Library at the University of Louisiana–Lafayette, the Schomburg Center for Research in Black Culture at the New York Public Library, and the New York Public Library for the Performing Arts. While I was in Chicago with my newborn daughter, I welcomed the opportunity to escape to the Newberry Library's beautiful sunny reading room to consult their excellent collection.

Of the many archivists and librarians I worked with, several stood out as providing crucial assistance: Leslie Rowland, with incredible skill and patience, guided me through the Freedmen's Papers at University of Maryland; George Ewert was my knowledgeable and generous guide at the Museum of Mobile. I spent substantial time with the knowledgeable Ed Frank, who helped me navigate the Meriwether Papers at the Special Collections at the McWherter Library at the University of Memphis. At small, local collections, which are often disorganized, dedicated guides are particularly crucial. Director Ola Jean Kelly helped me make my way through the files of the Union County (South Carolina) History Museum. When I showed up looking for local archives at the Giles County (Tennessee) Public Library, they called local historian Bob Wamble, who showed up with his arms full of binders of impressive research.

Although network analysis only plays a role in a single chapter of this book, learning to create and manipulate that network represented at least half of the work that went into this book. My father gets credit for turning me on to social network analysis. I remember calling him after a day of research in South Carolina, talking about how I had no idea what to do with the goldmine of information about people's relationships to one another that I was finding. He recalled that back in graduate school he had learned about something called a sociogram that might be just the thing. Over the next years I worked to learn network analysis. I attended several valuable training sessions; the most useful of these by far was a seminar at UCLA led by Tim Tangherlini funded by the National Endowment for the Humanities. There I not only learned a great deal more about network analysis itself but also formed ties with other humanities scholars engaged in network analysis whose work continues to inspire me, such as Javier Cha, Jack Chen, Song Chen, Matt Erlin, Anne Helmreich, Sarah Horowitz, Rob Nelson, and Colin Wilder.

Even with this training and support, I could not have moved forward on the project without the generous interventions of several people adept at network analysis and database work. Tom Lombardi, his whiteboard, and I spent hours together while I sought to clarify what I had and what, in network terms, I wanted to do. Patrick Juola and I spent some whiteboard time as well, and he even occasionally loaned me his computer science students. Patrick Doreian and I met multiple times over the years looking at how my project might tie into larger ideas in network math. Hossein Azari Soufiani and I spent many pleasant hours on the phone and in Cambridge working to translate between the language of network statistical analysis and the language of humanistic description. While I have not in this book done the ambitious things with network analysis that Patrick Doreian and Hossein Azari Soufiani proposed, all of the time spent with them was immensely helpful in allowing me to conceive of the project and to understand the capacities of my tools.

When, after years of work on the database, I found to my surprise that I was not able to get it into a form that would allow Pajek to analyze it in the way I was hoping, old and true friend Jonathan Kastin swooped in like a coding hero to solve the problem with a query I gratefully dubbed "awesomequery." And Jotham Parsons, who had sort of vaguely thought about becoming a computer scientist before he entered history graduate school, came to realize through the course of this project that he was glad that he hadn't. Nevertheless, he responded gamely and effectively to any number of pleas for technical assistance.

I benefited from financial support, which allowed me some course release time, travel funding, and training. The Harry Frank Guggenheim

Foundation Research Grant enabled me to take a semester away from teaching. Without this grant, I could not have produced the database that is at the core of chapter 6. A pre-tenure sabbatical semester allowed for another semester off. I received a Southern Studies Research Grant from the University of North Carolina at Chapel Hill to support research there. In addition, I enjoyed regular summer money from the University of Wisconsin–Oshkosh, including a semester leave for an Individual Planned Project. The Duquesne funding came from various sources, including a Presidential Fellowship, the Faculty Development Fund, the Wimmer Family Foundation Fund, and an internal National Endowment for the Humanities grant.

Throughout this process, I relied a great deal on the support of my colleagues. My wonderful former colleagues at the University of Wisconsin–Oshkosh, Franca Barricelli, Lane Earns, Stephen Kercher, Andrew O'Shaughnessy, Kim Rivers, and Tom Rowland, provided me with the support and encouragement to do the first few years' work on this project. Several of my colleagues, past and present, at Duquesne University have also given me their support during this process, whether by taking an interest in it and offering themselves as sounding boards or simply by being supportive presences as I juggled many responsibilities. I would particularly like to thank Jim Bailey, Greg Barnhisel, Tsekani Browne, Alima Bucciantini, Norm Conti, Mehmet Dosemeci, Laura Engel, Anna Haensch, Jean Hunter, Michael Irwin, Linda Kinnahan, Edith Krause, Christine Lorenz, Holly Mayer, Magali Michael, Sarah Miller, Lanai Rodemeyer, Julia Sienkewicz, and Elisabeth Vasko.

I could not have done this without the support of my friends, who sometimes talked me through the book in process and sometimes convinced me to talk about other things instead. Sarah Leaman, Steven Gorevich, and Susan Allen hosted me during my archive time in Washington, D.C., and New York City. I very much enjoyed Georgian wine on the roof of Susan's building after days in the windowless archives. During a hairy moment in the writing process, Sarah invited me to her Vermont cabin, made me coffee, and hustled me out onto the porch to write during the days, overlooking the mountains. Susan and Sarah maintained a perfect balance of patience and enthusiasm, while their own examples of professional dedication and inspiration helped me to keep my work steady and my aspirations high. I have found in Pittsburgh a group of brilliant and wonderful friends: Heather Arnet, Jenny Lee, David Shumway, Christine Lorenz, Jessie Patella, Melissa Tison, Mandy Perveiler, and Aran Jackson have been my friends, fellow travelers, and supporters as I balanced my writing with raising my family. And I could not have written this without PJ.

I also want to thank my fellow members of the Elsinore-Bennu Think Tank at the State Correctional Institution–Pittsburgh. The insights I have gained from my many conversations with Farukh, Fly, Khalifa, Malakai, Norm, Oscar, Sean, and Stephen about race, injustice, violence, and political culture have made this a better book.

It has been a great pleasure working with Brandon Proia, Mary Caviness, and the rest of the team at the University of North Carolina Press. In addition to providing professional and excellent editorial support, they have a particularly steady but upbeat and light-handed manner of encouraging the completion of work that I found to be very effective.

Jotham read every page of this book, helped me work through difficulties in my arguments, provided high-level technical assistance, and took care of the children and house while I went off on trips or focusing on writing. A true coparent, he has always helped me find space to keep pushing this book forward. I thank my sister, Carolyn; my brother-in-law, Eriks; and my excellent nieces, Magdalena, Annika, and Sabine, for their support and entertainment. Charles and Marjorie Parsons and Sylvia Parsons have fed, housed, inspired, and entertained me while I was writing and researching in Boston. My children, Charlotte and Nathaniel, have grown up with this book, which I began just before Charlotte was born. They have persevered through countless research trips and conferences and lots of "um, just a minute" from behind the laptop. Even as I write this acknowledgment, Charlotte is expressing her skepticism that I will ever actually finish the book.

I have dedicated the book to Carl Daniel Frantz and Janet Laing Frantz, my parents. They have done more than their share of stowing me securely away with my laptop and taking off with my children. But more than that, they raised me on family stories of a rural America in which people striving to live good lives struggled against poverty, violence, shame, ignorance, racism, and injustice, and they encouraged me always to look directly and fearlessly at the darker parts of our nation's past and present.

Notes

ABBREVIATIONS

BRFAL   Records of the Bureau of Refugees, Freedmen, and Abandoned
Lands, RG 105, U.S. National Archives and Records
Administration, Washington, D.C.

DMRL   David M. Rubenstein Rare Book and Manuscript Library, Duke
University, Durham, N.C.

FSSP   Freedmen and Southern Society Project, University
of Maryland, College Park

GSP   Governor Robert K. Scott Papers, Letters Received and Sent,
1868–1872, S516002, South Carolina Department of Archives
and History, Columbia

KK Report   U.S. Congress, *Testimony Taken by the Joint Select Committee on
the Condition of Affairs in the Late Insurrectionary States.* Vols. 2–13
(Washington: Government Printing Office, 1872)

Louisiana Report   *Report of the Joint Committee of the General Assembly of Louisiana on
the Conduct of the Late Elections and the Condition of Peace and Order
in the State* (New Orleans: A. L. Lee, 1868)

NARA   U.S. National Archives and Records Administration,
Washington, D.C.

Tennessee BRFAL Records of the Assistant Commissioner for the State
of Tennessee, microfilm 999, Bureau of Refugees, Freedmen,
and Abandoned Lands, RG 105, U.S. National Archives and
Records Administration, Washington, D.C.

Tennessee Report *Report of Evidence Taken before the Military Committee in Relation to
Outrages Committed by the Ku Klux Klan in Middle and West Tennessee
Submitted to the Extra Session of the Thirty-Fifth General Assembly
of the State of Tennessee September 2d, 1868* (Nashville: S. C.
Mercer, 1868)

UCCI   Union County Criminal Indictments, Court of General
Sessions, Union County, S.C., microfilm

1. Jim Downs, *Sick from Freedom*.

2. Testimony of John Childers, *KK Report*, 1723; Williamson, *After Slavery*, 97.

3. Williams, *They Left Great Marks on Me*.

4. Trotti, "The Scaffold's Revival," 195.

5. Roth, *American Homicide*, 352.

6. Keith, *The Colfax Massacre*; Hollandsworth, *An Absolute Massacre*; Ash, *Massacre in Memphis*.

7. Ayers, *Vengeance and Justice*, 161.

8. Sutherland, *A Savage Conflict*.

9. Vandal, *Rethinking Southern Violence*, 53; Harcourt, "Who Were the Pale Faces?"; Dauphine, "The Knights of the White Camelia and the Election of 1868."

10. Ayers, *Vengeance and Justice*, 159; Testimony of Simon Elder, *KK Report*, vol. 12, Miss., 2:732.

11. Trelease, *White Terror*, 118, 120, 122, 125, 130, 141, 149.

12. Ibid., 226, 246.

13. Ibid., 310–18, 336.

14. Ibid., 92; Weinfeld, *The Jackson County War*.

15. In that way, it complements the argument that the violence of slavery was entirely consistent with, and indeed constitutive of, modernity and capitalism. For a recent iteration of this argument, see Baptist, *The Half Has Never Been Told*.

16. Scholars have made a similar argument about the lynchings that would follow the Ku-Klux era. See Goldsby, *Spectacular Secret*, 216; Hall, *Revolt against Chivalry*, 131, 133; and Ayers, *The Promise of the New South*. 17. Thank you to Brook Thomas, "Turner's 'Frontier Thesis' as a Narrative of Reconstruction," for inspiring this idea.

18. Roark, *Masters without Slaves*, 196–200.

19. I use the gendered "freedmen" here rather than "freedpeople" because, while women were frequently targeted by Klansmen and were sometimes themselves important Klan supporters, Klan discourse was very largely about manhood and citizenship, and the work of the Klan was largely about including men in and excluding men from a body of civic activities and relationships that were imagined by Ku-Klux as a male domain.

20. Haworth, *Reconstruction and Union*, 43–47. See also William Watson Davis, *The Civil War and Reconstruction in Florida*, 557–64.

21. Du Bois, *Black Reconstruction*, 131.

22. Several important works written in the last two decades have included substantial treatments of the Reconstruction-era Klan. Scott Nelson's *Iron Confederacies* reads the Klan as enabled by but also motivated in part by resistance to the economic centralization the new railroad companies represented. Steven Hahn's *A Nation under Our Feet* is interested in the development of black associational life in the South and in the Klan's role in undermining it. Carole Emberton, *Beyond Redemption* interrogates the meanings of Ku-Klux violence to participants and the broader national audience as they negotiated the meanings of citizenship. I have become increasingly convinced of the importance of Mitchell Snay, *Fenians, Freedmen, and Southern Whites*,

which analyzes the discourse of nationalism and the strength of separatism in the later nineteenth century through the lens of the Klan and other groups. Stephen Prince's *Stories of the South* treats the idea of the Ku-Klux, as contrasted with the carpetbagger, in the national press. Many other works have thematized Klan testimony. Lou Falkner Williams, *The Great South Carolina Ku Klux Klan Trials*, is a substantial legal history of ambitious but largely fruitless efforts to convict and punish Ku-Klux. Kidada Williams, *They Left Great Marks on Me*, includes an important chapter on Ku-Klux testimonies, drawn from the more extensive treatment in her dissertation. Hannah Rosen, *Terror in the Heart of Freedom*, reads Klan violence as an effort to undermine black men and women's civic competency. Kwando Kinshasa's fascinating but often overlooked *Black Resistance to the Ku-Klux Klan* focuses on many moments in which black southerners physically resisted Klan attacks or even counterattacked Klan groups. Others have explored the Reconstruction-era Klan as part of the larger story of the development of postwar forms of racial violence. Bruce Baker's *This Mob Will Surely Take My Life* includes a chapter focused largely on the Union County, South Carolina, Ku-Klux. Christopher Waldrep's *The Many Faces of Judge Lynch* describes the failure of the Ku-Klux to gain enough local approbation to be validated as a "lynch mob." Still others have focused in on the Klan in particular regions. Daniel Weinfeld's *The Jackson County War* is a powerful account of the Florida Klan in that area. Aaron Astor, *Rebels on the Border*, tackles the (later, more amorphous) Klan in the border states. See also influential treatments of the Klan in several other broad works, including Fitzgerald, *The Union League Movement in the Deep South*; Gregory Downs, *After Appomattox*; Summers, *The Ordeal of the Reunion*; Egerton, *The Wars of Reconstruction*; and Blight, *Race and Reunion*. Finally, well-researched popular books, including Jerry West's *The Reconstruction Ku Klux Klan in York County, South Carolina* and J. Michael Martinez's *Carpetbaggers, Cavalry, and the Ku Klux Klan*, also bring important approaches and insights to the topic, and recover compelling narratives.

23. Trelease, *White Terror*, 75–76. He is citing Reed, "What I Know of the Ku Klux Klan."

24. For a fascinating insight on Trelease's time in Greensboro, see interview with Allen W. Trelease conducted by Natalie E. Davis, October 2, 2006, Oral History Collections, UNCG Digital History Collection, http://libcdm1.uncg.edu/cdm/ref/collection/OralHisCo/id/7107.

25. Ben Runkle, Chief Superintendent, Chief Superintendent's Office, Memphis, Tenn., to Bvt. Major Gen. C. B. Fisk, May 23, 1866, Tennessee BRFAL, Roll 34, Target 2, Reports of Outrages, Riots, and Murders, 1866–68 (Series 3394, or Press Copies of Letters Sent 3518).

26. Thank you to Brian Fonken for this insight.

CHAPTER 1

1. Mrs. S. E. F. Rose, based on a letter from Major James R. Crowe reprinted in her text, places the beginning in the winter of 1865–66. Rose, *Ku Klux Klan*, 18. The May date is given in William Thomas Richardson, *Historic Pulaski, Birthplace of the Ku-klux: Scene of Execution of Sam Davis* (W. T. Richardson, 1913), 13, and in Lester and

Wilson, *Ku Klux Klan*, 53. The date of "1867" is given in "Mr. Frank McCord Tells What He Knows about the Kuklux," *Pulaski Citizen*, photocopy of a clipping of a December 18, 1892, letter from Frank McCord, Fayetteville, Tenn., Robert Wamble Personal Papers, Pulaski, Tenn.

2. "The fight was very desperate and sanguinary. The Confederate generals led their men in the repeated charges, and the loss among them was of unusual proportions. Grant, *Personal Memoirs*, 535–36.

3. Kidada Williams, *They Left Great Marks on Me*, 26.

4. Letter from John A. Jackson to Brig. Gen. Clinton B. Fisk, December 25, 1865, J-56, Registered Letters Received, Series 3379, Office of the Assistant Commissioner of Tennessee, BRFAL (FSSP A6058).

5. Letter from John A. Jackson to Brig. Gen. Clinton B. Fisk, December 25, 1865.

6. Letter from Cornelius Brown and Other Citizens to Brig. Gen. Clinton B. Fisk, March 8, 1866, Box 5, B-84 (1866), Registered Letters Received, Series 3379, Office of the Assistant Commissioner of Tennessee, BRFAL (FSSP A6230).

7. Resolution from Henry Webb and others, submitted to Brig. Gen. Clinton B. Fisk, March 26, 1866, filed as M-89 (1866), Registered Letters Received, Series 3379, Office of the Assistant Commissioner of Tennessee, BRFAL (FSSP A6294).

8. Blight, *Race and Reunion*, 113.

9. Letter from Col. J. R. Lewis, Chief Superintendent of Nashville Sub-District, to Brig. Gen. Clinton B. Fisk, July 24, 1866, L-91 (1866), Box 7, Registered Letters Received, Series 3379, Office of the Assistant Commissioner of Tennessee, BRFAL (FSSP A6285).

10. Monthly Report for Williamson and Giles Counties for December 1866 submitted by Captain George E. Judd (Superintendent) to Captain Michael Walsh (Chief Superintendent), December 31, 1866, J-63, Registered Letters Received, Series 3570, Subassistant Commissioner of the Subdistrict of Nashville, Tennessee, BRFAL (FSSP A6482).

11. Letter from Captain George E. Judd (Agent) to Captain Michael A. Walsh (Subassistant Commissioner), May 14, 1867, Box 88, No. 453, Registered Letters Received, July 1866–September 1868, Series 3570, Subassistant Commissioner of the Subdistrict of Nashville, Tennessee, BRFAL (FSSP A6488).

12. Blight, *Race and Reunion*, 113, includes a sound description of the racial situation in Pulaski at the time of the Klan's emergence. Monthly Report for Williamson and Giles Counties for December 1866 submitted by Captain George E. Judd (Superintendent) to Captain Michael Walsh (Chief Superintendent), December 31, 1866.

13. "High-Handed Robbery," *Pulaski Citizen*, January 17, 1867, 3.

14. John A. Jackson to Clinton B. Fisk, December 25, 1866.

15. Severance, *Tennessee's Radical Army*, 87.

16. Lester and Wilson, *Ku Klux Klan*, 55–56; "Luther McCord: Brother's Historical Sketch and Tribute," *Pulaski Citizen*, September 20, 1900; Susan Lawrence Davis, *Authentic History*, 17, 19.

17. "Luther McCord: Brother's Historical Sketch and Tribute," *Pulaski Citizen*, September 20, 1900.

18. Mildred Ezell Reynolds, "My Memoirs," p. 4, typescript, Garrett Family Papers, Filson Historical Society, Louisville, Ky.

19. Rose, Ku Klux Klan, 18.

20. Horn, Invisible Empire, 113.

21. "Shooting," Pulaski Citizen, July 27, 1866, p. 3.

22. Early-twentieth-century historians were the first professional historians to tell the story of the Ku-Klux. Yet even these earliest historians consistently emphasized that the beginnings of the Ku-Klux were "innocent," meaning purely frivolous and free of political intention, even though Ku-Klux founders would very soon discover and exploit its political utility. William Garrett Brown, The Lower South in American History, 202; William Archibald Dunning did apologize to his readers up front that they might perceive him as slighting "the picturesque details of Ku-Klux operations." Dunning, Reconstruction, xvi. Revisionist historians took a considerably dimmer view of the Ku-Klux, and one might expect they would have questioned the innocent origins idea. A few did: John Hope Franklin argued that these men "could hardly have been unaware of what they were doing. Even if they were bored and impatient with life, as has been claimed in their defense, this was nothing new for young bloods in the village of Pulaski, Tennessee. Nor were wanton attacks on helpless Negroes new." Franklin, Reconstruction, 154.

23. Trelease, White Terror, 5.

24. "Origin of the Ku Klux Klan," letter to the Nashville Banner from James R. Crowe, Sheffield, Ala., n.d., Giles County Historical Society Archives, Pulaski, Tenn.

25. "Mr. Frank McCord Tells What He Knows about the Kuklux."

26. Lester and Wilson, Ku Klux Klan, 53.

27. Lapsley David McCord, "Red Gown," unpublished manuscript, Ku-Klux Collection, Missouri Historical Society, St. Louis.

28. Testimony of Daniel Coleman, KK Report, vol. 9, Ala., 2:660.

29. Lester and Wilson, Ku Klux Klan, 21.

30. Edward Harcourt, one of the recent scholars to reflect most closely on the Tennessee Ku-Klux's beginnings, and skeptical of the "innocent origins" account, points out that both that Giles and neighboring counties were singled out by Freedmen's Bureau agents as centers of political resistance by 1866—before the Ku-Klux's apparent politicization—and were known to be harboring gangs of young men eager and willing to violently disrupt Reconstruction. Analyzing the similar "Pale Faces" group, Harcourt notes that the founding members were politically minded and civically engaged adult men. Harcourt, "Who Were the Pale Faces?," 42.

31. "Fire at Pulaski," Pulaski Citizen, May 18, 1867, p. 3.

32. "Amusement Wanted," Pulaski Citizen, January 11, 1867, p. 3.

33. "Giles County," Nashville Union and Dispatch, October 8, 1867, p. 1.

34. Ryan, Civic Wars; Susan G. Davis, Parades and Power.

35. "Grand Memphis Tournament," Memphis Public Ledger, May 16, 1866, p. 2. Weinfeld, The Jackson County War, 105. Paul Christopher Anderson's "Rituals of Horsemanship" has an excellent discussion of the relationship of the Klan to tournaments.

36. "The Tableaux Last Week," *Pulaski Citizen*, May 4, 1866, p. 2; "Tournament at Clarksville," *Pulaski Citizen*, May 11, 1866, p. 2.

37. "Amusement Wanted," *Pulaski Citizen*, January 11, 1867, p. 3.

38. "To the Maimed Confederate Soldiers of Giles County," *Pulaski Citizen*, May 4, 1866, p. 3.

39. "The Tableaux Last Night," *Pulaski Citizen*, May 4, 1866, p. 2.

40. Lester and Wilson, *Ku Klux Klan*.

41. Giddens, *The Consequences of Modernity*, 21.

42. From an incidence of .00015 percent of all printed words in 1810, it would climb to .00041 in 1870, then would peak around 1880 at .00053. Google n-grams search, U.S.-published texts, "restlessness" 1800–1900 (accessed June 21, 2014).

43. Lester and Wilson, *Ku Klux Klan*, 48.

44. *Pulaski Independent Citizen*, April 8, 1859, p. 1. (In the antebellum period, the paper was titled the *Pulaski Independent Citizen*. After the war, as it fell in lockstep with the Conservative/Democratic Party, it dropped "Independent." Fuller Ossoli, *Women in the Nineteenth Century*.

45. Quist, *Restless Visionaries*, 72–74.

46. "Luther McCord: Brother's Historical Sketch and Tribute," *Pulaski Citizen*, September 20, 1900, p. 1.

47. "Editorial Excursions," *Pulaski Independent Citizen*, May 25, 1860, p. 3.

48. "Major Jack Dowling on Secession," *Pulaski Independent Citizen*, March 22, 1861, p. 1.

49. Based on my reading of the uses of "boredom" in the Gale-Cengage collection of Nineteenth-Century U.S. Newspapers (accessed August 1, 2014).

50. Benjamin, *Arcades Project*, cited in Goldstein, *Experience without Qualities*, 2.

51. Goldstein, *Experience without Qualities*, 120–24.

52. Ibid., 124.

53. *Edgefield (S.C.) Advertiser*, March 25, 1868, p. 2.

54. Lester and Wilson, *Ku Klux Klan*, 57; Green, *Recollections of the Inhabitants*, 136.

55. Ibid., 48.

56. Graham, *The Handbook of Standard or American Phonography*.

57. Cmiel, "'A Broad Fluid Language of Democracy,'" 913–36.

58. "Spiritualism," *Pulaski Independent Citizen*, December 10, 1858, p. 1; "Colored Logic," February 18, 1859, p. 1; "The Arkansas Traveler" (reprinted from the *Knickerbocker*), March 25, 1859; Polly Muggins, "Perils of Teaching Grammar," April 8, 1859, p. 1; "Oh, How Vulgaw!," September 30, 1859, p. 1; "Darkey Dialogue," February 3, 1860, p. 3; "Dutch Lottery Dialogue," May 4, 1860; "The Negro Patient," July 27, 1860, p. 1; "Major Jack Dowling on Secession," March 22, 1861, p. 1. For Reconstruction-era examples, see "Thixton: The Possible Origin of an Original Word," *Memphis Daily Appeal*, November 3, 1872, p. 4; "Origin of Words," *Memphis Avalanche*, November 28, 1872, p. 2.

59. Testimony of Daniel Coleman, KK Report, vol. 9, Ala., 2:660.

60. "What Does It Mean?," *Pulaski Citizen*, March 29, 1867, p. 3.

61. Lester and Wilson, *Ku Klux Klan*, 58–59.

62. "Letter from New York," *Atlanta Daily Sun*, October 21, 1871, p. 3.

63. "Mother Goose and Her Friends," in Venable, *The School Stage*, 39.

64. Allen Trelease amorphously suggests that "generals, politicians, and vigilantes . . . took over the organization in 1867 and 1868" and also that "vigilantism did become a serious business within the Klan a year later [than June 1866]. . . . Exactly when, how, and why [the transition] happened can only be inferred from very fragmentary evidence most of it provided by Lester and Wilson. . . . Some of their details, especially dates, are inaccurate." Trelease, *White Terror*, 5, 10. Mentioning the emergence of bands of "postwar regulators or vigilantes" throughout the South, Trelease says, "This apparently is what the Ku Klux Klan was coming to be by the spring of 1867. Its operations cannot have been very extensive or spectacular; the fact would have been reported if they were." Trelease, *White Terror*, 11. The early origins of the Pulaski Klan are only tangential to other recent scholars. Steven Hahn writes of Ku-Klux "and allied organizations" that "in late 1867 and 1868, they spread across the South with great speed." Hahn, *A Nation under Our Feet*, 268.

65. "Sensation Story," *Pulaski Citizen*, June 29, 1866, p. 1.

66. "What Does It Mean?," *Pulaski Citizen*, March 29, 1867, p. 3.

67. *Pulaski Citizen*, April 5, 1867, p. 4; "Ku-klux," *Pulaski Citizen*, May 3, 1867, p. 4.

68. Trelease, *White Terror*, 14.

69. Horn, *Invisible Empire*, 33; Trelease, *White Terror*, 14–20.

70. Lester and Wilson, *Ku Klux Klan*, 40.

71. Ryland Raldoph Sr. to Mr. Walter Fleming, August 21, 1901, Walter Lynnwood Fleming Papers, New York Public Library, New York.

72. Lester and Wilson, *Ku Klux Klan*, 135.

73. Ibid., 150.

74. Ibid., 137.

75. Ibid., 138.

76. Ibid., 139.

77. Ibid., 142.

78. Macoy, *The Masonic Manual*, 20, 25, 39.

79. Lester and Wilson, *Ku Klux Klan*, 136.

80. Rose, *Ku Klux Klan*, 22.

81. Lester and Wilson, *Ku Klux Klan*, 37, 84.

82. *Pulaski Citizen*, May 24, 1867, p. 3.

83. Trelease, *White Terror*, 14.

84. Trelease, and others following him, do not place any of the Confederate notables who were later associated with Ku-Klux leadership at the meeting. For that matter, he does not definitively place anyone there. Trelease concedes, "Whether the prominent men who were interested participated directly or guided the activities from a distance, we do not know." Trelease, *White Terror*, 14.

85. Rose, *Ku Klux Klan*, 22.

86. Lester and Wilson, *Ku Klux Klan*, 85.

87. Trelease is confident in this, though he acknowledges that he cannot identify any given point by which Forrest was definitively already involved. He believes, based on much later writings of John W. Morton, that it was probably May 1867. Trelease, *White Terror*, 20.

88. Preface by Lee Meriwether in Elizabeth Avery Meriwether, *Recollections of 92 Years, 1824–1916*.

89. Immediately after asserting that Forrest was at some point installed as the head of the Klan, Trelease writes that "a good deal has been written about the Klan's further organization at the top levels, but most of it lacks substantiation, and much of it is clearly fictitious." Trelease, *White Terror*, 20.

90. Richardson, *Historic Pulaski*, 7.

91. *The Daily South Carolinian*, July 6, 1866, p. 2, described one parade thusly: "Guzzling, gunpowder, perspiring negroes, hot lemonade, cold blackberry pies, unwholesome ginger-bread, overheated heroes and fat, fly-disturbed artillery horses, shoals of ragged juvenile freedmen, a brass band and a spreadeagle orator, black, red, yellow, white, or of some neutral tint, with the addition of heat, dust and smell, are all that is left of the Fourth of July."

92. Reynolds, "My Memoirs."

93. "Mr. Frank McCord Tells What He Knows about the Kuklux."

94. "Ku-klux. Grand Demonstration Wednesday Night," *Pulaski Citizen*, June 7, 1867.

95. Lester and Wilson, *Ku Klux Klan*, 95.

96. Ibid., 93.

97. Richardson, *Historic Pulaski*, 7.

98. Trelease, *White Terror*, 21.

99. Richardson, *Historic Pulaski*, 25.

100. "Knights of the Golden Circle, or Something Else," *Pulaski Citizen*, August 23, 1867, p. 2.

101. "Editor Citizen" and "Giles County: Radical Slanders Refuted," *Pulaski Citizen*, September 6, 1868, p. 2.

102. "Official: The Biggest Lie Yet to Be Hatched," *Pulaski Citizen*, September 6, 1868, p. 3.

103. Testimony of Captain J. J. Mankins (Tennessee Militia), *Sheafe v. Tillman* in *Miscellaneous Documents from the House of Representatives of the Second Session of the Forty-First Congress*, 264–65. Mankins claims that he first learned of the Ku-Klux while he was stationed in Pulaski in the spring of 1867.

104. Harcourt, "Who Were the Pale Faces?," 44. H. A. Eastman's December 1867 report from Columbia is cited in Michael Walsh to W. P. Carlin, January 8, 1868, Tennessee BRFAL, Roll 34, Reports of Outrages, Riots, and Murders, 1866–68.

105. H. A. Eastman, Report of Murders Committed during the Year Ending July 1, 1868, "List of Murders in Counties of Maury and Marshall, Tennessee from July 1st, 1867 to July 1st, 1868," Tennessee BRFAL, Roll 34, Reports of Outrages, Riots, and Murders, 1866–68.

106. Testimony of George F. Bowles (Giles County), 3; Testimony of Anderson Cheatham (Maury County), 11; and Testimony of Charles Marchbanks (Warren County), 47, *Tennessee Report*.

107. Testimony of Pink Harris (Giles County), 5–6; Testimony of Moses Boddy (Giles County), 64; and Testimony of Walter Scott (Giles County), 35, *Tennessee Report*.

108. Testimony of William Wyatt (Lincoln County), 15; Testimony of Richard Moore (Lincoln County), 46; Testimony of Charles E. Robert (Maury County), 55; Testimony of Nim Wilks, 13; and Testimony of Jacob M. Davis (Tipton County), 32, *Tennessee Report*. "List of Murders in Counties of Maury and Marshall, Tennessee, from July 1st, 1867 to July 1st, 1868," H. A. Eastman, Columbia, Tennessee, August 12, 1868, Tennessee BRFAL, Roll 34, Reports of Outrages, Riots, and Murders, 1866–68.

109. Lester and Wilson, *Ku Klux Klan*, 70.

110. Ibid., 84.

111. Trelease writes with characteristic caution, "It is impossible to say now how far the order had spread by this time, but probably not very far," and calls them dismissively "the bizarre band of secret regulators around Pulaski," but he does tacitly accept (by presenting Lester and Wilson's account and providing no alternative) the claim that the reorganization was motivated by those "alarmed by the tendency to violence within the order" and that it was at this meeting that the Ku-Klux was handed into the keeping of "men of far greater prestige and authority whose influence extended throughout the states." In fact, though, there is no evidence of a tendency to violence before spring 1867, and very little indeed to prove early organization. Trelease, *White Terror*, 13. My own article, "Midnight Rangers," also simply accepted Lester and Wilson's account.

112. "Proclamation of the Grand Cyclops," *Pulaski Citizen*, June 14, 1867, p. 4.

113. *Pulaski Citizen*, June 21, 1867, p. 3.

114. "KuKlux," *Pulaski Citizen*, July 26, 1867, p. 4.

115. *Pulaski Citizen*, August 23, 1867, p. 4.

116. *Pulaski Citizen*, September 6, 1867, p. 3.

117. Testimony of Capt. Mankins, *Sheafe v. Tillman*, 266.

118. "Obnoxious," *Pulaski Citizen*, December 20, 1867, p. 3.

119. "The Tournament," *Pulaski Citizen*, November 15, 1867, p. 3.

120. Resolution by Henry Webb and others submitted to Brig. Gen. Clinton B. Fisk, March 26, 1866, M-89 (1866), [filed as "Meble"], Registered Letters Received, Series 3379, Office of the Assistant Commissioner of Tennessee, BRFAL (FSSP 6294).

121. "Statement of attack on the house of Amos Kimble on the night of July 15th and firing on himself and family by parties supposed to be the same that murdered Dudley Kimble," sent from Colonel J. R. Lewis (Chief Superintendent, Nashville Sub-District) to Brig. Gen. Clinton B. Fisk, July 24, 1866 (statement written July 18, 1866), L-91 (1866), Registered Letters Received, Series 3379, Office of the Assistant Commissioner of Tennessee, BRFAL (FSSP A6285).

122. Letter from Captain George E. Judd (Agent) to Captain Michael A. Walsh (Subassistant Commissioner), May 14, 1867.

123. Ibid., including Monthly Report for Williamson and Giles Counties for January 1867, January 31, 1867, J-3 (1867), Box 87, Registered Letters Received, July 1866–September 1868, Series 3570, Subassistant Commissioner of the Subdistrict of Nashville, BRFAL (FSSP A6482).

124. *Pulaski Citizen*, August 23, 1867, p. 4.

125. "From Tennessee," *Milwaukee Daily Sentinel*, August 22, 1867, p. 4. (This had been printed in Nashville exchange on August 20, 1867.)

126. "The KuKlix [sic] Klan of Pulaski," *Nashville Union and Dispatch*, August 21, 1867, p. 3.

127. "Another Radical Lie Nailed," *Nashville Union and Dispatch*, August 31, 1867, p. 1.

128. "Giles County: Radical Slanders Refuted," *Nashville Union and Dispatch*, September 4, 1867, p. 1.

129. "Lance and Saber," *Nashville Union and Dispatch*, November 10, 1867, p. 3.

130. "Maury County," *Nashville Union and Dispatch*, December 18, 1867, p. 2.

131. "Maury County," *Nashville Union and Dispatch*, December 25, 1867, p. 1.

132. *Winchester Home Journal*, September 19, 1867, p. 2.

133. "Another Radical Lie Nailed," *Weekly Union and American* (Nashville, Tenn.), September 5, 1867, p. 1. I have not done a comprehensive search of national press coverage of the Klan. No doubt, there are other examples that I have not found. I am confident, though, that they are very few and scattered.

134. "Negro Outrages in Tennessee," *New York World*, December 17, 1867. Thank you to Mark Summers for this reference.

135. *Tuscaloosa Independent Monitor*, January 1, 1868, cited in Trelease, *White Terror*, 84–85. (I cannot find an extant copy of the issue of the *Monitor*.)

136. "Mr. Frank McCord Tells What He Knows about the Kuklux."

137. Lester and Wilson, *Ku Klux Klan*, 95.

138. Rose, *Ku Klux Klan*, 23–24.

139. "Negro Outrages in Tennessee," *The World* (New York, New York), December 17, 1867, p. 2. Thank you to Mark Summers for letting me know about this important article, and to Paul Friedman at the New York Public Library for going above and beyond the call of duty to find and scan it for me.

140. Captain Michael Walsh to William. P. Carlin, January 11, 1868, Registered Letters Received, Series 3379, Office of the Assistant Commissioner of Tennessee, BRFAL, Roll 34, Reports of Outrages, Riots, and Murders, 1866–68.

141. Ibid.

142. Letter from Captain George E. Judd (Agent) to Captain Michael A. Walsh (Subassistant Commissioner), May 14, 1867.

143. Captain Michael Walsh to William P. Carlin, January 11, 1868.

144. "The Riot—a Base Fabrication," *Pulaski Citizen*, January 17, 1868, p. 3.

145. Tennessee BRFAL, Roll 34, Reports of Outrages, Riots, and Murders, 1866–68.

146. *Proceedings of the State Convention of the Colored Citizens of Tennessee*, 4.

147. Testimony of Idel Brite, *Tennessee Report*, 40.

148. *Pulaski Citizen*, July 3, p. 3; testimony of H. H. Aynett, *Tennessee Report*, 60.

149. Walter Lynnwood Fleming Papers, MssColl 1029, Manuscripts and Archives Division, New York Public Library.

150. Reynolds, "My Memoirs," 4.

CHAPTER 2

1. Testimony of Caswell Holt, *KK Report*, vol. 2, N.C., 1:341–42.

2. Testimony of Columbus Jeter, *KK Report*, vol. 6, Ga., 1:561.

3. Testimony of Henry Hamlin, *KK Report*, vol. 9, Ala., 2:857.

4. Testimony of Betsey Westbrook, *KK Report*, vol. 9, Ala., 2:1243.

5. For an analysis of the collective fear created by Klan attacks, see Blight, *Race and Reunion*, 117–18.

6. Testimony of Henry B. Whitfield, *KK Report*, vol. 11, Miss., 1:427.

7. Testimony of John Talliaferro, *KK Report*, vol. 11, Miss., 1:239.

8. Testimony of *KK Report*, vol. 7, Ga., 2:603.

9. Baker, "Lynching Ballads."

10. UCCI, Box 36, Roll 4020; Box 38, Roll 5165; Box 38, Roll 4858; Box 37, Roll 4419; Box 40, Roll 6256; Box 36, Roll 3615; Box 36, Roll 3934; Box 38, Roll 5216.

11. Testimony of H. W. Guion, *KK Report*, vol. 3, S.C., 1:261.

12. November 29, 1868, Diary of Octavia Wyche Otey, Folder 45, Wyche and Otey Family Papers, Southern Historical Collection, University of North Carolina at Chapel Hill.

13. "Do you suppose those negroes really believe anything of that kind?" Testimony of John H. Christy, *KK Report*, vol. 6, Ga., 1:239.

14. On the Klan's relationship to charivari, see Flynn, "The Ancient Pedigree of Violent Repression," in Fraser and Moore, *The Southern Enigma*, 189–98. For accounts of the tradition of rough music in the United States, see Roediger, *The Wages of Whiteness*, 100–111; Susan G. Davis, *Parades and Power*, 73–111; Pencak, Dennis, and Newman, *Riot and Revelry in Early America*; Kenny, *Making Sense of the Molly Maguires*, 11. For European roots, see Natalie Zemon Davis, "The Reasons of Misrule."

15. Scott, *Domination and the Arts of Resistance*, 181. Whistling, William Pierson points out, was one of the many Klan performative elements that seemed to much more closely resemble an African than a European tradition. Pierson, *Black Legacy*, 155.

16. Harris, *Exorcising Blackness*. Brundage, *Lynching in the New South*, 17–48, argues that only those lynchings carried out with the broad participation of the whites in a community tended to partake of ritual.

17. On the reconfiguration of southern white manhood in the Reconstruction era, see Edwards, *Gendered Strife and Confusion*, 107–29, 161–77; Whites, *The Civil War as a Crisis in Gender*, 132–59.

18. Whites, *Civil War as a Crisis in Gender*, 96–131.

19. Baptist, *The Half Has Never Been Told*; Nelson, *Iron Confederacies*, 112.

20. Testimony of John Childers, *KK Report*, vol. 10, Ala., 3:1720.

21. "Brick Pomeroy's Description of the Black Crook," *Daily Phoenix*, February 12, 1867, p. 2.

22. Halttunen, *Confidence Men and Painted Women*; see also Johnson, *River of Dark Dreams*, 150.23. "Turner Masquerade Ball," *Cairo Evening Bulletin*, February 18, 1870, p. 3; "Grand Masquerade Ball," *Daily Ohio Statesman*, September 29, 1868, p. 2; "Theatre Francais," *New York Tribune*, December 18, 1868, p. 7.

24. Tom Hood, "Hunting Him Down: A Sensation Story for the Christmas Season," *Philadelphia Evening Telegraph*, December 24, 1869, p. 4.

25. Testimony of J. J. Hinds, *Report of Joint Committee on Outrages*, 7.

26. Testimony of Aaron V. Biggerstaff, *KK Report*, vol. 2, N.C., 1:485.

27. "1870–1872 Ku Klux Klan Hood/Mask," North Carolina Museum of History, 1996.102.1a.

28. Testimony of Samuel Bonner, *KK Report*, vol. 3, S.C., 1:578. Pierson, *Black Legacy*, 150, notes that these horns, like so many performative elements of the early Klan, evoke African or Caribbean origins. I would suggest that this is probably correct, but that these influences may have been largely conveyed through minstrelsy.

29. Testimony of Isham Henry, *KK Report*, vol. 9, Ala., 2:1199.

30. Testimony of Jacob Montgomery, *KK Report*, vol. 4, S.C., 2:696.

31. Testimony of J. Thomson Hughes, *KK Report*, vol. 4, S.C., 2:1093.

32. Testimony of Daniel Coleman, *KK Report*, vol. 9, Ala., 2:661. See also testimony of Hon. Peter M. Dox, *KK Report*, vol. 8, Ala., 1:457; testimony of Joseph F. Galloway, *KK Report*, vol. 12, Miss., 2:663; testimony of Warren Jones, *KK Report*, vol. 7, Ga., 2:690; and testimony of Charles Smith, *KK Report*, vol. 7, Ga., 2:599.

33. Fry, *Night Riders*, 138.

34. When a group of Ku-Klux attacked Alabama freedman William Ford, for instance, "some said they came from Nashville, and some down from off the moon." Testimony of William Ford, *KK Report*, vol. 9, Ala., 2:681; testimony of G. Wiley, *KK Report*, vol. 12, Miss., 2:1154; testimony of William H. Oglesby, *KK Report*, vol. 7, Ga., 2:1004; testimony of Thomas M. Drennon, *KK Report*, vol. 6, Ga., 1:404.

35. Dean Reynolds's Alabama attackers first claimed to be from hell, then claimed to be from the moon. Written affidavit of Dean Reynolds, *KK Report*, vol. 9, Ala., 2:1186. See also testimony of G. Wiley, *KK Report*, vol. 12, Miss., 2:1154; testimony of Henry Hamlin, *KK Report*, vol. 9, Ala., 2:857; "Ku Klux Outrages in Wayne County, N.C."; "Ku Klux Klan Papers, Depositions, etc. 1869–1870," William Woods Holden Papers, 1841–1929 [manuscript], DMRL; testimony of Joseph Gill, *KK Report*, vol. 9, Ala., 2:813.

36. "The Devil Turned Loose," *Pulaski Citizen*, March 9, 1866, p. 1. The paper later reported the apprehension of this "devil," who had been frightening people from their homes in this fashion in order to steal from them. "The 'Kentucky Devil' Arrested," *Pulaski Citizen*, April 13, 1866, p. 1.

37. While one purpose of assumed accents was probably disguise, there were a number of ways to disguise one's voice. Some Ku-Klux communicated through whistles. Others spoke in very high or very low pitches or through mouthpieces or horns. Testimony of James Moss, *KK Report*, vol. 9, Ala., 2:919. Those Ku-Klux who adopted accents that their victims identified as foreign chose among many options to assume the guise of foreigners. Testimony of James A. Justice, *KK Report*, vol. 2, N.C., 1:118; testimony of John Lipscomb, *KK Report*, vol. 4, S.C., 2:670; testimony of Reuben Bryant, *KK Report*, vol. 4, S.C., 2:677.

38. Testimony of Warren Jones, *KK Report*, vol. 7, Ga., 2:690.

39. J. P. Flournoy Sr., "The True Story of the Jones-Hill Mob by an Eye Witness" (typewritten bound manuscript), p. 156, Alfred Flournoy Sr. Family Papers, 1824–1944, Louisiana State University Archives, Baton Rouge.

40. Testimony of Sarah A. Allen, *KK Report*, vol. 12, Miss., 2:779.

41. Testimony of Joseph F. Galloway, *KK Report*, vol. 12, Miss., 2:663; testimony of John Coley, *KK Report*, vol. 6, Ga., 1:365.

42. Testimony of Edward E. Holman, *KK Report*, vol. 11, Miss., 1:352.

43. Testimony of Gadsden Steel, *KK Report*, vol. 4, S.C., 2:233.

44. Testimony of Columbus Jeter, *KK Report*, vol. 6, Ga., 1:560.

45. Testimony of Samuel Ghoulson, *KK Report*, vol. 12, Miss., 2:856.

46. Testimony of Sandy Sellers, handwritten unidentified trial transcript, p. 1, Ku Klux Klan Collection, DMRL.

47. Letter from Henry [?] to Andrew McCollum, April 16, 1868, from Louisiana State Seminary [near Alexandria], Folder 21, Andrew McCollum Papers, Southern Historical Collection, University of North Carolina at Chapel Hill.

48. "The Devil Turned Loose," *Pulaski Citizen*, March 9, 1866, p. 1.

49. Testimony of James A. Justice, *KK Report*, vol. 2, N.C., 1:116.

50. Testimony of William H. English, *KK Report*, vol. 10, Ala., 3:1438.

51. Cockrell, *Demons of Disorder*, 30–61.

52. Testimony of Thompson C. Hawkins, *KK Report*, vol. 9, Ala., 2:1326.

53. Testimony of John H. Wager, *KK Report*, vol. 9, Ala., 2:933.

54. Testimony of Austin Pollard, *KK Report*, vol. 12, Miss., 2:1109.

55. "Kuklux Klan," *Pulaski Citizen*, June 7, 1867, p. 4.

56. Testimony of John R. Taliferro, *KK Report*, vol. 11, Miss., 1:228.

57. Testimony of William Miller, *KK Report*, vol. 8, Ala., 1:9.

58. "Ku-klux Chronicles: Captain Shotwell's Story of the Klans," M. S. Shotwell Scrapbook, Folder 29, Box 4, Shotwell Family Papers, Southern Historical Collection, University of North Carolina at Chapel Hill.

59. Testimony of John Dunlap, *Tennessee Report*, 19.

60. Testimony of John Taylor Coleman, *KK Report*, vol. 9, Ala., 2:1048–49.

61. Testimony of Reuban Bryant, *KK Report*, vol. 4, S.C., 2:682.

62. Letter from Wentworth, N.C., July 13, 1869, to Tho. Settle from Tho. A. Ragland, C. J. L. Williams, Z. Groom, William Woods Holden Collection, DMRL. Here, Ku-Klux were forcing their black victim to act not only like circus performers but also like animals, a practice with a deep history in slavery. Johnson, *River of Dark Dreams*, 188–91.

63. Testimony of William A. Bolt, *KK Report*, vol. 4, S.C., 2:1121.

64. Lapsley David McCord, "Red Gown," p. 39, unpublished manuscript, Ku-Klux Collection, Missouri Historical Society, St. Louis.

65. Schechner, *Between Theatre and Anthropology*, 40; Turner, *From Ritual to Theatre*, 84, and *The Anthropology of Performance*, 25. Barbara Babcock-Abrahams made a similar point in "'A Tolerated Margin of Mess,'" arguing that "at the center of [the trickster's] antinomian existence is the power derived from his ability to live interstitially, to confuse and to escape the structures of society and the order of cultural things" (148).

66. "Death of an Old Citizen," *Mobile Daily Register*, June 14, 1870 (Mardi Gras, 1869–1871, Vertical File, Historic Mobile Preservation Society).

67. Testimony of Caleb Jenkins, *KK Report*, vol. 4, S.C., 2:697. Drew Faust discusses a wartime instance of carnivalesque cross-dressing in Spartanburg, S.C. Faust, *Mothers of Invention*, 229–30.

68. Nineteenth-century Jamaican carnival featured a "Koo-Koo" boy, and the traditional Bulgarian carnivalesque wildman a "Kuker." Kinser, *Carnival, American Style*, 216–23.

69. Letter from Avery Meriwether to Lee Meriwether, February 5, 1877, Folder 51, Box 1, Meriwether Family Papers, Mississippi Valley Collection, University of

Memphis, Memphis, Tenn. It becomes clear from a second exchange that the book referred to is the Klan play. See letter from Avery Meriwether to Rivers Meriwether University of Memphis, February 25, 1877, ibid.

70. Testimony of Sally Bedell, reprinted in *Radical Rule*, 59, 61.

71. Testimony of Joseph Gist, *KK Report*, vol. 4, S.C., 2:1061.

72. Testimony of Christine Page, *KK Report*, vol. 4, S.C., 2:1142–1144.

73. Testimony of William Bolt, *KK Report*, vol. 4, S.C., 2:1121.

74. Testimony of James Gaffney, *KK Report*, vol. 4, S.C., 2:617; testimony of John Lipscomb, *KK Report*, vol. 4, S.C., 2:667.

75. Testimony of John Christy, *KK Report*, vol. 6, Ga., 1:245.

76. "Belonged to Ku-klux-Klan: Houston Man Tells of His Experiences as a Member of That Famous Organization," *Mobile Daily Herald*, October 27, 1907.

77. Testimony of John Christy, *KK Report*, vol. 11, Miss., 1:144.

78. Midcentury minstrel groups frequently called themselves "serenaders." See, for instance, posters for the Boston Museum performance of Horn, Wells and Briggs' Celebrated Troupe of Ethiopian Serenaders, July 17, 1851: "8th Season Boston Museum. No. 368 . . . Last night but one of Horn, Wells, and Briggs' Ethoiopian serenadres! Benefit of Eve Horn! . . . August 1st, 1851," Series 1, no. 17161; and the Boston Museum performance of New Orleans Serenaders: "Seventh season Boston Museum. No. 348. . . . Second week of the engagement of the celebrated opera troupe of New Orleans Serenaders (July 20, 1850)," American Broadsides and Ephemera, Series 1, no. 17149, New York Public Library for the Performing Arts Research Collection, New York, N.Y.

79. Testimony of Henry Kidd, *KK Report*, vol. 9, Ala., 2:869.

80. August 6, 1867, and September 1, 1869, Samuel Agnew Diary, Southern Historical Collection, University of North Carolina at Chapel Hill.

81. "Ku-klux Chronicles."

82. Testimony of Elias Hill, *KK Report*, vol. 5, S.C., 3:1407.

83. Testimony of Samuel Horton, *KK Report*, vol. 9, Ala., 2:729.

84. Fry, *Night Riders*, 129; Flynn, "The Ancient Pedigree of Violent Repression," 192–93; Fossett, "(K)night Riders in (K)night Gowns."

85. Testimony of John J. Neason, *KK Report*, vol. 3, S.C., 1:42.

86. Testimony of Commodore Perry Price, *KK Report*, vol. 3, S.C., 1:297.

87. Testimony of Joseph Gill, *KK Report*, vol. 9, Ala., 2:813.

88. Testimony of Eli Barnes, *KK Report*, vol. 7, Ga., 2:955.

89. Testimony of John Dunlap, *Tennessee Report*, 18.

90. Testimony of A. B. Martin, *KK Report*, vol. 6, Ga., 1:549.

91. Testimony of Lieutenant F. B. Taylor, *KK Report*, vol. 6, Ga., 1:504.

92. *KK Report*, vol. 4, S.C., 2:605.

93. Greenberg, *Honor and Slavery*, 26–31; Faust, *Mothers of Invention*, 228.

94. Lott, *Love and Theft*; Natalie Zemon Davis, *Society and Culture in Early Modern France*, 124–51; Susan G. Davis, "'Making Night Hideous.'"

95. "The Negro Question Again," *Knoxville Whig*, September 27, 1865, p. 2. For earlier American precedents, see Susan G. Davis, *Parades and Power*, 81, 84, 106.

96. Testimony of Essic Harris, *KK Report*, vol. 2, N.C., 1:87.

97. Testimony of Mary Ann Norvill, *KK Report*, vol. 2, N.C., 1:473.

98. Testimony of Martha Hendricks, *KK Report*, vol. 6, Ga., 1:520.

99. Testimony of John H. Christy, *KK Report*, vol. 6, Ga., 1:245.

100. Robuck, *My Own Personal Experience*, 15. The loose-fitting, corsetless Mother Hubbard was associated with prostitution in the 1880s (so, well after the dress was given but well before Robuck described the event in his memoir). It seems likely that Robuck was retrospectively adding the sexual insult. Thank you to Mara Keire for the lead on Mother Hubbards. Sharon E. Wood, *Freedom of the Streets*, 5.

101. This line of five brothers is a version of a minstrel band, with Ku-Klux filling the structural role of the "end man" and the mother as the interlocuter.

102. Meriwether, *The Ku Klux Klan*, 4, 15.

103. Ibid., 42.

104. Ibid., 47.

105. "Minnesota," *Milwaukee Sentinel*, February 16, 1872, p. 3. Roediger, *Wages of Whiteness*, 105–9. Cockrell, *Demons of Disorder*, 46, discusses the Klan's emergence from this tradition; see also 50–54.

106. Pfeifer, "The Origins of Post-Bellum Lynching," 194.

107. "Removing Tan," *Pulaski Citizen*, April 26, 1867, p. 1.

108. *KK Report*, vol. 3, S.C., 1:393.

109. Ibid., 421; testimony of Robert Abercrombie, *KK Report*, vol. 9, Ala., 2:1113; testimony of Betsey Westbrook, *KK Report*, vol. 9, Ala., 2:1243–44; testimony of William Miller, *KK Report*, vol. 8, Ala., 1:3; testimony of Mary Campbell, *KK Report*, vol. 8, Ala., 1:149; testimony of William Burnside Anderson, *KK Report*, vol. 3, S.C., 1:290; testimony of Cornelius McBride, *KK Report*, vol. 11, Miss., 1:327.

110. "The New Rebellion," *New York Tribune*, November 4, 1868, p. 3.

111. Testimony of Mary Brown, *KK Report*, vol. 6, Ga., 1:376.

112. For allegations of black Klans, see testimony of William D. Simpson, *KK Report*, vol. 5, S.C., 3:1311; testimony of Alexander P. Wylie, *KK Report*, vol. 5, S.C., 3:1429; testimony of O. C. French, *KK Report*, vol. 11, Miss., 1:19; testimony of Charles Baskerville, *KK Report*, vol. 11, Miss., 1:375.

113. Testimony of Joe Brown, *KK Report*, vol. 6, Ga., 1:503. For an instance of such blackfaced spying in antebellum Louisiana, see Barde, *The Vigilance Committees of the Attakapas*, 217–18. Also see a reference to a claim to convincing blackface performance in Silver, "Making Minstrelsy of Murder," 352.

114. Piersen, *Black Legacy*, 150–53.

115. Lhamon, *Raising Cain*, 42.

116. Michaels, "The Souls of White Folk."

117. Testimony of William M. Champion, *KK Report*, vol. 3, S.C., 1:366. This is discussed in Fry, *Night Riders*, 111.

118. Testimony of Lewis Perkins, *KK Report*, vol. 12, Miss., 2:899.

119. Testimony of E. H. Chambers, *KK Report*, vol. 7, Ga., 2:602.

120. Ladurie, *Carnival in Romans*; Scott, *Domination and the Arts of Resistance*, 178–91; Natalie Zemon Davis, "The Reasons of Misrule"; Bakhtin, *Rabelais and His World*. Castle, *Masquerade and Civilization*, 88, argues that elites dressing as nonelites, unlike its opposite, did not threaten to existing power structures.

121. Cockrell, *Demons of Disorder*, 53, cautions against reading blackface minstrelsy as pure inversion, 160.

122. Lott, *Love and Theft*, 25, 52, 123–24.

123. Silver, "Making Minstrelsy of Murder," 345.

124. Roediger, *Wages of Whiteness*, 107.

125. Natalie Zemon Davis, *Society and Culture in Early Modern France*, 149.

126. Bederman, *Manliness and Civilization*, 217–32.

127. Cockrell, *Demons of Disorder*, 53.

128. Testimony of Elias Thomson, *KK Report*, vol. 3, S.C., 1:411.

129. Testimony of Dick Wilson, *KK Report*, vol. 5, S.C., 3:1741. The same testimony is printed in U.S. Circuit Court (4th Circuit), *Proceedings in the Ku Klux Trials at Columbia, S.C.*, 283.

130. Bederman, *Manliness and Civilization*, 77–120, 182.

131. According to Greenberg, since a gentleman's honor was determined by people's response to those parts of him that were visible, "to wear a mask was no shame for a man of honor; the horror was to be unmasked—to be publicly shamed and exposed as a man who dressed as a woman." Greenberg, *Honor and Slavery*, 15, 25.

132. Testimony of Columbus Jeter, *KK Report*, vol. 6, Ga., 1:560–62.

133. Testimony of Martha Hendricks, *KK Report*, vol. 6, Ga., 1:520.

134. Letter from Minor Meriwether to Avery Meriwether, April 23, 1869, Camp Ten Miles from Macon, Ala., Folder 50, Box 1, Meriwether Family Collection, Special Collections, University of Memphis, Memphis, Tenn.

135. Bond cited in Gillette, *Retreat from Reconstruction*, 28.

136. Lhamon, *Raising Cain*, 45.

137. *Franklin (La.) Planters' Banner*, December 7, 1870, p. 2. Actually, the "white showman" controlling the animals/ freedmen in this metaphor were northern rather than southern whites, who were thereby threatening to cause a racial uprising against southern whites. Earlier that year, the same newspaper had reviewed Dan Rice's circus by snidely suggesting of the performing horses that "if that kind of training becomes general, Congress will doubtless apply the Fifteenth Amendment to those progressive animals." "The Circus," *Franklin (La.) Planters' Banner*, March 30, 1870, p. 3.

138. Ritvo, *Animal Estate*, 219. Ritvo says that nineteenth-century zoos "reenacted and celebrated the imposition of human structure on the threatening chaos of nature."

139. Testimony of Eliza Lyon, *KK Report*, vol. 9, Ala., 2:1263.

140. Testimony of Anderson Ferrell, *KK Report*, vol. 7, Ga., 2:619.

141. Cockrell, *Demons of Disorder*, 33.

142. Phelan, *Mourning Sex*, 3, 12.

143. Testimony of Barclay Martin, *Tennessee Report*, 33.

144. Testimony of Samuel Stewart, *KK Report*, vol. 7, Ga., 2:597.

145. Scarry, *The Body in Pain*, 59; Emberton, *Beyond Redemption*, 76; Blight, *Race and Reunion*, 118.

146. Silver, *Minstrelsy and Murder*, 343.

147. Clinton, "Bloody Terrain," 323; Fitzgerald, *The Union League Movement*, 218, 221.

148. See "Telegraphic Correspondence to the Chronicle and Sentinel from Atlanta," *Daily Chronicle and Sentinel*, September 1, 1868, p. 4. "The scene which

is presented in this body [the House of Representatives] during the burlesque attempts at speech-making by Cuffee is ludicrous in the extreme."

149. Prince, *Stories of the South*, 73.

150. Testimony of James H. Alston, *KK Report*, vol. 9, Ala., 2:1019.

151. Testimony of Major Gardiner, *KK Report*, vol. 9, Ala., 2:862.

152. Prince, *Stories of the South*, 73.

153. Testimony of Reuben Sheets, *KK Report*, vol. 7, Ga., 2:651; Trelease, *White Terror*, 56–58.

154. Testimony of James H. Alston, *KK Report*, vol. 9, Ala., 2:1019.

155. Testimony of Elias Thompson, *KK Report*, vol. 3, S.C., 1:411.

156. This evokes Saidiya Hartman's discussion of the importance of pleasure in the construction of blackness: if Ku-Klux used pain to mark the black body as subjected, a victim's laughter, his claim of pleasure at the moment of the attack, was destabilizing. Hartman, *Scenes of Subjection*, 58.

157. Prince, *Stories of the South*, 75; Kidada Williams, *They Left Great Marks on Me*, 47.

158. Testimony of Henry B. Whitfield, *KK Report*, vol. 11, Miss., 1:425.

159. Testimony of Wiley Hargrove, *KK Report*, vol. 10, Ala., 3:1994.

160. Testimony of Peyton Lipscomb, *KK Report*, vol. 9, Ala., 2:952.

161. Testimony of Joseph Miller, *KK Report*, vol. 4, S.C., 2:601.

162. Testimony of Andrew J. Flowers, *KK Report*, vol. 13, Fla., 43.

163. Kidada Williams, *They Left Great Marks on Me*, 49. I am approaching these silences differently from Williams, who also notes that many witnesses engaged in "collective silence" about their pain and reads the silence as a "decision . . . to move on from violent attacks by never reliving them." The approaches are different but compatible.

164. Testimony of Augustus Blair, *KK Report*, vol. 9, Ala., 2:674.

165. Silver, *Minstrelsy and Murder*, esp. 86.

166. Kidada Williams, *They Left Great Marks on Me*, 5.

167. Testimony of Jerry Clowney, *KK Report*, vol. 5, S.C., 3:1860 (this is a reprint of the November 1871 South Carolina trials).

168. Elias Thompson, *KK Report*, vol. 3, S.C., 1: 411.

169. Testimony of Sir Daniel, *KK Report*, vol. 9, Ala., 2:994.

CHAPTER 3

1. Testimony of Jackson Surratt, *KK Report*, vol. 3, S.C., 1:524. As a correspondent to the *Chicago Times* reported, "The negroes . . . come out [of testimony] with smiling faces, and one, showing a roll of greenbacks in his greasy fingers, with more than average display of teeth, was heard to say 'Fore God, master, I let the Klues whip me agin for all dis money.'" "Seeking for Ku-Klux," *Chicago Times*, July 21, 1871, p. 3.

2. Testimony of Marcus M. Wells, *KK Report*, vol. 2, N.C., 1:226.

3. Testimony of James L. Grant, *KK Report*, vol. 2, N.C., 1:235.

4. Carole Emberton has noted, "When allowed to testify to their own experiences, southern blacks did so only within very tight parameters set by the

congressional investigating committees, who often made it clear that they found black voices unreliable or even unbelievable." Emberton, *Beyond Redemption*, 7, 53.

5. Testimony of Clem Bowden, *KK Report*, vol. 3, S.C., 1:382.

6. Testimony of John Dunlap, *Tennessee Report*, 18.

7. Testimony of James H. Alston, *KK Report*, vol. 9, Ala., 2:1019.

8. Gregory Downs, *Declarations of Dependence*, 118. "Free Tobe" McMullen was an example of this. Testimony of Isham McCrary, *KK Report*, vol. 3, S.C., 1:542. See also *KK Report*, vol. 2, N.C., 1:135; testimony of John Johnson, *KK Report*, vol. 7, Ga., 2:868.

9. Testimony of John Johnson, *KK Report*, vol. 7, Ga., 2:868.

10. Testimony of Robert W. Flournoy, *KK Report*, vol. 11, Miss., 1:84.

11. Testimony of Walter Scott, *Tennessee Report*, 35.

12. Testimony of Henry Lowther, *KK Report*, vol. 6, Ga., 1:357.

13. Testimony of J. B. Carpenter, *KK Report*, vol. 2, N.C., 1:25.

14. Testimony of T. J. Downey, *US v. Randolph Shotwell*, reprinted in *KK Report*, vol. 1, N.C., 1:437.

15. Testimony of Robert W. Flournoy, *KK Report*, vol. 11, Miss., 1:83.

16. *Milwaukee Daily Sentinel*, August 2, 1870, p. 2. Broomall, "Personal Confederacies," 239.

17. Nelson, *Iron Confederacies*, 99–114; Fitzgerald, *The Union League Movement*, 37–38, 101–7, 111–12, 213–33.

18. Fitzgerald, *The Union League Movement*, 37; Saville, *The Work of Reconstruction*, 183.

19. Fitzgerald, *The Union League Movement*, 215–24.

20. Saville, *The Work of Reconstruction*, 146–48; Hahn, *A Nation under Our Feet*, 273.

21. Burton, "Race and Reconstruction," 33; Saville, *The Work of Reconstruction*, 167–69; Testimony of Walter Scott, *Tennessee Report*, p. 36.

22. Tennessee General Assembly, *Senate Journal of the Extra Session*, 148.

23. Testimony of Henry Flowers, *KK Report*, vol. 13, Fla., 43.

24. Lewis, "The Democratic Partisan Militia and the Black Peril," 148, discusses Klan attacks on prepolitical black organizations and leaders in Kentucky. See also Emberton, *Beyond Redemption*, 89.

25. Hahn, *A Nation under Our Feet*, 173.

26. Johnson, "On Agency," 118.

27. Hartman, *Scenes of Subjection*, 65–70.

28. Hahn, *A Nation under Our Feet*, 196–97, 222.

29. Testimony of J. R. Smith, *KK Report*, vol. 11, Miss., 1:74.

30. Testimony of Lemuel Wilson, *KK Report*, vol. 13, Fla., 197.

31. Testimony of Henry B. Whitfield, *KK Report*, vol. 11, Miss., 1:436.

32. Testimony of Henry Lowther, *KK Report*, vol. 6, Ga., 1:359.

33. Testimony of Alfred Richardson, *KK Report*, vol. 5, Ga., 1:2, 3, 16.

34. Testimony of George W. Houston, *KK Report*, vol. 9, Ala., 2:998.

35. Testimony of Andrew J. Flowers, *KK Report*, vol. 13, Fla., 43.

36. Ibid., 45.

37. Weinfield, *The Jackson County War*, 83–87, includes an excellent narration of these events. See also Testimony of Henry Reed, *KK Report*, vol. 13, Fla., 111–12.

38. Hennessey, "Racial Violence during Reconstruction," 100.

39. Fitzgerald, "The Ku Klux Klan," 188; Fitzgerald, *The Union League Movement*, 215.

40. Testimony of James R. Taliaferro, *KK Report*, vol. 11, Miss., 1:238.

41. Testimony of Simon Elder, *KK Report*, vol. 7, Ga., 2:733.

42. Bardaglio, *Reconstructing the Household*, 162–64; Schwalm, *A Hard Fight for We*, 204–7.

43. Rosen, *Terror in the Heart of Freedom*, 7, 208–20. For an earlier incisive discussion of this, see Lou Falkner Williams, *The Great South Carolina Ku Klux Klan Trials*, 32–36. Clinton, "Bloody Terrain," 329; Edwards, *Gendered Strife and Confusion*, 197.

44. Rosen, *Terror in the Heart of Freedom*, 208.

45. "Cuffee's Brilliant Idea," *Pulaski Citizen*, March 8, 1867, p. 1.

46. Tennessee General Assembly, *Senate Journal of the Extra Session*, 134. For a discussion of freedmen sleeping out to avoid the Klan in Claiborne Parish, Louisiana, see *Louisiana Report*, 48.

47. "South Carolina Kuklux," *New York Times*, July 11, 1871, p. 4.

48. Testimony of John Dunlap, *Tennessee Report*, 19.

49. Testimony of Henry Hamlin, *KK Report*, vol. 9, Ala., 2:857.

50. Testimony of Simon Elder, *KK Report*, vol. 7, Ga., 2:732.

51. Testimony of Hannah Tutson, *KK Report*, vol. 13, Fla., 59. See also testimony of Andrew J. Flowers, *KK Report*, vol. 13, Fla., 47.

52. Cardyn, "Sexualized Racism / Gendered Violence," 813–35.

53. Testimony of Eli Hood, *KK Report*, vol. 3, S.C., 1:569.

54. Nelson, "Livestock, Boundaries, and Public Space in Spartanburg."

55. *Louisiana Report*, 23; testimony of Luther R. Smith, *KK Report*, vol. 8, Ala., 1:103.

56. Testimony of Gilbert Akin, *Tennessee Report*, 29.

57. Testimony of Lewis Stegall, *Tennessee Report*, 29.

58. Testimony of Henry Hamlin, *KK Report*, vol. 9, Ala., 2:858.

59. Summary of testimony of Nim Wilkes: "They treated my wife very cruelly, and threatened to hang her if she did not tell where I was." Tennessee General Assembly, *Senate Journal of the Extra Session*, 141.

60. Testimony of Edmund Gray, *KK Report*, vol. 12, Miss., 2:894.

61. T. J. Downey, reprint of Randolph Shotwell testimony, *KK Report*, vol. 2, N.C., 1:437. The friend was James Justice. Statement of Edwin G. Brown, Moses Tucker, Sam Harwell, and Taylor Bennet of Giles County: "They took Sam Harwell from his house, and beat him for refusing to tell where another slave was concealed." Tennessee General Assembly, *Senate Journal of the Extra Session*, 153.

62. Testimony of Willis Smith, *KK Report*, vol. 4, S.C., 2:613.

63. Testimony of Pinkney Dodd, *KK Report*, vol. 3, S.C., 1:417.

64. Testimony of William Ford, *KK Report*, vol. 9, Ala., 2:681.

65. Testimony of Hampton Hicklin, *KK Report*, vol. 5, S.C., 3:1566.

66. Testimony of Jackson Surratt, *KK Report*, vol. 3, S.C., 1:521.

67. Carnes, *Secret Ritual*, 19–20, 54.

68. Prince, *Stories of the South*, 70.

69. Anonymous, *Horrible Disclosures*, 26, 35.

70. Anonymous, *The Masked Lady of the White House*, 44.

71. James Broomall has recently explored the emotional power of these initiation rituals to defeated white southerners seeking "rebirth." "Personal Confederacies," 241–47.

72. Testimony of James E. Boyd, p. 4, *State v. William Andrews et al.*, Ku Klux Klan Collection, DMRL.

73. *Yale Pot-Pourri*, 1868, 61.

74. Carnes, *Secret Ritual*, 116–23.

75. Testimony of Columbus Jeter, *KK Report*, vol. 6, Ga., 1:565.

76. "Seeking for Ku-klux," *Chicago Times*, July 21, 1871, p. 3.

77. Emberton, *Beyond Redemption*, 6.

78. Stepto, *From Behind the Veil*, 45.

79. McBride, *Impossible Witnesses*, 20.

80. Some assert that freedpeople more consistently insisted on the political nature of the Klan. Prince, *Stories of the South*, 73. I agree that freedpeople in this testimony usually supported the account that the Klan was politically driven, but suggest that they were doing so in large part at the behest of congressmen who were eliciting that interpretation.

81. Testimony of Hon. A. J. Applegate, *Report of the Joint Committee of Outrages*, 63.

82. Testimony of Landon Gentry, *KK Report*, vol. 3, S.C., 1:205.

83. Testimony of Benjamin Horton, *KK Report*, vol. 9, Ala., 2:743.

84. Testimony of Samuel Horton, *KK Report*, vol. 9, Ala., 2:734; testimony of Benjamin Horton, *KK Report*, vol. 9, Ala., 2:743.

85. McBride, *Impossible Witnesses*, 22.

86. Testimony of Samuel Horton, *KK Report*, vol. 9, Ala., 2:729.

87. Testimony of William Shapard, *KK Report*, vol. 9, Ala., 2:746.

88. Testimony of Augustus R. Wright, *KK Report*, vol. 6, Ga., 1:105.

89. "Domestic News: Return of the Ku-klux Committee from South Carolina," *New York Times*, July 30, 1871, p. 1.

90. Testimony of Julius Cantrell, *KK Report*, vol. 3, S.C., 1:422.

91. Testimony of Margaret Blackwell, *KK Report*, vol. 3, S.C., 1:374.

92. Ibid., 1:376.

93. Hodes, *White Women, Black Men*, 161–62, describes the treatment of "bad white women" in the testimony.

94. Testimony of Margaret Blackwell, *KK Report*, vol. 3, S.C., 1:378.

95. Twenty-five-year-old Jacin Blackwell appears as a farmer without property living with a sixteen-year-old female in a house adjacent to that headed by forty-year-old Elizabeth Blackwell, no property, in which then thirteen-year-old Margaret Blackwell lived. *1860 South Carolina Census*, Cowpens, Sheet 291, B Reel, M653-1226, p. 191.

96. Testimony of J. B. Evans, *KK Report*, vol. 2, N.C., 1:192. Congressmen took a good deal of testimony on the Biggerstaff attack, and throughout, Blair attempted to rescript it as a personal rather than political attack. See Testimony of Margaret Biggerstaff, *KK Report*, vol. 2, N.C., 1:483.

97. Trouillot, *Silencing the Past*, 2.

98. Hannah Rosen makes this observation of freedwomen's rape testimony. Rosen, *Terror in the Heart of Freedom*, 224.

99. Emberton, *Beyond Redemption*; Rosen, *Terror in the Heart of Freedom*, 222–41; Kidada Williams, *They Left Great Marks on Me*, 27–52.

100. Kidada Williams, *They Left Great Marks on Me*, 8. This term is borrowed from Baptist, "'Stol and Fetched Here,'" 243–74.

101. Testimony of John Childers, *KK Report*, vol. 10, Ala., 3:1722.

102. Ibid.

103. Rosen, *Terror in the Heart of Freedom*, 229–30.

104. Testimony of Isham McCrary, *KK Report*, vol. 3, S.C., 1:551.

105. Testimony of Charlotte Fowler, *KK Report*, vol. 3, S.C., 1:388.

106. Kidada Williams, *They Left Great Marks on Me*, 35.

107. Ibid., 5.

108. Scott, *Domination and the Arts of Resistance*.

109. Testimony of Hilliard Bush, *KK Report*, vol. 9, Ala., 2:691. Here the congressman questioning him wonders how he could claim to be a political leader, "being unable to read or write and having none of the ordinary sources of obtaining information." Bush claimed, to his unimpressed questioner, that though he was unlearned, he turned to God for wisdom. I am indebted to Rosen's application of the idea of "counternarrative" to Klan testimony. Rosen, *Terror in the Heart of Freedom*, 226.

110. The best discussion of Republican papers in the South during these years is Abbot and Quist, *For Free Press and Equal Rights*.

111. Ibid., 61.

112. Nelson, "Livestock, Boundaries, and Public Space in Spartanburg," 322.

113. Testimony of Tilda Waltham, *KK Report*, vol. 6, Ga., 1:408.

114. Testimony of Robert Fullerlove, *KK Report*, vol. 10, Ala., 3:1653.

115. Testimony of William Burnside Anderson, *KK Report*, vol. 3, S.C., 1:293.

116. Testimony of Henry T. Johnson, *KK Report*, vol. 9, Ala., 2:1352.

117. Testimony of Major Gardiner, *KK Report*, vol. 9, Ala., 2:862.

118. Testimony of Lydia Anderson, *KK Report*, vol. 11, Miss., 1:510, 512.

119. Testimony of Betty Kinney, *KK Report*, vol. 6, Ga., 1:535.

120. Testimony of Hampton Hicklin, *KK Report*, vol. 5, S.C., 3:1572.

121. Testimony of Edmund Gray, *KK Report*, vol. 12, Miss., 2:894.

122. Testimony of Wiley Strong, *KK Report*, vol. 9, Ala., 2:668.

123. Testimony of Mary Ann Norvill, *KK Report*, vol. 2, N.C., 1:473.

124. Testimony of George W. Garner, *KK Report*, vol. 3, S.C., 1:393.

125. Testimony of John L. Coley, *KK Report*, vol. 6, Ga., 1:364.

126. Testimony of Henry Reed, *KK Report*, vol. 13, Fla., 111.

127. Testimony of John Lewis, *KK Report*, vol. 3, S.C., 1:436.

128. Testimony of Augustus Blair, *KK Report*, vol. 9, Ala., 2:675.

129. Testimony of George W. Houston, *KK Report*, vol. 9, Ala., 2:1001.

130. Testimony of Abram Colby, *KK Report*, vol. 7, Ga., 2:696.

131. Testimony of James Hicks, *KK Report*, vol. 12, Miss., 2:891.

132. Testimony of Henry Giles, *KK Report*, vol. 9, Ala., 2:1011.

133. Testimony of John L. Coley, *KK Report*, vol. 6, Ga., 1:364.

134. Ibid.

135. Testimony of John Lewis, *KK Report*, vol. 3, S.C., 1:438.

136. Testimony of Willis Butler, *KK Report*, vol. 3, S.C., 1:440.

137. This testimony evokes Earl Lewis's idea of the homeplace so evocatively applied to this testimony by Kidada Williams, *They Left Great Marks on Me*, 21–22.

138. Testimony of John Lewis, *KK Report*, vol. 3, S.C., 1:438.

CHAPTER 4

1. Prince, *Stories of the South*, 65.

2. Ibid., 53.

3. "From North Carolina," *New York Times*, August 29, 1865, p. 1.

4. Hacking, *The Taming of Chance*, 3.

5. Doyle, "The Five Orange Pips."

6. "The Pulaski Riots—Tennessee Chivalry Fighting for Miscegenation," *New York Tribune*, January 18, 1868, p. 2; "The Ku-Klux Klan," *New York Times*, January 20, 1868, p. 2.; "The 'Ku-klux' Gang Again," *New York Tribune*, January 20, 1868, p. 5; "A Dangerous Organization," *Milwaukee Daily Sentinel*, January 21, 1868, p. 2.

7. "From Tennessee," *Milwaukee Daily Sentinel*, August 22, 1867, p. 4 (printed in Nashville exchange on August 20, 1867).

8. "The Ku-Klux Klan," *New York Times*, January 20, 1868, p. 2.

9. "Terrorism in Tennessee," *New York Tribune*, March 24, 1868, p. 4.

10. "The News," *Milwaukee Daily Sentinel*, January 31, 1868, p. 1.

11. "The Ku-klux-Klan: More Outrages," *Milwaukee Daily Sentinel*, February 1, 1868, p. 1.

12. On March 18, the *New York Tribune*, responding to an article in the *New York World*, was the first of the papers to refer to Democratic papers' stories about the Klan. *New York Tribune*, March 18, 1868, p. 4. A week later, and more than two months after the Klan's premier in the major Republican papers, the Democratic *Chicago Times* included its first two mentions of the Klan. "From Tennessee," *Chicago Times*, March 19, 1868; "Memphis," *Chicago Times*, March 19, 1868.

13. "Proceedings of the Military Commission," *Weekly Georgia Telegraph* (Macon), July 10, 1868, p. 3.

14. "The South: Orders for the Suppression of the Ku-Klux Klan," *Chicago Times*, April 7, 1868, p. 1; "The Ku-Klux Klan," *New York Times*, April 7, 1868, p. 1; "General Sheppard Indicates the Ku Klux Klan by Name," *New York Tribune*, April 7, 1868, p. 5; "General Meade's Orders Followed by Orders of General Sheppard of Alabama," *New York Tribune*, April 7, 1868, p. 5.

15. *Tennessee Report*.

16. *Report of the Joint Committee on Outrages*.

17. Prince, *Stories of the South*, 62–63.

18. "Terrible Murder in Marshall County," *Milwaukee Daily Sentinel*, February 11, 1868, p. 1.

19. "Strange Scene at a Funeral—the Ceremonies of the Ku Klux Klan," *Milwaukee Daily Sentinel*, March 9, 1868, p. 2.; "Lynching by the Ku-Klux Klan in Tennessee,"

Milwaukee Daily Sentinel, March 10, 1868, p. 1; "An Old Murder Confessed," *New York Tribune*, March 18, 1868, p. 3.

20. "A Supposed Member of the Ku Klux Klan Shot Dead by a Negro at Memphis, Tennessee," *New York Times*, March 19, 1868, p. 5; "From Memphis," *Milwaukee Daily Sentinel*, March 19, 1868, p. 4.

21. Halttunen, *Murder Most Foul*.

22. "Ku-klux in Tennessee," *Milwaukee Daily Sentinel*, September 8, 1868, p. 2.

23. "Chicago Men Victims of the Ku-klux in Mississippi," *New York Times*, March 28, 1871, p. 1.

24. "Ku-klux Outrages," *Milwaukee Daily Sentinel*, March 18, 1869, p. 4.

25. Pike, *Metropolis on the Styx*; Reynolds, *Beneath the American Renaissance*; Denning, *Mechanic Accents*.

26. "A Member of the Order," in *An Authentic Exposition of the "K.G. C." Knights of the Golden Circle*, 29. See also *Narrative of Edmund Wright*.

27. "Object of the Kuklux Klan—Its Extent in Tennessee," *New York Times*, February 10, 1868, p. 2.

28. "A Richmond View of the Ku-klux Outrage in West Virginia," *New York Times*, March 13, 1870, p. 3.

29. "South Carolina Ku-klux," *New York Tribune*, November 16, 1871, p. 2.

30. "The Telegraphic Electioneering Machine," *Milwaukee Daily Sentinel*, October 26, 1868, p. 2.

31. *Tuscaloosa Independent Monitor*, January 1, 1868, cited in Trelease, *White Terror*, 84–85 (I cannot find an extant copy of the issue of the *Monitor*); "The North Carolina Constitution," *New York Times*, March 24, 1868, p. 5.

32. "Latest General News," *New York Tribune*, March 25, 1868, p. 1.

33. *New York Tribune*, April 6, 1868, p. 4; "Washington—Affairs at the National Capital," *New York Times*, April 7, 1868, p. 1.

34. "Terrorism in Tennessee," *New York Tribune*, March 24, 1868, p. 4; "Brownlow and the Ku Klux Klan," *Chicago Times*, March 30, 1868, p. 1.

35. "Editorial Paragraphs, Etc.," *New Orleans Crescent*, March 12, 1868, p. 4.

36. "Scraps and Facts," *Yorkville (S.C.) Enquirer*, March 19, 1868, p. 2.

37. "Home News," *New York Tribune*, March 31, 1868, p. 8.

38. "Origin of the Klan—Interest in the Organization Dying Out," April 6, 1868, *New York Tribune*, p. 5.

39. "Our Washington Letter," *Milwaukee Daily Sentinel*, April 13, 1868, p. 2.

40. "City Matters," *Milwaukee Daily Sentinel*, September 5, 1868, p. 1..

41. "House," *Chicago Times*, March 29, 1871, p. 1.

42. "Ku Klux Klan: Atrocious Attack on Citizen of Long Island," *New York Tribune*, August 28, 1868, p. 1.

43. "Local Items," *Daily Phoenix*, March 15, 1868, p. 2.

44. "*The New Orleans Times* . . . ," *New York Tribune*, November 12, 1868, p. 4.

45. "Political," *Milwaukee Daily Sentinel*, November 7, 1871 p. 1; "The Invisible Empire," *New York Times*, November 11, 1871, p. 2.

46. "South Carolina Ku-klux," *Milwaukee Daily Sentinel*, November 7, 1871, p. 3. Reprinted from *Columbia Phoenix*; *New York Tribune*, January 3, 1872, p. 4.

47. James L. Huston argues that the new capacities of the bureaucratic state were the only potentially effective answer to southern white postwar violence. Huston, "An Alternative to the Tragic Era," 404.

48. "Forty First Congress, Second Session," *New York Times*, March 22, 1870, p. 1.

49. "The Conventions," *New York Times*, September 23, 1869, p. 1.

50. Prince, *Stories of the South*, 65.

51. "The New Federal System," *Chicago Times*, March 1, 1871, p. 1; "The Condition of the South," *Chicago Times*, January 29, 1871, p. 10.

52. "Alabama Correspondence," *Memphis Public Ledger*, April 11, 1868, p. 1.

53. "North Carolina," *Milwaukee Daily Sentinel*, July 18, 1870, p. 2. (reprinted from *New York Herald*); "Troubles in North Carolina," *Milwaukee Daily Sentinel*, July 27, 1870, p. 5 (reprinted from *Chicago Tribune*); "North Carolina Troubles," *New York Times*, August 4, 1870, p. 5; "The War in North Carolina," *New York Times*, August 2, 1870, p. 5; *New York Times*, September 27, 1870, p. 4.

54. Brisson, "Civil Government Was Crumbling around Me," 144.

55. "Gov. Holden Arming a Company of Negroes," *New York Tribune*, October 26, 1869, p. 1; "Kuklux War," *New York Times*, October 30, 1869, p. 3; "Putting the Niggers Through," *Chicago Times*, July 9, 1870, p. 8; "The Situation in North Carolina," *Chicago Times*, August 2, 1870, p. 2.

56. "The Campaign: Speech of Hon. William S. Groesbeck," *Chicago Times*, September 14, 1871, p. 2.

57. "A Cry from South Carolina," *New York Tribune*, May 3, 1871, p. 1.

58. "There Is No Longer Room for Doubt . . . ," *New York Tribune*, August 8, 1872, p. 4.

59. "The Ku-Klux Klan in Kentucky: Democratic Eleventh-Hour Protests," *New York Times*, January 29, 1871, p. 8; Blain, "Challenge to the Lawless"; From J. J. Gainey, November 16, 1870, Box 13, Folder 8, GSP.

60. Brisson, "Civil Government Was Crumbling around Me," 138; Massengill, "The Detectives of William Woods Holden, 1869–1870."

61. "Testimony in Relation to the Alleged Safe-Burglary at the Office of the States Attorney, Washington D.C.," 249; "North Carolina: A Search for Ku-klux," *New York Tribune*, September 4, 1872, p. 3.

62. "The Kuklux: Arrest of a Gang, With their Disguises, in North Carolina. How They Were Entrapped," *New York Times*, August 15, 1871, p. 5. "Outrage by the Tennessee Ku-klux," *New York Tribune*, January 16, 1869, p. 5; "The News," *Milwaukee Daily Sentinel*, January 16, 1869, p. 1. "Ku-klux," *Milwaukee Daily Sentinel*, March 23, 1868, p. 2; "Band of Ku-klux Captured in North," *New York Tribune*, August 15, 1871, p. 5; "Stifling the Ku-klux," *New York Times*, October 11, 1871, p. 5.; "Washington News," *New York Times*, October 20, 1871, p. 1.

63. "Washington—The Ku-klux," *New York Tribune*, November 4, 1871, p. 1.

64. "From Alabama," *Milwaukee Daily Sentinel*, November 12, 1868, p. 4..

65. "Democratic Anxiety for the Constitution," *New York Times*, June 15, 1871, p. 4.

66. "The Enforcement Act: Report of Mr. Akerman on the Ku-klux Trials," *New York Times*, January 16, 1872, p. 2.

67. *New York Tribune*, October 18, 1872, p. 4; "Washington—Reckless Public Printing," August 10, 1872, p. 8.

68. "Washington," *Chicago Times*, August 28, 1871, p. 1.

69. Richardson, *To Make Men Free*, 91–93, and Blight, *Race and Reconstruction*, 124–27, describe Greeley's turn away from Klan enforcement. "The Campaign," *Chicago Times*, September 14, 1871, p. 2; "The Ku Klux Clan Bill," *Chicago Times*, September 15, 1871, p. 3.

70. "The Ku Klux Troubles," *Chicago Times*, October 24, 1871, p. 1.

71. "Spartanburg Ku-klux: How the Law Is Administered," *New York Tribune*, November 24, 1871, p. 2. This piece is not sympathetic to the aims of the Ku-Klux, but it does express this concern about overzealous prosecution.

72. "Final Work of the Liberal Canvass," *New York Tribune*, July 29, 1872, p. 1.

73. *Chicago Times*, October 13, 1868, p. 4; "Our Colored Ku-klux," *Chicago Times*, June 30, 1869, p. 6; "Negro Ku-klux," *Chicago Times*, September 13, 1869, p. 5; "An Outrageous Affair," *Chicago Times*, May 18, 1870; "Putting the Niggers Through," *Chicago Times*, July 9, 1870, p. 8.

74. "Hell at the Sound," *Chicago Times*, July 24, 1868, p. 6; "Outlawry in Kentucky," *Chicago Times*, February 15, 1870, p. 8.

75. "Tennessee," *Chicago Times*, January 12, 1869, p. 8.

76. "Ku Klux Outrages," *Chicago Times*, February 24, 1871, p. 4.

77. "House," *Chicago Times*, January 24, 1871, p. 1.

78. "The Ku-klux Investigation," *Chicago Times*, July 3, 1871, p. 8.

79. "Political," *New York Tribune*, March 20, 1868, p. 5.

80. "Tennessee: Political Troubles Anticipated," *New York Times*, August 14, 1868, p. 5.

81. "Onondoga County," *New York Times*, October 27, 1871, p. 5.

82. "North Carolina Campaign," *New York Times*, July 25, 1872, p. 5.

83. "Ballots and Bayonets," *Milwaukee Daily Sentinel*, July 30, 1868, p. 2.

84. "The Chahoon Case," *Milwaukee Daily Sentinel*, February 7, 1871, p. 2.

85. "Forty-Second Congress," *New York Times*, February 10, 1872, p. 3; "42nd Congress," *New York Tribune*, February 10, 1872, p. 1; "Wade Hampton," *Milwaukee Daily Sentinel*, February 16, 1872, p. 2.

86. "Wisconsin—What the World Predicts," *Milwaukee Daily Sentinel*, July 18, 1868, p. 2.

87. "Washington," *New York Tribune*, April 15, 1871, p. 7.

88. "Political," *New York Tribune*, March 20, 1868, p. 5.

89. "The Social Oppression in Kentucky," *Milwaukee Daily Sentinel*, September 1, 1868, p. 2.

90. *New York Tribune*, May 2, 1868, p. 4; "The Blood-Sucker's Triumph," *New York Tribune*, May 2, 1868, p. 4.

91. "Ratification of the Fourteenth Article," *Milwaukee Daily Sentinel*, July 18, 1868, p. 2; "Drift of Political Discussion: Tammany Illustrates This Democracy," *New York Tribune*, July 29, 1871, p. 5; "A Protest," *Milwaukee Daily Sentinel*, August 28, 1871, p. 2.

92. "The Ohio Campaign," *Morning Republican*, September 11, 1871, p. 1.

93. "The Ku-klux Outrages," *Milwaukee Daily Sentinel*, February 27, 1871, p. 2.

94. Baker, *This Mob Will Surely Take My Life*.

95. "Political," *New York Tribune*, February 20, 1871, p. 4.

96. *Milwaukee Daily Sentinel*, December 28, 1870, p. 2; "North Carolina," *New York Tribune*, December 30, 1870, p. 5.

97. Reprinted in "Ku Klux Klan," *Anderson Intelligencer*, April 1, 1868, p. 4.

98. *Chicago Times*, June 3, 1871, p. 4.

99. "Washington," *Chicago Times*, March 28, 1871, p. 1.

100. "Thugs in Congress," *Chicago Times*, April 11, 1871.

101. "The Ku-klux: North and South," *Chicago Times*, March 22, 1871, p. 4.

102. "Speech of S. F. Carey," *New York Tribune*, September 13, 1871, p. 2.

103. "42nd Congress, 1st Session," *New York Tribune*, March 24, 1871, p. 8; "Washington," *Milwaukee Daily Sentinel*, March 24, 1871, p.1. Blight, *Race and Reunion*, 115–17, discusses the depiction of the federal government's Enforcement Acts as despotism.

104. *Chicago Times*, April 1, 1871, p. 1.

105. See, for instance, "Sumner and the President," *Bangor (Me.) Daily Whig and Courier*, April 13, 1871, p. 1.

106. "Sumner and San Domingo," *New York Times*, March 28, 1871, p. 2.

107. "Washington," *Chicago Times*, March 28, 1871, p. 1.

108. "The Government and Household of the Grand Radical Empire," *Daily Phoenix* (reprinted from *New York Herald*, January 18, 1868, p. 1). The same article was excerpted at length in the *Memphis Public Ledger*, January 21, 1868, p. 1.

109. Testimony of David T. Corbin, KK Report, vol. 3, S.C., 1:74.

110. Bryant, *Experience of a Northern Man among the Ku-klux*, 15.

111. Testimony of Mankins, *Sheafe v. Tillman*, 264.

112. *Speech of the Honorable Charles H. Porter of Virginia*, 4.

113. "The Ku-klux," *New York Tribune*, November 13, 1871, p. 1.

114. I base my estimate of Klan mention frequency over time on the chronology of newspaper coverage of the Klan and a tally of the number of articles containing the words "Klux," "kuklux" or "Ku-Klux" in the Gale-Cengage Nineteenth-Century Newspapers database, in the Gale-Cengage database, and in the Proquest Historical *New York Tribune* and Historical *New York Times* databases. While these databases are imperfect (due to the limitations of optical character recognition software, particularly with fading or damaged newsprint), they do well showing broad patterns. This method, counting by name, will leave several articles out: articles describing events that some historians, but not the writer of the piece, would label "Ku-Klux"; or that some contemporaries, but not the writer of the piece, would label "Ku-Klux"; or articles in which the writer deliberately or inadvertently did not apply the term "Ku-Klux" to an event both he and his readers would have understood to be such. Since I am primarily interested in the circulation of the term, and the way in which its use impacted the practice and meaning of violence, I do not find dropping these stories to be problematic.

115. Zuczek, *State of Rebellion*, 95.

116. Rable, "Forces of Darkness, Forces of Light"; U.S. Congress, *Supplement to the Congressional Globe*, 227.

117. U.S. Congress, *Supplement to the Congressional Globe*, 471, 474.

118. Ibid., 207, 208.

119. Ibid., 167.

120. Ibid., 308.

121. For a mention of the publication of a "Full Expose" of the Klan by Paschen and Carr, see "K. K. K.," *Milwaukee Daily Sentinel*, June 6, 1868, p. 1. An ad for the book *The Ku-Klux Klan Outdone* appeared in the *New York Tribune*, July 4, 1868, p. 6; "Bryant's Operahouse," *New York Times*, May 31, 1868, p. 7, mentions that Bryant's Minstrels would be performing a new number called the "Ku Klogs Klan."

122. Scalpel [Edward H. Dixon], *The Terrible Mysteries of the Ku Klux Klan*, 38.

123. A Late Member, *The Oaths, Signs, Ceremonies and Objects of the Ku-Klux Klan*, 28.

124. "A. Head Exposes the Ku Klux Klan," *Daily News and Herald*, April 29, 1868, p. 1.

125. "The Anniversaries," *New York Tribune*, May 15, 1868, p. 2.

126. "The Impeachment: After the Adjournment," *New York Tribune*, May 18, 1868, p. 1.

127. "A Missive from one of Andrew Johnson's Friends," *Milwaukee Daily Sentinel*, March 28, 1868, p. 2.

128. "The New Rebellion—Alabama," *New York Tribune*, November 2, 1868, p. 1; "The New Rebellion—Tennessee," *New York Tribune*, November 2, 1868, p. 2.

129. "Texas: The Murder of the Hon. George W. Smith of Texas," *New York Tribune*, November 29, 1868, p. 1; "News," *Milwaukee Daily Sentinel*, October 23, 1868, p. 1; "Arkansas," *New York Tribune*, October 31, 1868, p. 3.

130. "A New Rebellion," *New York Tribune*, November 4, 1868, p. 3; "Brutal Assault," *Milwaukee Daily Sentinel*, November 4, 1868, p. 1.; "City Matters," *Milwaukee Daily Sentinel*, November 4, 1868, p. 1.

131. "A Democratic Attempt to Kill Thirty-Six Republican Girls," *Milwaukee Daily Sentinel*, October 22, 1868, p. 2.

132. "From Madison," *Milwaukee Daily Sentinel*, November 2, 1868, p. 4.

133. "Grand Republican Demonstration: Catskill, New York," *New York Times*, October 31, 1868, p. 2.

134. "A. Johnson to the Rescue," *Milwaukee Daily Sentinel*, October 27, 1868, p. 2.

135. *Chicago Times*, November 6, 1868, p. 4.

136. "Outrageous Conduct of the Militia," *Pulaski Citizen*, September 13, 1867, p. 3.

137. "North Carolina Troubles," *New York Tribune*, July 30, 1870, p. 5; "North Carolina Troubles: Governor Holden Explains His Position," *New York Times*, August 4, 1870, p. 5.

138. "Troubles in North Carolina," *Milwaukee Daily Sentinel*, July 27, 1870, p. 2. This claim is plausible: General Meade, as early as May 1868, reluctantly authorized the limited arrest of "parties on the suspicion of their having knowledge of the subject," though he balked at a widespread use of this practice. U.S. Army, Department of the South, *Major General Meade's Report on the Ashburn Murder*, 24.

139. "The War in North Carolina," *New York Times*, August 2, 1870, p. 5; "North Carolina Troubles," *Milwaukee Daily Sentinel*, August 2, 1870, p. 2.; "North Carolina: Colonel Kirk's Mode of Procuring Testimony," *New York Times*, August 4, 1870, p. 5.

140. "A Portion of South Carolina in Insurrection," *New York Tribune*, March 10, 1871, p. 1; "Political," *Milwaukee Daily Sentinel*, March 10, 1871, p. 2.

141. "Washington—a Last Warning for the Ku-klux," *New York Tribune*, May 5, 1871, p. 1.

142. *Chicago Times*, September 8, 1871, p. 4.

143. "Further Arrests in Union," *Daily Phoenix*, March 10, 1872, p. 2.

144. "President's Message," *Milwaukee Weekly Sentinel*, December 12, 1871, p. 2.

145. "Political Miscellany," *New York Tribune*, October 18, 1872, p. 2.

146. "A Juvenile Enemy," *New York Tribune*, October 17, 1872, p. 4.

147. "The Kuklux: Kuklux Prisoners en Route for a Northern Prison—A Sorry-Looking Assembly," *New York Times*, January 27, 1872, p. 7.

148. There were 263 mentions of acts of Ku-Klux violence versus 335 references to arrests, trials, imprisonments, or pardons.

149. Richardson, *Death of Reconstruction*, 84–85.

150. Ibid.,, 89–95.

151. Letter from U. S. Grant to House of Representatives, April 19, 1872, reprinted in Gannon, *The GAR v the Ku-klux*, 2.

152. "More Arrests," *Daily Phoenix*, May 25, 1872, p. 3 (reprinted from Union [S.C.] *Times*).

153. "North Carolina," *New York Tribune*, July 30, 1872, p. 4.

154. "The North Carolina Election Frauds," *New York Tribune*, August 24, 1872, p. 2; "North Carolina—a Search for Ku-klux," *New York Tribune*, September 4, 1872, p. 3.

155. "The Ku-klux Troubles," *Chicago Times*, October 24, 1871.

156. *New York Sun*, June 12, 1872, p. 1.

157. "Duty of the Democracy," *New York Tribune*, June 19, 1872, p. 2.

158. McPherson, "Grant or Greeley," 43.

159. *New York Tribune*, August 12, 1872, p. 4; "Gerrit Smith," *Lowell (Mass.) Daily Citizen*, August 27, 1872, p. 2; "Gerrit Smith to Horace Greeley," *Daily Evening Bulletin*, October 7, 1872, p. 1.

160. "The Ku-klux Prisoners in the Albany Penitentiary," *Boston Daily Advertiser*, August 16, 1872, p. 4; "The National Capital," *New York Times*, August 13, 1872, p. 5; *New York Tribune*, August 14, 1872, p. 4; "The Ku-klux Prisoners in the Albany Penitentiary," *New York Tribune*, August 14, 1872, p. 1; "The Imprisoned Ku-klux," *New York Times*, August 14, 1872, p. 5.

161. "An Anxious Executive," *New York Tribune*, September 30, 1872, p. 5.

162. "Washington," *Milwaukee Daily Sentinel*, August 16, 1872, p. 1; "Washington News," *New York Times*, August 17, 1872, p. 1; "The Ku-Klux Prisoners," *Milwaukee Daily Sentinel*, August 31, 1872, p. 1.

163. Zuczek, *State of Rebellion*, 122. "The Ku-Klux Klan Broken Up: Present Policy of the Government," *Evening Star* (Washington, D.C.), July 31, 1873, p. 1. Gillette, *Retreat from Reconstruction*, 161.

CHAPTER 5

1. Summers, *A Dangerous Stir*, 252–54, includes a brief discussion of Ku-Klux skepticism. Other historians have also noticed and noted the existence of Ku-Klux denial. For instance, in his article on the Enforcement Acts in Mississippi, Stephen Cresswell notes, "Many Southerners claimed that the Ku Klux was a figment of the Northern imagination." Cresswell, "Enforcing the Enforcement Acts," 428.

2. Richard D. Brown, *Knowledge Is Power*. Recent work in the digital humanities on citation networks promises to open up this field tremendously. See Smith, Cordell, and Dillon, "Infectious Texts."

3. Cohen, *States of Denial*, 21–50. This is arguably not a perfect fit, since the northerners who largely embraced this denial had not themselves experienced or witnessed Klan trauma. I would claim both that the trauma was continuous with the war and that many northerners experienced it as their own because of their identity with the nation.

4. "Domestic News: Return of the Ku-klux Committee from South Carolina," *New York Times*, July 30, 1871, p. 1.

5. "The Fight between the Kuklux and Troops in Arkansas," *New York Times*, November 19, 1868, p. 1; "A Portion of South Carolina in Insurrection," *New York Tribune*, March 10, 1871, p. 1; "The Kuklux: Progress of the Work of Suppressing the Rebels in South Carolina," *Milwaukee Daily Sentinel*, October 23, 1871, p. 1.

6. For a Ku-Klux killed while in disguise, see "A Supposed Member of the Ku-Klux Klan Shot by a Negro," *Daily National Intelligencer* (Washington, D.C.), March 20, 1868, p. 2.

7. Cresswell, "Enforcing the Enforcement Acts," 428.

8. "Through the South," *New York Tribune*, July 7, 1869, p. 2. On Pike, see Baker, *What Reconstruction Meant*, 15, 16.

9. "Mr. Greeley in the South," *New York Tribune*, March 23, 1871, p. 5.

10. "Through the South," *New York Times*, May 22, 1871, p. 2.

11. "The Ku-klux," *New York Tribune*, November 13, 1871, p. 1; "Through the South," *New York Tribune*, April 27, 1871, p. 1; "North Carolina," *New York Tribune*, September 4, 1872, p. 3; "In Georgia," *New York Tribune*, June 9, 1871, p. 2.

12. Summers, *The Press Gang*, 201, notes that reporters tended to downplay Klan violence and attributes it to their reliance on local white informants. K. Stephen Prince, in an unpublished conference paper, "The Paper Klan," discusses sensationalized Klan rhetoric as an expression of northerners' anxieties about the South. Waldrep, *The Many Faces of Judge Lynch*, 68–97, analyzes Klan efforts to portray themselves as representatives of public sentiment, and how the "lynching narrative" developed in the postwar years.

13. Jeffreys-Jones, *The FBI*, 17–26; Xi Wang, *The Trial of Democracy*, 95, 96; Swinney, "Enforcing the Fifteenth Amendment," 25–55.

14. For Merill's reports, see Letters Received by the Office of the Adjutant General (Main Series), Microfilm Series M-666-A, Reel 26, NARA.

15. "Ku-Klux Klan: Arrest of a Den of Them in Memphis," *Milwaukee Daily Sentinel*, April 25, 1868, p. 2.

16. Lou Falkner Williams, *The Great South Carolina Ku Klux Klan Trials*, 47.

17. *Bangor Daily Whig and Courier*, October 14, 1871, p. 3; Lou Falkner Williams, *The Great South Carolina Ku Klux Trials*, 45; "A Band of Ku-klux Captured in North Carolina," *New York Tribune*, August 15, 1871, p. 5.

18. Lou Falkner Williams, *The Great South Carolina Ku Klux Klan Trials*, 44, 45.

19. U.S. Circuit Court (4th Circuit), *Proceedings in the Ku Klux Trials at Columbia, S.C.*

20. Senate Reports, 42nd Cong., 2d Sess., No. 41: *Report of the Joint Select Committee to Inquire into the Condition of Affairs in the Late Insurrectionary States* (13 vols., Serials 1484–96) (Washington, 1872).

21. "K: K: K:," *Daily Arkansas Gazette*, April 11, 1868, p. 1.

22. "Arrest of Supposed K. K. K.s," *Edgefield (S.C.) Advertiser*, April 8, 1868, p. 1.

23. "The Ku Klux Klan Humbug," *Daily News and Herald*, April 2, 1868, p. 2.

24. See *Report of the Joint Select Committee*, 1:289–588.

25. "Congressional," *Milwaukee Daily Sentinel*, April 5, 1870, p. 3.

26. Cohen, *States of Denial*, 112, 113.

27. Beecher, "What We Heard at the South," 330.

28. *Daily Arkansas Gazette*, June 4, 1871, p. 2.

29. Gillette, *Retreat from Reconstruction, 1869–1879*, 46–48, 54–55.

30. "South Carolina," *New York Times*, April 26, 1868, p. 10.

31. "Minor Topics," *New York Times*, May 12, 1868, p. 4.

32. "The Kuklux Bugbear," *New York Times*, October 4, 1870, p. 4. In one of the few Klan stories published in 1869, the *Times* denied the legitimacy of a report of a Ku-Klux attack on a railroad in Barnett, Ga., as "without foundation. "Affairs in Georgia," *New York Times*, February 12, 1869, p. 2. For other examples of Klan skepticism, see "Georgia: From Our Special Correspondent," *New York Times*, April 12, 1871, p. 2.

33. "Terrorism in Tennessee," *New York Tribune*, March 24, 1868, p. 4.

34. "The Kuk-Klux-Klan [sic]," *New York Tribune*, April 6, 1868, p. 4. See also the *Tribune*'s dismissal of A. J. Fletcher's Klan testimony, *New York Tribune*, April 9, 1870, p. 4.

35. "North Carolina," *New York Tribune*, August 9, 1870, p. 5; *New York Tribune*, September 21, 1870, p. 4.

36. "Through the South," *New York Tribune*, April 26, 1871, p. 4.

37. Greeley, *Mr. Greeley's Letters from Texas and the Lower Mississippi*, 49.

38. *Daily Arkansas Gazette*, June 4, 1871, p. 2.

39. Greeley, *Mr. Greeley's Letters from Texas and the Lower Mississippi*, 50.

40. "Warning to Southern Men," *New York Tribune*, July 13, 1872, p. 4.

41. "North Carolina," *New York Tribune*, July 29, 1872, p. 1.

42. "The New Rebellion," *New York Tribune*, October 21, 1868, p. 2. See also "Southern Sentiment," *New York Times*, March 20, 1871, p. 5.

43. "Whitewashing the Kuklux," *New York Times*, April 15, 1871, p. 4.

44. "Out of their Mouths," *Milwaukee Daily Sentinel*, April 12, 1871, p. 3 (reprinted from the *New York Tribune*); "From Dixie," *Milwaukee Daily Sentinel*, February 10, 1871, p. 2.

45. "Washington," *Milwaukee Daily Sentinel*, March 7, 1871, p. 1; "Conservative Innocence—No Kuklux—No Outrages—Another Story from a Victim," *New York Times*, July 7, 1871, p. 1. "Let the American People Ponder," *Milwaukee Daily Sentinel*, August 1, 1871, p. 2, lists eleven things that, thanks to the congressional testimony, they now know without a doubt about the Klan.

46. "Ku-kluxism," *Milwaukee Daily Sentinel*, May 25, 1871, p. 2.

47. "Some Light on the Kuklux Question," *New York Times*, October 6, 1871, p. 4.

48. "Retribution," *Milwaukee Sentinel*, October 13, 1871, p. 2.

49. "Gen. Forrest," *New York Times*, September 14, 1868, p. 5.

50. Swinney, "Enforcing the Fifteenth Amendment," 209, 210.

51. For allegations of torture, see U.S. Congress, Senate, *Congressional Globe*, 42nd Cong., 1st sess., p. 301.

52. "XLIId Congress—Ist Session," *New York Tribune*, May 31, 1871, p. 4.

53. "Washington," *Milwaukee Sentinel*, January 26, 1872, p. 1.

54. "News by Telegraph," *Boston Daily Advertiser*, August 2, 1871. One of the many ways in which Van Trump's account of the Union County killings lacks credibility is that he repeatedly refers to the whole thing as occurring in Chester County.

55. *New York Tribune*, October 19, 1868, p. 4. Here the *Tribune* is taking issue with Klan deniers, criticizing their too-easy dismissal of Klan evidence as the products of Republican imagination.

56. "South Carolina—The Terrorism in the State—Letter to Hon. Reverdy Johnson," *Weekly Telegraph* and *Journal and Messenger* (both Macon, Ga.), November 7, 1871, p. 1.

57. "The Ku-klux Trials Ended," *Daily Arkansas Gazette*, January 19, 1872.

58. Parsons, "Midnight Rangers."

59. "Pompey Squash's Trilogy: A Drama of Yorkville S.C.," *Weekly Telegraph* and *Journal and Messenger* (both Macon, Ga.), January 9, 1872, p. 1 (reprinted from the *World*).

60. "K. K. K," *Daily News and Herald*, April 17, 1868, p. 4.

61. "A. Head Exposes the Ku Klux Klan," *Daily News and Herald*, April 29, 1868, p. 1.

62. "Say More," *Bristol News*, November 16, 1868, p. 1.

63. "Multiple News Items," *New-Orleans Commercial Bulletin*, April 11, 1868, p. 1.

64. "Stray Notes," *New York Tribune*, July 31, 1868, p. 3.

65. *Branson's North Carolina Business Directory for 1869*, 167.

66. Warden, *Ku Klux Klan: Comic Song*; Buell, *Buell's Ku-klux-Klan Songster*. The Buell quote was also cited in Prince, "The Paper Klan."

67. "General Notes," *New York Tribune*, January 9, 1869, p. 2; Crew, *Ku Klux Klan Sheet Music*, 6, 9; "General Notes," *New York Tribune*, March 17, 1869, p. 2.

68. "Our Letter Bag," *Our Boys and Girls*, July 11, 1868, vol. 4, p. 447.

69. "Washington," *Milwaukee Sentinel*, April 3, 1871, p. 1.

70. *Yale Pot-pourri 1868–69*, 50, 61; "Letter to the Editor," *Daily Chronicle and Sentinel* (Augusta, Ga.), October 29, 1868, p. 3; "Base Ball Match," *Bangor (Me.) Daily Whig and Courier*, June 8, 1868, p. 3; "The C. C. C.," *Milwaukee Daily Sentinel*, August 25, 1868, p. 1; *The Dartmouth* 5 (May 1871), p. 196. Another example (in Covington, Georgia) is given in Ayers, *Vengeance and Justice*, 156.

71. "Local and Other Items," *Bangor Daily Whig and Courier*, March 21, 1872, p. 3.

72. *New York Tribune*, March 13, 1872, p. 4.

73. "Stray Notes," *New York Tribune*, July 31, 1868, p. 3. Ayers, *Vengeance and Justice*, 156, includes another example of a Klan-themed ad, for confections.

74. Rourke, "Miss Rourke Replies to Mr. Blair."

75. Rourke, *American Humor*, 48, 49.

76. "The Kuklux," *Morning Republican*, March 20, 1868, p. 2.

77. "The Kluxlux [sic] Klan," *Daily News and Herald*, March 24, 1868, p. 1.

78. "A Supposed Member of the Ku Klux Klan Shot by a Negro," *Daily National Intelligencer* (Washington, D.C.), March 20, 1868, p. 3; "Killed in a Mask: Tragical Result of a Practical Joke," *Daily National Intelligencer*, March 23, 1868, p. 3.

79. "Minor Topics," *New York Times*, April 9, 1868, p. 4.

80. Pomery, Brick Dust, 80–81.

81. "Another Ku-klux Outrage," Fairfield (S.C.) Herald, June 8, 1870, p. 1.

82. "The Kuk-Klux-Klan," New York Tribune, April 6, 1868, p. 4.

83. "Horrible Disclosures," New York Tribune, August 12, 1872, p. 4.

84. "South Carolina," New York Times, August 9, 1869, p. 2.

85. "K: K: K:," Daily Arkansas Gazette, April 11, 1868, p. 1.

86. "Details of Eastern News," Daily Evening Bulletin (San Francisco), April 9, 1868, p. 1.

87. "K. K. K.," Daily News and Herald, April 2, 1868, p. 4.

88. "The Ku Klux Klan," Charleston Courier, April 4, 1868, p. 4.

89. "K-uKlux [sic] Again," Morning Republican, January 27, 1869, p. 2.

90. See, for instance, "A Member," The K. K. K. Exposed!, 15; Anonymous, Horrible Disclosures, 79; "Scalpel, M. D.," Terrible Mysteries of the Ku-Klux Klan, 16, 17.

91. A Late Member, The Oaths, Signs, Ceremonies and Objects of the Ku-Klux Klan, 5.

92. Parrish, Details of an Unpaid Claim on France for 24,000,000 Francs, 5.

93. Alexander, Poor Ellen Stuart's Fate, or, Victim of the Free Love Institute in Oneida, N.Y.; Anonymous, The Masked Lady of the White House.

94. Anonymous, Horrible Disclosures, 69.

95. Tennessee General Assembly, Senate Journal of the Extra Session, 7.

96. "The Maine Canvas," New York Tribune, August 31, 1872, p. 4. This was only one of several uses of men in Klan costume by the stalwarts during the election season. See, for instance, the performance of "The Song of the Ku Klux" by the "Idlewild Quartet," dressed in "full Klan costume," at an October 26, 1872, rally in New York City. "Political," New York Times, October 25, 1872, p. 5; "Campaign Notes," New York Tribune, September 26, 1872, p. 4.

97. The rest of the sentence severely moderates this extreme claim with a "waged, on the most part, by worthless individuals, but having its root in a bad public sentiment and the sympathies of influential classes." "The Political Campaign of 1872," 418.

98. "The Campaign," New York Tribune, October 7, 1868, p. 2.

99. "Working Up a Sensation," Daily News and Herald, April 11, 1868, p. 2.

100. "XLIId Congress—1st Session," New York Tribune, March 31, 1871, p. 4.

101. "Condensed Congress," 30. Masson, Our American Humorists, 34, describes the funding and staffing of the journal.

102. "No Title," Lowell (Mass.) Daily Citizen and News, April 10, 1868, p. 2.

103. "Ku-kluxism," May 25, 1871, p. 2.

104. "Ku-klux," Once a Week, May 27, 1871, 507–8. This British article debated the meaning of the Klan—"Don't believe nearly half the stories you will hear about Ku-klux. But then, sir, they are not all false"—and concluded that the reason it had been so difficult to suppress the Klan is that "Ku-klux is a ghost of the Civil War; and a ghost, sir, will defy creation."

105. "South Carolina," New York Times, December 14, 1868, p. 2.

106. "The Carnival," Memphis Avalanche, February 14, 1872, p. 4.

107. Ibid.

108. "High Carnival," Memphis Daily Appeal, February 14, 1872, p. 4.

109. We cannot know whether the men dressed as Ku-Klux in this parade sponsored by prominent Klan supporters were actually Ku-Klux, though it seems likely.

On the connection between New Orleans Mardi Gras and vigilante groups, see Roach, *Cities of the Dead*, 261, 262; Gill, *Lords of Misrule*, 86, 104–8. A New York City German society hosted a carnival in the same year, which similarly boasted, "K. K. s dressed in the horrible style accredited to these terrible being by the Africans." "Arion Maskers," *Mobile Daily Register*, February 14, 1872, p. 2.

110. "The Carnival," *Memphis Avalanche*, February 14, 1872, p. 4.

111. Mitchell, *All on a Mardi Gras Day*, 135, discusses the New Orleans carnival convention of prostitutes cross-dressing and driving about in carriages.

112. For a description of a similar Klan portrayal in an 1873 Louisville Mardi Gras parade, see "Carnival Ball at Louisville," *Frank Leslie's Illustrated Newspaper*, March 22, 1873, p. 27.

113. Black, *The Prevalence of Humbug*, 139.

114. Milburn and Conrad, *The Politics of Denial*, 3.

115. Hofstadter, *The Paranoid Style in American Politics*; David Brion Davis, *The Slave Power Conspiracy and the Paranoid Style*; Summers, *A Dangerous Stir*.

116. White, "The Value of Conspiracy Theory," 5.

117. "Trouble at the South," *New York Tribune*, March 10, 1871, p. 4. Here the Tribune is complaining about suppression of Klan evidence by the Democratic papers rather than about fabrication of Klan evidence by Republicans, but the rhetoric is the same.

118. Halttunen, *Confidence Men and Painted Women*; Johnson, *River of Dark Dreams*, 126–28.

119. Novick, *That Noble Dream*, 45.

120. "Outrage at the South," *New York Tribune*, June 16, 1871, p. 4.

121. "The Blind Who Would Not See," *New York Tribune*, November 18, 1871, p. 4.

122. Newspapers often used their defense of their own journalistic integrity to set up a class of political insiders and outsiders. "Journalism—South Carolina," *New York Tribune*, March 7, 1872, p. 4, for instance, insisted that though the *New York World* had accused them of partisanship, "the more intelligent [readers], however, know better; and time will enlighten more and more of those who are, at the moment, deceived and misguided."

123. Mische, "Cross-Talk in Movements," 264.

124. Brundage, *Where These Memories Grow*, 4.

125. Baker, *What Reconstruction Meant*, 7.

126. See, for instance, "More about the K. K. K.," *Salt Lake Daily Telegraph*, April 21, 1868, p. 2 (reprinted from the *New York World*).

127. "South Carolina," *New York Times*, August 9, 1869, p. 2.

128. "The Ku-klux Trials Ended," *Daily Arkansas Gazette*, January 19, 1872.

129. Beecher, "What We Heard At the South," 330.

130. Brundage, *Where These Memories Grow*, 7.

131. Blight, *Race and Reunion*, 50, 51.

132. Ibid., 60, 61.

133. "Universal Amnesty," *New York Tribune*, April 11, 1871, p. 4.

134. Silber, *The Romance of Reunion*.

135. Cohen, *States of Denial*, 10, 11, 64.

CHAPTER 6

1. Feaster, *A History of Union County*, 108–14; Baker, *This Mob Will Surely Take My Life*, 9–42; Nelson, *Iron Confederacies*, 115–38.

2. *A Compendium of the Ninth Census*, 1870, 584.

3. *Ninth Census of the United States Statistics of Population*, 370.

4. "The State vs the Bodies of Twenty Negro Children, Property of Governor John," UCCI Box 38, Roll 5237.

5. UCCI, Box 34, Roll 2834; UCCI, Box 34, Roll 2942; UCCI, Box 34, Roll 2993; UCCI, Box 35, Roll 3300.

6. UCCI, Box 34, Roll 2804; UCCI, Box 34, Roll 2819. UCCI, Box 34, Roll 2824.

7. UCCI, Box 34, Roll 3020.

8. UCCI, Box 35, Roll 3364.

9. Hadden, *Slave Patrols*, 130–31.

10. John [?] to Brevet Major S. Walker, March 9, 1866, enclosed in Adelbert Ames to Colonel [M. Binger], n.d., Letters and Reports Received Relating to Freedmen and Civil Affairs, Series 4112, RG 393, Part I, Department of South Carolina, Records of U.S. Army Continental Commands, 1821–1883, NARA.

11. Letter from Lieut. A. Wattison to Lieut. George W. Iden, Office of the Provost Marshal, March 5, 1866, unregistered, not numbered; and letter from Bvt. Maj. General Adelbert Ames to Lt. Col. W. L. M. Burger, March 9, 1866, unregistered, not numbered, Letters and Reports Received Relating to Freedmen and Civil Affairs, Series 4112, RG 393, Part I, Department of South Carolina, Records of U.S. Army Continental Commands, 1821–1883, NARA.

12. Adelbert Ames, "List of Outrages Committed by White Persons against Black in the District of West. SC since the Surrender of Johnston's Army," Reports of Outrages. This is neither numbered nor dated, but labeled "encl." It must have been written at the end of 1866. A barely decipherable penciled line under the title says "Dist. of Western [SC?] Nov–Dec. 66." It is filed among other reports of outrages in Letters and Reports Received Relating to Freedmen and Civil Affairs, Series 4158, Box I, RG 393, Part I, Department of South Carolina, Records of U.S. Army Continental Commands, 1821–1883, NARA. Storey, *The Story of the Maine Fifteenth*, 168–70. The list of Slickers was provided to me by Tim Linder, whose descendants are among those considered to have been in the group. This list is in several local histories, including Feaster, *A History of Union County*, 109, and Charles, *A Narrative History of Union County, South Carolina*, 216.

13. Letter from A. P. Caraher to Bvt Lt Col H. W. Smith June 29, 1866, Letters Sent, Unionville S.C. Subdistrict 1866, No. 2, Microfilm, Roll 106, M 1910, BRFAL; "Report of the Operations of Freedmen's Bureau, Condition of the Freedmen, etc. in Mil. Post of Unionville. SC for May 31, 1866," not numbered, Letters and Reports Received Relating to Freedmen and Civil Affairs, Series 4112, RG 393, Part I, Department of South Carolina, Records of U.S. Army Continental Commands, 1821–1883, NARA. 14. UCCI, Box 35, Roll 3455, October 18, 1861.

15. UCCI, Box 35, Roll 3455.

16. UCCI, Box 35, Roll 3550 (L44212). The authoritative treatment of Saxe's history, thoroughly researched and vividly told, is Cashin, "A Lynching in Wartime Carolina," 109–32, 121.

17. Cashin, "A Lynching in Wartime Carolina," 121; UCCI, Box 35, Roll 3550.

18. Faucett's degree in a two-mode network of the county was 47, Skelton's 49.

19. For a hands-on introduction to network analysis, see de Nouy, Mrvar, and Bategelj, *Exploratory Social Network Analysis with Pajek*, 143–53.

20. UCCI, Box 34, Roll 3061; UCCI, Box 36, Roll 3966.

21. UCCI, Box 35, Roll 3434.

22. UCCI, Box 34, Roll 3084; UCCI, Box 34, Roll 2974.

23. Evans, *Confederate Military History*, 5:608.

24. UCCI, Box 38, Roll 5102; UCCI, Box 38, Roll 5100.

25. From Thos. J. Greer, March 14, 1871, Box 15, Folder 18, GSP; UCCI, Box 36, Roll 4026.

26. UCCI, Box 34, Roll 2803; UCCI, Box 34, Roll 3035.

27. UCCI, Box 35, Roll 3130.

28. UCCI, Box 34, Roll 2804.

29. UCCI, Box 36, Roll 3966.

30. Letter from A. P. Caraher to Bvt. Maj. H. Heide, February 17, 1868, Unionville, S.C., Subassistant Commissioner of Unionville, Letters Sent, South Carolina, vol. 278, Roll 106, Target 5, no. 46, BRFAL. In fact, Lydia Skelton did bring an indictment against Hughes, and Mary Davis stepped forward as a witness. UCCI, Box 37, Roll 4530.

31. UCCI, Box 37, Roll 4433.

32. UCCI, Box 36, Roll 3846; UCCI, Box 38, Roll 5045; UCCI, Box 37, Roll 4381; UCCI, Box 37, Roll 4581.

33. UCCI, Box 37, Roll 4740.

34. Caraher's words were extracted in Robert. K. Scott to Charleston [Sickles], "Report of Condition of Affairs of Bureau in State of So. Ca. for month of November 1866," Office of the Assistant Commissioner, South Carolina, BRFAL.

35. I ran a Louvain community detection algorithm to extract Faucett's associates. I then shrunk the network to members of that community and the partition of wealthy Union Countians. Finally, I ran the Louvain community detection algorithm on the combined group.

36. Rogers claimed in at least one of the cases that it was a technicality—that his license had been applied for and paid for, but was pending. UCCI, Box 36, Rolls 3969a and 3969b.

37. UCCI, Box 34, Roll 3084; UCCI, Box 34, Roll 2974; UCCI, Box 35, Roll 3247.

38. Rubin, *South Carolina Scalawags*, 122.

39. Baker, *This Mob Will Surely Take My Life*, 15.

40. Nelson, *Iron Confederacies*, 124.

41. Letter from Sebastian Kraft, August 5, 1868, Box 1, Folder 27, GSP; Trelease, *White Terror*, xxx.

42. Letter from H. W. Duncan and Robert Martin, July 26, 1868, Box 1, Folder 17, GSP.

43. "Negro Violence Threatened in Union District—the Whites Refer the Matter to Governor Scott," *Daily Phoenix*, July 30, 1868, p. 2.

44. "Negro Troubles in Union," *Charleston Daily News*, August 10, 1868, p. 4. (reprinted from *Union [S.C.] Times*, August 7, 1868); "Negro Violence Threatened in Union District," *Edgefield (S.C.) Advertiser*, August 5, 1868, p. 4.

45. "Negro Violence Threatened in Union District," *Edgefield (S.C.) Advertiser*, August 5, 1868, p. 4.

46. Saville, *The Work of Reconstruction*, 192.

47. UCCI, Box 37, Roll 4618.

48. "Negro Troubles in Union," *Charleston Daily News*, August 10, 1868, p. 4.

49. Both of these women were later called as witnesses to the shooting, so they were probably, but not certainly, present. UCCI, Box 37, Roll 3574.

50. "Report of Mr. Hubbard," *Charleston Daily News*, September 5, 1868, p. 1.

51. UCCI, Box 36, Roll 3885, August 26, 1868. John Rogers and A. W. Thomson went Sartor's bond. UCCI, Box 36, Roll 3854, August 26, 1868; Box 37, Roll 4574, August 26, 1868.

52. UCCI, Box 36, Roll 3885.

53. UCCI, Box 36, Roll 3854.

54. *Reports and Resolutions of the General Assembly of the State of South Carolina*, 548.

55. Ibid.

56. Gregory Downs, *Declarations of Dependence*, 101–29.

57. Letter from Alex Walker to Governor, September 20, 1870, GSP.

58. Du Bois, *Black Reconstruction*, 428.

59. UCCI, Box 37, Roll 4530.

60. UCCI, Box 36, Roll 3721; UCCI, Box 36, Roll 3674.

61. UCCI, Box 36, Roll 3862.

62. UCCI, Box 36, Roll 4018.

63. UCCI, Box 38, Roll 4954. Joseph and Thomas Vanlew are important figures in this story. Their last name is spelled variably as Vanlew, Vanlue, and Van Lew.

64. "Affairs in Union," *Daily Phoenix*, November 17, 1870, p. 1; testimony of H. T. Hughes, *KK Report*, vol. 4, S.C., 2:1090.

65. Testimony of R. W. Shand, *KK Report*, vol. 4, S.C., 2:1013.

66. Union County Historical Foundation, *Voices of the Past*, 215.

67. Feaster, *A History of Union County*, 108.

68. Charles, *Narrative History of Union County*, 228.

69. Williamson, *After Slavery*, 263.

70. Zuczek, *State of Rebellion*, 81.

71. Baker, *This Mob Will Surely Take My Life*, 16–17. Zuczek, *State of Rebellion*, 56, 61–62, discusses 1868 Klan violence in the Upcountry but discusses Union as taking a slightly different approach (sabotaging the election process), without determining whether to label it "Klan" violence.

72. Testimony of Jesse Mabry, *Wallace v. Simpson, Evidence in the Contested Election Case in Fourth Congressional District of South Carolina*, December 22, 1869, 41st Cong., 2nd sess., Misc. Doc. 17, pt. 1, no. 1431, p. 31.

73. *Index to Miscellaneous Documents of the House of Representatives of the Second Session of the Forty-First Congress*, 29; testimony of Simon Farr, *Executive Documents Printed by*

Order of the House of Representatives during the Third Session of the Fortieth Congress, U.S. Congressional Serial Set, Vol. 1402, p. 48.

74. Testimony of Richard Kinyon, *Wallace v. Simpson*, 21.

75. *Miscellaneous Documents of the House of Representatives of the Second Session of the Forty-First Congress*, 559.

76. From D. D. Going, January 30, 1869, Box 5, Folder 19, GSP.

77. Trelease, *White Terror*, 351–52; from Alex Walker, Box 12, Folder 36, September 20, 1870, GSP.

78. H. H. Wilson to Capt. John B. Hubbard, September 21, 1870, S516002, Box 12, Folder 37, GSP.

79. Ibid..

80. UCCI, Box 35, Roll 3351.

81. UCCI, Box 35, Roll 3297.

82. UCCI, Box 35, Roll 3554.

83. UCCI, Box 35, Roll 3541; UCCI, Box 35, Roll 3422.

84. D. D. Going to Governor Scott, November 11, 1870, Box 13, Folder 6, GSP; UCCI, Box 38, Roll 5243.

85. UCCI, Box 34, Roll 2989.

86. Ibid.

87. 1870 Union County Census.

88. *Reports and Resolutions of the General Assembly of the State of South Carolina*, 688.

89. UCCI, Box 34, Roll 2942.

90. UCCI, Box 35, Roll 3266.

91. UCCI, Box 37, Roll 4152.

92. UCCI, Box 36, Roll 3622.

93. Testimony of Jesse Mabry, *KK Report*, vol. 5, S.C., 3:1081.

94. Ibid., 1082.

95. UCCI, Box 36, Roll 3855.

96. "More Arrests," Daily Phoenix, May 25, 1872, p. 3, Box 37, Roll 4125, *State v. Clough Bishop and Rufus Bishop, Assault with Intent to Kill*, December 28, 1870.

97. *Reports and Resolutions of the General Assembly of the State of South Carolina*, 128–29.

98. In his testimony, though, Robert Shand says that Mabry was "playing both fiddles," claiming to be a Republican to get "some money." Testimony of Robert Shand, *KK Report*, vol. 5, S.C., 3:1004. Presumably the money was his pay for serving as election manager and doing a few other small government jobs, including that of constable. Testimony of Jesse Mabry, *KK Report*, vol. 5, S.C., 3:1081.

99. UCCI, Box 36, Roll 4046.

100. UCCI, Box 36, Roll 3891.

101. Testimony of R. W. Shand, *KK Report*, vol. 4, S.C., 2:1040.

102. UCCI, Box 38, Roll 4909.

103. UCCI, Box 37, Roll 4525.

104. *Papers in the Case of Isaac G. McKissick v. A. S. Wallace*, 42nd Cong., 2nd sess., H. Doc 37 (Serial 1525), 10–25, 30, 36–38, cited in Zuczek, *State of Rebellion*, 82.

105. UCCI, Box 36, Roll 4023; *State v. Samuel Harris* and UCCI, Box 36, Roll 4033, *State v. Albert Martin, Assisted by Samuel Harris*.

106. UCCI, Box 38, Roll 4980, Assault with Intent to Kill, July 22, 1868.

107. UCCI, Box 37, Roll 4169.

108. "Arrests in Union," *Daily Phoenix*. October 23, 1871, p. 2.

109. "The Ku-Klux," *New York Tribune*, November 6, 1871, p. 1.

110. Testimony of Robert Shand, *KK Report*, vol. 4, S.C., 2:975.

111. Nelson, *Iron Confederacies*, 127; Testimony of Charles Near, UCCI, Box 37, Roll 4123.

112. There is an excellent account of this picket in Baker, *This Mob Will Surely Take My Life*, 23–24. See also Testimony of Sylvanus Wright, UCCI, Box 37, Roll 4123.

113. *A Compendium of the Ninth Census, 1870*; testimony of Fanny Davis, UCCI, Box 38, Roll 5128; Testimony of H. D. Hughes, UCCI, Box 37, Roll 4123; Testimony of Charles Near, UCCI, Box 37, Roll 4123.

114. *The State v. Murderers of Mat Stevens*, UCCI, Box 38, Roll 5129.

115. From Thos J. Greer, March 14, 1871, Box 15, Folder 18, GSP.

116. UCCI, Box 38, Roll 5128; testimony of Robert Greer, UCCI, Box 37, Roll 4123; testimony of William Faucett, UCCI, Box 37, Roll 4123; testimony of Eliza Chalk, *KK Report*, vol. 4, S.C., 2:1130.

117. *State v. The Dead Body of D. A. Smith*, UCCI, Box 38, Roll 5128.

118. Testimony of Eliza Chalk, *KK Report*, vol. 4, S.C., 2:1129.

119. Zuczek, *State of Rebellion*, 82.

120. "Transactions of Young Men's Associations," *Young Men's Magazine* 2 (July 1858), 142.

121 Testimony of Eliza Chalk, *KK Report*, vol. 4, S.C., 2:1130.

122. Ibid.

123. "Let Us Have Peace," *Charleston Daily News*, January 11, 1871, p. 1.

124. Testimony of Alfred Van Lew, *KK Report*, vol. 4, S.C., 2:1137.

125. Ibid.; testimony of Eliza Chalk, *KK Report*, vol. 4, S.C., 2:1128.

126. "Letter to the Editor," *Daily Phoenix*, January 14, 1871.

127. Testimony of Dr. A. W. Thompson, UCCI. Box 38, Roll 5127.

128. Testimony of Joseph Vanlew, UCCI, Box 38, Roll 5127.

129. UCCI, Box 38, Roll 4954.

130. Testimony of Simpson Bobo, *KK Report*, vol. 4, S.C., 2:802–3.

131. Testimony of Joseph Vanlew, UCCI, Box 38, Roll 5127.

132. Testimony of Sylvanus Wright, UCCI, Box 37, Roll 4123.

133. Testimony of Joseph Vanlew, UCCI, Box 38, Roll 5127.

134. UCCI, Box 36, Roll 3829, November 3, 1867.

135. Testimony of William Prater, UCCI, Box 38, Roll 5127.

136. Testimony of John Rodger, *KK Report*, vol. 4, S.C., 2:1080; UCCI, Box 37, Roll 4139.

137. Mrs. Mae E. Coddington Linder (wife of Dr. S. S. Linder) as dictated to her by former Sheriff J. G. Long, "The Ku Klux Klan," Ku Klux Klan, Vertical File, Union County Museum, Union, S.C.

138. "Who Were Driven from Union?," *Daily Phoenix*, January 14, 1871.

139. Baker, *This Mob Will Surely Take My Life*, 29.

140. From W. F. M. Williams, January 14, 1871, Box 14, Folder 3, GSP; From T. J. Greer, Probate Judge, January 24, 1871, GSP.

141. Testimony of Eliza Chalk, *KK Report*, vol. 4, S.C., 2:1133.

142. "The Best on the Road. G. G. Grady's American Circus," *Daily Phoenix*, January 19, 1871, p. 1; Lott, *Love and Theft*.

143. Testimony of Joseph F. Gist, *KK Report*, vol. 4, S.C., 2:1050.

144. Testimony of Christine Page, *KK Report*, vol. 4, S.C., 2:1142–44; testimony of William Bolt, *KK Report*, vol. 4, S.C., 2:1121. Page's testimony is cited in Pierson, *Black Legacy*, 148.

145. Testimony of Robert Shand, *KK Report*, vol. 4, S.C., 2:979.

146. *Union (S.C.) Times*, February 17, 1871, reprinted in Feaster, *History of Union County*, 113; Charles, *Narrative History of Union County*, 226.

147. "Another Mis-Trial: Disagreement of the Jury in the Roger Case," *Charleston Daily News*, April 24, 1872, p. 1.

148. The highest estimate I can find is "from 1,000 to 1,500," in Reynolds, *Reconstruction in South Carolina*, 185.

149. *Union (S.C.) Times*, February 17, 1871, reprinted in Feaster, *History of Union County*, 113–14; "The Ku Klux Trials," *Charleston Daily News*, April 23, 1872, p. 1.

150. Testimony of Simpson Bobo, *KK Report*, vol. 4, S.C., 2:802.

151. Robert Wallace Shand, "Incidents in the Life of a Private Soldier in the War Waged by the United States against the Confederate States, 1861–1865" (1907–8), p. 58, Robert W. Shand Papers, South Caroliniana Library, University of South Carolina, Columbia.

152. Testimony of Joseph F. Gist, *KK Report*, vol. 4, S.C., 2:1055.

153. Testimony of Robert Shand, *KK Report*, vol. 4, S.C., 2:983.

154. Supreme Court, U.S. Case No. 6200, *Ex Parte Jefferson Greer*.

155. UCCI, Box 36, Roll 3966, *State v. John C. Powell*.

156. "Political—North Carolina," *New York Tribune*, July 19, 1871, p. 4.

157. UCCI, Box 38, Roll 5128.

158. Testimony of Drury D. Going, *KK Report*, vol. 4, S.C., 2:1071.

159. Testimony of Robert Shand, *KK Report*, vol. 4, S.C., 2:990–91.

160. Shand, "Incidents in the Life of a Private Soldier," 58.

161. Union County Historical Foundation, *A History of Union County South Carolina*, 114.

162. *State v. Henry Cannon, Taylor Palmer, Fed. Green*, UCCI, Box 37, Roll 4123.

163. *Sumter Watchman*, March 22, 1871, p. 2.

164. Zuczek, *State of Rebellion*, 91.

165. Ibid., 92.

166. "South Carolina Kuklux: The Horrible Mutilation of the Body of a Colored Preacher," *New York Times*, July 11, 1871, p. 4.

167. Testimony of James Steadman, *KK Report*, vol. 4, S.C., 2:553.

168. Baker, *This Mob Will Surely Take My Life*, 39.

CHAPTER 7

1. "Local Items," *Daily Phoenix*, March 15, 1868, p. 2.

2. "K.-K.-K.," *Charleston Daily News*, March 24, 1868, p. 2.

3. *Daily Phoenix*, April 15, 1868, p. 1.

4. "Local Items," *Daily Phoenix*, April 18, 1868, p. 2.

5. "The Legislature," *Daily Phoenix*, July 22, 1868, p. 3.

6. *Daily Phoenix*, April 15, 1868, p. 1.

7. *Edgefield (S.C.) Advertiser*, March 25, 1868, p. 2.

8. "The Ku-Klux Klan: What Is It?," *Anderson Intelligencer*, April 19, 1868, p. 4. The first was "The Ku-Klux Klan," *Anderson Intelligencer*, April 1, 1868, p. 4.

9. *Daily Phoenix*, March 22, 1868, p. 3.

10. "Summary Vengeance upon a Negro in Tennessee," *Edgefield (S.C.) Advertiser*, August 12, 1868, p. 4.

11. "A Lady Outraged and Her Brother Murdered," *Daily Phoenix*, July 31, 1868, p. 1.

12. "K. K. K.," *Daily Phoenix*, April 30, 1868, p. 2.

13. "The Ku-klux-Klan," *Charleston Daily News*, September 4, 1869, p. 2.

14. "Satan Rebuking Sin," *Charleston Daily News*, October 31, 1870, p. 2.

15. "K. K. K," *Newberry (S.C.) Herald*, April 22, 1868, p. 2.

16. "De Large Negro Scare," *Newberry (S.C.) Herald*, July 29, 1868, p. 2.

17. "The Circus," *Charleston Daily News*, October 31, 1868, p. 3.

18. Testimony of Robert Shand, *KK Report*, vol. 4, S.C., 2:1005.

19. Burton, "Race and Reconstruction," 32.

20. Testimony of Robert Shand, *KK Report*, vol. 4, S.C., 2:1007–9.

21. "The Tools of Despotism," *Charleston Daily News*, October 25, 1871, p. 2.

22. U.S. War Department, *Annual Report of the Secretary of War*, 1:458; U.S. Congressional Serial Set, vol. 1367, *Executive Documents Printed by Order of the House of Representatives during the Third Session of the Fortieth Congress*.

23. *Message of Robert K. Scott*, 356.

24. Ibid.

25. "Testimony of John Hubbard," in *Report of the Joint Investigating Committee on Public Frauds*, 65.

26. Letter from Enoch Cannon to Governor Robert K. Scott, December 8, 1870, Box 13, Folder 22, GSP.

27. *Union (S.C.) Times*, August 7, 1868, as reprinted in "Negro Troubles in Union," *Charleston Daily News*, August 10, 1868.

28. Testimony of Robert Shand, *KK Report*, vol. 4, S.C., 2:974; *Reports and Resolutions of the General Assembly of the State of South Carolina*, 689; *Report of the Joint Investigating Committee on Public Frauds*, 713.

29. Letter from J. C. Bonsall to John B. Hubbard, 28–29.

30. UCCI, Box 38, Roll 4922.

31. UCCI, Box 36, Roll 3885. "From the State Capital," *Charleston Daily News*, September 5, 1868, p. 1.

32. From John B. Hubbard, September 21, 1870, Box 12, Folder 37, GSP.

33. From John B. Hubbard, February 15, 1871, Box 14, Folder 38, GSP.

34. Papers in the Case of *A. S. Wallace v. W. D. Simpson*, Fourth Cong. Dist., S.C., 41st Cong., 1st sess., Misc. Doc. 17, No. 1402, p. 2.

35. Charges, ibid., p. 2.

36. Ibid., p. 14.

37. Testimony of Richard Kinyon, ibid., p. 23.

38. Testimony of Simon Farr, ibid., p. 47.

39. Testimony of J. S. Mobley, ibid., p. 39.

40. Testimony of Samuel Nuckles, ibid., p. 57.

41. Testimony of P. J. O'Connell, ibid., p. 16.

42. Testimony of John L. Watson, ibid., p. 52.

43. Testimony of John Wesley Meade, ibid., p. 17.

44. Ibid., p. 49.

45. Testimony of Sancho Sanders, ibid., pp. 19–20.

46. Ibid., p. 33.

47. Testimony of H. C. Corwin, ibid., p. 44.

48. Testimony of John Bates, "Depositions Taken in Union County," *Miscellaneous Documents of the House of Representatives of the Second Session of the Forty-First Congress.*

49. Testimony of J. A. Walker, ibid., p. 29.

50. Testimony of Richard Kinyon, ibid., p. 23.

51. Testimony of Jesse Mabry, ibid., p. 31.

52. Testimony of Alfred Wright, ibid., p. 34.

53. "From the State Capital," *Charleston Daily News*, September 5, 1868, p. 1; "The Santuc Riot," *Charleston Daily News*, September 7, 1868, p. 2.

54. "Public Meetings in Anderson and Union—Reply of the Citizens to Governor Scott's Proclamation, Etc., Etc." *Charleston Courier*, October 31, 1868.

55. *Daily Phoenix*, October 28, 1868, p. 1.

56. "The Elections in the State," *Charleston Daily News*, November 6, 2013, p. 1.

57. There were incidents of collective violence during this period, of course, but none against people whom I can identify as either black or Republican.

58. UCCI, Box 36, Roll 3975.

59. UCCI, Box 37, Roll 4180.

60. UCCI, Box 36, Roll 3972.

61. Zuczek, *State of Rebellion*, 105.

62. Assault indictments in UCCI: 42 in 1868, 42 in 1869, 48 in 1870. Murder/attempted murder indictments: 12 in 1868, 14 in 1869, 16 in 1870. Larceny and arson indictments: 47 in 1868, 38 in 1869, 48 in 1870.

63. Anderson, "Rituals of Horsemanship."

64. "Grand National Tournament at Glenn Springs," *Daily Phoenix*, August 21, 1870, p. 3.

65. "Notice," *Daily Phoenix*, October 5, 1871, p. 2.

66. "Institute Fair," *Charleston Daily News* November 9, 1870, p. 3. For a discussion of the burlesque Klan figure at the tournament, see Anderson, "Rituals of Horsemanship," esp. 219.

67. "To the Colored People of South Carolina," *Sumter Watchman*, September 21, 1870, p. 2.

68. "Troubles in the State," *Keowee Courier* (Pickens Court House, S.C.), November 4, 1870, p. 3.

69. *Daily Phoenix*, September 11, 1870, p. 2.

70. Testimony of Robert Shand, *KK Report*, vol. 4, S.C., 2:1005.

71. Reprinted as part of testimony of William Irwin, *KK Report*, vol. 4, S.C., 2:864.

72. "Astounding Development," *Sumter Watchman*, September 21, 1870, p. 2 (reprinted from the *Daily Phoenix*).

73. UCCI, Box 36, Roll 3975; UCCI, Box 38, Roll 3867.

74. "The Negro Ku-klux. Effects of the Confidential Circular. Its Teachings at Work. More Light upon a Dark Subject," *Charleston Daily News*, October 4, 1870, p. 4.

75. Ibid.

76. T. J. Mackey to Scott, September 16, 1868, Box 2, Folder 22, GSP. Cited in Zuczek, *State of Rebellion*, 59–60.

77. *Daily Phoenix*, January 17, 1871, p. 2.

78. "Police Intelligence," *New York Herald*, May 3, 1856, p. 4; "An Affair of Honor in New York," *New York Herald*, July 30, 1856, p. 1.

79. "Nicaragua. Re-Enforcements for Walker," *New York Tribune*, January 30, 1856, p. 6; "The Nicaragua Filibusters," *New York Daily Tribune*, January 10, 1856, p. 7; "Fenian Convention," *New York Sun*, August 25, 1868, p. 3.

80. "City Politics and Politicians," *New York Herald*, October 17, 1870, p. 3.

81. "New Military Organization for the Protection of Municipal Rights and the South," *New York Times*, December 15, 1860, p. 4.

82. Snay, *Fenians, Freedmen, and Southern Whites*; Neidhardt, *Fenianism in North America*; Sullivan, *New Ireland*, 2:180; Anbinder, *Five Points*, 297; "Colonel J. E. Kerrigan's Career," *New York Times*, November 3, 1899, p. 7; "Telegraphic," *Louisiana Democrat*, November 18, 1868, p. 3; "Important from Washington," *New York Times*, January 7, 1862, p. 8; "Fenianism in New-York," *New York Times*, June 9, 1866, p. 5.

83. "Experience of New York Roughs in South Carolina," *Daily Phoenix*, January 24, 1871, p. 2 (reprinted from the *New York Sun*).

84. Testimony of Robert Shand, *KK Report*, vol. 4, S.C., 2:998.

85. Testimony of James Steadman, *KK Report*, vol. 4, S.C., 2:1016.

86. Quoted in the *Charleston Daily News*, December 30, 1870, p. 1.

87. "The Assassination Business," *Daily Phoenix*, January 31, 1871 (reprinted from *New York Sun*, January 24, 1871).

88. "The Disorders in Union County: The Facts of the Case," *Charleston Daily News*, December 29, 1870, p. 1.

89. *Report of the Joint Investigating Committee on Public Frauds*, 723.

90. "The Disorders in Union County," *Charleston Daily News*, December 29, 1870, p. 1.

91. Originally printed as "A War in South Carolina: Governor Scott Recruiting in New York City," *The Sun*, January 16, 1871, p. 1, reprinted as "A Monstrous Story: The Experience of New York Roughs in South Carolina," *Charleston Daily News*, January 19, 1871, p. 1.

92. Kelly, "Class, Factionalism, and Radical Retreat," 207.

93. Testimony of H. T. Hughes, *KK Report*, vol. 4, S.C., 2:1093.

94. Union (S.C.) Times, January 6, 1871, as reprinted in Feaster, History of Union County, 113.

95. From T. J. Greer, January 28, 1871, Box 14, Folder 19, GSP.

96. Testimony of James Steadman, KK Report, vol. 4, S.C., 2:1020; testimony of Robert Shand, KK Report, vol. 4, S.C., 2:999.

97. Union (S.C.) Times, February 17, 1871, as cited in Feaster, A History of Union County, 113.

98. Union (S.C.) Times, January 6, 1871, as cited in Feaster, A History of Union County, 112.

99. Ibid., 113. McKnight was in tension with Faucett intimate Samuel Sumner, even accused of assaulting him (on the same day that Benjamin Scott was accused of assaulting Sumner, presumably the same incident) in 1858. Faucett had gone bond for Sumner on Scott's charge. UCCI, Box 35, Roll 3080, and Box 35, Roll 3081, both Assault and Battery, August 21, 1858.

100. "After a Storm There Is a Calm," Daily Phoenix, January 15, 1871, p. 2.

101. "Slaughter of Negroes," New York Times, February 15, 1871, p. 1; New York Tribune, February 15, 1871, p. 4; "Ku-klux Outrages in South Carolina," New York Tribune, February 15, 1871, p. 5; "Charleston," Milwaukee Daily Sentinel, February 15, 1871, p. 1; "Outrages in North Carolina," New York Tribune, February 17, 1871, p. 5 (This article combines a report on an attack in North Carolina with a report on the South Carolina attack); "The Ku-klux," New York Tribune, February 23, 1871, p. 1.

102. Document entered into testimony of H. T. Hughes, KK Report, vol. 4, S.C., 2:1092.

103. "After the Storm There Is a Calm," Daily Phoenix, January 15, 1871, p. 2; "A Voice from Union," Daily Phoenix, February 14, 1871, p. 2; "The Ku Klux Proclamation," Daily Phoenix, February 15, 1871, p. 2.

104. Testimony of James Steadman, KK Report, vol. 4, S.C., 2:1003.

105. "How Ku-klux Stories Originate," Daily Phoenix, February 17, 1871, p. 3.

106. Grant, Papers of Ulysses S. Grant, 21:260–62; from Thomas Wilkes and Samuel Nuckles, March 2, 1871, Box 15, Folder 9, GSP; from L. C. Carpenter, February 21, 1871, Box 14, Folder 40, GSP.

107. Zuczek, State of Rebellion, 98; Lou Falkner Williams, The Great South Carolina Ku Klux Klan Trials, 44–46.

108. "The Ku-klux," New York Times, July 30, 1871, p. 1; Zuczek, State of Rebellion.

109. Daily Phoenix, February 23, 1871 (reprinted from Charleston Daily News).

110. Testimony of Robert Shand, KK Report, vol. 4, S.C., 2:977.

111. Testimony of Joseph F. Gist, KK Report, vol. 4, S.C., 2:1055. "The Cowardly Murders in Union," Charleston Daily News, February 15, 1871, p. 2, similarly casts doubt on the "Ku-klux" identity of these attackers, referring to them as "so-called Ku-klux" despite their own self-identification, and despite the fact that they perfectly fit national definitions of Ku-Klux.

112. Testimony of Robert Shand, KK Report, vol. 4, S.C., 2:978.

113. Ibid., 2:980, 986.

114. Ibid., 2:972.

115. Testimony of James Steadman, KK Report, vol. 4, S.C., 2:1033.

116. Ibid., 2:1032; UCCI, Box 37, Roll 4123.

117. Testimony of Robert Shand, *KK Report*, vol. 4, S.C., 2:970.

118. Testimony of James Steadman, *KK Report*, vol. 4, S.C., 2:1018.

119. Reprinted in the *Daily Phoenix*, February 17, 1871, p. 3, cited in testimony of Robert Shand, *KK Report*, vol. 4, S.C., 2:1001.

120. UCCI, Box 38, Roll 3100.

121. Testimony of James Steadman, *KK Report*, vol. 4, S.C., 2:1013, 1026; testimony of Robert Shand, *KK Report*, vol. 4, S.C., 2:969.

122. Testimony of James Steadman, *KK Report*, vol. 4, S.C., 2:1013. The militia attacks on Hughes and Faucett's home had been published in the "Affairs in Union," *Daily Phoenix*, November 17, 1870, p. 1.

123. UCCI, Box 36, Roll 3840, July 9, 1867.

124. UCCI, Box 36, Roll 4038, July 22, 1869.

125. "Assault on the Ku-klux Committee," *Milwaukee Daily Sentinel*, August 1, 1871; *Chicago Times*, July 27, 1871, p. 4; "Domestic News: Return of the Ku-klux Committee from South Carolina, What They Learned from the Victims . . . ," *New York Times*, July 30, 1871, p. 1.

126. Testimony of James Steadman, *KK Report*, vol. 4, S.C., 2:1014.

127. Ibid., 2:976.

128. Testimony of Robert Shand, *KK Report*, vol. 4, S.C., 2:978.

129. Ibid., 976.

130. Ibid., 970.

131. Ibid., 977.

132. Ibid., 978.

133. Testimony of H. D. Byron, Greenville, S.C., July 27, 1878, p. 12.

134. Unionville S.C. Station, October 31, 1871, November 30, 1871, December 31, 1871, February 29, 1872, March 31, 1872, April 30, 1872, May 31, 1872, June 30, 1872, July 31, 1872, August 31, 1872, December 1, 1872. See Captain F. H. French, Military Post of Unionville, South Carolina, Reports from U.S. Military Posts, 1800–1916, microfilm 617, Roll 1313, RG 105, NARA; *Report of the Joint Investigating Committee on Public Frauds*, 5.

135. "The Ku-Klux," *New York Tribune*, November 6, 1871, p. 1.

136. "The Ku-Klux," *Milwaukee Daily Sentinel*, November 13, 1871, p. 1.

137. "Washington," *Chicago Times*, November 20, 1871, p. 1.

138. "War on the Ku-Klux," *New York Tribune*, November 19, 1871, p. 5.

139. Lou Falkner Williams, *The Great South Carolina Ku Klux Klan Trials*, 49; "Jottings about the State," *Charleston Daily News*, November 19, 1872, p. 1; *Ex Parte T. Jefferson Greer*, Supreme Court U.S. Case No. 6200, Supreme Court of the United States No. 617 (1872).

140. UCCI, Box 36, Roll 4045; UCCI, Box 36, Roll 4046.

141. UCCI, Box 36, Roll 3829, Grand Larceny (November 3, 1867); UCCI, Box 37, Roll 4381.

142. UCCI, Box 36, Roll 3874; UCCI, Box 38, Roll 5294.

143. UCCI, Box 36, Roll 3975.

144. "The Ku-Klux," *Milwaukee Daily Sentinel*, October 31, 1871, p. 1.

145. "The Ku Klux Trials," *Charleston Daily News*, April 23, 1872, p. 1.

146. *Charleston Daily News*, May 1, 1872; "The Ku Klux Trials," *Charleston Daily News*, April 23, 1872, p. 1.

147. UCCI, Box 36, Roll 3800.

148. UCCI, Box 38, Roll 4949.

149. "The North Carolina Desperados," *Anderson Intelligencer*, March 7, 1872, p. 1. A very similar article, "Black Kuklux," *Daily Phoenix*, February 27, 1872, p. 4 (reprinted from the *New York Journal of Commerce*).

150. "South Carolina: Grant's War of Revenge upon the People of That State," *Atlanta Daily Sun*, March 17, 1872, p. 2.

CONCLUSION

1. Babcock-Abrahams, "A Tolerated Margin of Mess," 154.

2. Disguised vigilantism did continue on a much smaller scale. The Molly Maguires, for instance, reportedly blackened their faces during some of their attacks, though they were not reported to have worn women's dresses. Kenny, *Making Sense of the Molly Maguires*, 11.

3. UCCI Box 38, Roll 5287.

4. UCCI, Box 37, Roll 4525.

5. UCCI, Box 38, Roll 5310.

6. UCCI, Box 38, Roll 4949.

7. UCCI, Box 37, Roll 4150; UCCI, Box 37, Roll 4056.

8. UCCI, Box 39, Roll 5725.

9. UCCI, Box 37, Roll 4430.

10. "State News," *Orangeburg News*, February 7, 1874, p. 3.

Bibliography

PRIMARY SOURCES

Baton Rouge, La.
    Louisiana State University Archives
        Alfred Flourney Papers
Chapel Hill, N.C.
    Southern Historical Collection, University of North Carolina
        Samuel Agnew Diary
        Andrew McCollum Papers
        Shotwell Family Papers
        Wyche and Otey Family Papers
College Park, Md.
    University of Maryland
        Freedmen and Southern Society Papers
Columbia, S.C.
    South Carolina Department of Archives and History
        Governor Robert K. Scott Papers
Durham, N.C.
    David M. Rubenstein Rare Book and Manuscript Library, Duke University
        William Woods Holden Papers
        Ku Klux Klan Collection
Louisville, Ky.
    Filson Historical Society
        Garrett Family Papers
Memphis, Tenn.
    Mississippi Valley Collection, University of Memphis
        Meriwether Family Papers
New York, N.Y.
    New York Public Library
        Walter Lynnwood Fleming Papers
Pulaski, Tenn.
        Giles County Historical Society Archives
        Robert Wamble Personal Papers
St. Louis, Missouri
    Missouri Historical Society
        Ku-Klux Collection
Washington, D.C.
    U.S. National Archives and Records Administration

Records of the Bureau Refugees, Freedmen, and Abandoned Lands, Record
Group 105.
Records of United States Army Continental Commands, 1821–1920, Record
Group 393.

GOVERNMENT DOCUMENTS

A Compendium of the Ninth Census, 1870. Washington: Government Printing Office,
1872.
Condition of Affairs in Georgia. House of Representatives, 40th Cong., 3d sess., Misc.
Doc. No. 52. Congressional Serial Set, 1385.
*Message of Robert K. Scott, Governor of South Carolina, with Accompanying Documents,
Submitted to the General Assembly of South Carolina at the Regular Session November 1869.*
Columbia, S.C.: John W. Denny, Printer to the State, 1869.
*Miscellaneous Documents from the House of Representatives of the Second Session of the Forty-
First Congress, 1869–1870.* No. 152, Digest of Election Cases. Cases of Contested
Elections in the House of Representatives from 1865 to 1871, Inclusive.
Washington: Government Printing Office, 1870.
Ninth Census of the United States Statistics of Population. Washington: Government
Printing Office, 1872.
*Records of the Assistant Commissioner for the State of Tennessee Bureau of Refugees, Freedmen,
and Abandoned Lands, 1865–1869.* National Archives, microfilm publication M999,
Roll 34.
*Report of Evidence Taken before the Military Committee in Relation to Outrages Committed
by the Ku Klux Klan in Middle and West Tennessee Submitted to the Extra Session of the
Thirty-Fifth General Assembly of the State of Tennessee September 2d, 1868.* Nashville:
S. C. Mercer, 1868.
*Reports of the Committees of the House of Representatives for the First Session of the Forty-Third
Congress 1873–1874.* Washington: Government Printing Office, 1874.
Report of the Joint Committee on Outrages. Montgomery, Ala.: Jno G. Stokes, State
Printers, 1868.
*Report of the Joint Investigating Committee on Public Frauds and Election of Hon J. J. Patterson
to the United States Senate, Made to the General Assembly of South Carolina at the Regular
Session 1877–1878.* Columbia, S.C.: Calvo & Patton, State Printers, 1878.
*Report of the Joint Select Committee to Inquire into the Condition of Affairs in the Late
Insurrectionary States.* 13 vols., Serials 1484–96. Washington: Government Printing
Office, 1872.
*Reports and Resolutions of the General Assembly of the State of South Carolina at the Regular
Session 1870–1871.* Columbia, S.C.: Republican Printing Company, 1871.
*Speech of the Honorable Charles H. Porter of Virginia, delivered in the House of Representatives,
April 4, 1871.* Washington: F. and J. Rives and George F. Bailey, 1871.
Tennessee General Assembly. *Senate Journal of the Extra Session of the Thirty-Fifth General
Assembly.* Nashville: E. G. Eastman, 1868.
"Testimony in Relation to the Alleged Safe-Burglary at the Office of the United
States Attorney." Washington, D.C. Congressional Series of United States Public

Documents, Reports of the Committees of the House of Representatives for the
First Session of the Forty-Third Congress, Vol. 1627, Report No. 785.

U.S. Army, Department of the South. *Major General Meade's Report on the Ashburn
Murder*. N.p: 1868.

U.S. Circuit Court (4th Circuit). *Proceedings in the Ku Klux Trials at Columbia, S.C., in
the United States Circuit Court, 4th Circuit, November Term, 1871*. New York: Negro
Universities Press, 1969.

U.S. Congress. *Supplement to the Congressional Globe Containing the Proceedings of the
Senate Sitting for the Trial of Andrew Johnson, President of the United States*. 40th Cong.,
2d sess., 1868.

————. *Testimony Taken by the Joint Select Committee on the Condition of Affairs in the Late
Insurrectionary States*. Washington: Government Printing Office, 1872.

U.S. War Department. *Annual Report of the Secretary of War*. Vol. 1. Washington:
Government Printing Office, 1868.

PERIODICALS

Anderson Intelligencer
  (Anderson Court House, S.C.)
Atlanta Daily Sun
Boston Daily Advertiser
Charleston Courier
Charleston Daily News
Chicago Times
Daily Arkansas Gazette (Little Rock)
Daily Chronicle and Sentinel (Augusta, Ga.)
Daily News and Herald (Savannah, Ga.)
Daily Phoenix (Columbia, S.C.)
Edgefield (S.C.) Advertiser
Lowell (Mass.) Daily Citizen
Memphis Avalanche

Memphis Daily Appeal
Memphis Public Ledger
Milwaukee Daily Sentinel
Mobile (Ala.) Daily Register
Morning Republican (Little Rock, Ark.)
Nashville Union and Dispatch
Newberry (S.C.) Herald
New York Herald
New York Sun
New York Times
New York Tribune
Sumter Watchman (Sumterville, S.C.)
Union (S.C.) Times

PUBLISHED PRIMARY SOURCES

Alexander, Charles Wesley. *Poor Ellen Stuart's Fate, or, Victim of the Free Love Institute in
Oneida, N.Y.: A True and Thrilling Account of Miss Ellen Stuart's Captivity in a Free Love
Institute, and Her Tragic Escape and Sufferings*. Philadelphia: Cooperative Publishing
House, 1868.

Anonymous. *Horrible Disclosures: A Full and Authentic Exposé of the Ku Klux Klan*.
Cincinnati, 1868.

Anonymous. *The Masked Lady of the White House, or, The Ku-Klux-Klan: A Most Startling
Exposure of the Doings of This Extensive Secret Band, Whose Mysterious Lodges Exist in
Every City and County in the Land*. Philadelphia: [C. W. Alexander], 1868.Barde,
Alexandre. *The Vigilance Committees of the Attakapas: An Eyewitness Account of Banditry
and Backlash in Southwestern Louisiana*. Annotated and edited by David C. Edmonds

and Dennis Gibson; translated by Henrietta Guilbeau Rogers. Lafayette, La.: Acadiana Press, 1981.

Beecher, Mrs. H. W. "What We Heard at the South." *Christian Union* 3, no. 21 (May 24, 1871): 330.

Buell, E. C. *Buell's Ku-klux-Klan Songster.* New York, 1868.

Branson's North Carolina Business Directory for 1869. Raleigh: J. A. Jones, 1869.

Bryant, Benjamin. *Experience of a Northern Man among the Ku-klux, or, The Condition of the South.* Hartford: Published by the author, 1872.

"Condensed Congress." *Punchinello* 1, no. 2 (April 9, 1870): 30.

Davis, William Watson. *The Civil War and Reconstruction in Florida.* New York: Columbia University Press, 1913.

Doyle, Arthur Conan. "The Five Orange Pips." *The Strand* 2 (July–December 1891): 481–91.

Dunning, William Archibald. *Reconstruction: Political and Economic: 1865–1877.* New York: Harper & Brothers, 1907.

Evans, Clement Anselm. *Confederate Military History,* vol. 5. Atlanta: Confederate Publishing Company, 1899.

Fleming, Walter L. *The Ku-Klux Testimony Relating to Alabama, Published in Gulf States Historical Magazine, November, 1903.* Montgomery, 1903.

Fuller Ossoli, Margaret. *Women in the Nineteenth Century, and Kindred Papers Relating to the Sphere, Condition and Duties, of Women.* Edited by Arthur B. Fuller. Boston: John P. Jewett, 1855.

Gannon, W. H. *The GAR v the Ku-klux.* Boston: W. F. Brown, 1872.

Gillette, William. *Retreat from Reconstruction.* Baton Rouge: Louisiana State University Press, 1979.

Graham, Andrew Jackson. *The Handbook of Standard or American Phonography.* New York: Andrew J. Graham, 1858.

Grant, Ulysses S. *Papers of Ulysses S. Grant.* Vol. 21, November 1, 1870–May 31, 1871. Edited by John Y. Simon. Carbondale: Southern Illinois University Press, 1998.

————. *Personal Memoirs.* New York: Penguin, 1999.

Greeley, Horace. *Mr. Greeley's Letters from Texas and the Lower Mississippi, to Which Are Added His Address to the Farmers of Texas and His Speech on His Return to New York.* New York: Tribune Office, 1871.

Green, John Patterson. *Recollections of the Inhabitants, Localities, Superstitions, and Kuklux Outrages of the Carolinas by a "Carpet-Bagger" Who Was Born and Lived There.* Cleveland: n.p. 1880.

Haworth, Paul Leland. *Reconstruction and Union, 1865–1912.* New York: Henry Holt, 1912.

A Late Member. *The Oaths, Signs, Ceremonies and Objects of the Ku-Klux Klan: A Full Exposé.* Cleveland, 1868.

Macoy, Robert. *The Masonic Manual, Revised Edition.* New York: Clark and Maynard, 1867.

"A Member of the Order." *An Authentic Exposition of the "K.G. C." Knights of the Golden Circle, or a History of Secession from 1834–1861.* Indianapolis: C. O. Perrine, 1861.

"A Member." *The K. K. K. Exposed!* Cleveland, 1868.

Meriwether, Elizabeth Avery. *The Ku Klux Klan; or, The Carpetbagger in New Orleans.* Memphis: Southern Baptist Publication Society, 1877.

———. *Recollections of 92 Years, 1824–1916.* Nashville: Tennessee Historical Commission, 1958.

Narrative of Edmund Wright; His Adventures with and Escape from the Knights of the Golden Circle. New York: R. W. Hitchcock, 1864.

Parrish, Robert. *Details of an Unpaid Claim on France for 24,000,000 Francs.* Philadelphia: n.p., 1869.

"The Political Campaign of 1872." *North American Review* 237 (October 1872): 418.

Pomery, Mark Mills. *Brick Dust.* New York: G. W. Carleton, 1871.

Proceedings of the State Convention of the Colored Citizens of Tennessee, Held in Nashville, Feb. 22d, 23d, 24th, & 25th, 1871. Nashville: C. LeRoi, 1871.

Radical Rule: Military Outrage in Georgia. Arrest of Columbus Prisoners. Louisville, Ky.: John P. Morton, 1868.

Reed, John C. "What I Know of the Ku Klux Klan." *Uncle Remus' Magazine* 1, no. 8 (January 1908): 24–26.

Robuck, J. E. *My Own Personal Experience and Observation as a Soldier in the Confederate Army during the Civil War, 1861–1865 also during the Period of Reconstruction— Appending a History of the Origin, Rise Career and Disbanding of the Famous Ku-Klux Klan, or Invisible Empire. Exactly Why, When and Where It Originated.* N.p., 1900.

Scalpel, M. D. [Edward H. Dixon]. *The Terrible Mysteries of the Ku Klux Klan: A Full Exposé.* New York, 1868.

Story, Henry Augustus. *The Story of the Maine Fifteenth: Being a Brief Narrative of the More Important Events in the History of the Fifteenth Maine Regiment.* Bridgeton, Me.: Press of the Bridgeton News, 1890.

Sullivan, Alexander Martin. *New Ireland: Political Sketches and Personal Reminiscences.* Vol. 2. London: Sampson Low, Marston, Searle, and Rivington, 1878.

Tourgée, Albion. *A Fool's Errand: By One of the Fools.* New York: Fords, Howard, and Hulbert, 1879.

Venable, W. H., ed. *The School Stage: A Collection of Juvenile Acting Plays.* Boston: Van Antwerp, Bragg, 1873.

Warden, D. A. *Ku Klux Klan: Comic Song.* Philadelphia, 1868.

SECONDARY SOURCES

Abbot, Richard H. *For Free Press and Equal Rights: Republican Newspapers in the Reconstruction South.* Edited by John W. Quist. Athens: University of Georgia Press, 2004.

Anbinder, Tyler. *Five Points: The 19th Century New York City Neighborhood That Invented Tap Dance, Stole Elections, and Became the World's Most Notorious Slum.* New York: Simon and Shuster, 2001.

Anderson, Paul Christopher. "Rituals of Horsemanship: A Speculation on the Ring Tournament and the Origins of the Ku Klux Klan." In *Weirding the War: Stories from the Civil War's Ragged Edges,* edited by Stephen Berry, 215–33. Athens: University of Georgia Press, 2011.

Ash, Steven. *A Massacre in Memphis: The Race Riot That Shook the Nation One Year after the Civil War*. New York: Hill and Wang, 2014.

Ayers, Edward L. *The Promise of the New South: Life After Reconstruction*. New York: Oxford University Press, 1992.

———. *Vengeance and Justice: Crime and Punishment in the Nineteenth-Century American South*. New York: Oxford University Press, 1985.

Babcock-Abrahams, Barbara. "'A Tolerated Margin of Mess': The Trickster and His Tales Reconsidered." *Journal of the Folklore Institute* 11, no. 3 (1975): 147–86.

Baker, Bruce. "Lynching Ballads in North Carolina." Master's thesis, University of North Carolina at Chapel Hill, 1995.

———. *This Mob Will Surely Take My Life: Lynchings in the Carolinas, 1871–1947*. New York: Continuum, 2008.

———. *What Reconstruction Meant: Historical Memory in the American South*. Baton Rouge: Louisiana State University Press, 2007.

Bakhtin, Mikhail. *Rabelais and His World*. Translated by Helene Iswolsky. Cambridge, Mass.: MIT Press, 1968.

Baptist, Edward. *The Half Has Never Been Told: Slavery and the Making of American Capitalism*. New York: Basic Books, 2014.

———. "'Stol and Fetched Here': Enslaved Migrations, Ex-slave Narratives, and Vernacular History." In *New Studies in the History of American Slavery*, edited by Edward E. Baptist and Stephanie M. H. Camp, 243–74. Athens: University of Georgia Press, 2006.

Bardaglio, Peter. *Reconstructing the Household: Families, Sex, and the Law in the Nineteenth-Century South*. Chapel Hill: University of North Carolina Press, 1995.

Benjamin, Walter. *Arcades Project*. Translated by Rolf Tiedemann. Cambridge, Mass.: Harvard University Press, 1999.

Behrend, Justin. *Reconstructing Democracy: Grassroots Black Politics in the Deep South after the Civil War*. Athens: University of Georgia Press, 2015.

Bederman, Gail. *Manliness and Civilization: A Cultural History of Gender and Race in the United States, 1880–1917*. Chicago: University of Chicago Press, 1996.

Berg, Manfred. *Popular Justice: A History of Lynching in America*. Lanham, Md.: Ivan R. Dee, 2011.

Black, Max. *The Prevalence of Humbug and Other Essays*. Ithaca, N.Y.: Cornell University Press, 1986.

Blain, William T. "Challenge to the Lawless: The Mississippi Secret Service, 1870–1871." *Mississippi Quarterly* 31, no. 2 (1978): 229–40.

Blight, David. *Race and Reunion: The Civil War in American Memory*. Cambridge, Mass.: Harvard University Press, 2001.

Brisson, Jim D. "Civil Government Was Crumbling around Me: The Kirk Holden War of 1870." *North Carolina Historical Review* 88, no. 2 (2011): 123–63.

Broomall, James J. "Personal Confederacies: War and Peace in the American South, 1840–1890." Ph.D. diss., University of Florida, 2011.

Brown, Richard D. *Knowledge Is Power: The Diffusion of Information in Early America, 1700–1865*. New York: Oxford University Press, 1989.

Brown, William Garrett. *The Lower South in American History*. New York: Macmillan, 1903.

Brundage, William Fitzhugh. *Lynching in the New South*. Urbana: University of Illinois Press, 1993.

———. *Where These Memories Grow: History, Memory, and Southern Identity*. Chapel Hill: University of North Carolina Press, 2000.

Burton, Vernon. *In My Father's House Are Many Mansions: Family and Community in Edgefield, South Carolina*. Chapel Hill: University of North Carolina Press, 1987.

———. "Race and Reconstruction: Edgefield County, South Carolina." *Journal of Social History* 12, no. 1 (Autumn 1978): 31–56.

Cardyn, Lisa. "Sexualized Racism / Gendered Violence: Outraging the Body Politic in the Reconstruction South." *Michigan Law Review* 100 (February 2002): 675–867.

Carnes, Mark C. *Secret Ritual and Manhood in Victorian America*. New Haven, Conn.: Yale University Press, 1989.

Cashin, Joan E. "A Lynching in Wartime Carolina: The Death of Saxe Joiner." In *Under Sentence of Death: Lynching in the South*, edited by William Fitzhugh Brundage, 109–31. Chapel Hill: University of North Carolina Press, 1997.

Castle, Terry. *Masquerade and Civilization: The Carnivalesque in Eighteenth-Century English Culture and Fiction*. Stanford, Calif.: Stanford University Press, 1986.

Charles, Allan D. *A Narrative History of Union County, South Carolina*. Spartanburg: Reprint Company, 1987.

Clinton, Catherine. "Bloody Terrain: Freedwomen, Sexuality and Violence during Reconstruction." *Georgia Historical Quarterly* 76 (1992): 313–32.

Cmiel, Kenneth. "'A Broad Fluid Language of Democracy': Discovering the American Idiom." *Journal of American History* 79, no. 3 (December 1992): 913–36.

Cockrell, Dale. *Demons of Disorder: Early Blackface Minstrels and Their World*. New York: Cambridge University Press, 1997.

Cohen, Stanley. *States of Denial: Knowing about Atrocities and Suffering*. Cambridge, U.K.: Polity, 2001.

Cresswell, Stephen. "Enforcing the Enforcement Acts: The Department of Justice in Northern Mississippi, 1870–1890." *Journal of Southern History* 53 (August 1987): 421–40.

Crew, Danny O. *Ku Klux Klan Sheet Music: An Illustrated Catalogue of Published Music, 1867–2002*. Jefferson, N.C.: McFarland, 2003.

Daston, Lorraine, and Peter Galison. *Objectivity*. Cambridge, Mass.: MIT Press, 2010.

Dauphine, James G. "The Knights of the White Camelia and the Election of 1868: Louisiana's White Terrorists; A Benighting Legacy." *Louisiana History: The Journal of the Louisiana Historical Association* 30 (Spring 1989): 173–90.

Davis, David Brion. *The Slave Power Conspiracy and the Paranoid Style*. Baton Rouge: Louisiana State University Press, 1970.

Davis, Janet. *The Circus Age: Culture and Society under the American Big Top*. Chapel Hill: University of North Carolina Press, 2002.

Davis, Natalie Zemon. "The Reasons of Misrule: Youth Groups and Charivaris in Sixteenth-Century France." *Past and Present* 50 (February 1971): 41–75.

———. *Society and Culture in Early Modern France.* Stanford, Calif.: Stanford University Press, 1975.

Davis, Susan G. "'Making Night Hideous': Christmas Revelry and Public Order in Nineteenth Century Philadelphia." *American Quarterly* 34 (1982): 185–99.

———. *Parades and Power: Street Theater in Nineteenth Century Philadelphia.* Philadelphia: Temple University Press, 1986.

Davis, Susan Lawrence. *Authentic History, Ku Klux Klan 1865–1877.* New York: American Library Service, 1924.

Denning, Michael. *Mechanic Accents: Dime Novels and Working-Class Culture in America.* New York: Verso, 1987.

De Nouy, Wouter, Andrej Mrvar, and Vladimir Bategelj. *Exploratory Social Network Analysis with Pajek.* 2nd ed., rev. and exp. New York: Cambridge University Press, 2011.

Downs, Gregory P. *After Appomattox: Military Occupation and the Ends of War.* Cambridge, Mass.: Harvard University Press, 2015.

———. *Declarations of Dependence: The Long Reconstruction of Popular Politics in the South, 1861–1908.* Chapel Hill: University of North Carolina Press, 2011.

Downs, Jim. *Sick from Freedom: African American Illness and Suffering during the Civil War and Reconstruction.* New York: Oxford University Press, 2012.

Du Bois, W. E. B. *Black Reconstruction: An Essay toward a History of the Part Which Black Folks Played in the Attempt to Reconstruct Democracy in America, 1860–1880.* New York: Harcourt, Brace & Company, 1935.

Edwards, Laura F. *Gendered Strife and Confusion: The Political Culture of Reconstruction.* Urbana: University of Illinois Press, 1997.

Egerton, Douglas R. *The Wars of Reconstruction.* London: Bloomsbury, 2014.

Emberton, Carole. *Beyond Redemption: Race, Violence and the American South after the Civil War.* Chicago: University of Chicago Press, 2013.

Evans, Clement Anselm. *Confederate Military History.* Vol. 5. Atlanta: Confederate Publishing Company, 1899.

Faust, Drew. *Mothers of Invention: Women of the Slaveholding South in the American Civil War.* Chapel Hill: University of North Carolina Press, 1996.

Feaster, William Rice. *A History of Union County.* Union County Historical Foundation, 1977.

Fitzgerald, Michael W. "Ex-Slaveholders and the Ku Klux Klan: Exploring the Motivations of Terrorist Violence." In *After Slavery: Race, Labor, and Citizenship in the Reconstruction South*, edited by Bruce E. Baker and Brian Kelly, 143–58. Gainesville: University Press of Florida, 2013.

———. "The Ku Klux Klan: Property Crime and the Plantation System in Reconstruction Alabama." *Agricultural History* 71, no. 2 (Spring 1997): 186–206.

———. *Splendid Failure: Postwar Reconstruction in the American South.* Lanham, Md.: Ivan R. Dee, 2007.

———. *The Union League Movement in the Deep South: Politics and Agricultural Change during Reconstruction.* Baton Rouge: Louisiana State University Press, 2000.

Flynn, Charles L., Jr. "The Ancient Pedigree of Violent Repression: Georgia's Klan as a Folk Movement." In *The Southern Enigma: Essays on Race, Class, and Folk Culture,*

edited by Walter J. Fraser Jr. and Winfred B. Moore, 189–98. Westport, Conn.:
   Greenwood, 1983.

Foner, Eric. *Reconstruction: America's Unfinished Revolution, 1863–1877*. New York:
   Harper Perennial Classics, 2002.

Fossett, Judith Jackson. "(K)night Riders in (K)night Gowns: The Ku Klux Klan,
   Race, and Constructions of Masculinity." In *Race Consciousness: African American
   Studies for the New Century*, edited by Judith Jackson Fossett and Jeffrey A. Tucker,
   35–49. New York: New York University Press, 1997.

Franklin, John Hope. *Reconstruction: After the Civil War*. Chicago: University of Chicago
   Press, 1961.

Fry, Gladys-Marie. *Night Riders in Black Folk History*. 1975; reprint, Chapel Hill:
   University of North Carolina Press, 2001.

Giddens, Anthony. *The Consequences of Modernity*. Boston: Polity, 1990.

Gill, James. *Lords of Misrule: Mardi Gras and the Politics of Race in New Orleans*. Jackson:
   University Press of Mississippi, 1997.

Gillette, William. *Retreat from Reconstruction, 1869–1879*. Baton Rouge: Louisiana
   State University Press, 1979.

Goldsby, Jacqueline. *A Spectacular Secret: Lynching in American Life and Literature*.
   Chicago: University of Chicago Press, 2006.

Goldstein, Elizabeth S. *Experience without Qualities: Boredom and Modernity*. Stanford,
   Calif.: Stanford University Press, 2005.

Graham, Shawn, Ian Milligan, and Scott Weingart. *The Historian's Macroscope: Big
   Digital History*, www.themacroscope.org.

Greenberg, Kenneth S. *Honor and Slavery: Lies, Duels, Noses, Masks, Dressing as a Woman,
   Gifts, Strangers, Death, Humanitarianism, Slave Rebellions, the Pro-slavery Argument,
   Baseball, Hunting, and Gambling in the Old South*. Princeton, N.J.: Princeton
   University Press, 1996.

Hacking, Ian. *The Taming of Chance*. Cambridge: Cambridge University Press, 1990.

Hadden, Sally E. *Slave Patrols: Law and Violence in Virginia and the Carolinas*. Cambridge,
   Mass.: Harvard University Press, 2001.

Hahn, Steven. *A Nation under Our Feet: Black Political Struggles in the Rural South from
   Slavery to the Great Migration*. Cambridge, Mass.: Harvard University Press,
   2003.

Hale, Grace Elizabeth. *Making Whiteness: The Culture of Segregation in the South,
   1890–1940*. New York. Pantheon, 1998.

Hall, Jacqueline Dowd. *Revolt against Chivalry: Jessie Daniel Ames and the Women's
   Campaign against Lynching*. New York: Columbia University Press, 1979.

Halttunen, Karen. *Confidence Men and Painted Women: A Study of Middle-Class Culture in
   America, 1830–1870*. New Haven, Conn.: Yale University Press, 1986.

———. *Murder Most Foul: The Killer in the American Gothic Imagination*. Cambridge,
   Mass.: Harvard University Press, 2000.

Harcourt, Edward. "Who Were the Pale Faces? New Perspectives on the Tennessee
   Ku Klux." *Civil War History* 51, no. 1 (March 2005): 23–66.

Harris, Trudier. *Exorcising Blackness: Historical and Literary Lynching and Burning Rituals*.
   Bloomington: Indiana University Press, 1984.

Hartman, Saidiya V. *Scenes of Subjection: Terror, Slavery, and Self-Making in Nineteenth-Century America*. New York: Oxford University Press, 1997.Hennessey, Melinda Meek. "Racial Violence during Reconstruction: The 1876 Riots in Charleston and Cainhoy." *South Carolina Historical Magazine* 86, no. 2 (April 1985): 100–112.

Hodes, Martha. *White Women, Black Men: Illicit Sex in the Nineteenth-Century South*. New Haven, Conn.: Yale University Press, 1997.

Hofstadter, Richard. *The Paranoid Style in American Politics and Other Essays*. London: Jonathan Cape, 1966.

Hollandsworth, James G., Jr. *An Absolute Massacre: The New Orleans Race Riot of July 30, 1866*. Baton Rouge: Louisiana State University Press, 2001.

Horn, Stanley. *Invisible Empire: Story of the Ku-Klux Klan, 1866–1871*. Boston: Houghton Mifflin, 1939.

Huston, James L. "An Alternative to the Tragic Era: Applying the Virtues of Bureaucracy to the Reconstruction Dilemma." *Civil War History* 51, no. 4 (December 2005): 403–15.

Jeffreys-Jones, Rhodri. *The FBI: A History*. New Haven, Conn.: Yale University Press, 2007.

Johnson, Walter. "On Agency." *Journal of Social History* 37, no. 1 (Fall 2003): 113–24.

————. *River of Dark Dreams*. Cambridge, Mass.: Harvard University Press, 2013.

Keith, LeeAnna. *The Colfax Massacre: The Untold Story of Black Power, White Terror, and the Death of Reconstruction*. New York: Oxford University Press, 2008.

Kelly, Brian. "Class, Factionalism, and the Radical Retreat: Black Laborers and the Republican Party in South Carolina, 1865–1900." In *After Slavery: Race, Labor, and Citizenship in the Reconstruction South*, edited by Bruce E. Baker, 199–220. Gainsville: University Press of Florida, 2013.

Kenny, Kevin. *Making Sense of the Molly Maguires*. New York: Oxford University Press, 1998.

Kinser, Samuel. *Carnival, American Style: Mardi Gras at New Orleans and Mobile*. Chicago: University of Chicago Press, 1990.

Kinshasa, Kwando Mbiassi. *Black Resistance to the Ku Klux Klan in the Wake of the Civil War*. New York: McFarland, 2008.

Ladurie, Emmanuel Le Roy. *Carnival in Romans*. Translated by Mary Feeney. New York: G. Braziller, 1980.

Lemercier, Claire. "Formal Network Methods in History: Why and How?" This version might be slightly revised before publication in Georg Fertig (ed.), *Social Networks*, . . . 2011. <halshs-00521527v2>HAL Id: halshs-00521527 https:// halshs.archives-ouvertes.fr/halshs00521527v2. Submitted on 7 December 2011.

Lester, J. C., and D. L. Wilson. *Ku Klux Klan: Its Origin, Growth, and Disbandment*. With introduction by Walter L. Fleming. 1884. Washington: Neale, 1905.

Lewis, Patrick A. "The Democratic Partisan Militia and the Black Peril: The Kentucky Militia, Racial Violence, and the Fifteenth Amendment, 1870–1873." *Civil War Era* 56, no. 2 (June 2010): 145–74.

Lhamon, W. T., Jr. *Raising Cain: Blackface Performance from Jim Crow to Hip-Hop*. Cambridge, Mass.: Harvard University Press, 1998.

Lott, Eric. *Love and Theft: Blackface Minstrelsy and the American Working Class*. New York: Oxford University Press, 1995.

Martinez, Michael J. *Carpetbaggers, Cavalry, and the Ku Klux Klan: Exposing the Invisible Empire during Reconstruction.* Lanham, Md.: Rowman & Littlefield, 2007.

Massengill, Stephen E. "The Detectives of William Woods Holden, 1869–1870." *North Carolina Historical Review* 62 (October 1985): 448–87.

Masson, Thomas L. *Our American Humorists.* New York, 1922.

McBride, Dwight A. *Impossible Witnesses: Truth, Abolition, and Slave Testimony.* New York: New York University Press, 2001.

McPherson, James M. "Grant or Greeley: The Abolitionist Dilemma in the Election of 1872." *American Historical Review* 71, no. 1 (October 1965): 43–61.

McWhiney, H. Grady, and Francis B. Simkins. "The Ghostly Legend of the Ku-Klux-Klan." *Negro History Bulletin* 14 (February 1951): 109–12.

Meriwether, Elizabeth Avery. *Recollections of 92 Years, 1824–1916.* Nashville: Tennessee Historical Commission, 1958.

Michaels, Walter Benn. "The Souls of White Folk." In *Literature and the Body: Essays on Populations and Persons,* edited by Elaine Scarry, 185–209. Baltimore: Johns Hopkins University Press, 1988.

Milburn, Michael A., and Sheree D. Conrad. *The Politics of Denial.* Cambridge, Mass.: MIT Press, 1998.

Mische, Ann. "Cross-Talk in Movements: Reconceiving the Culture-Network Link." In *Social Movements and Networks: Relational Approaches to Collective Action,* edited by Mario Diana and Doug McAdam, 258–80. New York: Oxford University Press, 2003.

Mitchell, Reid. *All on a Mardi Gras Day: Episodes in the History of New Orleans Carnival.* Cambridge, Mass.: Harvard University Press, 1999.

Neidhardt, Wilfried. *Fenianism in North America.* State College: Penn State University Press, 1975.

Nelson, Scott. *Iron Confederacies: Southern Railways, Klan Violence, and Reconstruction.* Chapel Hill: University of North Carolina Press, 1999.

———. "Livestock, Boundaries, and Public Space in Spartanburg: African American Men, Elite White Women, and the Spectacle of Conjugal Relations." In *Sex, Love, Race: Crossing Boundaries in North American History,* edited by Martha Hodes, 313–27. New York: New York University Press, 1999.

Newton, Michael. *The Invisible Empire: The Ku-Klux Klan in Florida.* Forward by Raymond Arsenault and Gary M. Mormino. Gainesville: University Press of Florida, 2001.

Novick, Peter. *That Noble Dream: The "Objectivity Question" and the American Historical Profession.* New York: Cambridge University Press, 1988.

Olsen, Otto H. "The Ku Klux Klan: A Study in Reconstruction Politics and Propaganda." *North Carolina Historical Review* 39, no. 3 (July 1962): 340–62.

Ortiz, Paul. *Emancipation Betrayed: The Hidden History of Black Organizing and White Violence in Florida from Reconstruction to the Bloody Elections of 1920.* Berkeley: University of California Press, 2005.

Parsons, Elaine Frantz. "Klan Skepticism and Denial in Reconstruction-Era Public Discourse." *Journal of Southern History* 77 (February 2011): 53–90.

———. "Midnight Rangers: The Costume and Performance of the Reconstruction-Era Ku-Klux Klan." *Journal of American History* 92, no. 2 (December 2005): 811–36.

Peek, Ralph L. "Lawlessness in Florida, 1868–1871." *Florida Historical Quarterly* 40 (October 1861): 164–65.Pencak, William, Matthew Dennis, and Simon P. Newman. *Riot and Revelry in Early America.* College Station: Penn State University Press, 2002.

Perman, Michael. *The Road to Redemption: Southern Politics, 1869–1879.* Chapel Hill: University of North Carolina Press, 1984.

Pfeifer, Michael J. "The Origins of Post-Bellum Lynching: Collective Violence in Reconstruction-Era Louisiana." *Louisiana History* 50, no. 2 (2009): 189–201.

Phelan, Peggy. *Mourning Sex: Performing Public Memories.* London: Routledge, 1997.

Pierson, William Dillon. *Black Legacy: America's Hidden Heritage.* Amherst: University of Massachusetts Press, 1993.

Pike, David L. *Metropolis on the Styx: The Underworld of Modern Urban Culture, 1800–2000.* Ithaca, N.Y.: Cornell University Press, 2007.

Prince, K. Stephen. "The Paper Klan: Northern Culture and the Ku Klux Klan, 1868–1872." Paper presented at annual meeting of Organization of American Historians, Seattle, Wash., March 26–29, 2009.

———. *Stories of the South: Race and the Reconstruction of Southern Identity, 1865–1915.* Chapel Hill: University of North Carolina Press, 2014.

Quist, John W. *Restless Visionaries: The Social Roots of Antebellum Reform in Alabama and Michigan.* Baton Rouge: Louisiana State University Press, 1998.

Rable, George. *But There Was No Peace: The Role of Violence in the Politics of Reconstruction.* Athens: University of Georgia Press, 1984.

———. "Forces of Darkness, Forces of Light: The Impeachment of Andrew Johnson." *Southern Studies* 17 (Summer 1978): 151–73.

Reynolds, David. *Beneath the American Renaissance: The Subversive Imagination in the Age of Emerson and Melville.* Cambridge, Mass.: Harvard University Press, 1988.

Reynolds, John S. *Reconstruction in South Carolina, 1865–1877.* 1905. New York: Negro Universities Press, 1969.

Richardson, Heather Cox. *The Death of Reconstruction: Race, Labor, and Politics in the Post-Civil War North, 1865–1901.* Cambridge, Mass.: Harvard University Press, 2001.

———. *To Make Men Free: A History of the Republican Party.* New York: Basic Books, 2014.

Richardson, William Thomas. *Historic Pulaski, Birthplace of the Ku-klux: Scene of Execution of Sam Davis.* N.p.: W. T. Richardson, 1913.

Ritvo, Harriet. *Animal Estate: The English and Other Creatures in the Victorian Age.* Cambridge, Mass.: Harvard University Press, 1987.

Roach, James. *Cities of the Dead: Circum-Atlantic Performance.* New York: Columbia University Press, 1996.

Roark, James L. *Masters without Slaves.* New York: Norton, 1978.

Roediger, David R. *The Wages of Whiteness: Race and the Making of the American Working Class.* London: Verso, 1999.

Rose, Mrs. S. E. F. [Laura Martin]. *The Ku Klux Klan or Invisible Empire.* New Orleans: L. Graham Company, 1914.

Rosen, Hannah. *Terror in the Heart of Freedom: Citizenship, Sexual Violence, and the Meaning of Race in the Postemancipation South.* Chapel Hill: University of North Carolina Press, 2009.

Rourke, Constance. *American Humor: A Study of the National Character*. Garden City, N.Y., 1931.

———. "Miss Rourke Replies to Mr. Blair." *American Literature* 4 (May 1932): 207–10.

Rubin, Hyman, III. *South Carolina Scalawags*. Columbia: University of South Carolina Press, 2006.

Ryan, Mary P. *Civic Wars: Democracy and Public Life in the American City during the Nineteenth Century*. Berkeley: University of California Press, 1997.

Saville, Julie. *The Work of Reconstruction: From Slave to Wage Labor in South Carolina, 1860–1870*. New York: Cambridge University Press, 1994.

Scarry, Elaine. *The Body in Pain: The Making and Unmaking of the World*. New York: Oxford University Press, 1987.

Schechner, Richard. *Between Theatre and Anthropology*. Philadelphia: University of Pennsylvania Press, 1985.

Schwalm, Leslie A. *A Hard Fight for We: Women's Transition from Slavery to Freedom in South Carolina*. Urbana: University of Illinois Press, 1997.

Scott, James C. *Domination and the Arts of Resistance: Hidden Transcripts*. New Haven, Conn.: Yale University Press, 1990.

Severance, Ben H. *Tennessee's Radical Army: The State Guard and Its Role in Reconstruction, 1867–1869*. Knoxville: University of Tennessee Press, 2005.

Silber, Nina. *The Romance of Reunion: Northerners and the South, 1865–1900*. Chapel Hill: University of North Carolina Press, 1993.

Silver, Andrew. "Making Minstrelsy of Murder: George Washington Harris, the Ku Klux Klan, and the Reconstruction Aesthetic of Black Fright." *Prospects* 25 (2000): 339–62.

———. *Minstrelsy and Murder: The Crisis of Southern Humor, 1835–1925*. Baton Rouge: Louisiana State University Press, 2006.

Smith, David A., Ryan Cordell, and Elizabeth Maddock Dillon. "Infectious Texts: Modeling Text Reuse in Nineteenth-Century Newspapers." Conference paper presented at IEEE Workshop on Big Data and the Humanities, Santa Clara, Cal., October 6–9, 2013. http://www.ccs.neu.edu/home/dasmith/infect-bighum-2013.pdf.

Smith, John David, and J. Vincent Lowery, eds. *The Dunning School: Historians, Race, and the Meaning of Reconstruction*. Lexington: University Press of Kentucky, 2013.

Snay, Mitchell. *Fenians, Freedmen, and Southern Whites: Race and Nationality in the Era of Reconstruction*. Baton Rouge: Louisiana State University Press, 2010.

Sommerville, Diane Miller. *Rape and Race in the Nineteenth Century South*. Chapel Hill: University of North Carolina Press, 2004.

Stepto, Robert B. *From behind the Veil: A Study of Afro-American Narrative*. 1979; reprint, Urbana: University of Illinois Press, 1991.

Summers, Mark Wahlgren. *A Dangerous Stir: Fear, Paranoia, and the Making of Reconstruction*. Chapel Hill: University of North Carolina Press, 2009.

———. *The Ordeal of the Reunion: A New History of Reconstruction*. Chapel Hill: University of North Carolina Press, 2014.

———. *The Press Gang: Newspapers and Politics, 1865–1878*. Chapel Hill: University of North Carolina Press, 1994.

Sutherland, Daniel E. *A Savage Conflict: The Decisive Role of Guerrillas in the American Civil War*. Chapel Hill: University of North Carolina Press, 2009.

Swinney, Everette. "Enforcing the Fifteenth Amendment, 1870–1877." *Journal of Southern History* 28 (May 1962): 202–18.

Thomas, Brook. "Turner's 'Frontier Thesis' as a Narrative of Reconstruction." In *Centuries' Ends, Narrative Means*, edited by Robert Newman, 117–40. Stanford, Calif.: Stanford University Press, 1996.

Trelease, Allen W. *White Terror: The Ku-klux Conspiracy and Southern Reconstruction*. Baton Rouge: Louisiana State University Press, 1971.

Trotti, Michael Ayers. *The Body in the Reservoir: Murder and Sensationalism in the South*. Chapel Hill: University of North Carolina Press, 2008.

Trotti, Michael Ayers. "The Scaffold's Revival: Race and Public Execution in the South." *Journal of Southern History* 45 (Fall 2011): 195–224.

———. "What Counts: Trends in Racial Violence in the Postbellum South." *Journal of American History* 100 (September 2013): 375–400.

Trouillot, Michel-Rolph. *Silencing the Past*. Boston: Beacon, 1995.

Turner, Victor. *The Anthropology of Performance*. New York: PAJ, 1988.

———. *From Ritual to Theatre: The Human Seriousness of Play*. New York: PAJ, 2001.

Union County Historical Foundation. *A History of Union County South Carolina*. Greenville, S.C.: A Press, 1977.

———. *Voices of the Past*. Greenville, S.C.: A Press, 1979.

Union County Historical Newsletter.

Vandal, Gilles. *Rethinking Southern Violence: Homicides in Post–Civil War Louisiana, 1866–1884*. Columbus: Ohio State Press, 2000.

Waldrep, Christopher. *The Many Faces of Judge Lynch: Extralegal Violence and Punishment in America*. New York: Palgrave Macmillan, 2002.

Wang, Xi. *The Trial of Democracy: Black Suffrage and Northern Republicans, 1860–1910*. Athens: University of Georgia Press, 1997.

Weinfield, Daniel. *The Jackson County War: Reconstruction and Resistance in Post–Civil War Florida*. Tuscaloosa: University of Alabama Press, 2012.

West, Jerry Lee. *The Reconstruction Ku Klux Klan in York County, South Carolina*. Jefferson, N.C.: McFarland, 2002.

White, Ed. "The Value of Conspiracy Theory." *American Literary History* 14, no. 1 (Spring 2002): 1–31.

Whites, Lee Ann. *The Civil War as a Crisis in Gender: Augusta, Georgia, 1860–1890*. Athens: University of Georgia Press, 1995.

Williams, Kidada. *They Left Great Marks on Me: African American Testimonies of Racial Violence from Emancipation to World War One*. New York: New York University Press, 2012.

Williams, Lou Falkner. *The Great South Carolina Ku Klux Klan Trials, 1871–1872*. Athens: University of Georgia Press, 1996.

Williamson, Joel. *After Slavery: The Negro in South Carolina during Reconstruction, 1861–1877*. New York: W. W. Norton, 1965.

Wood, Amy. *Lynching and Spectacle: Witnessing Racial Violence in America, 1890–1940*. New Directions in Southern Studies. Chapel Hill: University of North Carolina Press, 2011.

Wood, Sharon E. *The Freedom of the Streets: Work, Citizenship, and Sexuality in a Gilded Age City*. Chapel Hill: University of North Carolina Press, 2005.

Zuber, Richard L. *North Carolina during Reconstruction*. Raleigh: State Department of Archives and History, 1968.

Zuczek, Richard. *State of Rebellion: Reconstruction in South Carolina*. Columbia: University of South Carolina Press, 1996.

Index

Italicized page numbers refer to illustrations and illustration captions.

Gordon, George W., 31, 45–46
Gordon, Henry, 113
Goshen Hill, S.C., 238, 262
Goss, H. L., 248–49, 290
Goss, James H., 239, 292
Gowdeysville, S.C., 219, 240, 241, 301
Grant, James L., 110
Grant, Ulysses S., 146–47, 181, 201, 204;
    and Ku-Klux Klan suppression, 159,
    162, 167, 174–75, 177–80; analogized
    to the Ku-Klux Klan, 167; and elec-
    tion of 1872, 193, 197–98, 208–9
Gray, Edmund, 123, 139
Greeley, Horace, 159, 167, 201; as *New
    York Tribune* editor, 146, 184, 199, 213;
    and election of 1872, 162, 179–81,
    108–9; investigations and denial of
    Ku-Klux Klan, 184, 190, 192–93, 204
Green, Fed, 261
Green, Innes. *See* Byers, Thomas
Greene County, Ala., 86
Greer, Jason, 300
Greer, Robert, 223–24, 229, 244,
    247–51, 258, 260, 289–90,
    297–98, 300
Greer, Thomas Jefferson, 224–25, 228,
    244, 246, 254, 255, 258–60, 263,
    289–90, 297, 299, 307
Gregory, B. Frank, Jr., 224, 296, 300
Gregory, Adolphus (aka Dolphus), 221
Gregory, Horace, 282
Grisby, Judd, 67
Groesbeck, William S., 159
Guion, H. W., 76
Gustine, William, 163, 267

Hacking, Ian, 146
Hahn, Stephen, 116–17
Halttunen, Karen, 210
Hamlin, Henry, 73, 123
Hammond, Nelson, 275
Hampton, Mark, 233, 306
Hampton, Wade, 173
Hardy, Jim, 246, 251–52
Harris, Essic, 91

Harris, Pink, 56
Harris, Samuel, 243–44, 247, 301
Harris, William C., 300
Hartford (Conn.) Times, 179
Harvey, Charley Jeff, 237
Hawkins, Barby, 250
Hawkins, Edward, 224, 228, 258
Hawkins, James, 243–44
Hawkins, Moses, 244, 275–76
Hawkins, Silas, 243–44, 247,
    306–8
Hawkins, Thompson C., 85
Hawkins, Wade. *See* Johnson, Wade
Haworth, Paul, 16
Hendricks, Martha, 98, 100
Herndon, J. N., 255
Hicklin, Hampton, 124, 139
Hicks, James (aka Jim), 139, 141
Hill, Elias, 89
Hill, Lunney B., 256, 260–61
Hinds, J. J., 81
Historical network analysis of Union
    County, S.C., 217–18, 223, 228–30,
    259–60, 349 (n. 35)
Hix, Joseph, 235–36
Hoar, George Frisbee, 196
Hobson, Ephram, 233
Hobson, Frank, 233
Hofstadter, Richard, 153
Holden, William Woods, 159–60, 166,
    174, 192
Holt, Caswell, 72
Horn, Stanley F., 16, 31
Horton, Samuel, 130
Hubbard, John B., 237, 271–74, 278,
    284–88
Hudspeth, James, 220
Huggins, Allen, 152
Hughes, Moses C., 223
Hughes, H. Thomas "Tom" (aka
    Thompson), 224, 226, 227, 229,
    235, 236, 247, 250, 251, 253, 254,
    255, 256, 258–61, 296, 299
Hughes, William, 307
Humphries, W. D., 301

44–45, 49–50, 53, 57, 60–62, 72, 216, 323 (n. 111); disbandment of, 45; development of as violent, political organization, 54; as defining communities, 75, 78, 95, 101–8, 112, 126, 212, 213; costume and behavior of, 76–77, 81, 84–85, 87, 89–90, 95–99; recognition of attackers by victims, 97–100; isolation of victims of, 114, 120–23; destroy black autonomy, organizations, and community, 114–20, 121, 122, 123; as synecdoche, 144–45; press coverage of, 145–50, 154–59, 173, 266–69; sensational and comic framing of, 197–206; in Union County, 216–18, 237–49, 250–62, 265–69, 274–77, 280–89, 294, 302, 308
Ku-Klux Kaleidoscope (newspaper), 198
Kunan, Alfred. *See* Keenan, Alfred

Lacrosse (Wisc.) Democrat, 278
Lamb, Robert, 299
Lambert, Calvin, 64
Lansing (Mich.) Republican, 205
Laurens County, S.C., 234, 239, 249–50, 272, 275, 286, 288
LeMaster, Richard, 306
Lester, John C., 30–41, *33*, 43–45, 50–53, 57–58, 62
Lewis, Albert, 301
Lewis, John, 141–42
Lewisburg, S.C., 267
Lhamon, W. T., Jr., 94, 99
Lincoln County, Tenn., 56
Lindsey, Edward, 238
Lipscomb, Peyton, 104
Little, William, 301
Littlefield, William, 226
Little Rock (Ark.) Republican, 166, 200, 202
Loblic, Samuel, 271
Long, James Gideon, 216, 238
Long, J. C., 237
Long, Monro, 243
Lott, Eric, 95

Louisville Courier, 156
Lowell (Mass.) Daily Citizen and News, 205
Lowndes County, Miss., 141
Lowther, Henry, 118–19
Lyles, Aaron, 234
Lyles, J. Bank, 216, 237–38
Lynching, 88, 101, 151, 260, 267, 290, 303, 304; of Sax Joiner, 222, 249, 268
Lynneville, Tenn., 50

Mabry, Jesse, 241, 242, 271, 275, 276–77
Madison County, Ala., 73
Mankins, J. J., 55, 59
Marchbanks, Charles, 56
Mardi Gras, 26, 87, 206, 305
Marion (S.C.) Star, 202
Marshall County, Tenn., 55, 148–49, 51
Martial law, 159, 174, 292
Martin, Albert, 243–46, 306
Martin, Cansada, 220
Martin, Robert, 231–32
Martin, Sam, 244
Maury County, Tenn., 55, 56, 61–62, 63, 64, 65, 66, 148, 149
Maryville (Tenn.) Republican, 136
McBeth, John, 244
McCord, Frank O., 27, 29–34, *33*, 36, 39–41, 45, 51–52, 59, 62–66, 147
McCord, Lapsley, 31–32, 39, 86
McCord, Luther, 30–31, 39, 41, 53, 64, 68, 147
McCrary, Isham, 135
McCullough, William F., 220
McDaniel, Thomas, 296
McKissick, Amos, 256
McKissick, Hezekiah, 220
McKissick, Isaac G., 238, 243, 248–49, 254, 260, 261, 263, 279, 290, 298, 299, 301
McKissick, Joseph, 300
McKissick, John P., 256, 259, 281
McKnight, Robert, 290
McMahan, Hattie, 219
McNally, Thomas, 254, 259
McNease, Andrew, 281, 307

Nichols, Matt (son), 140
Nichols, William, 301
Noland, G. Stout, 299
Noland, Isaiah, 246
North American Review, 204
Noxubee County, Miss., 86
Nuckles, Samuel, 275, 292

Oconee County, S.C., 275
O'Connell, P. J., 275
Odd Fellowship, 49, 65
Optic, Oliver, 199
Orangeburg News, 308
Outlaw, Wyatt, 115
Owens, Alfred B., 240–41, 261, 273,
    280, 300, 304

Pacolet, S.C., 281
Page, Christine, 255
Page, Richard, 238
Pale Faces, 6, 16
Palmer, Ben, 306
Palmer, Major, 247–48
Palmer, Taylor, 246, 261
Park, Pat, 306
Parker, J. Reese, Jr., 220
Parker, Walton, 220
Parker, William R., 220
Parr, Benjamin, 246, 282
Parr, Dele, 246
Parrish, Robert, 203
Peeler, Gilbert, 219
Philadelphia Daily Evening Telegraph, 81
Pierson, William D., 94
Pike, Albert, 29
Pike, James S., 184
Pinkney, S.C., 224, 233, 238,
    240–41, 307
Plug-Uglies, 94
Poland, Luke, 131
Pomeroy, Brick, 79, 201
Poole, Isaac, 276
Porter, Charles, 168
Porter, Jed P., 238, 240–41, 275,
    276, 300

Powell, John, 226
Powell, William, 247
Prater, Emma, 253–54, 301
Prater, William, 253–54
Prescript, 19, 31, 45–49, 53–54, 62, 153
Price, Thomas J., 144
Prince, Stephen, 144
Prior, Miles, 108
Pulaski, Tenn., 27–28, 146, 147, 155,
    215, 237; origin of Ku-Klux Klan in,
    7, 20–21, 41–57, 72, 187; motiva-
    tion for Ku-Klux Klan in, 20–21,
    30–40, 94; racial violence in, 29, 59;
    Ku-Klux Klan in, 64–66, 67, 68, 72,
    79, 81, 85, 88
Pulaski (Tenn.) Citizen (alternately Pulaski
    Independent Citizen), 27–29; as mouth-
    piece of early Pulaski Ku-Klux Klan,
    38–39; unsuccessful at publicizing
    early Ku-Klux Klan, 54; Ku-Klux
    Klan developed as political and
    violent by, 57, 63–64; fabrications
    about Ku-Klux in early articles of, 62

Rable, George, 170
Race riots, 4, 19, 29–30, 66, 234,
    261–62, 288
Racial violence, 3–10; in Giles County,
    Tenn., 29, 54, 59, 63–64, 68; in
    Union County, 23, 216–20, 231–33,
    239; as Ku-Klux Klan violence, 7,
    240–41, 244, 251, 267, 276–77. See
    also Collective violence; Ku-Klux Klan
Radical Ku-Klux Klan, 279, 280–83,
    286–87
Randolph, Ryland, 46, 62
Ray, James, 248
Raymond, Henry J., 184
Raymond, Henry W., 184
Reconstruction, 11–12, 24–25, 145, 177;
    Ku-Klux Klan during, 1, 10, 13, 17, 21,
    77–78, 87, 305–6; African American
    organizations during, 2, 96, 121;
    racial violence during, 3–4, 6; in
    Giles County, Tenn., 32–35, 39, 70;

and Ku-Klux Klan costumes, 94, 303;
Radical Reconstruction, 110, 230;
Ku-Klux Klan skepticism and denial
during, 181, 209–11, 213–14; in Union
County, S.C., 219, 230, 236, 242, 270,
305–6
Reed, Henry, 120
Reed, Richard, 30, 33, *33*, 35
Reid, L. Dow, 234
Reynolds, Lucy, 64
Reynolds, Mildred Ezell, 31, 51, 69
Rhodes, Dangerfield "Danger," 27–28,
31–32
Rhodes, Orange. *See* Jones, Orange
Richardson, Alfred, 119
Richardson, Heather Cox, 176
Richardson, W. T., 53–54
Richmond Dispatch, 198, 268
Richmond (Ky.) Register, 163
Richmond Whig, 154
Robert, Charles E., 56
Robinson, Benjamin, 244–47, 259
Robinson, John, 269
Robuck, J. E., 92, 94
Rodger, John (aka Rogers), 235, 293, 300
Roediger, David, 93
Rogers, Calvin, 120
Rogers, James Rice, 228, 229, 239, 242,
250–51, 254, 258–59, 260, 279, 287,
289, 296, 300
Rose, S. E. F. (Laura), 31, 49–50, 62
Rosen, Hannah, 121, 134
Rourke, Constance, 199
Rubin, Hyman, 230
Runkle, Benjamin, 19

Salter, Wade. *See* Sartor, Wade
Sanders, John, 225, 246, 258, 297
Sanders, Sancho, 275
Sanders, W. H., 296
Sanders, Wesley, 297
Santuc, S.C., 238, 272, 282, 301
Sartor, Christopher, 220
Sartor, John Harrison, 233, 273
Sartor, Richard "Dick," 282

Sartor, Wade (aka Wade Salter), 301
Saulsbury, Willard, 188
Savannah (Ga.) Daily News and Herald, 188,
198, 200, 205
Sax(e). *See* Joiner, Sax
Scarry, Elaine, 102
Schechner, Richard, 86
Schurz, Carl, 147
Scott, Ellison, 236, 256
Scott, James, 77
Scott, John (senator), 166, 292, 296–98
Scott, John Wesley, 243
Scott, Robert K., 240, 268, 290–92,
299; as Union County governor,
230–34, 242–43, 254–55; Ku-Klux
Klan investigations organized by,
270–73, 278, 284–88; criticism of,
278, 280–81
Scott, Walter (author), 15, 41, 43
Scott, Walter (Giles County), 56, 114
Scruggs, James, 59
Secret Service, 149, 160, 178–80, 185
Seward, William, 171
Shand, Robert, 236, 257, 260, 269, 270,
271, 285, 293–96, 298
Sheldon, D. H., 269
Shelmar, Gilbert. *See* Chalmers, Gilbert
Sherman, William T., 147, 190
Shotwell, Randolph, 86, 88
Simmons, Benjamin, 256
Simpson, William D., 239, 274
Sims, Charles, 216, 237
Skelton, John, 223–24, 226
Skelton, Lydia, 226, 235, 236
Smith, Asa, 221
Smith, Billy, 221
Smith, Daniel, 248
Smith, Elipas, 221
Smith, Gerrit, 179
Smith, John R., 296
Snoddy, Sam, 141
Sons of Temperance, 65
Spartanburg County, S.C., 104–5, 124,
128–29, 132, 136, 141, 155, 162, 257,
279, 281, 292, 299